Futureproof

GLOBAL INSECURITIES

A series edited by Catherine Besteman

Futureproof

Security Aesthetics
and the
Management
of Life

Edited by
D. Asher Ghertner,
Hudson McFann,
and Daniel M. Goldstein

Duke University Press
Durham and London
2020

© 2020 Duke University Press
All rights reserved
Designed by Drew Sisk
Typeset in Portrait Text by Westchester Publishing Services

Cataloging-in-Publication Data is available at the Library
of Congress

ISBN 9781478006091 (hardcover: alk paper)
ISBN 9781478006909 (pbk: alk. paper)
ISBN 9781478007517 (ebook)

Cover art: Barbed wire samples from the Jack Chisholm
Fencing Collection, Museums Victoria. Photograph by
Michelle McFarlane. Copyright Museums Victoria / CC BY 4.0.
https://collections.museumvictoria.com.au/items/404382.

CONTENTS

Catherine Lutz

A Special Forces veteran and libertarian in Fayetteville, North Carolina, told me, years ago, that "defense is the first need of any organism." The thinkers in this volume follow him, if in a more critical vein, in seeing security as the guiding framework and dominant force for organizing collective life in our era. They encourage us to ask: How did this man come to feel that way about the nature of being human? How did many others come to operate within the strict limits of security discourses and to be presented with political, economic, and life constraints and choices structured by this guiding principle rather than another one? How did the number of things against which defense is thought to be needed expand so radically in this era as opposed to earlier ones?

This volume uses ethnographic perspectives and broadly distributed cases to help us look for the family resemblances among a variety of institutions and practices that are based in either the fear of distinct or inchoate threats or the desire for security, as those things are variously defined. Its authors want us to see security not simply as a *good* or as a *need* provided for, but as a *mode of power*, or an authorizing and coercive regime of governance. They want us to broaden our sense of what the relevant institutions and practices are that should be considered as based on a security paradigm. Widening the object of attention beyond the military and police, traditionally seen as a society's "security institutions," the chapters show us that security-seeking or security-marketing involves the quest for, or selling of, protection not just from military attack but also from disease, stranger danger in the park, home invasion and theft, the sudden collapse of stock or housing prices, and climate change. The quest, most prolifically, has become protection from the very idea of an unknown future, and often in contrast to a nostalgically reimagined past that was predictable or knowable.

Many aspects of our world and its recent history are evidence for the ubiquity of a security framework (even if not always with the same biological or evolutionary understanding as that Fayetteville resident). The signs of its omnipresence are not simply in how people talk with each other about their present and future fears or security aspirations. The symptoms include sharply rising budgets for the public and private employment of soldiers, police, transit security agents, and mercenary, paramilitary, and private security forces. They include remarkable new types of baroque weaponry, set in vast arsenals kept in perpetual readiness for use by both states and individuals. There is also the rising status and public visibility of more militant, protectionist/nationalist, and misogynist masculinities in political leaders and popular culture figures alike. They are in the normalized infrastructure of gates and walls; of antivirus software and passwords; of the literally millions of video cameras trained inside homes and businesses, above sidewalks and at borders, standing sentry; and in the broad-scale surveillance or digital scanning of populations via online data collection, computer algorithms, blood tests, airport scanners, and threat prevention investments on everything from the cellular to the bodily level and from the international to the planetary scale as climate engineers anxiously discuss how to prepare to secure our future from our past greenhouse gas emissions.

The innovation of this particular volume within the now mushrooming critical literature on security is to ask about the political aesthetics of these practices. Following Teresa Caldeira's (2000) pioneering work on the "aesthetics of security" in São Paulo, the contributors want to draw our attention to how it is that "security, as a form of power, operates through distinct aesthetic registers, including notions of beauty and taste, style and genre, form and appearance, representation and mimesis, and emotion and affect" (Ghertner, McFann, and Goldstein, this volume). They want us to see how people learn to make judgments of taste (variously in different communities) and to feel (whether anxiously or angrily or pleasurably) about the world in this register of judgment. When we go beyond seeing security as simply disciplinary, and come to see it as involving matters of distinction, per Pierre Bourdieu, we can discover more about the power and endurance and attractions, as well as the fragilities of modern militarism, for example. We are encouraged to look at the spatial or social location of aesthetic judgments which, in some communities, give elevated worth not just to the soldier but to those who know that a man in uniform is a beautiful thing, that a field of Arlington graves makes a tragically beautiful landscape, that video games involving danger and escape are more fun than others, that a refugee child in an ambulance promises to teach us about the goodness of the rescue, the truth of who the perpetrator is, and the beauty of youth that was and might yet be, or that an array of Transportation

Security Administration officers and machines is a comforting sight at best, an acceptable nuisance at worst. These modes of judgment educate many to see the publishing of a photograph of someone killed as a result of war or brutal policing as in "bad taste," and to see those who represent no threat because of their wealth or other modes of power as eminently beautiful and viewable.

While the chapters in this volume generally draw our attention to urban infrastructures and practices, we can also examine the media productions that so powerfully tutor collective taste in a world increasingly lived on-screen. Take the *New York Times* photographs of war examined by David Shields in his book *War Is Beautiful* (2015). Every photograph, war-related or not, is a teller of tales. It suggests an often complex event, with a history and a sequel, and its colors, composition, and subject matter propose how viewers ought to feel about what is happening. But most of us continue to see photos—and especially photojournalism—as thin slices of life, as objective records of the world out there. Text is widely approached with suspicion as to its writers' ideological bent, but images—whether because of their presumed objectivity or their aesthetic appeal—push those concerns to the side. The photos of war become that much more powerful in structuring our taste for security.

Shields (2015) looks at the fourteen years of *New York Times* front-page photos of images related to the wars in Afghanistan and Iraq; hundreds have been published from 2001 to the present. He writes emphasizing the *Times'* status as an American newspaper whose editors, through the years, have presumed the basic goodness of the U.S. government and its activities even when they have investigated its functionaries' failings. Shields arranges sixty-five of them, in rich color and large format, clustered by the implicit themes that give their viewers the overwhelming sense that war is a thing of some horrible or not-so-horrible beauty. America's longest and ongoing wars have been devastating in their human costs. By contrast, the *New York Times* photos, Shields shows, often focus on their rewards: on American power being exercised for good; on the Iraqi, Afghan, and American citizenry's love for the dead and wounded; and on the heroics and values of those who fight (and report on) them.

These themes are seen in recurring images of the striking natural world of a conquered "wilderness" in Iraqi deserts and Afghan mountains across which U.S. soldiers move, and Shields sees Hollywood as providing the templates for the *New York Times* photographers and picture editors through hundreds of war movies that focus on the pyrotechnics of blasting weaponry. These images include the warrior presented as an imposing father figure bringing protection and order, whether cradling a toddler or helping a comrade recover in a military hospital. There is beautiful religious imagery in pietà-like tableaus (an Iraqi man cradling the limp, bloody body of his brother) and stunning God's-eye views of leadership scanning for bad guys and securing the landscape (President Obama and General Petraeus surveying Baghdad rooftops by helicopter). Shields points to the inordinate number of photos of sweet and tragic-faced Afghan and Iraqi "womenandchildren" whose beauty and fragility make visible the need for their protection.

The evidence of death in these photos is more likely to be trails of blood on an Afghan hospital floor than butchered flesh. And it is more likely to be mourners collapsed on a coffin than ugly hysterical grief. What we find is love, art, nature, and religious sentiment rather than the revolting destruction of these things. These photos are evidence of the *New York Times'* complicity in the warmakers' desire to make each American war a "good" war, and war marketeers' knowledge of the common U.S. desire to construe the "securing of the globe" as beautiful, even when Americans regret or critique the wars that result. And they represent the epitome of high-brow, objectivist, Manhattan-based judgments of taste in security photographic style.

Security objects with such aesthetic qualities are consumed in vast quantities, some in the form of images, some in the form of documents like constitutions or political advertisements or immigration laws whose aesthetics we should understand as well. The security aesthetic in political life is not simply a beautiful design that enhances or markets a prosaic ideology; rather, "an ideology *is* an aesthetic system, and this is what moves or fails to move people, attracts their loyalty or repugnance, moves them to action or to apathy" (Sartwell 2010, 1). In looking at the aesthetics, we are reminded to continue to examine security as a *good*, both in the sense of a moral claim—the specifying of who or what places are dangerous and who (almost always paternally) protects—and in the sense of a commodity—this is the product being sold and this is who profits. As the editors of this volume argue, security is contested terrain, and those studying it have often focused on parsing and locating the moral claims and counterclaims involved. The commodity good, however, has received less attention. There are three sources of threat that the contemporary United States economy is focused on: the fear that racial others will enter or attack the United States (e.g., protection from which structures large parts of the federal budget), the threat and prevention of redistribution or property theft (evident in the one in four American workers who fall in the category of "guard labor" [Bowles and Jayadev 2004]), and the threat and prevention of illness both individual and pandemic (via the many medical surveillance and prevention allocations in the federal budget). Erased, however, are the ugly truths that the true threat of violence for many is untreated disease, the threat of arrest and incarceration, or the car crashes that killed 1.2 million globally last year and more Americans in the twentieth century than died in all the wars of that period.

People gradually become conversant in a new security language and come to "delight" in a new sense of what is beautiful about their preferred language and speakers of security speak. When Carol Cohn (1987) years ago identified the emerging security aesthetics of nuclear strategists in her classic article "Sex and Death in the Rational World of Defense Intellectuals," she made the point that gender was implicated in the abstractions, euphemisms, and sexual metaphors used in those strategists' technostrategic dialect. This is all the more important to understand when the Trump administration is virtually predicated on demonstrating that white men are in charge of security in every form, from rebordering the nation to securing life for the unborn.

Each of the chapters in this book explicitly or implicitly asks what an *anti*-security aesthetics would look like—how a tastefully subversive sensibility might be cultivated. The artist elin o'Hara slavick shows us one way in which representations of war can be made tastefully subversive in her remarkable series *Bomb after Bomb: A Violent Cartography*. slavick's aesthetic intentions are clear. The colorful and complex drawings of the many places the United States has bombed in its history are, in her words: "relatively abstract—and I say relatively because there *are* some recognizable cartographic, geographic and realistic details like arrows, borders and airplanes, and as in war, civilians are rendered invisible. I employ abstraction to reach people who might otherwise turn away from realistic depictions. People approach abstraction with fewer expectations and defenses. I want to reach people who have not made up their minds, who long for more information, the people who vote and want to believe that we are living in a democracy but are filled with fear and doubt" (slavick 2007, 97). The drawings are also "beautifully aerial to seduce and trap the potentially apathetic viewer so that she will take a closer look, slow down, and contemplate the accompanying information that explains that what she is looking at may implicate her. I also chose the aerial view to align myself, as an American, with the pilots dropping the bombs, even though I would not, myself, drop them."

slavick's aesthetic is meant not just to draw attention to the moment of trauma or bombing, but to point as well to the long-term impact of having organized U.S. society around a view of security that makes war a self-evident good and allows it to provide the threat template for ever-widening obsessions and the products to cope with them. The contributors to this volume use a similarly subversive and accessible style and content to address an audience

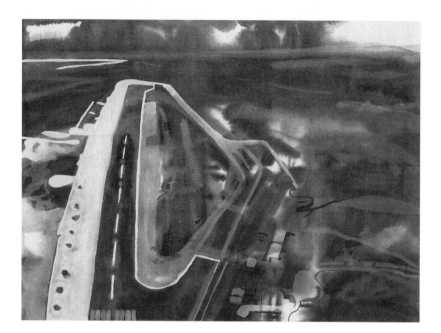

Figure F.1   elin o'Hara slavick, *Johnson Atoll, U.S., 1958–1962*. Mixed media on Arches paper. Image reproduced from slavick (2007).

that might be called into being in a world where the marketing of security goes far beyond war to the very imagination of the future as a whole.

REFERENCES

Bowles, Samuel, and Arjun Jayadev. 2004. "Guard Labor: An Essay in Honor of Pranab Bardhan." Working Paper 2004-15. University of Massachusetts at Amherst.

Caldeira, Teresa. 2000. *City of Walls: Crime, Segregation, and Citizenship in São Paulo.* Berkeley: University of California Press.

Cohn, Carol. 1987. "Sex and Death in the Rational World of Defense Intellectuals." *Signs* 12, no. 4: 687–718.

Sartwell, Crispin. 2010. *Political Aesthetics.* Ithaca, NY: Cornell University Press.

Shields, David. 2015. *War Is Beautiful: The* New York Times *Pictorial Guide to the Glamour of Armed Conflict.* New York: powerHouse Books.

slavick, elin O'Hara. 2007. *Bomb after Bomb: A Violent Cartography.* New York: Charta.

Security Aesthetics of and beyond the Biopolitical

*D. Asher Ghertner, Hudson McFann,
and Daniel M. Goldstein*

All things human hang by a slender
thread; and that which seemed to stand
strong suddenly falls and sinks in ruins.
—OVID

Security, we are told, is the defining characteristic of our age, the driving force behind the management of collective political, economic, and social life. Yet security resists definition, easily roaming across scales. Security is at once about protecting something as basic as an individual life—personal safety, both yours and mine—and as abstract as "our" collective defense—homeland security, public health, world peace. But security's aspirations are also grandiose, its justifications almost metaphysical. It seems to promise a forestalling of the inevitable death and decline of all that is "civilized" or "human," as per Ovid, a guardian against the barbarians at the gate, or in our midst. Incorporating all that people both yearn for and fear, security offers tremendous power to whomever can convincingly promise its delivery, proofing us against uncertain future perils. Thus, as both governmental technology and anticipatory device for defining and mediating potential future threats, security may very well be whatever the powerful say it is.

But such claims invite rebuttal, making security a highly contested terrain, closely keyed to sovereignty. While the state remains the principal actor in security production, the possibility exists for other aspirants to power to assert themselves by assuming the responsibility for providing security. This contestation occurs at different levels or scales, from the local to the national to the global. These include areas of intense social interaction, like schools, museums, and other public spaces; the contemporary cityscape, where street gangs, paramilitaries, mafias, ethnic organizations, and others establish sovereign claims through public performances of securitizing power; and spaces of social abandonment, such as vacant properties and buffer zones in conflict territories. Borders—both the "hard" systems of defensive fortification evident at international frontiers and the "soft" forms of border inspection practiced routinely in the interiors of nation-states—similarly condense and render visible security as an infrastructural apparatus for managing circulations, or managing the *perception* of circulations.

Notably, security's delivery is revealed through a negation: security is achieved when threats do not materialize and risks are obviated. Thus, doing security requires the constant staging of an absence, the performance of preemptive capacity, and the signaling of the potential to forestall or offset—encoded in objects (Advanced Warning Systems, inflatable life vests, razor wire), practices (airport screenings, border searches, a public "show of force"), and affects and imaginaries (collective fear, catastrophe scenarios, contingency plans). For this reason, we might consider security as much a sensibility as a calculative logic—something felt as much as thought. It is enacted through a population's collective recognition of risk and possibility, prompted through the bodily process of being squeezed through checkpoints, the awareness of being overseen by closed-circuit television, the fear generated in watching the Doppler radar of an approaching hurricane, or the sting of teargas. This sensory rooting suggests an analysis of security's aesthetic dimensions, observable in the menace of walls and fences, the reassuring display of an emergency landing card in a seat-back pocket, and the alarming image-figure of the "terrorist," "criminal," or "refugee" broadcast on the nightly news. The sensibility that such encounters provoke trucks in feelings of safety and apprehension, eliciting embodied reactions from a heterogeneous public implored to exchange its recognition of sovereign power for the sense, momentary and fleeting, of security.

This volume represents an intervention into the broad, interdisciplinary conversation about security and its societal expressions and effects, a conversation that has been ongoing since the dawn of the social sciences. The original Hobbesian and Lockean formulations of the social contract can, to an extent, be understood as agreements about security, or the willingness of a society to recognize sovereign authority in exchange for the policing of threats and the limitation of risk. More recently, during the Cold War and especially since the 9/11 attacks in the United States, the discussion about security has focused principally on conventional, biological, nuclear, and chemical attacks and terrorism as the preeminent national security threats. These threats are joined by concerns over pandemics such as SARS and swine flu in the sphere of biosecurity and attention to ecological catastrophe in the form of climate change, extreme weather events, and species extinction within environmental security debates. This post-9/11 discussion, dominated by political science and international studies, has tended to collapse security—as a broad approach to governing risk (Foucault 2007)—into a narrower problematization of challenges to state sovereignty in an era of the global war on terror. As Joseph Masco (2014) notes of the U.S. embrace of terror as the organizing concern of security policy, emotional management and threat awareness have, since 9/11, evolved as central components of the Western social contract. Leviathan is said to be under threat from all sides, often from sources that only the state security apparatus is able or allowed to know about. Threats to Leviathan stand in for threats to collective life, and the security of the state acquires such existential significance that the everyday violences people experience in regimes of securitized control are deemed of secondary concern.

The chapters in this volume, by contrast, train attention on these violences of everyday life and the ways in which security is lived and felt. The volume thus resists transhistorical or nation-centric notions of security and, through ethnographic analysis, shows how hard-edged logics of control—such as border hardening or landslide mapping—become far less determinate as they are perceived and experienced on the ground. While engaging security as "a biopolitical problem of the protection and betterment of a population's essential life processes in an indeterminate world" (Grove 2012, 140), the volume therefore attends to forms of securing the future that draw on nonquantifiable modes of governing. Here, we refer to both the means by which even calculable risks—assessable using biopolitical techniques like statistics, forecasting, and insurance—come to be governed by sensory processes that do not depend on techniques of risk assessment, as well as the forms of imminent threat that exceed biopolitical calculation, even when they are the central focus of security logics like preparedness and preemption (B. Anderson 2010; Collier 2008; Samimian-Darash and Rabinow 2015). Vulnerable lives are hence "futureproofed" not only by making risks measurable and therefore governable, but also by cultivating, through forms of sensory training, anticipatory subjectivities attuned to the possibility of unpredictable events.

We are concerned, then, with the question: How do we comprehend the sensory, symbolic, and affective experiences integral to the regulation of bodies and spaces, the delimitation of threats and vulnerabilities, and the securing of sovereign command through the promise of "proofing" society against future perils? The contributors to this volume respond to this question by providing ethnographic analyses of what we call *security aesthetics*. In asking what security looks, feels, sounds, smells, and even tastes like, we treat aesthetics in its broadest sense as the domain of sense perception, which includes the range of affective and intellectual faculties that combine to transform how the material world strikes the surface of the body into subjective judgments of taste. Derived etymologically from the Greek *aisthetikos*, meaning "sensitive, or pertaining to sense perception" (which is further derived from and relationally linked to *aisthēta*, "perceptible things"), aesthetics in its original sense rejects a dualistic outlook of viewer and viewed, subject and object, reason and feeling, instead foregrounding the experience of human design and the sensory world more broadly as grounded in a material-affective encounter through which judgments of beauty and order are formed (Guyer 2005; Manovich 2017). Security, in the pages that follow, lies in this domain between affect and order, sense and judgment, and inclination and directive, building from a classical *aesthetics* that antedates Alexander Baumgarten's eighteenth-century use of the word to develop the philosophy of artistic taste with which it is popularly associated today.

More specifically, we take up Jacques Rancière's (2004, 12) elaboration of the aesthetic as the "distribution of the sensible," by which he means "the system of self-evident facts of sense perception that simultaneously discloses the existence of something in common"—a shared aesthetic disposition, a normative arrangement of intelligibility—as well as "who can have a share in what is common to the community." The distribution of the sensible hence shapes how differently placed parts of the community see and can be seen, as well as what they can say; what gets recognized as speech versus mere noise; and who is authorized to speak in sensible terms.

Rancière's conceptual elaboration of aesthetic politics is rooted in the Aristotelian notion of citizenship as the act of partaking in government, a partaking that is prefigured by an "apportionment of parts and positions" determining those "who have a part in the community of citizens." The distribution of the sensible is thus at once *inclusionary*, building a shared "community of sense" (Rancière 2009) or an agreed upon set of terms and categories of sensible action, and *exclusionary*, as it rests on a prior social distribution of subjects, some external to the sphere of citizenship—the "part with no part." This broad framing accepts that aesthetic judgments have a necessary normative grounding, conditioned by cultures of practice, social conventions, and discourses of beauty, status, and order—what together might be called "the terms of sensi-

4

bility" (Ghertner 2015). It further recognizes the profound political stakes of how these terms of sensibility are codified and reconfigured—the domains of aesthetic consensus and dissensus that Rancière (2010) places at the center of his analysis of political hegemony. This capacious starting point allows us to consider how security, as a form of power, operates through distinct aesthetic registers, from notions of beauty and taste to style and genre, form and appearance, representation and mimesis, and emotion and affect.

To break this down further, we distinguish three intersecting modalities for framing and understanding security aesthetics: designing fortresses, screening threats, and calibrating vulnerabilities. By *designing fortresses*, we refer to the ways in which interventions in built form deploy visual and other sensory signals to fashion aesthetic norms about how security looks, sounds, and feels. Alongside, and often through, disciplinary techniques of defensive enclosure—such as the erection of walls or the installation of barbed wire— the cultivation of a fortress aesthetic enables the landscape to "speak," deterring threats and simulating order by prompting the viewing public to respond to normative standards of appearance. "Fortresses," then, refers not only to discrete residential, commercial, or governmental structures or territories designed to impose constraints through the power of the environment, but also to the broader sensory coding of security logics into the design of physical, geographical, and infrastructural milieux.

By *screening threats*, we mean the surveillant conversion of corporeal and spatial imagery into ostensibly self-evident, impartial, and predictive knowledge of dangerous aberration, as well as the material and symbolic systems developed to anticipate and respond to deviance. At the same time, we acknowledge more everyday forms of screening, from mundane acts of reading strangers as one navigates a city sidewalk to more patterned, but nevertheless ordinary, considerations of how investors and homeowners assess neighborhood safety in making locational decisions. Surveillance, though typically an apparatus of control directed by state security-making entities, here also operates as a tool of self-securitization by those located outside of, or parallel to, the state.

By *calibrating vulnerabilities*, we refer to the social regulation of how risks are recorded, imagined, and affectively experienced, often through sensory projections of a threatening Other. This includes a consideration of a range of signals, signs, codes, and sensory schemes for developing securitized ways of seeing and feeling, concentrated and honed in the practices of security experts, but more widely disseminated into a securitized public capable of sensing insecurity even when it is not rationally known.

Taken together, these modalities concern not only the ways in which security-aesthetic rhetorics and practices are instituted and normalized, but also how they are variously challenged, appropriated, and manipulated—or perceived and responded to in sometimes unexpected ways. In what follows, we provide a conceptual genealogy for understanding these three modalities in order to demonstrate that a concern with security aesthetics has long been central to security studies—although it has been, we argue, insufficiently analyzed. Attention to these modalities and their histories and various forms also provides a framing for the substantive chapters that follow, which themselves define and periodize security differently. While each chapter, like any given security apparatus, necessarily elicits different processes of aestheticization, each chapter also explicates the operation of the modalities of security aesthetics we introduce here. With an empirical focus on a range of security practices—including biosecurity, border and territorial security, cybersecurity, environmental security, neighborhood and school safety, and residential tenure security—they thus offer readings of twenty-first-century security as a sensory terrain shaped by affect, image, and form as much as rationalities, restrictions, and rules.

DESIGNING FORTRESSES: BUILDING AND MANAGING SECURE SPACES

> We have to do something about it, and we have to start by building a wall—a big, beautiful, powerful wall. It can have a gate. It can have a door. We'll let people in legally, but we have to stop what's happening to our country because we're losing our country.
>
> —DONALD TRUMP, INTERVIEWED ON *THE O'REILLY FACTOR*, AUGUST 18, 2015

In her landmark article in *Public Culture* in 1996, Teresa Caldeira used the phrase "aesthetics of security" to capture how visual rhetorics of status and taste shaped the segregation of urban space through a proliferation of "fortified enclaves" in São Paulo and, by extension, other cities undergoing rapid demographic and political transformation. For Caldeira (2000, 292), as she later put it in *City of Walls*, "aesthetics of security" refers to "a new code for the expression of distinction," one which "encapsulates elements of security in a discourse of taste and transforms it into a symbol of status." In locating this shift, in the 1980s and 1990s, toward an increasingly insular city marked by the precipitous obliteration of public space, Caldeira drew parallels between São

Paulo and Los Angeles, which Mike Davis (1990, 226) had earlier identified as a "fortress city" in which "the neo-military syntax of contemporary architecture," exuding a palpable hostility toward the street, combined with intensified policing and surveillance to partition the urban landscape (see also Low 1997; Penglase 2014).

Echoing broader studies of disciplinary architectures (e.g., Foucault 1977), which differentiate between physical controls that prohibit "risky" forms of behavior and psychosocial controls operationalized through human sensory reactions to the environment (Habraken 1998), Davis's and Caldeira's early formulations of security aesthetics evoke classical treatments of aesthetics as a domain concerning judgments of taste. Articulated most forcefully by Kant (1790, 52), judgments of taste differ from more ordinary judgments by their implicit claim to a type of universal validity, requiring agreement by others: "When [a man] puts a thing on a pedestal and calls it beautiful, he demands the same delight from others. . . . He blames them if they judge differently, and denies them taste, which he still requires of them as something they ought to have." The demand for recognition and agreement gives the aesthetic a normative power, which, as Bourdieu (1986) elaborates, can be used to train perceptions by correcting or dismissing "bad" judgments of taste.

The social function of security technologies—including gates, walls, barbed wire, and the broad design features through which spaces are seen as properly securitized—operates through similar logics of correcting aesthetic deviance and retraining improper judgment. Caldeira (2000, 295), for example, notes how residents of São Paulo initially found the securitization of houses strange but gradually became literate in "the new code of distinction," recognizing how well-enclosed spaces became key markers of status, separating private residences from the precarious housing found in the low-income neighborhoods, or favelas (see also Fischer, McCann, and Auyero 2014). Security technologies, then, are called upon not for purely disciplinary functions (e.g., imposed order or total surveillance) but as a means of producing a shared mode of public judgment that allows observers to participate in private practices of display, arrangement, and order that invariably contrast with the practices of those outside that community—those without taste, or with bad taste (see Dinzey-Flores 2013; Ghertner 2012). Those so classified may be regarded as suspicious, with a tendency to exhibit other failures of moral judgment, including a propensity for criminality, and hence themselves come to embody security threats. In a gated community, manicured lawns and uniform design standards contrast with the "less orderly" outside, which comes to be seen as a space of risk and uncertainty (Goldstein 2012). In Trump's United States, the "beautiful" wall—translated in the Department of Homeland Security's bidding process as a declaration that wall designs shall be judged, in part, based on "aesthetics" (U.S. Customs and Border Protection 2017)—operates as an idealized image of national sovereignty, despite its necessarily limited power to thwart what Wendy Brown (2014) calls "waning sovereignty."

The aesthetics of security within a disciplinary mode thus imposes a spatialized sense of order, a normativizing knowledge, and a visual grid of what does and does not belong, such that "the aesthetics of the proper" (Mirzoeff 2011, 3) establishes a feeling of what is right, even in the absence of the total surveillance upon which discipline is based. As George Kelling and James Wilson (1982) put it in their "broken windows" theory—which begins from the criminological idea that unrepaired windows in a neighborhood signal neglect and encourage further criminality—the landscape communicates, informing onlookers of acceptable behavior. Broken windows, here, are taken to indicate a visual coding of the street in a manner akin to Jane Jacobs's (1961, 32) classic account of sidewalk safety. For Jacobs, having "eyes on the street," untrained except in a shared sense of civility, became an informal means of social regulation maintained through "an intricate, almost unconscious, network of voluntary controls and standards among people." Oscar Newman's (1973, 4) theory of "defensible space" built upon this in seeking to incorporate what he called "corrective prevention" into the design of public housing projects. Falling under what is now known as "crime prevention through environmental design" (see Jeffrey 1971), space is securitized to the extent that one can "design-out" crime (Coaffee 2009). This technical end is achievable, in Newman's model, through designs attentive to four characteristics of defensible space: territoriality, natural surveillance, image, and milieu. Territoriality involves the deployment of real and symbolic barriers to establish "zones of influence," enhancing residents' "proprietary attitudes"—their feelings of territorial control and responsibility for maintaining security—while conveying a sense of dominion to would-be intruders (Newman 1973, 53). Figure I.1 shows this at work, introducing to a New York City public housing project a propriety security aesthetic based on white picket fencing, microspatial differentiation, and a linear geometry that clearly distinguishes inside from outside. This figure, taken from Newman's *Creating Defensible Space* handbook—published in 1996 by the U.S. Department of Housing and Urban Development—shows how the introduction of leading lines divides open space, building in natural surveillance that allows an onlooking subject to quickly identify spatial transgression. The third characteristic, image, employs design techniques, such as white picket fencing, to reduce the stigma attached to public housing projects,

BEFORE

AFTER

Figure I.1   A site redesign carried out by Oscar Newman (1996, 76) in a New York City Housing Authority project in the South Bronx. Newman describes the redesign as delivering "territoriality" by allowing residents to assert "control of the space and activities *outside* their dwellings," while improving "image" by cultivating a residential environment "that enhances their self-image and evokes pride." The "bottom line," according to Newman: "By subdividing and assigning all the previous public grounds to individual families, we have removed it from the gangs and drug dealers."

as well as the sense of isolation and vulnerability felt by residents and signaled to outsiders. Finally, the fourth characteristic, milieu, involves "geographical juxtaposition" with adjacent areas deemed to be safe, such as the positioning of building entrances so they face public streets.

While Jacobs and Newman, for different reasons and toward different ends, celebrated public civility and community-based policing as resources of collective problem solving and inclusive city making, others have emphasized how civility and beauty can become tools of control used to banish those reliant on public space (e.g., Harms 2013; Sorkin 2008). Ghertner's (2015) formulation of "aesthetic governmentality," for example, shows how bourgeois codes of civility were translated into a governing aesthetic used to evaluate the legality of urban spaces in Delhi, India. Amidst a crisis of calculative governmentality—which allowed slum dwellers to tamper with or expose the false premises of governmental records and thereby perpetually block demolition orders against them—the Indian judiciary shifted the epistemological basis of government to allow settlements to be declared illegal because, quite simply, they *looked* illegal. This was possible due to a reintroduction of colonial-era logics of nuisance law, which read not just objects or actions but whole population groups as potential nuisance categories. As a necessary defense of what Ghertner calls the "propriety of property" and bourgeois civility, slums were increasingly cast as insecure objects, nuisances to be managed rather than citizens entitled to governmental programs of improvement. In line with broader writing on (post)colonial urbanism, Ghertner thus shows how contemporary urban improvement programs continue to rely on colonial strategies of municipal control that use hygiene, order, and beauty as techniques of exclusion (cf. W. Anderson 1995; Kooy and Bakker 2008).

The proliferation of a type of "securitarian visuality" (Ivasiuc 2019), in which Jacobs's "eyes on the street" get weaponized into instruments of surveillance and fortress defense, can be tied more directly to what Neil Smith (1996) famously diagnosed as the revanchist city, oriented toward punishing those deemed obstacles to sanitized images of the bourgeois city. This is part of a global surge in efforts to produce the city anew through "vigilant visualities," or a watchful politics traceable to "the 'behind the blinds' surveillance of 1950s suburban neighbourhood watch" (Amoore 2007, 216). Whether through municipal efforts to create visibly vendor-free zones in historically informal market spaces of Cochabamba, Bolivia (Goldstein 2016), or "zero tolerance" policing that vilified key figures of disorder (the squeegee man, the turnstile jumper, the panhandler) in 1990s New York City, urban revanchism promising a new, more beautiful, and safe city is underpinned by a security aesthetic of fortress design.

The projection of security through fortress design and spatial management, though, can generate symbolic meanings and lived sentiments that conflict with the very logics driving securitization, challenging the terms of sensibility not only among those outside of them (the informal vendor, slum dweller, or migrant), but also within. Lisa Benton-Short (2007), for example, explores the increased presence of "hypersecurity" measures at the National Mall in Washington, DC. Although laden with symbolism evoking ideals of democracy and freedom, the mall has become increasingly partitioned by Jersey barriers (dividers made of plastic or concrete and used to separate lanes of traffic), bollards, and fencing. Here, "the aesthetics of security," Benton-Short (2007, 442) argues, was "at odds with the iconography of the Mall" and raised questions about its future as a public, democratic space. Trevor Boddy (2008) has described this highly visible temporary fortification, exemplified by the Jersey barrier, as a kind of "fear theming" or "architecture of dis-assurance." He suggests that after 2005, when the National Capital Planning Commission issued new design standards for construction on the mall, urban antiterrorism measures began shifting to an "architecture of reassurance" (cf. Marling 1997) as they became more permanent and less visible.

To account for this mutable relationship between security architecture's visibility and the feelings it may induce, Jon Coaffee, Paul O'Hare, and Marian Hawkesworth (2009) have devised a "spectrum of visible security" that ranges from conspicuous techniques of fortressing (e.g., walls and fences) to features that are visible but whose security purpose may not be immediately apparent (e.g., bollards, ornamental barriers) to deliberately concealed features (e.g., collapsible pavement). In so doing, they call attention to a series of "aesthetic paradoxes," that is, possible disjunctions between the messages transmitted through security features and the differentiated ways in which they are interpreted and responded to in everyday life. The management of public life, then, increasingly rests on the ability of security regimes to mediate these aesthetic paradoxes via effective threat screening and identification, balancing architectural and other experiential projections of control with the management of risky bodies, spaces, and behaviors.

SCREENING THREATS: RECOGNIZING RISK IN BODIES, SPACES, AND BEHAVIORS

It is not incidental that Michel Foucault (2007) introduces his framing of security through a discussion of the unique challenges associated with urban density and the complex social economy that emerged in the eighteenth-century city. The explosion in trade between city and country, the collapse of the old "walled city" wherein internal and external elements could be clearly ordered and separated, and the intricate conjugation of bodies, diseases, and resources circulating in and through urban markets made the functional differentiation of spaces imagined by, and required of, sovereign and disciplinary power impossible to maintain. This more polyfunctional urban milieu, an admixture of elements that made life itself contingent upon a range of aleatory mechanisms, was inherently unpredictable. So, instead of planning or controlling a *space*, security mechanisms would need to work upon and through the *milieu*, aiming to modify not discrete territorial units so much as the regulating logics of how people and things moved and interacted with each other—to manage what Foucault (2007, 20) called "an indefinite series of mobile elements."

The figures of the crowd, the street, the slum, and the market/bazaar, in both metropole and colony, litter nineteenth-century reports prepared by public health experts, police, architects, and planners, appearing as dense, shadowy webs only partially intelligible to a technologically advancing surveillance apparatus (see Dubber and Valverde 2008; Joyce 2003; Osborne 1996). The challenge for security mechanisms was to take the crowd, that indefinite series of mobile elements, and transform it into a population, an aggregate body abstracted from the "indefinite series." Security, as a mode of power necessary for the emergence of modern governmentality, thus begins with an explicitly calculative techne premised on statistical and actuarial logics that use a synoptic gaze to capture not every detail, but rather aggregate patterns concerning, inter alia, health, reproduction, criminality, and hygiene. This synoptic gaze makes action possible through a probabilistic rationality capable of governing through powers of normalization, a form of visibility used to track and improve the overall conditions of the population's welfare—to, for example, target the likelihood of criminal recidivism among victims of child abuse or bring the high rate of mortality from smallpox among infants into line with the rate found in the general population (Foucault 1977, 2007). For Foucault (2007, 63), the ability to treat the statistical normal—in the sense of a numerical distribution of the characteristics of a population—as a social norm or target of population governance means that the probabilistic gaze, focused on the likelihood of a particular individual or group having a certain social trait, can easily reduce to the normative gaze, dispensing with or forgetting the statistical construction of group attributes and naturalizing them as sociological or ecological truths. Ecological, economic, or epidemiological mechanisms of risk are then socially mapped as biological attributes of risky social groups, or people who live or work in proximity to risks—from slum dwellers to waste pickers to residents of ethnic enclaves and townships (see Baviskar 2003; Jaffe

2016). The "criminal type" and "potential terrorist" thus sit between probabilistic risk assessment and normative judgment of risky characters.

The projection of social deviance and the reenactment of a normative classificatory aesthetics is evident in what Allen Feldman (2005) calls the "actuarial gaze," a set of visual arrangements mobilized to sense and anticipate danger, and thereby exact optical command over everyday life. Building on Ulrich Beck's (1992) observation that the sphere of risk transcends the human sensorium due to the inherent imperceptibility of numerous threat potentials (e.g., radiation or air pollution), Feldman (2005, 206) theorizes the actuarial gaze as "the prosthetic extension of the human sensorium." This point is illustrated by U.S. Air Force drone targeting and surveillance in Afghanistan, which deploys a particularly potent form of mechanized threat screening (Gregory 2011; Gusterson 2016). Ethnographic research shows that the highly mediated "drone stare" participates in "an actuarial form of surveillance," mobilizing "categorical suspicion" to anticipate and manage risk (Wall and Monahan 2011, 240). Trained to mistrust their own perceptions, drone operators rely on the technologically mediated surveillance that drones offer as a means to detect threats "on the ground." Mere sight is no guarantee, then, for "objects become rifles, praying a Taliban signifier, civilians 'military-aged males,' and children 'adolescents'" (Gregory 2011, 203).

An earlier instance of "social sorting," to use David Lyon's (2007) phrase, is detailed by Allan Sekula (1986) in his illuminating essay on the advent of criminal portraiture in the nineteenth century, when photography intersected with numerical methodologies, incorporating techniques of physiognomy and phrenology, to regulate social life. Sekula focuses on two figures, Alphonse Bertillon, a Paris police clerk, and Francis Galton, the founder of eugenics and a key figure in the formalization of modern statistics. Whereas for Bertillon the photograph was indexical, of use for identifying individual criminals and potential recidivists, for Galton photographic images could be symbolic and typological, offering a means to generalize about heredity and race.

Thus, Bertillon's "signaletic notice," or "Bertillonage," combined anthropometric measurement and what are now known as "mug shots" to amass elaborate archives of individual criminal bodies that, before the criminological use of the fingerprint, could be used to confirm an association between a criminal suspect and a criminal record. Galton, by contrast, folded images of multiple bodies into composite portraits, which yielded average types, he claimed, through a kind of "pictorial statistics" (see Figure I.2). Rapists, in other words, had a particular look that, through pictorial rendering, would allow the police to profile

13

INTRODUCTION

Figure I.2
Francis Galton's
demonstration of
composite portraiture,
suggesting how
"criminal types" and
others prone to set
pathologies and
maladies could be
visually derived from
photographic case
records. Metropolitan
Museum of Art.

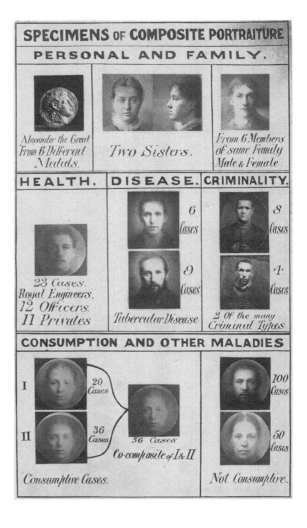

other potential offenders. Despite their differences, both approaches, Sekula (1986, 11) shows, ultimately derived from "the belief that the surface of the body, and especially the face and the head, bore the outward signs of inner character."

Despite the discrediting of phrenology, anthropometry, and racial forensics, the racialized schema of perception that they helped build remains embedded in contemporary criminal forensics' presumption that identity is unequivocally indexed to a biological self. The normative physiognomy of the social body hence continues to underlie the perceived objectivity of fingerprinting and other biometric techniques of "reading" the body's form. As

Frantz Fanon (1952, 111) puts it in his account of epidermalization, or the reduction of the human subject to her skin color: "Below the corporeal schema I had sketched [there is] a historico-racial schema. The elements I had used had been provided for me . . . by the other, the white man, who had woven me out of a thousand details, anecdotes, stories. I thought that what I had in hand was to construct a physiological self, to balance space, to localize sensations, and here I was called on for more." Fanon's confirmation of the characterological secrets that lie hidden beneath the surface of the body, of the semiotics of Blackness produced out of "a thousand details, anecdotes, stories," mirrors biometric technology's continual reliance on the statistical knowledge of anthropometry. Building on Lewis Gordon's (2006) notion of "white prototypicality," Simone Browne (2015) notes how "the racially saturated field of visibility" (Butler 1993) associated with social schemas of perception gets mapped into biometric technologies, producing what she calls digital epidermalization, that is, "the exercise of power cast by the disembodied gaze of certain surveillance technologies that can be employed to do the work of alienating the subject by producing a truth about the racial body and one's identity despite the subject's claims" (Browne 2015, 110). What Browne's concept of "digital epidermalization"—and the broader concept of "racializing surveillance" within which it is embedded—provides is a recognition that the actuarial gaze often reduces to the racializing gaze. Or, as John Fiske (1998) puts it, "Today's seeing eye is white." The same could be said of the biometric eye.

Epidermalization applies not just to visual technologies but to the whole forensic practice of reading the body, including fingerprinting, that most scientific of technologies (Breckenridge 2014). Describing the "cold hit" linking Brandon Mayfield to a partial fingerprint pulled from a bag of detonators recovered near the 2004 Madrid train bombings, Simon Cole (2006), for example, notes how a biometric match of this sort can actually generate the very suspiciousness of facts that might otherwise seem innocuous. Even in the face of strong exculpatory evidence, Mayfield was deemed suspicious and imprisoned for nineteen days based upon a potential fingerprint match and a post hoc profile: he had converted to Islam, had an Egyptian wife, and had ballistics expertise through his prior service in the U.S. Army. Despite the perceived "mechanical objectivity" of information technology and presumed infallibility of fingerprinting—reflected in the FBI's declaring Mayfield a "100% identification" with the Madrid partial print—the Spanish National Police eventually found the true source of the print, a Moroccan national living in Spain. The wrongful detention of Mayfield leads Cole to conclude that the only reasonable basis for the mismatched fingerprint was that the "suspicious information"—the "dark matter" of racialized optics that Browne (2015) argues underpins the entire surveillance apparatus—about Mayfield's profile leaked into the laboratory. If in Western philosophy Descartes's "malicious demon" (Ewald 2002) represents the ever-present threat that the rational subject's senses will fall victim to perceptual illusion, here the demon takes the form of the rational security apparatus itself. The "leak" of the racialized gaze into actuarial and forensic modes of securitization is most starkly evident in policies of racial profiling, where white prototypicality leads to the "illicit appearance" of Blackness (Gordon 2012)—which, much like the figures of the immigrant and refugee, produces Blackness as prototypically criminal.

The question of prototypicality—raised to a pseudo-science in Galton's forensic photography and still "leaking" into biometric technology today—confirms the continual blurring of superficially aesthetic readings of the body when prototype is reduced to phenotype, as well as the actuarial logic of security. The probabilistic interpretation that it was likely a Muslim who triggered a bomb in Madrid allowed an actuarial-security logic to appear to underpin assumptions about the character of a Muslim convert. The schematic racism implicit in prototypicality, though, in the Mayfield case and more generally, allows the racial-aesthetic logic to transcend the actuarial-security one, an exaggerated version of which appeared in President Trump's executive orders banning refugees and immigrants from Muslim-majority countries, even though zero terrorist attacks had been perpetrated on U.S. soil by citizens of the listed countries. A further example of the racial-aesthetic logic of profiling is provided through the statistical fact that the Transportation Security Administration (TSA) stops and frisks black women at airports nine times more frequently than it does white women, even though the former are found carrying contraband less than half as often as the latter (Browne 2015, 132). While travelers "with 'risky' surnames and meal preferences" tend to experience more intensive surveillance than others during air travel, the risk of "travelling while black" is registered here in the material-aesthetic surface of hair, or what R&B singer Solange Knowles called out in a clever play on words, "Discrim-FRO-nation," which she tweeted in 2012 after the TSA searched her for having her hair combed out (see Bennett 2005, 129–133). In Knowles's case, epidermalization was anatomized to a single body extension, deemed risky, as the TSA put it, due to its "puffiness." This marks a visual transposition of the security question "Does this person show signs of distress and agitation?"—which underpins the practice of remotely screening airline passengers' emotional states to detect "abnormal behavior" before it materializes as security breach (Maguire 2014; see also Maguire and Fussey 2016)—to "Did this person comb her hair like a criminal?"

Didier Fassin and Estelle d'Halluin (2005), writing on applications for asylum in France, see the body's surface emerging as another kind of evidence in security theater. They detail how more restrictive immigration controls since the 1980s, combined with growing suspicion toward asylum seekers and their biographies, have heightened the evidentiary value of medical certificates in asylum seekers' applications. Specifically, Fassin and d'Halluin see the rise of a new form of bodily governmentality, as asylum seekers are increasingly expected to display wounds to medical experts in order to verify their persecution—and thus demonstrate their eligibility for refugee status (see also Ticktin 2011). The display of the body to screening is also at issue in Rachel Hall's (2015) work on the "aesthetics of transparency," a rationality of government that seeks to produce docile citizens, willfully visible to biometric screening at airports, while projecting an image of the war on terror's enemies, in contradistinction, as "irredeemably opaque" (76).

Threat screening, though, is not only about how sovereign powers manage threat propensities. It is also an everyday navigational tactic by which those living in infrastructure-scarce environments outmaneuver (often state-induced) precarity by constantly experimenting with styles of communication, movement, and exchange to bypass or minimize risk and open up opportunity. While new forms of self-presentation, collaboration, and display are constantly necessary in the informal economies he studies, AbdouMaliq Simone (2004, 2010) offers a range of generative concepts for tracing how seemingly discrete styles of managing rhetorical situations—for example, how to make an illegal operation appear legitimate—add up to a genre of sorts, a mode of speaking or acting that people learn to mimic, weave together, and manipulate (see Bakhtin 1983). Under the rubric of "people as infrastructure," Simone shows the endless variation, evolution, and recombination of codes of practice required to read and navigate sources of collaboration or threat. To the extent that these styles of practice—seemingly parochial and unpredictable on their own—reference socially inferred conventions, they become cultural genres facilitating rich networks of economy and allowing a strong sense of security to be maintained outside of state-sovereign command (Simone 2010, 192).

CALIBRATING VULNERABILITIES: FASHIONING AN AURA OF (IN)SECURITY

In his writings on security, Foucault (2007) identifies two general conditions to which security mechanisms must necessarily respond, one juridical-moral and one cosmological-political. The first is evil human nature, implying that certain actors within the population will inevitably do things antagonistic to the goals of overall social welfare, and the second is "bad fortune," a concept requiring acceptance of inevitably undesirable outcomes (e.g., that the weather will sometimes be bad or that terrorists might someday pick your city). Security seeks to isolate evil and forestall misfortune, an important means of which is the calibration of vulnerabilities and the modification of sensory schemas of perception. For our purposes, this marks a point of departure for exploring the forms of aesthetic training central to the production of securitized publics, "communities of sense" (Rancière 2009) perceptually and affectively disposed to share in governmental schemes of sensing threat, but also prone to exceeding or reworking those schemes (Masco 2014; Pedersen and Holbraad 2015).

In contrast to juridical and disciplinary power, which focus on a possible event and seek to prevent that event from ever occurring, security, Foucault (2007, 37) writes in relation to food scarcity, tries to arrive at an apparatus (*dispositif*) for transforming scarcity into a nonevent. In this case, the apparatus was the "liberal" repeal of market restrictions (price ceilings, restrictions on hoarding or exports) and a system of *laisser-aller*, letting things take their course—quite the opposite of how we understand security mechanisms to operate with reference to the types of crises more prominent in security discourse today. And yet the central feature of how the event is transformed into a nonevent remains located in a process of displacing danger onto the biopolitical outside, the part of society *not* to be defended, the evil. As Foucault (2007, 42) puts it, the security event is split: the specific "scarcity-scourge disappears, but scarcity that causes the death of individuals not only does not disappear, it must not disappear." By allowing certain people to die of hunger, the scarcity event, a wider scourge, is avoided. In this manner, what would normally pass as an event is rendered nonevental through a partitioning of the pertinent from the nonpertinent, the human from the nonhuman (Mbembe 2003). The section of society reduced to bare life must be aesthetically rendered grotesque—the not-quite-human object of revulsion or unease (Agamben 1998; see also McFann 2014). Produced through a distortion or exaggeration of a human form, the grotesque is what one sees and tries to, but cannot quite, turn away from, arousing feelings of both fear and amusement in the observer (Kristeva 1982; Ruskin 1851).

Didier Bigo (2002), writing on the "governmentality of unease," details how the "transversal" figure of the immigrant, rooted in the myth of the state-as-body, allows politicians and a transnational field of security professionals to frame political problems in terms of threatening "penetrations," foreign breaches of bodily integrity. This pliant framing, Bigo argues, structures political thinking and discourse in a way that allows for endless adaptation and coordination across contexts, for the word "immigrant" may incorporate a seemingly limitless range of threats under the same sign. And yet, while migration flows can never be completely controlled, politicians and security professionals act on the basis that territorial control *is* possible, so that a sense of unease may be continually reproduced and cited to justify new security measures. Indeed, because fear gathers in proportion to the indeterminacy of the threat, the very amorphousness of the immigrant figure facilitates its instrumental mobilization, both as a scapegoat for policy failures and as the constitutive outside that reaffirms the body politic.

The slippage of signs and the nebulousness of risk may combine to propagate fear. Sara Ahmed (2004, 119) argues that emotions like hate and fear do not reside within individual subjects but rather circulate through "affective economies" and therefore "work by sticking figures together," such as the asylum seeker and the terrorist (see also Puar 2008), "a sticking that creates the very effect of the collective." In a commensurate vein, Brian Massumi (2005, 32, 40) has written on the color-coded Homeland Security Advisory System, created in the aftermath of 9/11, arguing that it was designed "to calibrate the public's anxiety" through a form of affective training. Without form or content, the alerts depended on fear in a solely anticipatory register, detached from any specific threat or experience of danger, such that fear could now "self-cause." In this sense, as a form of what Cindi Katz (2007) calls "banal terrorism," vulnerabilities are calibrated through the production of an atmosphere of fear, using visual and other sensory means to call into existence a generalized anxiety and simultaneously demanding the opening up of bodies to an array of forms of sensory training, or subtler sensory attunements to the security atmosphere (Stewart 2011; Turner and Peters 2015). At the level of national security practice, this is what Joseph Masco (2014) calls "national security affect." Masco specifically shows how the U.S. security apparatus mobilized 9/11 as an "ongoing existential danger," inserting Cold War–era nuclear fear into the twenty-first-century U.S. regime of counterterror. Echoing Foucault, Masco argues that the global war on terror rests upon "the promise of a world without events"—a war carried out on and through negative affects, in which the perpetual experience of insecurity is managed through a vague promise that that experience can be eliminated.

Barbara Sutton (2013), writing about perceptions of street violence in Colombia, describes a further attunement to a threatening environment through what she calls a "fashion of fear," represented by the downscaling of security design from the gated community to the bulletproof car and all the way down to the body through a different type of banal security object: fashionable armored clothing. As the pervasive logic of borders and fences becomes attached to the problem of moving and being present in threatening public spaces, how one dresses and self-presents becomes a domain of status that simultaneously reworks security into a question of individual choice and personal responsibility, rather than state violence or structural inequality. Security, then, is available for purchase, and ballistic apparel tells parents to either live in fear or take charge of their own lives, outfitting their children in shielded backpacks and polka-dotted bulletproof vests as a way to live securely and attractively.

A likewise illuminating perspective on vulnerability calibration is offered by Brent Steele (2010) in his writing on the "aesthetics of insecurity," a sensory domain he distinguishes to account for how collective bodies, including but not limited to the nation-state, fashion self-images through "aesthetic power." David Murakami Wood and Abe Kioyshi (2011) provide a similar articulation of what they call an "aesthetic of control" in Japan, whereby nostalgia for a mythologized past—a pre-1964 "Beautiful Japan" imagined to be clean and free of crime—serves to displace present anxieties about the future. Thus, just as visibility is produced via technocratic surveillance or public service announcements enjoining residents to see and anticipate danger, disappearance is enforced through intensified policing involving the displacement of homeless encampments whose presence sullies the idealized urban order (see also Jusionyte and Goldstein 2016).

In another context, but echoing Steele's broader claim, Katya Mandoki (1999, 78) explores how the Nazis used techniques of visibility to feign an aura of collective security. The regime engaged the aesthetic, she writes, through a series of substitutions—religion by art, art by propaganda, propaganda by indoctrination, culture by monumentalism, politics by aesthetics, and, finally, aesthetics by terror—"to frame the shapelessness of the masses and fabricate their fictitious image as an ordered, steady and invulnerable organisation." Yet, as Hudson McFann and Alexander Hinton (2018) argue, the pursuit of a pure, utopian order by genocidal regimes is always haunted by an "impassability," as their revolutionary visions are inevitably undermined by the threats they must continually produce. In the case of the Cambodian genocide, the focus of their analysis, just as the Khmer Rouge sought to create a pure, uniform society, the regime was undone by the threatening excess—various forms of "detritus," including physical garbage of the prior regime and its polluting traditions and incorrigibles—that it had to manifest in order to legitimize its violent transformation of Cambodia.

The challenge of instituting durable forms of aesthetic consensus is more evident with threats of long or unknown duration. For example, the field of nuclear semiotics arose in 1981 when the Human Interference Task Force

Figure I.3 "Landscape of Thorns," concept by Michael Brill and art by Safdar Abidi. This image depicts a hypothetical landscape rendered as unnatural and evil, with jagged and unwelcoming features that its designers thought would deter future human entrance, even in the absence of shared cultural conventions or criteria for assessing evil. Image reproduced from Trauth, Hora, and Guzowski (1993, F-61).

(HITF) was established by the U.S. Department of Energy to search for ways to reduce the chances of future humans unintentionally entering radioactive waste isolation zones. The project was continued in 1991 when a group of linguists, astrophysicists, architects, and artists were invited to the New Mexico desert to visit the Waste Isolation Pilot Plant, the only permanent repository for nuclear waste in the United States. The panel was assigned the task of devising a system to communicate to people, ten thousand years in the future, that entry into the waste zone was dangerous. Given this long time horizon, the existence of a shared language, standardized criteria of aesthetic judgment, or even cultural translatability could not be assumed, leading the panel to conclude that visual storytelling was the most viable solution. One proposal was to design a "landscape of thorns"—fifty-feet-high concrete spires with sharp points jutting out at different angles—aimed at scaring people away from a dangerous place, but worries crept in that this engineered landscape itself would become an attraction (see Figure I.3).

Earlier, philosophers Françoise Bastide and Paolo Fabbri (1984) had proposed a solution under the HITF that a breed of cat be genetically engineered to change color when exposed to radiation. Released into the wild, this new "radiation cat" would serve as a living Geiger counter, visually symbolizing risk when it turned an "unnatural" color. Proliferating songs, legends, and folklore about these "evil" creatures would create, they suggested, a durable culture of avoidance toward the distorted felines, passing the fear they elicited onto the spaces they occupied. Here, then, the juridical-moral concept of evil was deployed to avert the cosmological-political appearance of misfortune.

Sensory warning systems often rely on environmental signals rather than human modifications of species form. The growth of water lilies, which are drawn to warming waters, and the increased pollen production from common ragweed, caused by warming soil and higher atmospheric carbon dioxide concentrations, are two examples of aesthetic harbingers of climate change (Ziska et al. 2003). The earlier seasonal appearance of bright white and purple water lily blooms or their discovery in more northern locations tells the trained eye that temperatures are rising. The more intense irritation in the eyes and the more aggressive sneezes an allergic body experiences to higher pollen counts tell the body of environmental change. Scientific usage of satellite imagery of glacier retreat further functions as a "fingerprint" of global warming—as distinct from, yet often complementary to, calculative assessments of atmospheric temperature or snow mass.

SECURITY AESTHETICS AND THE MANAGEMENT OF LIFE

Each of the chapters that follow shows how the three modalities of security aesthetics charted above intermix in the making of differently imagined futures, illuminating the complex interplay of sense perception and articulated reason in how security apparatuses operate. They provide ethnographic illustrations of security aesthetics at work in diverse geographic and social situations, deepening and extending our framing conceptions through their context-specific interventions.

Victoria Bernal's chapter begins with a close reading of three recent museum exhibits unique in the U.S. context for focusing on cybersecurity. Responding to what she calls "digital opacity," Bernal shows how each exhibit uses distinct aesthetic techniques to make visible "the elusive digital." The first exhibit, Weapons of Mass Disruption, is aligned with the U.S. national security apparatus and develops a "masculine, futuristic geek" tech aesthetic. This exhibit trains audience members to fear future cyberattacks as the digital equivalent of nuclear warfare, while encouraging faith in government agencies to protect society from them. The Cyber Detectives exhibit, by contrast, uses low-tech analogs—including wooden keys as passwords and rotating dials to simulate cryptography—to depict the internet as a mechanical system that individual citizens can and should game and secure through routine practice. The third exhibit, Covert Operations, features internationally renowned artists and deploys a revelatory and dystopian aesthetics characterized by a pedagogical overtone meant to shock viewers into questioning the overreach of surveillance technology. As is typical of the curatorial space of the museum, the aesthetic orientation of the three displays is transparent and easily intelligible, supplemented by voiceovers, instructional text, or artists' statements. And yet, as Bernal argues, the ability of audiences to step into any of these orientations and seamlessly partake in their narratives suggests that the content of cybersecurity—including normative questions of what it is and should be—is as malleable as its form, making security aesthetics perhaps the key terrain for contesting how our digital lives are managed.

Shifting from elusive digital security threats to immediately recognizable environmental dangers, from landslides and floods to household accidents, Austin Zeiderman's chapter shows how vulnerabilities calibrated through decades of exposure have produced what he calls an endangered city. Contrasted with "danger," which indicates the presence of a specific, identifiable threat, "endangerment" refers to "the more general condition of being threatened," even after the concrete dangers that may have once placed lives at risk have subsided. Building on Bogotá's housing agency's own practice of sensory training—what it calls *sensibilización*—Zeiderman describes how a securitized urban citizenry is made through its response to public service announcements and environmental security programs. As an effort to raise awareness, make the public conscious of risk, and train perceptions, sensibilización, Zeiderman shows, shapes the political terrain on which poor *bogotanos* occupying flood- and landslide-prone hillsides pursue state care, having to identify and perform their endangerment to secure benefits. In Bogotá, systems of social inclusion and exclusion are hence increasingly conditioned upon "individual and collective abilities to perceive and respond to signs of danger."

Ieva Jusionyte considers security aesthetics less as a system of state provisioning than as a tool of violent exclusion, studying how border enforcement maims immigrant bodies while concealing its very techniques of violence through facade embellishments, architectural design, and the weaponization of topography. The border fence in Nogales, Arizona, along the U.S.-Mexico border is thus depicted by the U.S. Department of Homeland Security as an "aesthetically pleasing" infrastructural deterrent to potential border crossers, a means both of screening threats and building a national fortress. However, its actual effect, Jusionyte shows, drawing from ethnographic research with emergency responders, is to push would-be border crossers either into the deep desert, where they are more likely to suffer from dehydration or other environmentally induced illnesses, or over the top of the wall, where they suffer a range of injuries delivered by the tactical infrastructure that the wall and surrounding terrain jointly constitute. Security aesthetics here naturalizes injury as a feature of border life, concealing state-enforced environmental violence and rendering broken ankles and amputated fingers signs of illegal entry—a civil offense less than a humanitarian disaster.

Whereas Jusionyte's chapter focuses on futureproofing the U.S. border from the perceived threat of Central American and Mexican immigrants, Jon Carter's chapter turns to the everyday violence of Honduran neighborhoods, where the competing sovereignties of gangs and the militarized police compel youth to lie, hide, and sometimes flee north toward the United States. Tracing the shifting security aesthetics of more than fifteen years of anti-gang policing, Carter describes futureproofing as an art of survival premised on different, sometimes competing, forms of aesthetic labor and display. Ranging from the retelling of public secrets to the construction of personal security archives and the utilization of scannable police uniforms, Carter notes how the ability to read who is or is not police, gang, or both underpins an entire theater of security practice. Semiotic ambiguity was not always the norm, though, as prior to the adoption of tough-on-crime Mano Dura policing policies in 2003, youth transformed their bodies into a semiotic surface for expressions of counter-state security aesthetics, tattooing their faces with gang insignia as an act of refusal. Dissimulation and concealment—and when that is not enough, flight out of the country—are the new techniques through which ordinary residents stage security, leading Carter to turn ethnographic attention away from resistance and toward resilience and deferred surveillance as the means by which communities pursue safety.

Rivke Jaffe's chapter focuses on the sensorial politics of difference within don-controlled inner-city "garrisons" in Kingston, Jamaica. Examining how "Downtown" and "Uptown" Kingstonians—the former typically lower-income and darker in complexion than the latter—experience safety within these spaces, Jaffe shows how differentiated uses of security aesthetics relate to the formation of distinct but overlapping political communities. Political and gang graffiti, party anthems, arrangements of bodies, manners of speaking and greeting, hand signals, preferred reggae or dancehall sounds, and (non)uses of street signage thus weave together styles of garrison aesthetics, a set of material-affective relations not entirely dissimilar to those of the military base to which the term originally referred. However, rather than associating these aesthetic regimes only with feelings of fear, she emphasizes their function in generating positive sensations of safety, comfort, and familiarity for those within shared communities of sense, and further considers how modifications in the environmental intensities of sound and heat can shift the atmosphere of security to welcome Uptowners into the more culturally "authentic" Downtown. An analysis of security aesthetics, Jaffe thus suggests, helps move beyond rigid categories of race or neighborhood hierarchy, while also highlighting the built environment as a more-than-material domain of security practice.

Remaining alert to the aesthetic order of the street, Zaire Z. Dinzey-Flores and Alexandra Demshock ask what security looks, sounds, and feels like in gentrifying Brooklyn, New York. They do so by examining how real estate property listings depict and rebrand historically black neighborhoods as "safe" for affluent, mostly nonblack families. Focusing on the narrative and pictorial staging of interior residential spaces, but refusing to separate these more obvious strategies of interior design from the staging of neighborhoods, the authors consider how neighborhoods and their residents are arranged, organized, and pictured as part of what they call "the furnishings of safety." Just as a skilled stager might emphasize the original woodwork or iconic stone of an historic home, the reputation of "Do or Die Bed-Stuy"—the infamous name given to the once-gunfire-ridden-but-now-gentrifying neighborhood of Bedford-Stuyvesant—is not completely elided in neighborhood staging. Rather, real estate agents incorporate the neighborhood's history into a process of "narrative renovation" that invites would-be buyers to participate in neighborhood improvement while gaining the cultural cache of becoming an owner in a not-yet-discovered area. Through this and other aesthetic techniques, such as "picturing quietness" and "creating pre-fab escape hatches," real estate practice rests on racialized logics of public appearance and street order, but it spins them into lifestyle amenities perfectly suited to you, the self-conscious "American Gentrifier."

Turning to a radically different staged space, Rachel Hall explores the realist aesthetics of active-shooter drills executed in grade schools in the United States. Using the theatrical techniques of scripting, mise-en-scène, blocking, prop work, makeup, and improvisation, school boards willingly subject young children to worst-case scenarios—replete with fake blood, live ammunition, and unknown "intruders"—as a means to prepare them for the real thing. Noting how school drills have shifted from an older logistics paradigm, characteristic of the venerable fire drill, to an aesthetic one wherein students and teachers enter the mimetic world of scenario play, Hall argues that active-shooter drills function in a performative space that is variably "world-reflecting" and "world-simulating." That is, while they draw on references to an external reality of gun violence, which justifies the need for the drills, they also operate by forcing students to "submit to experiential training in which they play the potential victims of future acts of gun violence." Calling into question the security logic that has led more than two-thirds of U.S. schools to subject their children to an immersively traumatic experience, Hall challenges the aesthetics of the current security ethos of preemption, noting how efforts to "harden" children's psyches in anticipation of the "real event" ignore the very real violence of the performance itself and instill a tragic sensibility in one of our most important civic spaces.

Limor Samimian-Darash remains focused on the aesthetics of preemption in her chapter on the establishment of rules for Dual Use Research of Concern following a scientific lab's successful transformation of H5N1 avian influenza virus into an aerosol possibly transmissible among human beings. Tracing the ways in which the National Science Advisory Board for Biosecurity under the U.S. National Institutes of Health responded to the realization that biosecurity threats could emerge within the scientific community, rather than from the outside, she describes a shift in the aesthetics of biosecurity from danger, premised on a list of known possible threats, to risk—and, in parallel, from designing fortresses to screening threats. Yet because potential uncertainties, in which threats are not typically predictable, had to be rendered perceptible in order to establish rules of regulatory oversight, uncertain threat potential was reduced to a list of possible pathogenic outcomes. This produced an inherent mismatch between the uncertain form of the threat and its tangible conceptualization/visualization. Thus, while biosecurity protocols were meant to capture the uncertain terrain of emergent scientific practice, they remained locked in a framework of danger premised on predictability and concrete form.

The absence of predictability serves as the starting point for AbdouMaliq Simone's study of everyday life in Jakarta. Exploring a variety of experiential and experimental modes of living that he terms "standby," Simone shows how rampant financialization and real estate speculation—along with competing systems of property inheritance and subdivision—have led to everything from the search for means of daily waste disposal to the possession of something as seemingly permanent as land title to be governed by an array of shifting associations. Dominated by a pervasive sense of provisionality and an absence of clear logics of regulatory oversight, living in standby becomes an improvisational practice out of which "a sense of security is anchored in a certain insecurity."

When lease agreements and infrastructures become open and temporally non-durable, and where symbolic and aesthetic markers of the urban have ever-shifting spatial and political coordinates, standby marks a way of anticipating opportunities to align oneself with "architectures of possibilities," or specific lines of association that make aggregated outcomes possible but not predictable. Judgments of taste, Simone thus concludes of the conditions of "the urban majority," are not about moral validity or aesthetic purity, but rather become a sorting mechanism for knowing when to follow a line or wait for another one.

Alejandra Leal Martínez, finally, explores the experiences of displacement among informal street vendors and parking attendants in a rapidly gentrifying area of Mexico City, where aesthetic consensus is both more consolidated and founded on sharper moral coordinates than in Simone's Jakarta. Leal Martínez finds that a dominant middle-class security aesthetic premised on an absence of social mixing and orderly sightlines has masked longer-standing economic security concerns behind the sheen of urban renewal projects—a transportation hub and mechanized parking meters. Asking how the disappearance of this older sense of security as a collective, common horizon has articulated with new urban securitization initiatives, she shows how a sanitized public plaza and sterile digital parking meters come to operate as signs of the city's global publicness. But the reimagining of the city as a securitized fortress along these lines also generates a new aesthetic paradox: the invisibilization of informal workers' status as urban citizens means that compensation and support that might facilitate their transition into less "disorderly" professions can be read only as a wasted handout. Aesthetic purification, Leal Martínez notes, therefore cannot be articulated as anything but spatial cleansing, despite the public discourses of democratization and sustainable development driving it.

REFERENCES

Agamben, Giorgio. 1998. *Homo Sacer: Sovereign Power and Bare Life*. Stanford, CA: Stanford University Press.

Ahmed, Sara. 2004. "Affective Economies." *Social Text* 22, no. 2: 117–139.

Amoore, Louise. 2007. "Vigilant Visualities: The Watchful Politics of the War on Terror." *Security Dialogue* 38, no. 2: 215–232.

Anderson, Ben. 2010. "Preemption, Precaution, Preparedness: Anticipatory Action and Future Geographies." *Progress in Human Geography* 34, no. 6: 777–798.

Anderson, Warwick. 1995. "Excremental Colonialism: Public Health and the Poetics of Pollution." *Critical Inquiry* 21, no. 3: 640–669.

Bakhtin, Mikhail M. 1983. "Epic and Novel." In *The Dialogic Imagination: Four Essays*, edited by Michael Holquist, 3–40. Austin: University of Texas Press.

Bastide, Françoise, and Paolo Fabbri. 1984. "Lebende Detektoren und komplementäre Zeichen: Katzen, Augen und Sirenen" [Living detectors and complementary signs: Cats, eyes and sirens]. *Zeitschrift für Semiotik* 6, no. 3: 257–264.

Baviskar, Amita. 2003. "Between Violence and Desire: Space, Power, and Identity in the Making of Metropolitan Delhi." *International Social Science Journal* 55, no. 1: 89–98.

Beck, Ulrich. 1992. *The Risk Society: Towards a New Modernity*. London: SAGE.

Bennett, Colin J. 2005. "What Happens When You Book an Airline Ticket? The Collection and Processing of Passenger Data Post-9/11." In *Global Surveillance and Policing*, edited by Elia Zureik and Mark Salter, 113–138. Portland, OR: Willan.

Benton-Short, Lisa. 2007. "Bollards, Bunkers, and Barriers: Securing the National Mall in Washington, DC." *Environment and Planning D: Society and Space* 25: 424–446.

Bigo, Didier. 2002. "Security and Immigration: Toward a Critique of the Governmentality of Unease." *Alternatives* 27: 63–92.

Boddy, Trevor. 2008. "Architecture Emblematic: Hardened Sites and Softened Symbols." In *Indefensible Space: The Architecture of the National Insecurity State*, edited by Michael Sorkin, 277–304. New York: Routledge.

Bourdieu, Pierre. 1986. *Distinction: A Social Critique of the Judgement of Taste*. London: Routledge.

Breckenridge, Keith. 2014. *The Biometric State: The Global Politics of Identification and Surveillance in South Africa, 1850–Present*. Cambridge: Cambridge University Press.

Brown, Wendy. 2014. *Walled States, Waning Sovereignty*. Brooklyn, NY: Zone Books.

Browne, Simone. 2015. *Dark Matters: On the Surveillance of Blackness*. Durham, NC: Duke University Press.

Butler, Judith. 1993. "Endangered/Endangering: Schematic Racism and White Paranoia." In *Reading Rodney King/Reading Urban Uprising*, edited by Robert Gooding-Williams, 15–22. New York: Routledge.

Caldeira, Teresa P. R. 1996. "Fortified Enclaves: The New Urban Segregation." *Public Culture* 8, no. 2: 303–328.

———. 2000. *City of Walls: Crime, Segregation, and Citizenship in São Paulo*. Berkeley: University of California Press.

Coaffee, Jon. 2009. "Urban Restructuring and the Development of Defensive Landscapes." In *Terrorism, Risk and the Global City: Towards Urban Resilience*, 13–37. Farnham, Surrey: Ashgate.

Coaffee, Jon, Paul O'Hare, and Marian Hawkesworth. 2009. "The Visibility of (In)Security: The Aesthetics of Planning Urban Defenses against Terrorism." *Security Dialogue* 40, nos. 4–5: 489–511.

Cole, Simon. 2006. "Brandon Mayfield, Suspect." In *Suspect*, edited by John Knechtel, 170–185. Cambridge, MA: MIT Press.

Collier, Stephen J. 2008. "Enacting Catastrophe: Preparedness, Insurance, Budgetary Rationalization." *Economy and Society* 37, no. 2: 224–250.

Davis, Mike. 1990. *City of Quartz: Excavating the Future in Los Angeles.* London: Verso.

Dinzey-Flores, Zaire Z. 2013. *Locked In, Locked Out: Gated Communities in a Puerto Rican City.* Philadelphia: University of Pennsylvania Press.

Dubber, Marcus D., and Mariana Valverde, eds. 2008. *Police and the Liberal State.* Palo Alto, CA: Stanford University Press.

Ewald, François. 2002. "The Return of Descartes's Malicious Demon: An Outline of a Philosophy of Precaution." In *Embracing Risk: The Changing Culture of Insurance and Responsibility*, edited by Tom Baker and Jonathan Simon, 273–301. Chicago: University of Chicago Press.

Fanon, Frantz. 1952. *Black Skin, White Masks.* New York: Grove Press.

Fassin, Didier, and Estelle d'Halluin. 2005. "The Truth from the Body: Medical Certificates as Ultimate Evidence for Asylum Seekers." *American Anthropologist* 107, no. 4: 597–608.

Feldman, Allen. 2005. "On the Actuarial Gaze: From 9/11 to Abu Ghraib." *Cultural Studies* 19, no. 2: 203–226.

Fischer, Brodwyn, Bryan McCann, and Javier Auyero, eds. 2014. *Cities from Scratch: Poverty and Informality in Urban Latin America.* Durham, NC: Duke University Press.

Fiske, John. 1998. "Surveilling the City: Whiteness, the Black Man and Democratic Totalitarianism." *Theory, Culture and Society* 15, no. 2: 67–88.

Foucault, Michel. 1977. *Discipline and Punish: The Birth of the Prison.* New York: Vintage Books.

———. 2007. *Security, Territory, Population.* New York: Palgrave Macmillan.

Ghertner, D. Asher. 2012. "Nuisance Talk and the Propriety of Property: Middle-Class Discourses of a Slum-Free Delhi." *Antipode* 44, no. 4: 1161–1187.

———. 2015. *Rule by Aesthetics: World-Class City Making in Delhi.* New York: Oxford University Press.

Goldstein, Daniel M. 2012. *Outlawed: Between Security and Rights in a Bolivian City.* Durham, NC: Duke University Press.

———. 2016. *Owners of the Sidewalk: Security and Survival in the Informal City.* Durham, NC: Duke University Press.

Gordon, Lewis. 2006. "Is the Human a Teleological Suspension of Man? Phenomenological Exploration of Sylvia Wynter's Fanonian and Biodicean Reflections." In *After Man, towards the Human: Critical Essay on the Thought of Sylvia Wynter*, edited by Anthony Bogues, 237–257. Kingston, Jamaica: Ian Randle.

———. 2012. "Of Illicit Appearance: The L.A. Riots/Rebellion as a Portent of Things to Come." *Truthout*, May 12. http://www.truth-out.org/news/item/9008-of-illicit-appearance-the-la-riots-rebellion-as-a-portent-of-things-to-come.

Gregory, Derek. 2011. "From a View to a Kill: Drones and Late Modern War." *Theory, Culture and Society* 28, nos. 7–8: 188–215.

Grove, Kevin. 2012. "Preempting the Next Disaster: Catastrophe Insurance and the Financialization of Disaster Management." *Security Dialogue* 43, no. 2: 139–155.

Gusterson, Hugh. 2016. *Drone: Remote Control Warfare.* Cambridge, MA: MIT Press.

Guyer, Paul. 2005. *Values of Beauty: Historical Essays in Aesthetics*. Cambridge: Cambridge University Press.

Habraken, N. J. 1998. *The Structure of the Ordinary: Form and Control in the Built Environment*. Cambridge, MA: MIT Press.

Hall, Rachel. 2015. *The Transparent Traveler: The Performance and Culture of Airport Security*. Durham, NC: Duke University Press.

Harms, Erik. 2013. "Eviction Time in the New Saigon: Temporalities of Displacement in the Rubble of Development." *Cultural Anthropology* 28, no. 2: 344–368.

Ivasiuc, Ana. 2019. "Sharing the Insecure Sensible: The Circulation of Images of Roma on Social Media." In *The Securitization of the Roma in Europe*, edited by Huub van Baar, Ana Ivasiuc, and Regina Kreide, 233–260. London: Palgrave Macmillan.

Jacobs, Jane. 1961. *The Death and Life of Great American Cities*. New York: Vintage Books.

Jaffe, Rivke. 2016. *Concrete Jungles: Urban Pollution and the Politics of Difference in the Caribbean*. New York: Oxford University Press.

Jeffrey, C. Ray. 1971. *Crime Prevention through Environmental Design*. Beverly Hills, CA: SAGE.

Joyce, Patrick. 2003. *The Rule of Freedom: Liberalism and the Modern City*. New York: Verso.

Jusionyte, Ieva, and Daniel M. Goldstein. 2016. "In/visible—In/secure: Optics of Regulation and Control." *Focaal—Journal of Global and Historical Anthropology* 75: 3–13.

Kant, Immanuel. 1790. *Critique of Judgment*. Oxford: Oxford University Press.

Katz, Cindi. 2007. "Banal Terrorism: Spatial Fetishism and Everyday Insecurity." In *Violent Geographies*, edited by Derek Gregory and Allan Pred, 349–361. New York: Routledge.

Kelling, George L., and James Q. Wilson. 1982. "Broken Windows: The Police and Neighborhood Safety." *The Atlantic*, March. https://www.theatlantic.com/magazine/ archive/1982/03/broken-windows/304465/.

Kooy, Michelle, and Karen Bakker. 2008. "Technologies of Government: Constituting Subjectivities, Spaces, and Infrastructures in Colonial and Contemporary Jakarta." *International Journal of Urban and Regional Research* 32, no. 2: 375–391.

Kristeva, Julia. 1982. *Powers of Horror: An Essay on Abjection*. New York: Columbia University Press.

Low, Setha M. 1997. "Urban Fear: Building the Fortress City." *City and Society* 9, no. 1: 53–71.

Lyon, David. 2007. "Surveillance, Security and Social Sorting: Emerging Research Priorities." *International Criminal Justice Review* 17, no. 3: 161–170.

Maguire, Mark. 2014. "Counter-Terrorism in European Airports." In *The Anthropology of Security: Perspectives from the Frontline of Policing, Counter-Terrorism, and Border Patrol*, edited by Mark Maguire, Catarina Frois, and Nils Zurawski, 118–138. London: Pluto.

Maguire, Mark, and Pete Fussey. 2016. "Sensing Evil: Counterterrorism, Techno-Science, and the Cultural Reproduction of Security." *Focaal* 75: 31–44.

Mandoki, Katya. 1999. "Terror and Aesthetics: Nazi Strategies for Mass Organisation." *Renaissance and Modern Studies* 42, no. 1: 64–81.

Manovich, Lev. 2017. "Aesthetics." In *Keywords for Media Studies*, edited by Laurie Oullette and Jonathan Gray, 9–11. New York: New York University Press.

Marling, Karal Ann, ed. 1997. *Designing Disney's Theme Parks: The Architecture of Reassurance*. New York: Flammarion.

Masco, Joseph. 2014. *The Theater of Operations: National Security Affect from the Cold War to the War on Terror*. Durham, NC: Duke University Press.

Massumi, Brian. 2005. "Fear (The Spectrum Said)." *positions* 13, no. 1: 31–48.

Mbembe, Achille. 2003. "Necropolitics." *Public Culture* 15, no. 1: 11–40.

McFann, Hudson. 2014. "Humans-as-Waste." In *Discard Studies Compendium*, edited by Max Liboiron, Michele Acuto, and Robin Nagle. https://discardstudies.com/discard-studies-compendium/#Humansaswaste.

McFann, Hudson, and Alexander Laban Hinton. 2018. "Impassable Visions: The Cambodia to Come, the Detritus in its Wake." In *A Companion to the Anthropology of Death*, edited by Antonius C. G. M. Robben, 223–235. Hoboken, NJ: Wiley-Blackwell.

Mirzoeff, Nicholas. 2011. *The Right to Look: A Counterhistory of Visuality*. Durham, NC: Duke University Press.

Murakami Wood, David, and Kiyoshi Abe. 2011. "The Aesthetics of Control: Mega Events and Transformations in Japanese Urban Order." *Urban Studies* 48, no. 15: 3241–3257.

Newman, Oscar. 1973. *Defensible Space: Crime Prevention through Urban Design*. New York: Macmillan.

——. 1996. *Creating Defensible Space*. Washington, DC: Office of Policy Development and Research, U.S. Department of Housing and Urban Development.

Osborne, Thomas. 1996. "Security and Vitality: Drains, Liberalism and Power in the Nineteenth Century." In *Foucault and Political Reason: Liberalism, Neo-Liberalism, and Rationalities of Government*, edited by Andrew Barry, Thomas Osborne, and Nikolas Rose, 99–122. Chicago: University of Chicago Press.

Pedersen, Morten A., and Martin Holbraad. 2013. "Introduction: Times of Security." In *Times of Security: Ethnographies of Fear, Protest and the Future*, edited by Martin Holbraad and Morten A. Pedersen, 1–27. New York: Routledge.

Penglase, Ben. 2014. *Living with Insecurity in a Brazilian Favela: Urban Violence and Daily Life*. New Brunswick, NJ: Rutgers University Press.

Puar, Jasbir K. 2008. "'The Turban Is Not a Hat': Queer Diaspora and Practices of Profiling." *Sikh Formations: Religion, Culture, Theory* 4, no. 1: 47–91.

Rancière, Jacques. 2004. *The Politics of Aesthetics*. New York: Continuum.

——. 2009. "Contemporary Art and the Politics of Aesthetics." In *Communities of Sense: Rethinking Aesthetics and Politics*, edited by Beth Hinderliter, William Kaizen, Vered Maimon, Jaleh Mansoor, and Seth McCormick, 31–50. Durham, NC: Duke University Press.

——. 2010. *Dissensus: On Aesthetics and Politics*. London: Continuum.

Ruskin, John. 1851. "Grotesque Renaissance." In *The Stones of Venice*, 236–243. Cambridge, MA: Da Capo Press.

Samimian-Darash, Limor, and Paul Rabinow, eds. 2015. *Modes of Uncertainty: Anthropological Cases*. Chicago: University of Chicago Press.

Sekula, Allan. 1986. "The Body and the Archive." *October* 39: 3–64.

Simone, AbdouMaliq. 2004. *For the City Yet to Come: Changing African Life in Four Cities*. Durham, NC: Duke University Press.

———. 2010. *City Life from Jakarta to Dakar: Movements at the Crossroads*. London: Routledge.

Smith, Neil. 1996. *The New Urban Frontier: Gentrification and the Revanchist City*. New York: Routledge.

Sorkin, Michael. 2008. "Introduction: The Fear Factor." In *Indefensible Space: The Architecture of the National Insecurity State*, edited by Michael Sorkin, vii–xvii. New York: Routledge.

Steele, Brent J. 2010. *Defacing Power: The Aesthetics of Insecurity in Global Politics*. Ann Arbor: University of Michigan Press.

Stewart, Kathleen. 2011. "Atmospheric Attunements." *Environment and Planning D: Society and Space* 29: 445–453.

Sutton, Barbara. 2013. "Fashion of Fear: Securing the Body in an Unequal Global World." In *Bodies without Borders*, edited by Erynn Masi de Casanova and Afshan Jafar, 75–99. New York: Palgrave Macmillan.

Ticktin, Miriam. 2011. *Casualties of Care: Immigration and the Politics of Humanitarianism in France*. Berkeley: University of California Press.

Trauth, Kathleen M., Stephen C. Hora, and Robert V. Guzowski. 1993. *Expert Judgment on Markers to Deter Inadvertent Human Intrusion into the Waste Isolation Pilot Plant*. Sandia National Laboratories report SAND92-1382/UC-721. https://prod-ng.sandia.gov/techlib-noauth/access-control.cgi/1992/921382.pdf.

Turner, Jennifer, and Kimberley Peters. 2015. "Unlocking Carceral Atmospheres: Designing Visual/Material Encounters at the Prison Museum." *Visual Communication* 14, no. 3: 309–330.

U.S. Customs and Border Protection. 2017. "Design-Build Structure." Solicitation Number: 2017-JC-RT-0001. https://www.fbo.gov/index?s=opportunity&mode=form&id=f61a85538f383ec3ed9cac3c9e21d6fi&tab%20=core&_cview=1.

Wall, Tyler, and Torin Monahan. 2011. "Surveillance and Violence from Afar: The Politics of Drones and Liminal Security-Scapes." *Theoretical Criminology* 15, no. 3: 239–254.

Ziska, Lewis H., Dennis E. Gebhard, David A. Frenz, Shaun Faulkner, Benjamin D. Singer, and James G. Straka. 2003. "Cities as Harbingers of Climate Change: Common Ragweed, Urbanization, and Public Health." *Journal of Allergy and Clinical Immunology* 111, no. 2: 290–295.

The Aesthetics of Cyber Insecurity

Displaying the Digital in Three American Museum Exhibits

Victoria Bernal

Digital media raise new kinds of risks and new political questions about threats and security. There are aspects of digital media that make digital threats qualitatively different from crimes such as shootings, hijackings, bombings, and other more familiar threat scenarios Americans have been sensitized to, particularly since 9/11. One difference is at the sensory, experiential level where digital media pose perceptual challenges. Understanding issues of security involving digital media is difficult for ordinary people partly for aesthetic reasons. In this chapter I draw on the conceptualization of aesthetics put forward by D. Asher Ghertner, Hudson McFann, and Daniel M. Goldstein (this volume) where aesthetics provides a framework for considering sensory experience (how something looks, sounds, and feels) and for attending to the kinds of sensibilities that are invoked by certain performances, objects, and signals. The three modalities of security aesthetics outlined by Ghertner et al.—designing fortresses, screening threats, and calibrating vulnerabilities— help to reveal what is and what is not distinct about security in relation to the digital. The focus of my analysis is three American museum exhibits that deal with digital threats.

This chapter analyzes the overt representations and decodes the hidden cultural messages and values embedded in three exhibits: the Weapons of Mass

Disruption room at the International Spy Museum (hereafter "Spy Museum") in Washington, DC; the Cyber Detectives Exhibit at the Tech Museum of Innovation (hereafter "Tech Museum") in San Jose, California; and the traveling art exhibit Covert Operations, which I saw displayed at the San Jose Art Museum in California (although it was originally curated by Claire Carter at the Scottsdale Museum of Contemporary Art in Arizona). Given how entwined digital media are in people's daily lives, we might see discourses about digital threats as part of a sociotechnical imaginary that describes the world people now inhabit and envisions possible futures. The three museum exhibits each use distinct aesthetic techniques to present different narratives about the kinds of risks that should concern the public and to sensorily attune people to respond to them.

Museums might not be the most obvious venues for exploring the digital, since they are an old institutional form that historically has been slow to embrace the cutting edge of art, culture, and technology. Clearly museums are institutions of power and knowledge; they are pedagogical (Bennett 1995) and political institutions (Anderson 1991). The museum has been criticized for "presenting itself as the guardian of a separate realm of aesthetic experience, a neutral space," which "conceals its status as a political institution" that functions to reproduce the status quo (Hinderliter et al. 2009, 10). Yet the museum can also be seen as "a form of organization for possible social and cultural operations" (Hinderliter et al. 2009, 11). The museum itself constitutes an aesthetic form—one that is authoritative and elite. Museumgoers see exhibits on display, but the processes of curation and administration, and the debates and politics behind the decisions that produced the exhibits, are not visible. To enter a museum is to enter a space and time separate from the quotidian, and this decontextualized experience where one becomes especially attuned to one's own sense perception is part of what people seek when they go there.

As recent scholarship argues, aesthetics is not about abstract notions of beauty, nor is it purely about appearances; it is about how people's experiences of perception are related to norms and ethics, which contribute to the pleasure or discomfort they feel. Any aesthetic has a political dimension because it references "the historical configuration of social and perceptual experience" (Hinderliter et al. 2009, 5). Jacques Rancière's (2009) ideas about aesthetics as having to do with forms of visibility and intelligibility are pertinent to the project of analyzing how digital threats and security are imagined and experienced, and how they are given substance and communicated to the public by the exhibits I consider here. We might say, in other words, that these exhibits help construct a particular, securitized "distribution of the sensible," providing "terms of sensibility" (Ghertner 2015, 127) and possible conditions of consensus for reading and responding to digital threats.

Before analyzing the three museum exhibits, it is necessary to contextualize their efforts to represent the digital by considering the perceptual and representational challenges posed by digital media, situating the exhibits in wider discussions of security and aesthetics, and considering what is distinct about questions of security and threat involving digital networks.

DIGITAL OPACITY, THE EXPERIENTIAL GAP, AND DIGITAL THREATS

The way people usually experience digital media creates an illusion of privacy and safety. People engage with their devices and their online accounts in ways that make them appear to be separate and compartmentalized when, in fact, openness and connectivity are characteristic of the network and fundamental to how the internet works. I think of this as "the experiential gap" because people are receiving deceptive sensory cues when using digital media. The illusion may have become even more pronounced as smartphones and other personal devices have replaced public computers and internet cafes. The very term "personal" devices indeed suggests their discrete association with an individual. A text message or email one sends or receives appears to involve only the sender and the addressee. A person's possession of the device and what they experience suggests that they alone see what is on their screen and that only the intended recipient knows what has been sent. People relate to their devices as private and personal, and rarely does anything in their experience of digital media contradict the feelings of security and confidentiality. One example of an experience that does contradict the feeling of privacy is when someone searches for something online and later receives spam related to that search. In describing this experience, I have heard people say it feels "creepy" and even "scary." The creepiness and scariness of realizing one's online activities may not be private shows the degree to which people normally experience these as if they were confidential. While the 2013 revelations by Edward Snowden about the extensive reach of government surveillance programs and the 2018 scandal revealing Cambridge Analytica's lifting of tens of millions of Facebook profiles to try to sway the U.S. presidential election, in particular, informed the public that their digital lives actually are not private, this knowledge is purely intellectual and not something people can actually perceive when using their devices.

Another distinctive factor creating a sense of privacy and safety is what I term "the opacity of digital media." People see what is on their screens and the commands they execute, but they have no way of seeing what happens beyond or behind the screen when, for example, they send an email or text message.

Most people have very little knowledge of how the internet works even as they rely on it every day for many aspects of their lives. Their familiarity with digital media is largely confined to what they can see, hear, and touch, which has to do with the interfaces, applications, and hardware they use. The underlying codes, algorithms, and infrastructures are invisible and inaccessible to most people (Langlois, Redden, and Elmer, 2015; Parks and Starosielski 2015). Digital media are thus opaque in that their inner workings and extensive networks are not something users encounter or learn about through their ongoing experiences of using the media.

The experiential gap and digital opacity point to features of digital media that contrast with its celebrated features of interactivity and the empowerment associated with the decentralized participation it facilitates (Bernal 2014; Papacharissi 2015; Rosen 2012). Considerations of digital aesthetics, moreover, have mainly focused on the quality and characteristics of digital images and sounds. Aesthetics, as Sean Cubitt (2008, 28) points out, demands a wider scope, but "digital aesthetics has the uncomfortable job of looking at many things, from celnets to Internet governance, that simply cannot be seen or touched."

With regard to cybersecurity, the situation is further complicated by the fact that digital harm is often imperceptible. An account or device may be hacked, yet the owner remains unaware. One's data is collected (and perhaps shared, surveilled, or sold), but one still has it, and one experiences no change. Hacks, even those involving millions of accounts, such as the massive 2014 hack of Yahoo, which did not come to light until 2016, commonly go unnoticed for years. Digital media thus sustain an illusion of security and privacy because there is no experience of intrusion, interruption, or any other sensory cue. The 2013 Snowden revelations about the U.S. government's mass surveillance programs showed that corporations and the state could collect and store information on Americans' digital lives while people remained totally unaware of the data the National Security Agency was stockpiling on them (Greenwald 2015). One of the less recognized aspects of the Snowden revelations is that not only did Americans not know that the government was collecting their data; they did not know that many of these kinds of digital capabilities even existed. They did not know that data could be intercepted at key transfer points or that devices could be turned on remotely or that someone could witness their keystrokes as they typed.

The experiential gap, the opacity of digital media, and the imperceptibility of harm to the average person mean that it largely falls to experts to determine the nature of digital threats and to explain the risks and possible safeguards to the public. Screening threats and constructing security can never be a purely technical matter, however, regardless of how complex the technologies involved. Thus, while Americans have been increasingly exposed to discourses about cybersecurity, what it is that poses a threat, who or what is to be secured, and by what means remain ambiguous and contentious. A coherent common sense about these matters has yet to be established. For example, the FBI casts encryption as a threat and talks of the dangers of "going dark," while Apple's CEO Tim Cook, among others, argues that encryption is a fundamental cornerstone of security.

ANALOGIES, METAPHORS, AND THE ELUSIVE DIGITAL

There are inherent challenges in representing digital data and its circulation and storage. The lack of materiality makes representation through visual imagery problematic. In the aftermath of the Snowden revelations, for example, images of huge government buildings in the Utah desert used to store data became iconic symbols of mass surveillance. These immense and rather mysterious concrete forms seemed to suggest the grand scale of the surveillance operations, portending an ominous gravity—their size communicating the weightiness of the matter. Yet the image of these buildings told people very little. In some sense the buildings could be seen as standing in for everything the public does not know about the government's data collection.

Cultural reference points and legal ideas lag behind digital developments, so government officials, journalists, tech experts, and scholars addressing issues of digital surveillance and security resort to diverse images and metaphors to bridge old and new in order to communicate digital matters to the public. The images that have been invoked include needles in haystacks, backdoors, reading someone's mail, peering into bathrooms, and leaving keys under doormats. Many of these images are reassuring in their simplicity. While U.S. government officials invoke the threat of terrorism to defend mass surveillance, famously using the rationale that "we need a haystack to find a needle," others see these same actions as a threat to the public. One of the most alarming analogies comes from Bruce Schneier (2016, 3), who compares weakening encryption to poisoning restaurant goers:

> Of course, criminals and terrorists have used, are using, and will use encryption to hide their planning from the authorities, just as they will use many aspects of society's capabilities and infrastructure: cars, restaurants, telecommunications. In general, we recognize that such things can be used by both honest and dishonest people. Society thrives nonetheless because the honest so outnumber the dishonest. Compare this with the tactic of

secretly poisoning all the food at a restaurant. Yes, we might get lucky and poison a terrorist before he strikes, but we'll harm all the innocent customers in the process. Weakening encryption for everyone is harmful in exactly the same way.

These rather ill-fitting analogies of searching haystacks—in fact the proverb holds that you *can't* find a needle there—and eating in restaurants illustrate some of the conceptual imprecision and communicative challenges associated with questions of digital security.

Three significant museum exhibits have recently entered into this confusing and evolving societal conversation about what digital threats might look like and what exactly cybersecurity stands for. They each employ novel strategies to confront the aesthetic problems posed by representing the internet and associated threats, offering particular interpretations and experiences to the public. While Americans have been receiving diverse messages about these issues from a range of official and unofficial sources in various news media and television shows, museums offer a particularly interactive and immersive experience of images, texts, objects, and sounds, building a type of security atmosphere that works sensorily as well as narratively on its audience (Turner and Peters 2015). The museum experience blends leisure, entertainment, and education. Each of the three exhibits I analyze presents a different view of digital threats and our digital lives, and they do so through distinct aesthetic repertoires and techniques.

The Cyber Detectives exhibit is important not only for the unusual approach it takes to representing the digital, but because it bills itself as the very first museum exhibit focused on cybersecurity. Located in Silicon Valley in the San Jose Tech Museum, the Cyber Detectives exhibit is within walking distance of the San Jose Art Museum where the Covert Operations exhibit, explored below, was displayed in 2015. The contrast between how these two exhibits, available to the same public, dealt with questions of security and digital media was striking and seemed to call for comparative analysis. Before visiting these two exhibits, I had already been intrigued by the Spy Museum's dramatization of digital threats. These three exhibits together reveal the different aesthetic renderings of opaque digital threats and the different political stakes of how security is rendered intelligible.

The three exhibits articulate different messages, employ different aesthetic approaches, and loosely represent particular perspectives. The Spy Museum conveys a U.S. government national security perspective, whereas the Tech Museum reflects Silicon Valley tech culture—both of which are deeply involved in questions of cybersecurity. The Covert Operations exhibit, however, reflects a critical artist perspective, an outsider, nonexpert view in relation to government and technology industries. One might also describe the three museums as devoted respectively to entertainment (the Spy Museum), science (the Tech Museum), and art (the Art Museum), although each museum combines elements of all of these curatorial elements. In terms of the modalities of security aesthetics addressed by Ghertner et al. (this volume), "calibrating vulnerabilities" is particularly dominant in the Spy Museum's exhibit, while the Cyber Detectives exhibit creates experiences of "screening threats." The modality of Covert Operations is one of calibrating vulnerabilities, but vulnerabilities constructed in very different ways than those of the Spy Museum. The security aesthetics of "designing fortresses" is one that highlights what is distinct about digital security—its firewalls, antivirus protections, and other such fortifications are not physical barriers, and they are not visible (except to coders), yet the vocabularies and metaphors around them do participate in clear regimes of security aesthetics. The convergence and divergence among the aesthetic techniques and narratives of the three exhibits reveal the complex contours of struggles over competing visions of digital security, as well as differing understandings of the present world and the future. I begin the analysis with the Spy Museum, then explore the Cyber Detectives exhibit, before turning my focus to the art exhibit, Covert Operations.

CYBERWAR AND THE INTERNET AS WEAPON

The Spy Museum in Washington, DC, devotes one room to the twenty-first century, and its theme is the weaponization of the internet, addressed under the rubric "://Weapons of_Mass Disruption." This exhibit thus posits digital threats as the major challenge of our century and, through nuclear analogy, presents an apocalyptic view of the possible future. Joseph Masco's (2014, 2) exploration of the culture of the American national security state argues that "counterterror" following 9/11 has created an "unlimited space and time horizon for military state action" and "a world without borders, generating threats without limits." Cyberspace lends itself to new scenarios of danger on an expansive scale because it is already imagined as borderless, global, and future-oriented, offering a perfect field for the development of such threat imaginaries. The exhibit's immersive experience is designed to cause visitors to recalibrate their sense of the scale and significance of digital threats and to foster feelings of vulnerability.

In the museum, the visitor arrives at the Weapons of Mass Disruption room only after visiting the rest of the museum, having moved through a series of chronological exhibits. Tony Bennett (1995, 179) eloquently criticizes this conventional "narrative machinery" of museums as designed so the "ideologies of progress" and evolutionary narratives are "realized spatially in the form of routes that the visitor was expected—and often obliged—to complete." To fully understand the vision of the twenty-first century and digital media presented by the Spy Museum, it is helpful to first explore the context of the museum and the experience of its other exhibits. This museum, which opened in 2002, is a private institution, but its director and many of its key advisers are former government intelligence personnel. The museum's director spent thirty-six years at the CIA. According to its "History and Mission" statement, the museum draws on experts in the "Intelligence Community," and its list of advisers includes former directors of the FBI and the CIA.[1]

The Spy Museum's stated aim is to "educate the public about espionage and intelligence in an engaging way." Its mission statement asserts that the museum is "committed to the apolitical presentation of the history of espionage in order to provide visitors with nonbiased, accurate information." It also claims to provide a "global perspective." A former member of Russia's KGB and a former member of Britain's MI5 are also listed among the museum's advisers; however, the museum showcases the evolution of spying and intelligence largely from an American perspective. Exhibits are organized chronologically, and one of the earliest artifacts one encounters is a 1777 letter written by George Washington. What "global" and "apolitical" mean in this context is suggested by a sign at the entry to the first exhibit hall, "School for Spies," stating: "The skills you will discover are timeless, shared by spies of every land. . . . Learn them as if your life depended on it. Because it may." The museumgoer is thus invited to learn about spycraft as if training to become a spy. The sign also states that what is displayed in the museum are "not Hollywood inventions," although the exhibits nonetheless include artifacts from James Bond movies and photographic stills from *Get Smart*, the 1960s television comedy about spying. These, along with the pretense that visitors are training to be spies, lend a playful element to the presentation. The dominant aesthetic of the museum halls is ultramodern and hi-tech, much more in keeping with a science museum than a history museum. The visible materials are metallic, plastic, and glass, and the space has a spare, cold feel to it. It is a total environment; there is no natural light, nor any windows. Information and images are displayed on screens. In some sections it feels a bit like being inside a submarine or a spacecraft. If I had to coin a term for this aesthetic, I might call it "masculine futuristic geek" to denote the fact that it is not just masculine, hard-edged, and slick, but also techie and intellectual, with a hint of sci-fi. This interior design asserts a claim to power, authority, and the future. We, the museumgoers, are there to learn, to be guided through the rarified knowledge of spies.

Much of the spying and code-breaking the museum covers took place during actual wars, yet the focus of the exhibits is not on weapons and destruction, but rather on the intricate techniques and technologies of espionage, intelligence gathering, encryption, and code-breaking. These are illustrated with real artifacts used by spies, such as fake beards, bugging devices, and camera watches. The focus shifts abruptly in the final twenty-first-century room, which is devoted to the digital age. The first thing a visitor encounters is the title of the room, "://Weapons of_Mass Disruption." This phrase has been used by the Department of Defense in reference to the internet (Lawson 2013). As this title indicates, the exhibit presents the internet as a battleground and weapon of war. The aesthetics of this label itself is interesting for the way it combines nuclear-related text with symbols associated with the internet, a fusing of the fear of fission onto cyberspace. The nuclear analogy of the room's title is made more explicit in the exhibit description: "In earlier decades, we feared nuclear war," but "today computer networks in our homes, businesses and government are key targets for infiltration, espionage, and attack.... Cyberspace has become a battleground for the military, terrorists and spies." The exhibit accords little attention to the issues of secrecy, cryptography, surveillance, and leaking associated with information technologies, even though such issues are more in line with the museum's focus on spycraft and intelligence and more in keeping with the rest of the museum's exhibits.

To communicate its vision of digital threats, the twenty-first-century exhibit has to contend not only with the difficulty of representing cyberspace and digital networks, but also with portraying events that have not yet happened. The other exhibits in the museum are historical, organized around artifacts from the past, but this room is engaged in anticipating future threats. The exhibit ends up relying heavily on spoken narrative. The dominant feature is a video of "top experts," many of them current and former government officials, talking about the destructive threat posed by possible cyberattacks to infrastructures and to American life as we know it. The exhibit also displays a large map of the United States depicting the power grid, above which glowing letters pose the question: "Could power lines turn into battle lines?" (see Figure 1.1). For reasons unclear to me, but perhaps suggestive of the difficulty of illustrating the scenario of cyberwar with existing artifacts, the exhibit features several items from the James Bond film *Skyfall* (2012). Another artifact on display is a laptop said to have belonged to a notorious hacker. Yet, seeing an ordinary (dated) laptop tells the visitor nothing about the methods and skills

Figure 1.1   Weapons of Mass Disruption exhibit at the International Spy Museum, Washington, DC.

of hackers or about the workings of digital networks. This is an example of digital opacity—what one sees of and on a digital device is only a surface that does not provide clues to the capabilities it possesses.

Texts in the exhibit state that rampant looting and anarchy would break out in mere days were a cyberattack on infrastructure to cause electrical outages and shortages of goods. It is significant that, in this scenario, part of the danger Americans face is from what their fellow citizens would do in an emergency. Through constructing a chain reaction of human chaos, the internet is presented as a weapon of mass destruction that can quickly cause the collapse of American society. To heighten the sense of danger, the room suddenly goes completely dark at one point to simulate the experience of a cyberattack on the power grid. While the authoritative threat narrative of the video and references to "weapons" and "battle lines" are narratively alarming, the simulated attack attempts to overcome the experiential gap by supplying what is usually lacking where digital threats are concerned—something that can be directly experienced through the senses. This is an aesthetic of vulnerability, conveyed via an enveloping atmosphere intended to affectively jar the museumgoer. As the nuclear analogy suggests, fear of attack is not new to Americans. This exhibit is not creating a condition of fear where none existed; it is sounding the alarm about a new vector of vulnerability, a new kind of attack to fear by drawing upon a reserve of latent fear of unpredictable threats.

Clearly, the Spy Museum is partly, perhaps primarily, about entertainment, and being momentarily submerged in darkness can provide a thrill or at least a surprise. Yet the need for drama and entertainment value is not sufficient to account for the exhibit's overall focus on a catastrophic cyberattack. There is little emphasis on dramatic war scenarios in the earlier rooms that cover periods of actual warfare. In fact, a whole room is devoted to Bletchley Park, Alan Turing, and code-breaking, all of which can be seen as antecedents to the development of computing. These earlier exhibits also foreground intelligence—both in the sense of information gathering and human inventiveness. Yet these narratives are not drawn forward into the twenty-first-century room. Visitors are instead presented with the specter of a cyberattack on the United States and a vision of the internet as a dangerous weapon analogous to an atomic bomb. The content of the exhibit, moreover, makes clear that government experts have the important knowledge about threats and security. There is no encouragement of any form of agency on the part of museumgoers.

When I visited the exhibit in 2014, there was no mention of cybersecurity, nor of any other measures ordinary people might take to avert the doomsday scenario presented. The spycraft skills and techniques showcased in the earlier exhibits are not referenced. Ultimately the exhibit hails the viewer as a particular kind of securitized citizen, one whose sense of vulnerability is recalibrated in light of a potentially catastrophic future—and one who is expected to have faith that government experts can avert this future, if given the power to do so.

DIGITAL LOGICS AND PUZZLES

Spies and detectives have much in common, but the Cyber Detectives exhibit at the San Jose Tech Museum presents digital threats and cybersecurity in ways that contrast sharply with the aesthetics and narratives of Weapons of Mass Disruption. Cyber Detectives, which opened in 2015, bills itself as the first interactive exhibit on cybersecurity.[2] The Tech Museum exhibit is optimistic in its overall tenor, quite unlike the ominous atmosphere and warnings about cyberattacks offered by the Spy Museum. Significantly, the Cyber Detectives exhibit engages visitors in hands-on problem solving that foregrounds human agency and is designed to materialize aspects of the internet that are normally invisible. For the most part, it does so through specially designed analog artifacts that illustrate underlying principles of digital technology. Through analogous experience, the exhibit uses a mechanical style to overcome elements of the experiential gap and the opacity of digital media, but in doing so reduces abstract and systems-based risks into discrete, almost game-like objects.

Screens are barely present in the exhibit; it is as if the audience has stepped through to the world behind the screen, experiencing the principles and seeing the mechanisms by which computers and the internet work. The game-like environment makes sense given its target audience, which is more school-age than adult. Aesthetically, this is communicated in part by the way displays are labeled—in very large letters on brightly colored backgrounds. The method is generally one of learning by doing, as compared to receiving knowledge imparted by the authoritative voices of experts, as in the Spy Museum exhibit discussed above. The spirit of play is built up through interactive exhibits that take the form of puzzles or problems to be solved.

The exhibit physically shares with the Spy Museum a lack of any natural light, but without evoking the same feeling of enclosure. The space is much more open, with a very high ceiling, and the visitor moves freely from one station to another in a large area according to preference, rather than via the more curated, winding path through consecutive rooms found in the Spy Museum. The game-like experience of the Tech Museum exhibit is further enhanced through the scoring system visitors are offered based on tasks accomplished. Stations within the exhibit invite the visitor to accomplish particular tasks by manipulating physical objects. The first station one encounters upon entering teaches about the internet as a system. It consists of physical game pieces labeled "routers," "servers," and "firewalls" on a display table that lights up to show the connections between the pieces when they are placed on the board (see Figure 1.2). The lights indicate whether the data traveling between two pieces is corrupt. The goal is to get the system design configured so that it is interconnected but protected by firewalls.

This introduction to the internet offers a distinctly low-tech, 1980s-gameboard-like aesthetic. It eschews any form of technophilia, runs completely counter to the lure of flashy consumer goods like smartphones or tablet computers, and avoids any aura of awe about the wonders of computers. The museum materializes cyberspace, making it hands-on while also devoid of precious, fragile, or possibly intimidating technology. Throughout the exhibit, many objects are made of wood, a familiar and organic substance inviting tactile encounter and fiddling. In the router game, firewalls must be placed to reduce vulnerabilities, but here, like in the rest of the exhibit, there is no threat scenario, enemy, or danger other than "corrupt data." While the exercise is explicitly about screening threats, the nature of the threat is presented in technical,

Figure 1.2 Server display at the Cyber Detectives exhibit, Tech Museum of Innovation, San Jose, California. Photograph by author.

even benign terms. In some sense the threat comes from within, from the risks created by bad or faulty design.

The curator and developer of the exhibit, Michelle Maranowski, in a radio interview, says the exhibit has two goals: "to empower our guests with the tools to be safe online" and "to introduce our visitors to the idea of cybersecurity as a career" (Maranowski 2015). Maranowski has a degree in electrical engineering and has worked in Silicon Valley since 1997. What I experienced as games, she describes as "training," explaining that visitors assume the role of a new cybersecurity professional and enter "the training zone," where they learn skills, before entering "the mission zone," where they will apply them. This contrasts with the Spy Museum, where, after learning the tools and techniques of spycraft, the visitor is confronted with a digital threat scenario in which what they have seen (camera wristwatches, fake beards, and shoes with secret compartments) will be of no use.

Surprising to me is that Maranowski does not mention in the above interview the creative analog displays that are the most distinctive feature of Cyber

Detectives. One such station, Creating Code, represents the way computer programming works as a series of commands. The visitor confronts a machine-like wooden contraption whose various moving parts can be coordinated to propel a ball from start to finish. The visitor must set speeds and timing, choosing the right commands in the right sequence to get the contraption to complete the task. This involves step-by-step logic and trial and error to get everything configured correctly. In the process, it reveals the kind of precision that is needed when writing code because a computer follows your commands, not your intentions.

The exhibit's open, colorful, free-flowing design and use of game-like materials creates an aesthetic very different from the hi-tech, futuristic, hard-edged atmosphere at the Spy Museum. In contrast to the dark room, closed space, and aesthetic sense of unknown and unknowable vulnerability that engulfs and dwarfs the visitor in the Weapons of Mass Disruption room, the interactivity of the Cyber Detectives exhibit foregrounds the human, bringing the scale of the internet down and breaking it up into different components that can be manipulated. This gives the visitor a sense of control over technology, rather than being at its mercy. Where the temporality of the Spy Museum is progress oriented, futuristic (even when presenting historical artifacts), and predictive, the temporality of Cyber Detectives is the now. Visitors work their way through a series of hands-on experiences that need not follow a particular order, each involving different information and skills, but all set simultaneously in the time frame of the present.

At the Cryptography: Secure Exchange station the visitor is invited to "hack a secret message." Here, there are a series of large wooden dials that one can rotate in order to decode messages. Texts of the exhibit explain "symmetric" and "asymmetric" cryptography and how public and private keys work. One of the examples is called a "Cardon Grille," which the sign explains is an example of steganography, where holes in the grill reveal a secret message in a text. "Rail Fence" is an example of what they label a "transposition cipher," while "Caesar Cipher" is a substitution cipher. Significantly, although this exhibit teaches the concepts underlying digital encryption, it mentions nothing about end-to-end encryption or cell phone data, which have been hotly debated particularly in relation to the 2015 shooting in San Bernardino, which led to a standoff between Apple and the FBI. This omission may be because the exhibit was designed prior to the 2015 controversy and has not been updated, but it is also consistent with the way digital technology is decontextualized and depoliticized throughout the exhibit.

It is, thus, important to consider not only what the exhibit shows, but what is not addressed. There is nothing about politics, rights, war, or terrorism in the exhibit. Since the exhibit appeals to youth, it is surprising that it also makes no mention of digital privacy issues or sexting. An area called Passwords and Picking includes several stations, one of which involves a giant wooden lock and key, with wooden pins that visitors must manipulate to rekey the lock. The exhibit explains that "a key is similar to a password." I could not figure out how to work the wooden pins to rekey the lock, and a museum docent showed me and my companion how to do it. He then remarked, "Now I need your names to send to the FBI. We are creating criminals here." This informal, joking comment was the only thing encountered in the exhibit that raised the issue of government surveillance, an issue of increasing national and international concern.

One of the most elaborate features of Cyber Detectives is a group of four small rooms set up as offices where the visitor is given a mission to solve hacking problems by following various clues. A video says "welcome to cyberattack simulation center" and explains that a "vicious series of cyberattacks" have occurred on a recycling company and your mission is to stop them and identify "the criminals." Hackers are simply described as "criminals" in contrast to the Spy Museum, where hackers were presented as terrorists or dangerous enemies. In the interview mentioned earlier, Maranowski (2015) explains that the missions are based on actual events and designed to depict four basic kinds of attack: espionage, sabotage, social engineering, and financial hacks. In talking about such hackers, she says, "I call them criminals," and she refers several times to "good guys" and "bad guys," a reference that evoked for me a simpler, childish world of television Westerns and apolitical outlaws. "Bad guys" in this view are not a looming, amorphous, catastrophic threat of the twenty-first century but merely a fact of life, part of the mundane world that contains both good and bad. These are the perspectives on display in the mission zone of the exhibit.

Significantly, "the victim" of the hacking is a corporation, but not just any corporation; its business is recycling, so it is clearly a "good guy." Using skills gained in the training zone, and following clues and hints in each room (guided also by a recorded voice that ensures each visitor will succeed), the visitor solves the problem and gets the recycling company running again. One mission starts with the report that "criminals have installed malware" on Acme Recycling, which is interfering with the factory's operation. We must search a computer for malware. As an inside joke perhaps, the malware, we later discover, is named "stucksnet," an echo of Stuxnet, the infamous U.S. government malware that was used to attack Iran's nuclear plant.

For these missions, the museum creates an immersive environment that places the visitor in a simulated real-world situation with a domestic aesthetic. You do not enter a hi-tech command center with glossy computer screens.

Each mission is instead contained in a room set up to look like someone's very ordinary and homey office with a computer on a desk, some books on a shelf, and a photograph on the desk. The digital world of the internet is not experienced as a grand, futuristic presence, but is rather integrated as one facet of a familiar, workaday environment. The simulated offices are given a personal feeling and individualized through various accessories. On one desk there is a photograph of a pet chihuahua named Jorge, and "Jorge" turns out to be the password that works to access the computer. The computers in these rooms are not really operational; they are set up to display only specific information related to the mission. In another room "banking information has been stolen," and your mission is to "save the company from having its money stolen." Since these rooms are designed to depict contemporary life, they contain excess cultural information not directly relevant to cybersecurity. One includes an unfortunate gender stereotype, in which a woman customer calls the bank to complain about not being able to pay for a pedicure.

One of the other rooms features a desk on which the visitor sees a framed photo of a man who looks South Asian. The desktop computer displays a screen saver that to me looked like a photo of the Blue Mosque in Istanbul. Whether this was meant to suggest that "good guys" could be brown skinned and Muslim, or whether we are meant to see the mosque image as put there by the hacker, is not clear. Another desk is decorated in the style of a Silicon Valley techie, featuring books on stereotypical Bay Area leisure interests: coffee, whales, and hiking.

Cyber Detectives represents the internet as a logical system, presenting challenges and puzzles that are solvable through human ingenuity. It takes a novel approach through specifically designed artifacts that represent in simple, physical terms the way networks are organized, how code works, and some of the methods used to infiltrate systems and to secure digital data. The experience makes technology and digital threats unintimidating, in part through a low-tech, small-scale, and even homey, aesthetic. However, the exhibit approaches digital technology in a way that decontextualizes it from any social, political, or ethical issues or questions. The exhibit achieves its goal of empowerment, but its approach to empowerment is individualistic rather than social. This may reflect the neoliberal and even libertarian culture of Silicon Valley. In the interview mentioned above, curator Maranowski (2015) asserts that "as a user I have to be careful," reflecting a view of cybersecurity that places responsibility on the individual rather than on tech developers or government regulators. The museum's webpage about the exhibit says, "We are each responsible for protecting our own digital lives." Also on the webpage, under the title "Exploring Ethics and Cyber Security," are several links relating to issues of encryption and surveillance. However, these links take you off the museum's website to a Santa Clara University website, and there is no mention of these issues in the museum exhibit itself.

Depicting hackers as bad guys while setting up a corporation as the good guy/victim is a political choice, but there is no acknowledgment within the exhibit of any conflict or debates about digital technologies. Visitors are told nothing about the politics of digital rights, surveillance, the war on terror, or digital privacy. The digital risks or threats that are included in the exhibit are simply posed by "corrupt data" and "criminals." This is striking given that the exhibit opened two years after the 2013 Snowden revelations, which showed that corporations and the U.S. government were engaged in massive, secret digital data collection on average Americans.

The art exhibit Covert Operations was inspired in part by issues of government secrecy, and the form and content of its messages about digital threats present a sharp contrast with the security aesthetics of the Spy Museum and the Tech Museum.

SECURITY, POWER, AND VIOLENCE

Covert Operations was inspired, according to the blurb on its catalog, by the aftermath of 9/11 and seeks to pursue "the complicated intersection of freedom, security, secrecy, power and violence" (Carter 2014). It begins, therefore, by acknowledging the role of politics in the exhibit, something neither the Spy Museum nor the Tech Museum exhibits do. It also locates itself in a particular social, historical temporality—that of post-9/11 America. Covert Operations features the work of thirteen international artists "who have collected and revealed unreported information on subjects ranging from classified surveillance to terrorist profiling, narcotics trafficking to ghost detainees, and nuclear weapons to drone strikes." Based on this framing, one can juxtapose it with the Weapons of Mass Disruption exhibit, which likewise is engaged with a post-9/11 America-under-threat, yet one framed from the perspective of the CIA, the FBI, and other intelligence experts. In contrast to the ways the Spy Museum's exhibit assumes the viewpoint of U.S. intelligence, and with how the Tech Museum's exhibit depoliticizes digital technologies, the San Jose Art Museum's exhibit starts with the issues of government secrecy and power. While "information" is mentioned in the catalog blurb, digital media is not. Yet the digital has a strong place in the exhibit because of the subject matter addressed and also because some of the artists work in that medium. Unlike the other two museum exhibits described above, which do not have an associated publication, the catalog of Covert Operations is a large-format book of 124 pages that, along with images of the artwork, includes several essays that contextualize the project (Carter 2014). Before turning to the visitor experience of the exhibit, I analyze these texts.

The foreword to the catalog states: "This exhibition and publication focus on the time period after 9/11 and consider the methods, results, difficulties and limitations encountered by government agencies and private individuals to maintain safety and security" (Rodgers 2014, 9). It explains that the artists use "techniques that duplicate and/or parallel those deployed by governmental agencies to cover and uncover information" and notes that "every day, we hear new information about how we in the United States are involved in elaborate webs of misinformation and deception" (Rodgers 2014, 9, 10). In the prologue, curator Claire Carter begins by referencing geopolitics, the Cold War, and the threat of nuclear war as setting the stage for many of the artworks in Covert Operations. She mentions global superpowers' "increasingly sophisticated use of media, surveillance and government misinformation" (Carter 2014, 13). Immediately following the prologue is a two-page photo spread showing the Twin Towers on 9/11, with one tower burning as the second plane nears impact. Following this is Carter's essay, "Bearing Witness: Freedom, Security and Violence after 9/11," in which she writes that the artwork arises from the artists' "insistence upon civil rights protections, transparency, open government and adherence to human rights" (Carter 2014, 19).

Carter's essay discusses several of the artworks while contextualizing them with detailed explanations of the United Nations' Universal Declaration of Human Rights, the Geneva Conventions, and the U.S. Freedom of Information Act and the Patriot Act, including references to major court decisions and quotes from The 9/11 Commission Report. Carter (2014, 21) writes that "every effort has been made to verify the authenticity of the artists' information; no research was taken at face value. Works . . . that conflate historical facts and fictional narratives . . . were excluded." Such truth claims are rather unusual for an art exhibit. It is clear that Covert Operations aims to educate viewers about issues of security, surveillance, and state power. Cumulatively, the art in the exhibit suggests a dystopian world of hypersurveillance, borderless and lawless U.S. militarism, and government secrecy in relation to the public, a world that is deeply entwined with digital technology. In some ways this exhibit is kindred to the project of this volume, concerned to explore "how security looks, sounds, and feels." Art contains a reflexivity about representation that may facilitate a critical perspective. The standpoint of the artist looking at the world that comes through in Covert Operations contrasts with the scientific orientation of the Tech Museum or the expert perspective of the Spy Museum, where things are presented as self-evident, impartial, and unfiltered by any perspective. At the simplest level, the art museumgoer is made aware of the existence of different perspectives by the label accompanying each piece identifying the artist who made it.

Covert Operations is comprised of thirty-seven distinct artworks by thirteen different artists. One result of this is that the experience is less immersive than either Weapons of Mass Disruption or Cyber Detectives, where a unified vision is presented throughout. As staged by the San Jose Museum of Art, there was nothing distinctive or unusual in the way Covert Operations was presented as an art exhibit. It followed the conventional, neutral art museum format where the visitor moves through a series of galleries in which the various artworks are displayed, an aesthetic that gives prominence to the artwork itself rather than to its surroundings. The galleries feel light and airy with high ceilings, wooden floors, and white walls. In one sense, the dominant aesthetic of the experience is that of any contemporary art museum: a safe, serene, elite space that requires no vigilance on the part of visitors, freeing them to lose sense of their immediate surroundings as they allow themselves to be drawn into works of art.

Upon entering the exhibit, my attention is immediately drawn to the bright and moving lights on a large installation of industrial-style electronic signage arcing from the wall to the floor. Its LED lights display circulating messages in red, white, and blue. The scale and form of the signs as well as the brightness of the display and its continuous scroll suggest it has an important and up-to-date message. I struggle to read the messages, but the letters flash by and, although I can make out words, I am not able to follow the sentences they form or find the meaning of their content. Later, in the exhibit catalog I read that in making this piece, titled *Ribs*, Jenny Holzer used source material from declassified U.S. government documents, but broke up the texts into fragments. The catalog copy states that "by dematerializing official documents into the electronic signals interpreted by a computer and pushed through an LED sign, Holzer further dispersed their content" (Carter 2014, 60). Figure 1.3 shows this dispersal at work, depicting snippets of text whose banality is rendered eerie through word repetition and the installation's radiating effect. Considering this work in light of how its content was made, it seems to me that it performs a kind of Marshall McLuhan demonstration where the medium is the message, prompting the viewer to reflect on how messages get their meaning or their authority.

While still in the first gallery of the exhibit, suddenly the hushed ambiance in which I and other museumgoers are contemplating the art is eerily

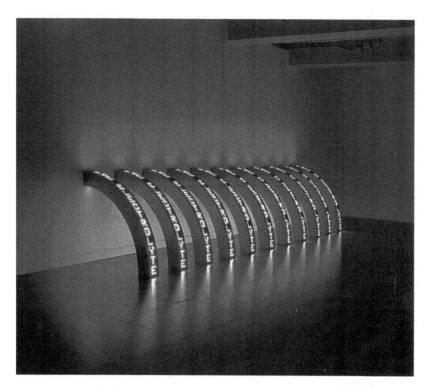

Figure 1.3 Jenny Holzer, *Ribs* (2010): eleven LED signs with blue, red, and white diodes. Image reproduced from Carter (2014, 61).

broken by a loud series of bell chimes. This aural disruption, I later learn, is from David Gurman's piece, *The Nicholas Shadow* (the title relates to an image of St. Nicholas on the bell). The artist has set up a huge bell to ring on the hour, chiming once for every civilian casualty in Iraq that day thus far. It is quite literally a death toll. The death count is updated hourly based on data accessed from the website Iraq Body Count (www.iraqbodycount.org) by a computer that also controls the bell. The chimes of the bell, by reaching the audience directly through the senses, communicate the losses in a way that is more powerful than statistics. In the museum, the way that sound carries across the rooms interrupts the separate space in which each artwork in turn holds the viewer's attention while they tune everything else out. Once every hour, the sound of the bell dominates and changes the atmosphere.

One could compare this experience to the sudden darkness in the Spy Museum. As in that experience, the element of surprise is significant. In the

Art Museum, it is mysterious because viewers may hear the chimes before they have reached the bell itself. When I heard it, it sounded vaguely to me like an alarm of some kind, a warning signal that someone had gotten too close to a piece of art or opened an emergency exit door perhaps. And perhaps it is meant to sound an alarm. This work does not make the workings of digital technology less opaque. However, it uses digital data to create a sensual, aural experience that physically conveys to us information that is hidden or oft-ignored, information that even when known may be difficult to fully perceive or feel. The catalog notes on this piece state that "the designer, technologist and installation artist David Gurman specializes in visualizing data" (Carter 2014, 64).

Several artworks are concerned with technologies' visual and data-gathering capabilities, addressing drones, satellites, and surveillance cameras. Other works address various forms of data, record-keeping, and documentation. Taryn Simon's photographic series *An American Index of the Hidden and Unfamiliar* includes an image of transatlantic undersea cables reaching land in New Jersey. The photograph shows industrial flooring and walls with five big cables coming up through the floor. This photograph, as Simon's title states, makes visible the "hidden and unfamiliar" infrastructure of digital networks that rely on physical cables that traverse the globe. The photo thus materializes the internet for the viewer, showing how it is bound to the earth and, particularly for the American viewer, how the internet is physically bound to the nation (the photo is part of an "American Index," and the label tells the viewer that the photograph was taken in New Jersey). This image can be seen as working against the opacity of digital media, revealing its material dimension. Another photograph in this series shows a church, which the label explains is part of a U.S. military set used for simulations of urban combat (see Figure 1.4). The next photo is a computer-generated image showing the same church with a burning car in front and terrorists aiming guns at civilians (see Figure 1.5). The effect of viewing these two images is disturbing, suggesting either that there is no safety anywhere, no line between civilian settings and battle zones, or more likely that the U.S. government views the world in terms of threat potentials and worse-case scenarios. In this latter sense, the viewer, through the images, is getting a chance to see things through the militaristic, hypersecuritized lens of the state, where what appears to be an innocent scene must always be read as waiting for an imminent attack.

"Camera Room, New Mexico, 2007" is part of David Taylor's series about the U.S. border, *Working the Line*. It is a poster-sized photographic print showing the inside of an office that is clearly conducting surveillance. Only one

person is visible, a man working at a desk off to one side. Computer screens dominate the image. Fourteen screens are arrayed in two rows across one wall of the office, each displaying a different, presumably live image, while another giant screen looms in the corner, overshadowing the man at the desk. We see him from the back, looking at four screens that occupy his desk, and we see three more digital screens displaying data and video feeds on another desk in the foreground. The room has no windows and most of the light in the room comes from the digital brightness of the screens. What we see is digital surveillance in practice, the visual data being streamed into this office on all of these screens suggests the power and ubiquity of surveillance. Just as Simon's piece showing the threatened church indicates how public and state perceptions of threats are engineered, here the actual mechanics of threat screening are shown in all their scary wonder. Yet we also see the screens and the work of surveillance as oppressive and dehumanizing to the surveillor. He is the lone, isolated human presence in this room, dwarfed by the technology that surrounds him. Thinking of this office in relation to those depicted in Cyber Detectives' simulations, we see how the aesthetics of the office contains a narrative about technology, threats, and humanity. In Cyber Detectives, one senses a human presence, even though no worker was present. The digital threat there is specific and easily handled, allowing the resumption of office normality. In Taylor's image, by contrast, we see a disturbing new normal where the threat is unspecified and ubiquitous, requiring constant surveillance everywhere and, what is worse, where the pursuit of security produces a miserable life. Taylor's image suggests a dystopian digital future, but as the title reminds us, it is already here in "Camera Room, New Mexico, 2007."

Entering another gallery of the exhibit one sees a large white wall covered with columns of text, long lists that make no sense. They are in alphabetical order. If you happen to look at the D's, they begin with "Dark Tea, Darwin, Data Clarity, Data Detective, Data Logic/RDS, Data Mining Suite, Data Serfer, Data Surveyor, Dataminer 3D, Datamite, Datascope, Datasurferplus, . . ." The D's end with "Dreamland." This is Trevor Paglen's work *Code Names, 2007–Present*.

55

THE AESTHETICS OF CYBER INSECURITY

Figure 1.4 (Opposite, top) Taryn Simon, *"World Church of God," Simulation Military Operations on Urban Terrain (MOUT), Fort Campbell, Kentucky* (2007). Image reproduced from Carter (2014, 97).

Figure 1.5 (Opposite, bottom) Taryn Simon, *Military Operations on Urban Terrain, Virtual Simulation, MetaVR, Brookline, Massachusetts* (2007). Image reproduced from Carter (2014, 97).

On seeing it, the viewer is confronted first by the sheer mass of material, the number of different names, and then, on closer inspection, by the strangeness of the names and phrases themselves, like "Crew Valiant," "Eelpot," "Moon Smoke," and "Omnidex." The grand size of the work gives the viewer a sense of the vast scale of covert government action, while the individual names invoke the mystery and secrecy that shrouds these programs. The knowledge that the government is working behind the scenes to maintain the status quo or protect the nation might, under some circumstances, be reassuring. But confronting the enormity of the hidden realms and the eeriness of the strange language has the opposite effect. The encounter is unsettling, seeming to contradict or belittle one's quotidian knowledge of the world through the evidence of this other unknown reality.

Even where the names make some kind of sense ("Geotagger," "Outlaw Hunter," "Pathfinder"), the viewer is prompted to wonder what these code names stand for. What activities were carried out by the U.S. government under "Granite Sentry," "Indigo Serpent," or "Looking Glass"? The exhibit label explains that the work is based on years of research and "includes the 2013 release of classified material by National Security Agency private contractor Edward Snowden." Paglen's work could be understood as another form of data visualization, translating knowledge about secret programs into a simple, powerful form: black text on a white background, which through its orderly alphabetized columns mimics the aesthetic and organizational form of a bureaucratic document. This is a deliberate symbolism, as the museum catalog states that "the stark black-and-white palette is fundamental to the work. The covert world is often referred to as 'black,' while sanctioned and acknowledged programs and activities are described as 'white'" (Carter 2014, 72).

Here, in seeing secret names revealed, the experience is not the thrill of unmasking or unveiling. Instead, the art invokes a kind of awe at the magnitude of hidden realms and secret codes that the viewer knows are operating even as they stand contemplating art in a museum. It is not the secret that is revealed so much as the practice of secrecy itself, here made into a spectacle. According to the catalog, this work is not finite, but an ongoing process to which Paglen makes additions and deletions.

Paglen's work *Lacross/Onyx II Passing through Draco* is a photograph of the night sky with what is described as a U.S. covert satellite streaking across it (see Paglen 2009 for details on his research and observational methods). Another photograph by Paglen in the exhibit is labeled *Untitled (Reaper Drone)*. This is a huge, beautiful image of a blood-red sky that appears empty. From the (un)title we know it is not. The work, thus, invites the viewer to inspect it very closely, searching the vast sky to discern the drone. Eventually, we locate it—way off to one side is a tiny, tiny object that is barely visible. Like a proverbial fly in the ointment, it is a speck that changes everything. We can no longer see the beauty of the infinite sky in the same way as before now that we have observed the drone's presence. That it is called a "Reaper Drone" is ominous, even to those who know nothing about this drone, harking as it does to the Grim Reaper. In fact, as the catalog explains, Reapers are also known as "hunter-killer" drones (also see Chamayou 2015). Paglen's photograph seems to warn the viewer not to be lulled by appearances, to heighten her senses, and to inspect closely. In fact, it trains the observer to screen for threats and abnormalities in the very act of viewing the work.

Covert Operations reveals the entanglement of digital media and power, particularly the power of the U.S. government. This exhibit, in some ways like Cyber Detectives, exposes the unseen workings of things about which most people have little knowledge and about which they are not even thinking. Where Cyber Detectives presented a simple, empowering version of security that each individual could provide for themselves, Covert Operations situates the viewer in complex networks of politics and technology, often operating without their knowledge or consent, with dangerous consequences for society. The dystopian atmosphere of Covert Operations shares something with the Weapons of Mass Disruption room, but while the Spy Museum's exhibit worked through an aesthetics of vulnerability, the art of Covert Operations is more of a call to critically examine state practices of surveillance and warfare. Like Paglen's *Untitled (Reaper Drone)*, the exhibit educates and empowers through engaging viewers in the experience of finding the hidden drone, perceiving the secret names, seeing the underground cables that support the network and the surveillance cameras that produce much more than security. Through various techniques and forms of data visualization, the art reaches people through their senses of sight and hearing, as well as through their intellect.

The artworks brought together in Covert Operations may not be seen together again, but the individual works will continue to be seen by publics in other shows, galleries, and museums, as well as in reproductions. I recently came across Taryn Simon's photograph of transatlantic cables as the frontispiece of a book (McLagan and McKee 2012). Individually the works of art have powerful effects, but putting them into conversation under the rubric Covert Operations foregrounded themes of secrecy and power. The dystopian aesthetics of the artworks are offset by the visual pleasures of experiencing art and by the demonstration of the magnitude and vitality of human creativity. Making art about threatening and disturbing subjects is a form of mastery and transformation. In this way, the exhibit, despite the threat of state overreach it constantly evokes, is thought-provoking and even inspiring, rather than depressing. If securitization works in part through normalizing certain ways of seeing and feeling, Covert Operations creates a disjuncture, a redistribution of the sensible, shifting one's sensory focus in ways that denaturalize the state-backed security consensus.

Viewers may be moved not only by what the artworks communicate, but by the actions taken by the artists in constructing these works. The artists' agency in researching and revealing hidden dimensions of contemporary life can serve as a model of individual agency even in the face of large-scale and complex processes. Nonetheless, there is a risk of overstating what a work of art or an entire exhibit achieves, and not only because, as the saying goes, "results may vary" among individual viewers. When curator Claire Carter (2014, 60) says Jenny Holzer's fragmenting of sentences from official documents in *Ribs* is "challenging the authorial voice behind the original document," she may be overly optimistic about the power of the artist and of artwork to speak back.

THE AESTHETICS OF UNCERTAINTY

"Cybersecurity" is no longer a term confined to military and technical specialists, having entered public discourse as a new buzzword with an associated growth industry now serving to identify digital risks and devise countermeasures against them. A whole range of digital threats are now part of our lexicon—ransomware, phishing, hacks, cyberattacks—even though the mechanics that lie behind them and actual effects they generate are often vague and unknown. Digital media are thus an example of complex systems that have profound consequences for people's lives, but which are difficult or impossible for them to perceive through direct experience, a condition framed by what I have called digital opacity and the experiential gap.

At present, the nature of digital threats and the meaning of cybersecurity have vague contours and lack clear definition. Questions of digital surveillance, drone warfare, and digital rights remain open to debate and deliberation. As the exhibits explored here demonstrate, there is an ongoing cultural struggle to grasp the meanings of security in a digital context. The three exhibits I have examined provide examples of the creative means necessary to translate and represent digital opacity in ways that facilitate understanding and agency. While each of these exhibits taken on their own could present a compelling picture of cybersecurity, when considered together, the fissures and ambiguities in defining risks and security in relation to digital media become apparent. This divergence and ambiguity is significant because at some point notions of cybersecurity may become firmly fixed and appear as common sense—like nuclear security became during the Cold War—while at this moment in history they remain in flux and contested, leaving open a range of possible futures for digital society. Analyzing the ways that digital threats are being conveyed to nonexperts hence sheds light on the processes through which dominant narratives are constructed and securitized ways of seeing and sensing are established and normalized.

The approach to security aesthetics adopted in this volume shows how diverse human sensory capacities are evoked and engaged to produce feelings of danger, safety, agency, and docility in subtle yet powerful ways, reaching beyond people's reasoning faculties. Through the different aesthetic modalities they employ and the divergent narratives they mobilize, the exhibits I have explored in this chapter collectively reveal the extent to which digital threats and possible responses to them remain in flux, not yet normalized to a set representational repertoire. This uncertainty suggests just how high the political stakes are in the various performances and enactments of digital security aesthetics at work today. The vastly different policy and legal landscapes emerging around digital privacy in the United States and the European Union, for example, suggest the profound divergence in how digital threats are perceived. The aesthetics of digital security thus promises to play a key role in establishing terms of sensibility for assessing our digital futures, and this chapter represents an effort to read how such security aesthetics are being performed in the contemporary cultural landscape of U.S. museums—an important pedagogical space that shapes and is shaped by other cultural performances, enactments, and narrations of security.

The three exhibits I have explored reflect different facets of the digital. Each also trains different modes of viewing cybersecurity, thereby advancing different sensory and discursive schemas for judging digital threats. Whether private companies' collection and disclosure of social media profiles is seen as an accidental breach of privacy or a deliberate manipulation of our digital lives, and whether the surveillance of cell phone records is registered as a necessary threat-screening measure or an attack on civil liberties, hence depends on the aesthetic regime through which cybersecurity is framed. What counts as a threat? What disclosures and forms of interconnection are acceptable? How is the monitoring and management of our digital lives rendered normal, and what visual, narrative, and affective arrangements provide us with the comfort to accept such monitoring and management? The experience of each of these three exhibits lends different answers to these questions, even if they together deliver an experience consistent with the recognition that ordinary citizens are not able to directly apprehend digital threats. Whereas Cyber Detectives presents digital technologies in a recursive field of technological puzzles and problem solving, Weapons of Mass Disruption represents the internet as a dangerous weapon that has already fallen into the wrong hands with potentially apocalyptic consequences. In contrast to this doomsday scenario, Cyber Detectives proposes an optimistic narrative of capacity building through which individuals master technology and solve emergent problems. This neoliberal vision assumes that individuals are able to solve societal problems, but does not account for the fact that infrastructures of information are becoming so complex that nonexperts cannot ever have such mastery. Covert Operations suggests that practices of security may themselves become threats and shows how the opacity of digital media is compounded by government practices of secrecy, which keep much of its activity and knowledge hidden from citizens. Each exhibit thus offers different ethical frameworks for relating state power to individual agency and technological innovation, showing how the future of our digital lives is necessarily emergent within regimes of security aesthetics.

ACKNOWLEDGMENTS

I am grateful to the Center for Advanced Behavioral Studies, Stanford University, for a fellowship that facilitated the larger research project upon which this chapter draws. I am very thankful to the editors of this volume for their work, and especially to D. Asher Ghertner for the generous attention he gave to multiple drafts of this chapter.

NOTES

1   All quoted text in this section is based on the exhibit descriptions in the Spy Museum and texts found on https://www.spymuseum.org/about, last accessed May 13, 2019.
2   All quoted text in this section is based on exhibit descriptions in the San Jose Tech Museum and texts found on https://www.thetech.org/plan-your-visit/exhibits /cyberdetectives, last accessed May 13, 2019.

REFERENCES

Anderson, Benedict. 1991. *Imagined Communities: Reflections on the Origin and Spread of Nationalism*. Rev. ed. London: Verso, 1991.

Bennett, Tony. 1995. *The Birth of the Museum: History, Theory, Politics*. London: Routledge.

Bernal, Victoria. 2014. *Nation as Network: Diaspora, Cyberspace, and Citizenship*. Chicago: University of Chicago Press.

Carter, Claire. 2014. *Covert Operations: Investigating the Known Unknowns*. Scottsdale Museum of Contemporary Art. Santa Fe, NM: Radius Books.

Chamayou, Grégoire. 2015. *A Theory of the Drone*. New York: New Press.

Cubitt, Sean. 2008. "Case Study: Digital Aesthetics." In *Digital Cultures: Understanding New Media*, edited by Glen Creeber and Royston Martin, 23–29. Maidenhead, Berkshire: Open University Press.

Ghertner, D. Asher. 2015. *Rule by Aesthetics: World-Class City Making in Delhi*. New York: Oxford University Press.

Greenwald, Glenn. 2015. *No Place to Hide: Edward Snowden, the NSA, and the U.S. Surveillance State*. New York: Picador.

Hinderliter, Beth, William Kaizen, Vered Maimon, Jaleh Mansoor, and Seth McCormick. 2009. "Introduction." In *Communities of Sense: Rethinking Aesthetics and Politics*, edited by Beth Hinderliter, William Kaizen, Vered Maimon, Jaleh Mansoor, and Seth McCormick, 1–30. Durham, NC: Duke University Press.

Langlois, Ganaele, Joanna Redden, and Greg Elmer, eds. 2015. *Compromised Data: From Social Media to Big Data*. New York: Bloomsbury.

Lawson, Sean. 2013. "Beyond Cyber-Doom: Assessing the Limits of Hypothetical Scenarios in the Framing of Cyber-Threats." *Journal of Information Technology and Politics* 10 (March): 86–103.

Maranowski, Michelle. 2015. "Cyber Detectives Exhibit Developer Talks about Cyber Security on 'Hot Tech, Cool Science.'" Soundcloud, August 27. https://soundcloud.com/the-tech-museum/cyber-detectives-exhibit-developer-talks-about-cyber-security-on-hot-science-cool-tech.

Masco, Joseph. 2014. *The Theater of Operations: National Security Affect from the War on Terror*. Durham, NC: Duke University Press.

McLagan, Meg, and Yates McKee. 2012. *Sensible Politics: The Visual Culture of Nongovernmental Activism*. New York: Zone Books.

Paglen, Trevor. 2009. *Blank Spots on the Map: The Dark Geography of the Pentagon's Secret World*. New York: Dutton.

Papacharissi, Zizi. 2015. *Affective Publics: Sentiment, Technology, and Politics*. Oxford: Oxford University Press.

Parks, Lisa, and Nicole Starosielski, eds. 2015. *Signal Traffic: Critical Studies of Media Infrastructures*. Urbana: University of Illinois Press.

Rancière, Jacques. 2009. "Contemporary Art and the Politics of Aesthetics." In *Communities of Sense: Rethinking Aesthetics and Politics*, edited by Beth Hinderliter, William Kaizen, Vered Maimon, Jaleh Mansoor, and Seth McCormick, 31–50. Durham, NC: Duke University Press.

Rodgers, Timothy. 2014. "Foreword." In *Covert Operations: Investigating the Known Unknowns*, edited by Claire Carter, 9–10. Scottsdale Museum of Contemporary Art. Santa Fe, NM: Radius Books.

Rosen, Jay. 2012. "The People Formerly Known as the Audience." In *The Social Media Reader*, edited by Michael Mandiberg, 13-16. New York: New York University Press.

Schneier, Bruce. 2016. "Security or Surveillance?" In *Don't Panic: Making Progress on the "Going Dark" Debate*, Harvard Berkman Center Report, February 1, app. A. https://cyber.harvard.edu/pubrelease/dont-panic/Dont_Panic_Making_Progress_on_Going_Dark_Debate.pdf.

Turner, Jennifer, and Kimberley Peters. 2015. "Unlocking Carceral Atmospheres: Designing Visual/Material Encounters at the Prison Museum." *Visual Communication* 14, no. 3: 309-330.

VICTORIA BERNAL

2

Danger Signs

The Aesthetics of Insecurity in Bogotá

Austin Zeiderman

Adorning a construction site in a gritty corner of central Bogotá is a billboard (Figure 2.1). The billboard contains the image of a fireman rescuing a young girl accompanied by text that translates into English as "Every day in Bogotá we conduct thirty-eight operations to protect the lives of our residents." The fireman is outfitted in full protective clothing, helmet, and respiratory apparatus, while the girl is in shorts, T-shirt, and tennis shoes. Female, young, helpless, scared, perhaps poor—she is a figure of extreme vulnerability. Her shirt and shoes are soiled, suggesting exposure to hardship or danger. The fireman, on the other hand, is male, confident, heroic, and strong. In contrast to the young girl in his arms, his body is erect and in motion. And stamped on his helmet is the official seal of the city government, identifying him as the personification of a patriarchal state committed to protecting the lives of its subjects, who appear here in a strikingly infantilized, feminized form.

On this billboard—or danger sign—the objective of protecting vulnerable populations is accompanied by its moral and political justification: "Porque es tu derecho!" ("Because it's your right!"). No one is asking, and yet the billboard preemptively responds to the implicit question: What authorizes the state to exercise its powers of protection? If the fireman were rescuing this young girl from a burning building, as might be inferred, she and her family would certainly be grateful. But there are other situations in which such intervention might not be welcome. The girl may be living in unsanitary conditions because her family is struggling to get by, and the government may be taking her into custody. Perhaps her home is in an area declared unsafe for habitation and the

Figure 2.1 "Every day in Bogotá . . ." Billboard in central Bogotá. Photograph by author, 2008.

household is being forcefully relocated. In these situations, one could imagine the demand to know what legitimates such interventions. Hence, the need to affirm that the state is working not, for example, to protect private property or to maintain social order, but rather to uphold the right to life.

What, exactly, is the threat from which the fireman is rescuing this young girl? We know not whether she is being saved from a blazing inferno, from a family unfit to care for her, from the destruction wrought by an earthquake, or perhaps even from a terrorist attack. The danger is imminent and demands action, and yet it remains invisible. Its identity is perhaps known only to those with the authority and expertise to define who or what is dangerous. The solid, yellow background out of which the fireman emerges is tabula rasa. Attributable to anyone or anything, the threat serves as a blank screen onto which viewers' fears may be projected. It is assumed that Bogotá is a city of dangers— explosions, landslides, robberies, murders, kidnappings—and that its inhabitants are perpetually under threat. Unlike the rights of the individual that legitimate the protective power of the state, the threat to which this power responds need not be explicitly affirmed.

I encountered this billboard in 2008, a moment at which Bogotá was safer than it had been for half a century. Compared to the turbulent 1980s and 1990s, crime and violence had dramatically decreased and security had improved. Yet there was something paradoxical about this change. Although the atmosphere in the city was more relaxed—outdoor cafés and restaurants were flourishing, public parks bustled with carefree activity—many of the old anxieties remained. It was as if Bogotá was still in the grip of a violent and dangerous past. Friends and strangers alike frequently urged me to see the city as a threat-ridden place and proposed strategies for negotiating it. On one level, such measures are ways of adapting to everyday life in a city generally understood to be fraught with danger. Not so long ago, Bogotá's homicide rate was one of the highest in the world, and assassinations, kidnappings, and bombings were almost routine. It stands to reason that those who lived through *this* Bogotá would orient their lives in relation to threats of many kinds, some more plausible than others. But why at a time when urbanists and security experts from around the world were heralding the dawn of a new age, indeed celebrating the "rebirth" of Bogotá, would this preoccupation with danger remain?

This paradox eventually prompted me to begin thinking less about "danger," and more about "endangerment." Though cognates, there is a subtle difference between the two terms. While both suggest the possibility of imminent harm, rather than its reality, "danger" often indicates a specific threat whereas "endangerment" refers to the more general condition of being threatened. As a result, the two states might be said to exist in different temporalities. Endangerment is durative and open-ended while danger is immediate and short-term. The latter often indexes a specific threat that may dissipate when time passes or conditions change. The temporality of endangerment, in contrast, is lasting: the possibility of injury is endured indefinitely, requiring subjects to recalibrate their perception of the city and their place within it.

Endangerment can be thought of more as a condition than an experience; indeed, it is what gives shape to experiences of the city. This distinction is important for understanding cultural, social, and political life in places like Bogotá where endangerment has outlasted immediate danger. The fact that trauma persists in the bodies and memories and attitudes of people who have experienced it is well known. So, too, is the fact that histories of violence often produce persistent cultures of fear that are difficult to dispel. The larger project from which this chapter is drawn extends such analyses to the domain of urban politics and government, to the relationship between the state and the citizen, to the city as a political community.[1] It explores the degree to which endangerment has conditioned politics in Colombia in the past and continues to do so in the present. Endangerment reveals how the state establishes and maintains its authority and legitimacy, how the government intervenes in the lives of its citizens, how those citizens inhabit the city as political subjects, and how those subjects position themselves when addressing the state. It offers a way of apprehending the politics of security and the government of risk, and their implications for contemporary cities and urban life.

This chapter deepens that analysis by focusing on what the editors of this volume call "security aesthetics." In developing this concept, D. Asher Ghertner, Hudson McFann, and Daniel M. Goldstein (this volume) take inspiration from Jacques Rancière's (2011, 9) understanding of aesthetics as the "configurations of experience that create new modes of sense perception and induce novel forms of political subjectivity." By foregrounding security's aesthetic dimensions, they draw attention to the "distribution of the sensible" as a process by which supposedly self-evident truths about things like threat, danger, and protection come to shape the social world. Of the three modalities of security aesthetics they identify, "calibrating vulnerabilities" denotes a field of action in which such truths are "instituted and normalized but also . . . challenged, appropriated, and manipulated—or perceived and responded to in sometimes unexpected ways." What makes this field of action so lively is its direct and consequential relationship to questions of political belonging within what Rancière (2009) calls the "community of sense." Like the concept of "endangerment," security aesthetics highlights the degree to which matters of inclusion and exclusion are predicated on individual and collective abilities to perceive and respond to signs of danger.

This chapter engages such a provocation in the following way. The first section after this introduction examines signs of danger appearing in Bogotá on billboards, at bus stops, and in print. Offering information, warnings, and advice to the casual viewer, these signs reflect official expectations for how society, the state, and the individual should perceive and respond to potential threats, from the exceptional to the routine. The second section turns to the practices through which government officials work to cultivate a sensibility toward insecurity in the domain of housing. The third section then traces a series of shifts in municipal housing policy that recast the terms of inclusion in the city by foregrounding the imperative to protect the lives of vulnerable populations from specific kinds of danger. The fourth section reveals how those subject to that imperative respond to it, sensing that the condition of endangerment is a route to recognition within the community of sense. The conclusion then draws out implications for critical analyses of security that target the subjective and affective transformations engendered by invocations of danger.

Throughout Bogotá, a variety of signs convey to the city's inhabitants the message that they are in danger. Occasionally the threats are visible, and they range from everyday household hazards to large-scale catastrophes. Take, for example, an image on a newspaper kiosk in the city center depicting a young girl in front of a stove (Figure 2.2, right). She is tilting a frying pan full of scalding hot oil toward her face. The warning, put out by the city government, informs us: "159 children suffered burns in the home last year." Adjacent to it is another one of a boy reaching for a pair of scissors and a knife lying at eye level on the kitchen counter (Figure 2.2, left). This sign also reports precise statistics of injury: "285 children suffered wounds from sharp objects in the home last year." And the message beneath both images indicates to whom these warnings are addressed: "Preventing household accidents is everyone's responsibility."

Like the billboard of the fireman rescuing the little girl, these signs reference a fundamentally patriarchal relationship between the state and its subjects—the latter are depicted as small children exposed to danger and in need of protective care. However, a number of features set them apart from the first image. First of all, the threat is readily apparent. Rather than an invisible danger that can refer to anyone or anything, encountered here are the everyday, household hazards of hot oil in a frying pan and an unprotected pair of scissors. These are not catastrophic events like fires or explosions, but rather regularly occurring accidents. Thus, the threat is domesticated and the home is identified as the space of danger. And this move to the private realm of the household also brings with it a shift in emphasis from protection to prevention, as well as a redirection of accountability. Rather than depicting a state saving the lives of its subjects, these signs maintain that preventing accidents in the home is "everyone's responsibility."

A different form of sensory attention is promoted by bus stops around town displaying the warning "An earthquake could occur at any moment." This portentous prognosis is followed by a list of "six smart moves (*jugadas maestras*) that could save your life" (Figure 2.3). These techniques for "mastering" danger range from securing furniture that might cause injury, defining evacuation routes, and preparing emergency supplies to reinforcing the home against seismic activity, locating safety zones, and carrying out damage inventories after the event. A handsome young man wearing the yellow vest typical of the Directorate of Emergency Prevention and Response (DPAE), the governmental agency sponsoring this campaign, points his finger directly outward from the sign toward the viewer.[2] And beneath the list of "smart moves" the

Figure 2.2
"Preventing
household accidents
is everyone's
responsibility."
Billboard in central
Bogotá. Photograph
by author, 2008.

public is expected to learn is the simultaneously reassuring and disconcerting motto "In Bogotá, we are preparing ourselves."

Responsibility is again directed to each and every individual, and the home is identified as the space of potential safety and danger. The state is personified not as a heroic protector or cautious caretaker, but as a technical adviser (again, male) telling people what to do to protect their own lives. Rather than depicting the governmental response to a catastrophic event that has already happened or reporting on the number of domestic accidents occurring in the previous year, the poster directs attention forward in time toward an unpredictable natural disaster—an earthquake that "could occur at any moment." Furthermore, this warning does not assert that lives would be protected by the state, but instead affirms that all *bogotanos* are, or at least ought to be, engaged in the ongoing and incomplete process of preparing themselves for an event that cannot be prevented and from which one must not expect protection.

Figure 2.3
"Six smart moves."
Billboard in central
Bogotá. Photograph
by author, 2008.

Occasionally threats are depicted in animated form, such as in the advertisement for an emergency hotline used to report suspicious activity (Figure 2.4). The heading reads: "I take the safe road. If you see something strange or dangerous, immediately dial 123." In the image, a tortoise is walking a dog on a city street. While doing so, the tortoise, whose gender is unspecified, encounters a male figure. The latter is dressed respectably in a business suit and is carrying a briefcase. But, in reality, he is a malicious, dark-faced wolf in sheep's clothing, hiding behind a white mask, and his briefcase contains an explosive device about to detonate. Recognizing the figure's true identity and intentions, the tortoise acts with the prudence and caution for which it is known proverbially and calls the emergency hotline. In its vigilance, the tortoise is doing a job that pertains to all responsible urban citizens. A message below the wolf tells us: "Security is a shared goal!"

This type of threat may be encountered anywhere in the public space of the city. One must, therefore, be on guard at all times. But the threat is

Figure 2.4
"I take the safe road."
Advertisement in
municipal government
newspaper. Secretaría
de Gobierno.

disguised—anyone could be a wolf—though the contrast between its face and mask indexes the racialized optics of safety and danger. Preventing such an attack depends on inculcating the public with suspicion, and it presumes the average citizen's ability to know how to detect and decipher danger signs. The threat is not an unpredictable future event, like an earthquake, for which one can only hope to be sufficiently prepared. Nor is it the sort of event whose probability can be calculated across the population, as with domestic accidents. It follows no discernible logic, but can be prevented if people are alert and act quickly and vigilantly. No heroic savior is swooping in to protect the vulnerable, nor are expert advisers working to ensure everyone's safety. Although the imperative to dial "123" invokes the ultimate power of the state to intervene, the job of providing security depends on each and every individual.

70

AUSTIN ZEIDERMAN

Figure 2.5 "Protect your family." Billboard in Bogotá's southern periphery.
Photograph by author, 2009.

A population of citizen watchdogs (or watch-tortoises, as the case may be) leads
to collective safety.

All the signs mentioned thus far appear in public places in and around
the city center. A final one, however, is set into the steep hillside of a self-built
settlement on the southern periphery of Bogotá (Figure 2.5). In contrast to
the others, this sign has only the solid orange background that convention-
ally accompanies warning messages overlaid with bold, block lettering. The
text communicates both a firm directive ("Protect your family") and a stern
admonition ("For your safety, do not purchase lots in zones of high risk [*zonas
de alto riesgo*]"). The sign identifies itself with the insignia of the municipal government of Bogotá as well as with the name of the local governing body. The
expertise required to determine risk is clearly in the hands of the state, as is
the authority to issue the prohibitive injunction against settling in a high-risk
zone. The threat, however, remains outside the frame.

Among government officials, "zona de alto riesgo" refers to a technical designation denoting an area vulnerable to landslides, floods, and other environmental hazards. Its meaning, however, is more ambiguous for local viewers:

it references the responsibility to protect one's family from danger and, since this area is unsafe, to look elsewhere for housing. The state asserts its knowledge of what must be done to ensure everyone's safety, and by informing the public it performs a protective function. But aside from providing a phone number to call for additional information, the sign instructs viewers that the ultimate responsibility for protecting life is theirs. Notably absent when compared to the previous examples are gestures to prevention; though it directs potential settlers away from this area, nothing is being done to reduce the probability of landslide. Preparedness is also sidelined, since there is no indication of how to get ready for an event that will likely, or perhaps inevitably, occur. The state, rather, accepts that a disaster may happen, and enjoins people to do what is prudent to protect themselves from it.

The sign's intended audience is not the average *bogotano*, as in the previous examples, but the poor and working-class settlers who either live in, or are likely to move to, the rough edges of the city. It implies that where the viewer is standing (or perhaps living) is unsafe. For those who know the area, the sign's location means something more. The ground on which it stands had been occupied by dwellings similar to those remaining adjacent to it. The families once living in them were relocated by the municipal government, and their shacks subsequently demolished. Since 2003, Bogotá's municipal housing agency, the Caja de la Vivienda Popular (lit., "Fund for Popular Housing"; "Caja," for short), has been in charge of resettling populations living in zones of high risk. Areas cleared of habitation are frequently "invaded," as they say, by others in need of a place to settle, hence the sign's prohibition against buying lots here. While the Caja subsidizes the relocation of those inhabiting the area at the moment it was designated a high-risk zone, it does not confer the same benefits on those who arrived after the fact. Simultaneously prohibiting some while entitling others, the resettlement program employs a combination of techniques in the name of safeguarding the lives of its subjects in the face of specific kinds of danger.

Taken together, these signs provide insight into the condition of endangerment in contemporary Bogotá. They operate literally as the "perceptible things"—or *aesthēta*, the Greek root of aesthetics—that attune viewers to surrounding risks, thereby enrolling them in an endangered community of sense. As signs, they convey the message that the city is a space of threat and imply that the pursuit of security ought to extend from the scale of the city down to that of the home. Alongside the more straightforward injunction to observe and report, these signs are aesthetic objects that perform the work of calibrating sensory perception to the dangers that inhere in an otherwise familiar milieu. Common to them is the assumption that life is not a resource to be prolonged, cultivated, or improved, but rather a precarious possession perpetually in danger of being harmed or taken away. However, their projections of threat differ, as do their ascriptions of authority and responsibility and their targets and techniques of intervention—all of which contain only somewhat consistent gendered and racialized connotations. References to the state's duty to actively protect lives and allusions to the imperative that people must be disciplined to avoid dangers run parallel to indications that free, autonomous individuals are responsible for preparing themselves for events likely to occur.

Confounding the epochal claims of some critical studies of risk and security, there is no overarching logic of power here that replaces what came before but rather an assemblage of overlapping technical, ethical, and political guidelines for how society, the state, and the individual are expected to behave. These signs suggest that the field of governmental intervention organized around the condition of endangerment is a problem space in which heterogeneous imperatives coexist and intersect (cf. Collier 2009). What is striking about these state-sponsored security aesthetics is how they hold these imperatives together, orienting those viewing them toward a milieu of potential threats and a set of prescribed responses. The next section elaborates on this point by drawing upon ethnographic research conducted alongside the social workers who manage the Caja's resettlement program for families living in recently designated zones of high risk. Based on daily interactions between government officials and this program's beneficiaries, as well as interviews with both groups, it highlights the state-subject relations accompanying the imperative to protect the lives of vulnerable populations from specific kinds of danger. By instituting a new regime for governing urban spaces and populations, this initiative contributes to the cultivation of forms of sensory perception attuned to threat and, ultimately, to the creation of an endangered community of sense. However, entitlements are distributed unevenly to members of that community on account of a sensory mismatch between the Caja's emphasis on environmental risk and residents' concern with other forms of insecurity.

MAKING SENSE

The warning signs analyzed above attest to the fact that the municipal government of Bogotá uses educational campaigns to raise awareness about danger among the general public. Instilling a collective ethos of risk management is a specific objective of the Caja's resettlement program. Caja staff refer to this as a process of *sensibilización*. Although no direct translation exists, the adjective *sensible* from which it derives equates to "sensitive," or the quality of being conscious of and responsive to one's surroundings. The closely related verb *sensibilizar* means "to make aware" or "to raise awareness." When the process of sensibilización is directed at an individual, it implies the need to educate someone to see, feel, or comprehend what is going on around them. When it involves a group of people or the general public, sensibilización aims to increase awareness of and responsibility for an issue, such as domestic violence or racial discrimination. The sensibility implied in both cases is perceptual, such as the ability to sense something in the external environment, as well as moral, as in expressing adequate concern for an existing problem. Echoing Rancière's (2011) emphasis on the sensible as the domain in which politics and aesthetics combine to produce boundaries that govern the social world, sensibilización sets the terms according to which the poor in Bogotá should behave in relation to future threats. In the context of risk management and housing policy in Bogotá, it determines who can be recognized as urban citizens.

The social workers who staff the Caja's field office in Ciudad Bolívar are charged with facilitating this sensibility among those subject to the resettlement program. As an informal policy guiding their work, sensibilización implies the formation of new values, behaviors, and concerns among the "at risk" population. A young social worker, who I will call Carmela, explained further, echoing the inculcation of personal responsibility advocated by the household accidents sign above.[3] A subjective transformation must take place, she said, "so that the families accept and participate in their own resettlement." This means that Carmela and her colleagues felt the responsibility to foster an awareness that their clients' lives may be in danger: "We work with quite a difficult population. Therefore, what one does as a social worker is make them conscious, that is, enable them to be conscious that the situation in which they are in risks their lives and the lives of their children, and that every time they go to work they don't know whether their children will arrive [home] safely, whether their children are alright, whether there will be some natural disaster, or whether their house will collapse." Although members of this population are routinely exposed to a wide range of threats—robbery, kidnapping, violence, landslide, extortion, sickness, and unemployment, among others—the Caja assumes the pedagogical role of educating them to be especially conscious of and concerned about environmental hazards.

Sensibilización carries the implicit assumption that those subject to the resettlement program (*beneficiarios*, or "beneficiaries") do not have the capacity to protect and care for themselves and that the municipal government must intervene on their behalf, such as in the billboard depicting the fireman rescuing the young girl.[4] But training beneficiaries to perceive their homes and neighborhoods as vulnerable, or "at risk," is also fundamentally about bringing them into an active partnership with the state. Caja staff often stress the concept of *co-responsabilidad*, or the responsibility shared between resettlement beneficiaries and municipal authorities, as in the emergency hotline flyer, which stated that "security is a shared goal." Yolanda, the coordinator of the Caja's field office in the peripheral locality of Ciudad Bolívar, explained this to me in the following terms:

> Let's say that there is a responsibility that applies as much to the state as to the families living in the high-risk area. The state did not put them there, nor will we solve their housing problems as a constitutional right. From the moment at which the zone of high risk is designated, carrying out the [resettlement] process should be the *co-responsabilidad* of the two parties. What does this entail? It entails that the families recognize that they are equally responsible: they have to submit the documentation required of them, show they were living there when the risk designation took place, prove that they possess titles corresponding to the property, search for alternative solutions, attend meetings, etc. In addition, it is their responsibility to be supportive (*solidario*) of the entire process.

In targeting a population assumed to be unable to recognize and respond to the dangers they face, and in training them to carry out their own relocation, the Caja distributed the responsibility for risk among individual households. In this sense, sensibilización resembles the technique of "responsibilization" (Rose 1999, 74), which has been a cornerstone of neoliberal reforms of the welfare state and of the relations of government associated with it. The poor and the vulnerable should no longer expect the state to provide them with security; they must learn to accept responsibility for their own protection by prudentially governing themselves. This model of state-subject relations is predicated on the calibration of vulnerabilities and the sensory attunement necessary to perceive them.

That said, it would be wrong to conclude that sensibilización is simply a discourse that uses fear and threat to create rational, responsible, and self-governing subjects. Caja staff also frequently emphasize the importance of educating members of the urban poor in the appropriate legal and political grammar in which to claim their rights. As another Caja social worker, Carlos, put it on one occasion: "It's about teaching them the rules of the game and how to play it." For example, Caja social workers often joke about their beneficiaries' misuse of bureaucratic terminology: saying *suicidio* (suicide) when they meant *subsidio* (subsidy), demanding *vivienda indigna* (wretched housing) instead of *vivienda digna* (decent housing), referring to their *previos* (an adjective meaning "previous") rather than their *predios* (lands), and mistaking Davivienda (a local bank) for the Caja de la Vivienda Popular and de Páez (a mountain in southern Colombia) for the DPAE. Ridiculing resettlement beneficiaries for their lack of fluency in bureaucratic language reinforces hierarchies between governors and the governed. But as Carlos implied, his job is to train beneficiaries to sense, speak, and act in ways necessary to be recognized as deserving of certain entitlements.

Other aspects of sensibilización aim to increase the state's presence in the lives of its subjects; the figure of the fireman rescuing the young girl personifies this imperative. According to Yolanda, the coordinator of the Ciudad Bolívar field office, "The sensibilización that I think is the most important in Ciudad Bolívar is that the people feel we are on their side . . . as friends and not as enemies. . . . I've noticed that in every meeting with the community, they expect to fight with the state because they believe state institutions are to be fought with. Therefore, I believe the most difficult work is to make them understand otherwise, that we have moved over to their side; which in other words is to 'sensibilize them' (*sensibilizarlos*) to a different model of government." Yolanda, like many Caja managers and staff, was a member of the Polo Democratico Alternativo, the left-of-center political party that occupied the mayor's office in Bogotá from 2004 to 2011. Teresa, director of the Caja's social team, told me that the resettlement program had been central to both Lucho Garzón's (2004–2007) and Samuel Moreno's (2008–2011) commitment to governing the city in the interest of the people and to building a political constituency among the urban poor. She reminded me of their campaign slogans—"Bogotá sin indiferencia" ("Bogotá without Indifference") and "Bogotá positiva" ("Positive Bogotá")—and emphasized that they were not empty rhetoric. "Truly," she said, "they represent the demands (*reivindicaciones*) of the communities."

During Enrique Peñalosa's firm term as mayor (1998–2002), Teresa told me, resettlement was not conceived in the same way. It required families to match their government subsidy with an equal amount of credit, and if they could not acquire the latter they would not qualify for the former. Many families were forced to relocate with only the value of their existing property (usually around 1 million pesos, or $500). As Teresa put it, "All you can do with a million pesos is move back to a zone of high risk. Garzón understood this," she underlined, "and pushed the City Council to double the subsidy. Since 2007, the program has taken off." Risk management provided a technical language in which to address the social and environmental problems of the urban periphery and achieve an electoral majority. Connecting the resettlement program and the process of sensibilización to the overall goal of increasing ties between the state and its subjects in the peripheral settlements of Bogotá, Teresa concluded: "This is the different model of government (*modelo de gobierno distinto*) I'm talking about." Instituting this model in the self-built settlements of the urban periphery is tied to the task of inculcating in residents the sense that their homes and neighborhoods look and feel insecure.

REGIMES OF HOUSING

The municipal agency Teresa worked for went through a series of shifts throughout the twentieth century. Public housing in Bogotá dates back to the epidemic of Spanish influenza in 1918–1919, which infected approximately 100,000 people in the capital city and took 1,500 lives (Pecha Quimbay 2008, 17–19). Medical experts and city councilmen argued that the disease had been spread by working-class neighborhoods with poor housing conditions, and legislation was passed requiring all municipal governments to dedicate a percentage of their overall budget to the provision of "hygienic housing for the proletariat (*habitaciones higiénicas para la clase proletaria*)" (Noguera 2003, 69). By the 1930s, public concern for hygiene was overshadowed by a state-led drive for economic modernization and the related imperative to house the growing population of urban industrial workers. When the Caja was created by an agreement between the national and municipal governments in 1942, its mandate was to build *barrios populares modelos*, or model neighborhoods for the popular classes (Pecha Quimbay 2008, 33–35). This lasted until 1959 when the Caja ceased constructing housing and instead began using public funds to acquire lands on the urban periphery where families with scarce resources could build their own homes. The category of *vivienda de interés social* (social interest housing) emerged in the 1960s amidst a concern for the living conditions not of workers but of low-income populations. Poverty alleviation overtook modernization as the municipal housing agency's orienting telos, and the "poor" displaced the "worker" as the target of government intervention.

In the 1980s, the Caja's mission shifted again, this time in the direction of slum eradication and upgrading. Municipal housing policy was no longer focused explicitly on workers or the needy, but rather on marginal spaces and populations in the rapidly urbanizing periphery of the city. The rationality of urban renewal current at that time saw the proliferation of *tugurios* (slums) and *invasiones* (illegal occupations) as problems of physical deterioration to be impeded. The Caja was charged with providing infrastructural improvements and legal recognition to some neighborhoods while facilitating the removal of others. Although the ratification of a new constitution in 1991 granted all Colombian citizens the right to *vivienda digna* (decent housing), the Supreme

Court subsequently ruled that the state could not be expected to guarantee this right to everyone living in substandard conditions.

Since the late 1990s, the Caja has had an altogether different mission: to protect the lives of populations living in Bogotá's zones of high risk by facilitating their relocation. Although the Caja's resettlement program coexists alongside other initiatives, such as neighborhood improvement and land titling, 70 percent of the agency's 2009 budget of $28 million was allocated to the resettlement of households located in areas vulnerable to landslides, floods, and other environmental hazards. As Teresa put it: "The Caja's objective is now to safeguard (*salvaguardar*) life; that is the priority, and in order to safeguard life it is necessary to guarantee that people do not inhabit properties in high-risk [zones]." Clarifying this recent transformation, she insisted that the Caja was no longer in the business of building houses for the poor: "Many families come to the Caja de la Vivienda saying: 'Listen, I don't have housing, I want a house, and you guys are the ones who give houses!' No, our principal objective with the resettlement program is now to protect lives in danger. This should lead us to compensate them for the housing they had, of course! But this does not correspond to a policy of public housing for the homeless (*la gente sin techo*)." As the political rationality shifted to risk management, so did the target of governmental intervention. Rather than organizing housing policy in terms of social class, political membership, or economic necessity, vulnerability became the primary criterion that determined one's eligibility to receive state benefits. "Life at risk" displaced "worker," "citizen," and "poor" as a new category of political recognition and entitlement. At a moment in which class-based demands for social transformation were perpetually in danger of being targeted as subversive—even to the point of being equated with the guerrilla insurgents who had themselves been relabeled "terrorist organizations"—risk management offered a seemingly neutral political idiom. In calculations of unequal exposure to environmental hazards, moderate and progressive mayoral administrations found a technical rationale for pursuing political ends, such as housing the poor, that had long been associated with the radical left.

That said, the application of risk management principles to housing regimes in Bogotá did not effect a wholesale transformation. For example, it is significant that the imperative to protect the life of the population in zones of high risk only applies to members of stratum 1 or 2 (Bogotá is zoned into six socioeconomic *estratos*; 1 and 2 are the lowest). So while governmental intervention no longer targets "poverty" and the housing conditions of the "poor," these priorities remain important to how Caja social workers understand and perform their jobs. Carlos once remarked to me that, in adopting risk management principles, his agency had found a way to give housing subsidies to disadvantaged families while remaining in compliance with the priorities of international development agencies and financial institutions, which were resolutely opposed to welfare state policies, while also avoiding accusations from the conservative political establishment. He did not go as far as to celebrate the Caja's resettlement program as a heroic act of local resistance to the hegemony of externally imposed models of development and to the authoritarian national state. But he did demonstrate that "risk" can function as a metonym for other social and political problems, and Caja officials stretch it beyond its usage as a technique for guiding action in the present according to predictive calculations of future harm.

In the government of risk in Bogotá, recognizably neoliberal principles (responsibilization, calculability, risk-taking, etc.) are occasionally mobilized in the service of state-based projects of social welfare that direct public expenditure to the housing conditions of the poor. For example, Carlos and I discussed the frequent practice of informally expediting the resettlement of families he deemed more needy or deserving, rather than those prioritized by technical risk calculations. However, when Caja social workers combine the imperatives of risk management and social welfare, this has a limited effect on the functioning of the resettlement program. The rise of the former imperative in Bogotá narrows the state's responsibility for other social problems like poverty, inequality, or forced displacement wrought by violence. For there are hundreds of thousands, if not millions, of *bogotanos* living in substandard or hazardous conditions, and yet only those few (approximately 10,000 households in 2008) officially included within the boundaries of zones of high risk, and not even all of them, are eligible for housing subsidies. These regimes of housing neither give "sustained attention to the welfare of the population" nor seek "to intervene in the living conditions of human beings as members of a social collectivity," as Andrew Lakoff (2007, 271) puts it. Risk management in Bogotá offers a politically safe way to address the social and environmental problems of the urban periphery, but ultimately works only to protect the lives of a small number of potential victims from a narrowly defined set of threats.

INVASIONS

Since 1950, Bogotá has grown from about seven hundred thousand inhabitants to over eight million, according to recent estimates, and the city continues to grow. Some migrants come to look for work, join their families, or pursue opportunities not available elsewhere. Many others, however, are *desplazados*, or victims of the armed conflict who have been forced to leave their homes. As a result, since the mid-1980s, Bogotá has received close to a million internal refugees fleeing violence (Consultoría para los Derechos Humanos y el Desplazamiento [CODHES] 2007, 42).[5] According to the municipal government, in the late 2000s an average of fifty-two displaced families arrived every day (*El Tiempo* 2009). Some rely on kinship ties for shelter, food, and employment. Those who have no one, or whose families cannot accommodate them, have to fend for themselves. Their first concern, inevitably, is where to spend the night.

Parts of the city are known to be receptive to the displaced—areas where one might set up camp for a few days without being hassled. Few and far between, however, are spaces in which to settle permanently. While finding a foothold in the city has always been a struggle for poor migrants, those arriving a decade ago had a better chance of acquiring a plot of land and building a humble shack. In the past, leftist political organizations frequently mobilized recent migrants to the city by helping them lay claim to the urban peripheries, build housing, and eventually equip them with infrastructure. The zones of high risk recently cleared by the municipal government are the few remaining areas in which squatting is still possible or where today's refugees can hope to settle for a small fee (CODHES 2007, 51). The very same zones evacuated by the government to protect people from one kind of threat have become, for this population, spaces of potential safety from an altogether different danger.

Some desplazados occupy evacuated zones of high risk hoping to access the municipal government's resettlement program. After all, becoming visible to the state as "lives at risk" entitles them to rights, such as decent housing, and to benefits from other governmental programs. Their pleas are successful if they can demonstrate exposure to environmental hazards, but most attempts to access housing subsidies by moving into zones of high risk are not. By law, the program applies to those living in these areas *before* they were designated high risk, and a number of techniques (such as examination of census records and aerial photographs) are used to verify this. Warning signs are placed throughout these areas to discourage further settlement. As I was told by one government official, "We are prepared to deal with people who try to take advantage of the state's goodwill by inserting themselves into the resettlement program." Those attempting to be recognized as lives at risk must be able to navigate this regulatory landscape. They must also enter the realm of security aesthetics and its endangered community of sense.

This became especially clear to me as I accompanied Tatiana and Miguel, two government technicians, on a trip to monitor an evacuated zone of high risk. About four months ago, Tatiana explained, a group of over a hundred settlers arrived in this area under cover of darkness with whatever building materials they could round up and by morning had constructed a cluster of makeshift shelters among the ruins of the former settlement. When local authorities tried to remove the *invasión*, representatives from the Personería de Bogotá—the municipal agency charged with defending human rights—arrived to support the settlers, saying that they were desplazados and could not be forced to relocate. Being officially recognized as belonging to this vulnerable population confers certain forms of governmental protection. But vulnerabilities are calibrated between human and nonhuman threats, and this calibration sets up a sensory regime that adjudicates the entitlements of citizenship to some and not others.

Toward the end of our long, rough ride, we came upon Mauricio, the head of the local *vigías ambientales*, or "environmental guards." These guards are municipal employees who patrol the steep hillsides of the urban periphery once they have been cleared of settlers. They are armed with pickaxes and shovels rather than badges and guns, but their mission is to secure these zones and prevent their future occupation. The environmental guards monitor daily for "invasions" and immediately alert the police if they find any.

Mauricio looked winded and concerned. There was another invasion last night, he said, and the police have just arrived to tell the *invasores* (invaders) to leave. Catching his breath, Mauricio then conveyed his assessment of the new arrivals: "It appears the desplazados who arrived a few months ago have turned this into a business. They are going around looking for other desplazados who have no place to live and offering to facilitate their settlement in this area in exchange for 40,000 pesos [$20]." Calling into question the motives behind the occupation, he continued: "They are telling all sorts of lies in order to make a few bucks. They claim the police cannot evict anyone who says they are a desplazado. And they are promising the desplazados that if they move into this area, they will be eligible for relocation subsidies." Conveying both disbelief and admiration, Mauricio stressed the degree to which an informal political hierarchy was taking shape: "There is even a guy who has given himself the title of Presidente de la Zona de Reubicación [President of the Relocation Zone]!"

Saying goodbye to Mauricio, we carried on toward the new settlement and, within a few minutes, arrived at a cluster of rudimentary shacks. Two light-skinned male police officers standing next to their motorcycles were immersed in a heated conversation with Catalina, a darker-skinned young woman in shorts and flip-flops—the typical attire of *tierra caliente*, or the hot lowlands, but not in Bogotá, and therefore a visible marker of her refugee status. Obviously new to the city, she looked frustrated and distraught. Tatiana got out of the truck and began to explain to Catalina that what the officers were saying is true: if she and the other "invaders" did not leave on their own accord, they would soon be evicted.

Catalina said she understood but that she had nowhere else to go. "I have documentation showing that I'm one of the displaced (*Tengo la carta de desplazado*)," she pleaded while gesturing to a paper she gripped as if it was her most important possession. Like the danger signs discussed above, this piece of paper was a concrete manifestation of the domain of security aesthetics in Bogotá. Tatiana examined the document, which was official proof that Catalina was a victim of the armed conflict, and wrote down her name and place of origin as she inquired further: "When did you arrive?" Catalina responded, "I've been in Bogotá for two weeks. I don't have anywhere else to go!"

"How many are there in your family?" "I have two children, so we're three . . . or four," Catalina said tentatively, not sure whether to count her husband. The urgency in her voice began to build:

> What else can we do? The government hasn't given us anything! We were forced from our home. It was a *zona roja* [an area in which active combat is taking place]. They threatened us and said they were going to kill us if we didn't leave, and that's how we ended up here. We want to go back, but we can't. The government says that we have to wait . . . that we should wait for assistance. But when? And what are we supposed to do in the meantime? We need a place to live! They are supposed to give us a new home because this is a relocation zone. It's a zone of high risk. There's water coming out of a broken water pipe and the ground is unstable. This area is not safe to live in.

Having heard Catalina's plea, in which she conveyed her sensory attunement to a range of threats, from political violence to environmental hazard, Tatiana interrupted:

> Look, this was declared a zone of high risk in 2004, after which point no one is allowed to live here. If you do, you are in violation of the law and ineligible for resettlement. Since this occupation occurred in the last seventy-two hours, we have the authority to evict you. It's our responsibility to evacuate this zone. It's as simple as that. That's why I am telling you to look for another place to live, because here . . . sooner or later they are going to kick you out. And if that happens, they're not going to come with two or three policemen, but many. They'll kick you out, and it won't be pretty (*Los van a sacar a las malas*).

Sensing that her bid to access the resettlement program had failed, Catalina reiterated that her status as one of the desplazados entitled her to benefits: "I have this document, and it means I have rights." Her vulnerability to human threats became the grounds for a different claim to protection—one that was ultimately incompatible with municipal housing policy—leaving Catalina in a precarious position. Tatiana responded, "Look, you know that unfortunately the internal conflict in this country is very complicated and that we have many desplazados. I am just informing you what's going to happen. I am making a suggestion. Go to another part of the city—I don't know, maybe in Soacha, or I don't know where. There are so many [displaced] people and the state doesn't have the resources to deal with them all. But at any moment, we are going to come with the backing of the police and they're going to kick you out and destroy everything you've got."

As far as I know, the police never did evict these desplazados. I returned two months later, and, although unable to locate Catalina, I found the settlement looking as it had before. The settlers told me that, like the group that had arrived four months earlier, they had been able to hold back the threat of eviction because of their officially documented status as members of the internally displaced population. For people like Catalina, membership within the political community of the city depends on the need for governmental protection. To be recognized as citizens with rights, they have to engage the state as lives at risk, for citizenship claims are predicated on vulnerability and mediated by exposure to danger. Although Catalina and her fellow settlers were successful at being recognized as desplazados, and were spared from eviction, they were unable to persuade the authorities that they were vulnerable to landslides and, thus, eligible for housing subsidies. Whereas the Caja's resettlement program targets those exposed to nonhuman dangers, vulnerability to a convergence of threats can make one eligible for and subject to an even broader extension of the state's protective care. However, the frames of political recognition linked to security aesthetics both include and exclude, especially when there is a sensorial mismatch between different forms of insecurity.

VULNERABLE INCLUSIONS

Engaging with the concept of security aesthetics, this chapter has shown how decades of armed conflict have led to the development of what I call an endangered city. In contrast to "danger," which indexes a discrete, identifiable threat, "endangerment" points to the more general condition of being threatened, which shapes the experience of urban life and configures modes of sensory perception, thereby shifting how people perceive the city and their place within it. Focusing on the work of municipal government agencies in Bogotá, this chapter has demonstrated how the endangered city is created and sustained long after immediate dangers have dissipated. Public information campaigns and risk management programs both engage in sensory training, or sensibilización, to cultivate an endangered community of sense. In the domain of housing, vulnerability to environmental hazards, such as landslides and floods, becomes the primary pathway to recognition as an urban citizen who is entitled to certain benefits. While some participate in the municipal government's risk management program to pursue strategic individual ends, doing so also contributes to the formation of a collective subjectivity organized around vulnerability. Inclusion and exclusion within the political community of the city are both predicated on the capacity to perform awareness of and exposure to specific dangers lurking on the horizon.

As a practice of calibrating vulnerabilities, the sensory training analyzed above occasionally aligns with the other modalities of security aesthetics contained in this volume—designing fortresses and screening threats. By building security logics into the management of the urban periphery, the municipal housing program erects walls, both geographical and institutional, that prevent certain people from accessing the benefits of urban citizenship. However, the barriers preventing some from establishing membership and entitlement also enable others to claim their rightful share within a community of sense organized around the condition of endangerment. Likewise, aesthetic norms dictating how security and insecurity look and feel effectively screen out exposure to environmental risk while normalizing social vulnerability. Yet identifying and responding to one kind of nonhuman threat, such as landslides and floods, often becomes a way to escape from an altogether different type of human danger, such as violence. Calibrating vulnerabilities, designing fortresses, and screening threats are three modalities of security aesthetics that do not always coalesce around a common purpose or produce a similar outcome.

The foregoing analysis has implications for critical studies of security that attend to the subjective and affective states engendered by pervasive invocations of imminent danger. Most scholars in anthropology, geography, and related disciplines offer what Clive Barnett (2015) calls a "dark interpretation" of security. According to this view, security is "viewed with deep suspicion as an extension of domination that impinges on the freedom of those subjected to its orderings" and is "subjected to a form of critique that privileges the tasks of exposure and revelation" (Barnett 2015, 260). Studies interested in subjectivity and affect, Barnett argues, agree that security logics aim to inculcate anxious and fearful states of mind, essentially foreclosing the space of the political by recourse to the logic of exception, the suspension of law, and the powers of emergency. While this style of thought does shed light on certain aspects of the politics of security in contemporary Colombia, it limits our ability to grasp the contingent and unpredictable ways security politics unfold in particular historical conjunctures.

In contrast to the "dark interpretation" of security, I advocate for an analysis that is at once more superficial and more substantive: more superficial, since it does not imply a deep-seated subjective transformation at the level of affect, emotion, or interiority; more substantive, since it centers on the material consequences of inclusion or exclusion within the political community of the city rather than the more abstract, metaphysical space of the political. Belonging to what I have been calling here an endangered community of sense requires competent and convincing enactments of sensitivity toward specific hazards lurking in the urban environment, yet it does not expect or demand a wholesale subjective or affective transformation. And while the security aesthetics I have analyzed above do delineate the boundaries of recognition, membership, and entitlement, especially for the displaced and the urban poor, and often along gendered and racialized lines, they are not the necessary manifestation of a political order founded on the abandonment of certain devalued forms of life. Empirically based ethnographies and genealogies of security are needed to account for practices though which the aesthetic values and norms governing political life get established, deployed, and contested.

NOTES

1   This chapter draws on material that appeared in my 2016 book, *Endangered City: The Politics of Security and Risk in Bogotá* (Durham, NC: Duke University Press).
2   The DPAE ceased to exist in 2010, when it was replaced by Fund for Emergency Prevention and Response (FOPAE).
3   All names used in the chapter are pseudonyms.
4   The official category of "beneficiary" (*beneficiario*) used by the resettlement program connotes one who holds an insurance policy, inherits a will, or receives welfare payments.
5   Precise figures on internal displacement in Colombia are difficult to attain. CODHES (2007) estimates that between 1985 and 2006 about 666,590 displaced persons arrived in the Bogotá metropolitan area. This estimate, they clarify, is conservative and the actual number was probably closer to one million. CODHES is an acronym that, in English, stands for Consultancy for Human Rights and Displacement.

REFERENCES

Barnett, Clive. 2015. "On the Milieu of Security: Situating the Emergence of New Spaces of Public Action." *Dialogues in Human Geography* 5, no. 3: 257–270.

Collier, Stephen J. 2009. "Topologies of Power: Foucault's Analysis of Political Government beyond 'Governmentality.'" *Theory, Culture and Society* 26, no. 6: 78–108.

Consultoría para los Derechos Humanos y el Desplazamiento. 2007. *Gota a gota: Desplazamiento forzado en Bogotá y Soacha*. Bogotá: Consultoría para los Derechos Humanos y el Desplazamiento.

El Tiempo. 2009. "Desplazados llegarían en masa." May 20.

Lakoff, Andrew. 2007. "Preparing for the Next Emergency." *Public Culture* 19, no. 2: 247–271.

Noguera, Carlos E. 2003. *Medicina y política: Discurso médico y prácticas higiénicas durante la primera mitad del siglo XX en Colombia*. Medellín, Colombia: Fondo Editorial Universidad EAFIT.

Pecha Quimbay, Patricia. 2008. *Historia institucional de la caja de la vivienda popular*. Bogotá: Alcaldía Mayor de Bogotá, D.C., Secretaría General, Archivo de Bogotá.

Rancière, Jacques. 2009. "Contemporary Art and the Politics of Aesthetics." In *Communities of Sense: Rethinking Aesthetics and Politics*, edited by Beth Hinderliter, William Kaizen, Vered Maimon, Jaleh Mansoor, and Seth McCormick, 31–50. Durham, NC: Duke University Press.

———. 2011. *The Politics of Aesthetics: The Distribution of the Sensible*. London: Continuum.

Rose, Nikolas. 1999. *Powers of Freedom: Reframing Political Thought*. New York: Cambridge University Press.

AUSTIN ZEIDERMAN

3

"We All Have the Same Red Blood"

Security Aesthetics and Rescue Ethics on the Arizona-Sonora Border

Ieva Jusionyte

MARCH 2017, WASHINGTON, DC

The U.S. Customs and Border Protection (CBP) issued the solicitation for proposals to design President Donald Trump's signature campaign promise: a "big, beautiful wall." The new barrier along the nearly 2,000-mile-long boundary with Mexico must be "physically imposing in height" and "constructible to slopes up to 45 percent," include "anti-climb topping features," "prevent digging or tunneling below it for a minimum of 6 feet," and able to "prevent/deter for a minimum of 1 hour the creation [of] a physical breach of the wall" using "sledgehammer, car jack, pick axe, chisel, battery operated impact tools, battery operated cutting tools, Oxy/acetylene torch or other similar handheld tools," while "the north side of wall (i.e. U.S. facing side) shall be aesthetically pleasing in color, anti-climb texture, etc., to be consistent with general surrounding environment" (CBP 2017). One of the requests was for a wall of "reinforced concrete," while the other left the material of the barrier unspecified.

The fortification had to be "humane": The proponents sought a structure that would not rely on razor wire or electric shocks to deter people from crossing. Michael Evangelista-Ysasaga (2017), whose grandparents came to the United States illegally, and who now owns a construction company that put in a bid to build the wall, told NPR: "We have several different options that meet what the government is wanting in terms of security but at the same time is a very humane obstruction. And I just didn't want to wake up on a Sunday morning and read about, you know, a dozen Guatemalan kids that were electrocuted or seriously injured. That would not have been something that my conscience would have—would allow." This double imperative of the wall—it must be effective at stopping unauthorized entry but also tasteful—called for a particular security aesthetic: a barrier designed to appear innocuous even though it is intended to harm.

MAY 2015, NOGALES, ARIZONA

The ambulance had just finished a run to the Border Patrol station—a seventeen-year-old Mexican boy the agents detained crossing through the desert earlier in the morning had a fever of 102 degrees Fahrenheit—and was returning to the firehouse when, at 11:07 A.M., the tones went off again. The Border Patrol requested assistance with a thirty-year-old female who had fallen off the fence near the corral west of town. The woman had a laceration to her forehead, we were told. The Border Patrol met us near the parking lot where semi tractor-trailers were picking up livestock. Agent Fernández wasn't sure whether the ambulance could get any closer to the scene. Neither were we. It was a steep dip, but Frank, who was driving, made it through. Once the ambulance parked alongside the fence, we noticed a man with a foot injury who was sitting on the bed of a Border Patrol truck. He must have been traveling together with our patient. Fernández pointed to a ditch a few dozen feet north of the wall. "She is down there," he said.

We descended a steep stony slope overgrown with shrub, and found Lupita sitting on the bottom of the ditch, on her bent right leg. She had a 1.5-inch laceration on her forehead, and her forehead was swollen. She said she couldn't get a grip of the fence when she climbed up, and fell, head first. She complained of lower back pain. She spoke in Spanish, so Scott, a paramedic, asked Agent Fernández to translate for him. Through Fernández, he asked Lupita what day of the week it was, where she came from, and whether she knew where she was. She was from Guerrero, she said. She was "at the border, in Nogales, in Arizona, in the United States." She was not so sure about the day of the week. Scott explained to the agent that these questions help him to evaluate patients' neurologic functions. Then he climbed up the slope to retrieve the equipment and call for backup.

I stayed in the ditch with Lupita and Agent Fernández. The stench of cattle dung was strong; flies were everywhere. She asked for water, and I explained that we could not give her any, per protocol, because she may need surgery. I asked whether she had any tenderness in her leg—an agent had told us that

Figure 3.1
Shoes left at the site where a Mexican woman fell off the border fence in Nogales, Arizona. Photograph by author, May 2015.

she couldn't stand on one of her feet and that she crawled all the way from the fence and down to the ditch to hide here. But Lupita said she didn't. She also said she couldn't remember whether she really landed head first or perhaps fell flat from the top—the details were blurry. It took about 5 minutes for the rest of the crew to arrive—Captain Lopez, Bojo, Alex, and Carlitos. Division Chief Castro also showed up. Scott was in charge of treatment: he started an IV, hooked it up to a bag of normal saline, and called for a dose of 5 milligrams of morphine. "You have to stay awake," he commanded. "Frank," he added, "translate this to her." Scott turned to his colleague, since he was one of only a few Anglos in the Nogales Fire Department and did not speak Spanish. "If you feel like you are falling asleep, you must let me know," he instructed the patient.

They put a cervical collar on Lupita's neck to protect her spine, but she started to gag, and Scott decided to take it off. Lupita closed her eyes and looked like she was dozing off, so the firefighters kept waking her up. They brought a Stokes basket—a litter used for rescue operations on difficult terrain—

and discussed the best route to carry her to the ambulance. The slope that we descended was too steep and unstable, with falling rocks and sand; on the other side, there was a fence surrounding the lot with tractor-trailers. The rescuers decided it was best to reach the end of the ditch, where they could climb up the slope easier and lift the patient across a barbed-wire fence. Six firefighters carried Lupita to the ambulance, their feet sliding on the rocks as they clambered up the slope. Once secured to the long spinal board and put onto the gurney, Lupita was transported by ambulance to a helipad, where the crew of *LifeLine 3* were already waiting for her. The mechanism of injury—falling from the height of over 20 feet—and the possibility of a traumatic brain injury meant that she had to be flown to the Level I trauma center at the University Medical Center in Tucson.

Back at the fire station, Captain Lopez left the record of the call in the red log book: "1107 M2 E2 B2 Dead End Freeport—Jumper/Head Injury."

———

This incident is one of several similar episodes recorded in my field journal. The present fence separating Nogales, Arizona, and Nogales, Sonora, comprised of concrete-and-rebar-filled vertical steel tubes, meets most of the desired specifications for President Trump's new barrier. Compared to an earlier landing mat construction, which people remember was colored like an old bruise, the present fence is also more "aesthetically pleasing" to residents of the region and national publics alike. The see-through barrier looks harmless; its capacity to injure rendered invisible (see Figure 3.1). Mutilated bodies of those who dare trespass disappear: some vanish in the desert only to turn up years later, when, despite the painstaking efforts of forensic anthropologists, their skeletons can rarely be identified; the emergency service providers scoop up others into ambulances and rush them to hospitals, where doctors mend broken bones and replenish those dehydrated bodies with fluids before immigration authorities lock them up in detention centers. Migrants injured by the border fence live in the shadows of the public sphere, with renal failure or a permanent limp, bound to a wheelchair or missing a hand. Some are afraid to seek treatment because they still don't have documents to live legally in the United States; others are unable to find or afford long-term care once deported to their country of origin. The barrier effectively neutralizes the menace of "illegal aliens" to the body politic. Within the broader scope of this volume, the ethnography of emergency responders illuminates the intersection between two modalities of security aesthetics: designing fortresses and screening threats.

Border-related trauma along the U.S. southern fringe is so common that it has become normalized. In Douglas, Arizona, about two hours east of Nogales, fire department personnel are dispatched to care for patients with orthopedic injuries—they call them "fence jumpers"—so frequently that they now refer to the cement ledge abutting the international wall as "ankle alley." "We help everyone. It's human nature to want a better chance of life. We all have the same red blood," Chief Mario Novoa said when he invited me for a ride along "ankle alley" in 2015. Fire departments in southern Arizona have been thrust into the mill of policies that target the U.S.-Mexico border as a source of threats. Trained as emergency medical technicians (EMTs) or paramedics, firefighters regularly rescue injured migrants who fall off the fence and those who are hurt in the desert; they fight wildland fires started by border crossers in distress as well as those used as diversion by smugglers; and, they go to the overcrowded Border Patrol station to take undocumented minors with seizures, fever, or heat illness to the hospital.[1] Their uniformed bodies, a symbol of heroism and strength (i.e., security) stand in contrast to the vulnerable and criminalized bodies of unauthorized migrants that they are called to help. Dispatched to correct the deleterious consequences of U.S. federal drug and immigration policies, emergency responders are caught between the government's "security logic" and their professional mandate to provide patient care, or "humanitarian reason" (Fassin 2012). They witness and experience firsthand the most palpable effects of border militarization—they know what injury looks like, smells like, and feels like in the field, before it is wrapped up in medical terminology and legal jargon to be hidden from public oversight. Thus, their work provides a unique angle from which to examine security aesthetics by focusing on the damage, both physical and legal, that material infrastructures do to human bodies.

The chapter is based on my ethnographic research with firefighters in southern Arizona and northern Sonora. I have been working in the region since early 2015 with the goal to examine the violent entanglement between statecraft, law, and topography. Firefighters are uniquely attuned to the characteristics of space and their training provides them with tactical advantage over the most challenging of environments and structural failures. Yet along the Arizona-Sonora border they must also navigate the complex political and legal landscape sliced by a symbolically charged international boundary. In this chapter, I focus on the material and aesthetic qualities of security; that is, on how its discursive and affective dimensions are anchored in urban and desert terrain. The concept of "tactical infrastructure," which the U.S. government uses to describe the assemblage of structures and technologies that enhance security, draws attention to the depoliticized and legal methods of deploying state violence against unauthorized migrants. This security assemblage is made up of parts that are scattered across the landscape and include elements of both natural and man-made environments, which provides the government with a convenient "moral alibi" when locating responsibility for migrant deaths. As Roxanne Lynn Doty (2011, 607) writes: "The raw physicality of some natural environments has an inherent power which can be put to use and can function to mask the workings of social and political power. In the case of U.S. border control strategy, geographic space has made it possible to suggest that the consequences in the form of migrant deaths result from 'natural causes'—e.g., extreme heat, dehydration, thirst, or exposure to the elements—thus deflecting official responsibility." In the Sonoran Desert, the four states of matter—earth, water, air, and fire—play key roles in producing "accidents" that injure and kill the unarmed. The border wall is specifically designed to perform what Achille Mbembe (2003, 21) calls "demiurgic surgery," severing the limbs of those who try to scale it. Using Eyal Weizman's (2014) concept of "forensis," which regards built environment as capable of structuring human action and conditioning incidents and events, I propose reading these injuries as state-effects. Critical anthropological analysis of the patterns of physical trauma on the U.S.-Mexico border allows us to trace the responsibility of the government for what it successfully presents as the unintentional consequences of security processes unfolding on a rugged terrain.

To begin with, I will review existing research that shows the risks and dangers that unauthorized migrants face when they travel across the border from Mexico to the United States. As scholars have argued, the hazards have intensified as a direct consequence of new security infrastructures and surveillance technologies put in place along the international boundary since the 1990s. The chapter then moves on to examine the peculiar position of emergency responders as frontline state actors whose rescue ethics relieves the damage caused by security aesthetics and inadvertently obscures the human costs of border militarization. Using data collected during ethnographic research in nine fire departments along the Arizona-Sonora border from 2015 to 2017, I will discuss the links between Border Patrol's tactical infrastructure and types of injuries that emergency responders often treat. I will finish the chapter by returning to the question about accidental versus intentional character of trauma and the implications of migrant injuries for our understanding of border security and its aesthetics.

TACTICAL INFRASTRUCTURE

Many life-threatening injuries in the U.S.-Mexico border space are not accidental. Rather, they result from structural conditions created by the escalation of violence and security enforcement. Criminalization of immigration, which

Figure 3.2   Mexican side of the border: CBP surveillance tower stands tall above the barrier separating Nogales, Sonora, and Nogales, Arizona. Photograph by author, October 2016.

accelerated in the 1990s and was further radicalized by concerns with terrorism in the aftermath of 9/11, led the U.S. government to designate its southwestern border with Mexico as a threat to homeland security. This justified the amassing of law enforcement resources to protect it and the waging in the borderlands of what has been likened to a low-intensity conflict (Dunn 1996). To deter unauthorized entry, the government has employed a combination of personnel, technology, and infrastructure, which made crossing the border considerably more difficult and dangerous (see Figure 3.2).

Fences and gates, roads and bridges, drainage structures and grates, observation zones, boat ramps, lighting and ancillary power systems, as well as remote video surveillance are part of the CBP's "tactical infrastructure," a term the agency uses to refer to an assemblage of materials and technologies that together "allow CBP to provide persistent impedance, access, and visibility, by making illicit cross-border activities, such as the funneling of illegal immigrants, terrorists, and terrorist weapons into our Nation, more difficult and time-consuming" (CBP 2012, n.p.). Installed on the frontlines of the U.S. government's converging "wars"—the "war on drugs," the "war on terror," and what looks like the "war on immigration"—tactical infrastructure harms the latter category—people—most. According to a 2009 Congressional Research Service Report, "Border fencing is most effective for its operational purposes when deployed along urban areas. . . . In rural areas, the [U.S Border Patrol] testified that it has a tactical advantage over border crossers because they must travel longer distances before reaching populated areas" (Haddal, Kim, and Garcia 2009). Containing such terms as "operational" and "deployed," the report conveys the language of war.

Nogales falls within the jurisdiction of Border Patrol's Tucson Sector, which covers 262 miles from the Yuma County line in the west to the Arizona-New Mexico state line in the east.[2] The area continues to be a major route for northbound migrants and drug and human smugglers: 63,397 unauthorized border crossers were apprehended there in 2015 (Montoya 2016). These numbers don't say much about anything. There's no hard formula to plug them into and calculate how many people and drugs get across. Yet this did not stop the federal agency from using them to justify projects that have converted southern Arizona into the testing ground for state-of-the-art security infrastructures and surveillance technologies. It began in the mid-1990s with the new national strategy to secure the U.S. southern border with Mexico. Operation Safeguard in Arizona was a replica of Operation Blockade/Hold the Line between El Paso, Texas, and Ciudad Juárez, Chihuahua, and Operation Gatekeeper on the San Diego-Tijuana border. This put into practice the Border Patrol's 1994 Strategic Plan, which assumed that "those attempting to illegally enter the United States in large numbers do so in part because of the weak controls we have exercised over the southwest land border in the recent past" (U.S. Border Patrol 1994, 4). The centerpiece of the plan was the "prevention through deterrence" program, which called for "bringing a decisive number of enforcement resources to bear in each major entry corridor." These resources—increased number of agents on the line, aided by the use of tactical infrastructure, such as landing mat fencing and stadium-style lighting, and technology, including night vision scopes and ground sensors—had to raise the risk of apprehension to the point where many would "consider it futile to attempt illegal entry." The plan predicted that, as a direct consequence of border security buildup in urban areas, "illegal traffic will be deterred, or forced over more hostile terrain, less suited for crossing and more suited for enforcement." So it was that in the 1990s the chain-link fence in Nogales was replaced by 12-foot-high steel panels.

"The threat and terrain dictates the strategy and equipment. . . . There is not one single piece of equipment or technology or infrastructure that is a panacea to border security," explained Manuel Padilla, the former chief of the U.S. Border Patrol's Tucson Sector (Trevizo 2015b). Announced in 2011 and expected

94

to be fully operational by 2020, the Arizona Border Surveillance Technology Plan is the most recent iteration in a series of attempts to secure the border: it consists of a combination of Integrated Fixed Towers, ground sensors that can detect a single person, and long-range night-vision scopes mounted on mobile surveillance trucks; the program will give Border Patrol "ninety percent situational awareness" (Trevizo 2015c). The defense company that won the government's bid—Israel's giant private military manufacturer Elbit Systems—has promised to bring to southern Arizona the same security technologies used in Gaza and the West Bank (T. Miller and Schivone 2015). Integrated fixed towers will be equipped with cameras that provide agents with high-resolution video that allows them to see whether someone is carrying a backpack or a long-arm weapon from up to 7.5 miles away. Seven such towers are already perched on the rolling hills surrounding Nogales. Thirty-one others will be constructed in Douglas, Sonoita, Ajo, and Casa Grande.

INHUMANE CONSEQUENCES

The trend of border militarization that began in the 1990s and escalated after 9/11—including the adoption of "prevention through deterrence" as the primary immigration enforcement strategy, the increase in the numbers of Border Patrol agents, the parallel amplification of the Mexican military after President Felipe Calderón assumed power and declared war on organized crime, and the blurring of lines between human smugglers and drug traffickers—have all added to the escalation of violence and resulted in a border-crossing experience that is extremely dangerous (Cornelius 2001; Doty 2011; Infante et al. 2012; Slack and Campbell 2016; Slack and Whiteford 2011). Like other urban areas that had traditionally been popular crossing corridors for unauthorized migrants, Nogales has been increasingly fortified (McGuire 2013; Nevins 2010). In addition to the obstacles presented by the fence, border crossers were subjected to "the thickening of delinquency" (Rosas 2012) that thrived on the neoliberal frontier—gang violence, kidnapping, extortion, rape, and other forms of illegalities. As the Border Patrol's plan predicted, "illegal traffic" was "forced over more hostile terrain, less suited for crossing and more suited for enforcement." Unable to cross through towns, unauthorized migrants were funneled to less policed passages through the Sonoran Desert.

Such stringent security policies are directly linked to the routinization of migrant deaths. A report prepared by the American Civil Liberties Union (ACLU) claims that the deaths of an estimated 5,607 unauthorized migrants between 1994 and 2009 were a predictable and inhumane outcome of border security policies (Jimenez 2009, 7–8). Since 2001, the Pima County Medical

Examiner's Office identified more than 2,500 human remains in the Tucson Sector alone (Blust 2016). As migrants who are trying to cross into the United States are being pushed into geographically and environmentally difficult desert and mountain areas in southern Arizona, they have come to rely on guides linked to drug cartels, which can lead to robberies, kidnapping, physical abuse, and rape. Some get lost or are abandoned by smugglers, especially when they are injured or in distress. Most deaths occur due to environmental factors, primarily from exposure to extreme heat or cold (temperatures can reach over 120 degrees Fahrenheit during summer days and drop below freezing during winter nights) and dehydration, as people typically never carry enough water to sustain themselves on a multiday crossing (de León 2012). Researchers and activists who work on recovering, identifying, and repatriating migrant remains note that, besides existing diseases, other common causes of death while crossing the border include blunt force injuries, train and motor vehicle accidents, gunshot wounds, natural disasters such as fires, and drowning in rivers and irrigation canals (Jimenez 2009). Referring to these deaths as a result of "natural causes" or "unintended effects" of "prevention through deterrence" deflects official responsibility.

There are specific patterns of suffering that can be traced back to border securitization and militarization and that reveal the border crossing to be a well-structured violent social process. Drawing on ethnographic and archaeological data from the Undocumented Migration Project in the Sonoran Desert, Jason de León (2012, 2015) has shown how "use-wear" of objects that migrants take with them to avoid being caught by border enforcement agents—black plastic water jugs, cheap sneakers, darkly colored clothes—act on people's bodies, causing particular types of injuries. All migrants are made vulnerable through encounters with the Border Patrol, coyotes, bandits, and traffickers, but women, children, and monolingual indigenous people face the greatest risk (Slack and Whiteford 2011). Those traveling from Honduras, El Salvador, or other countries south of Mexico may get mutilated if they fall off the freight trains colloquially known as "La Bestia" (the beast), which they take to reach the U.S. border. Wendy Vogt (2013) has shown how the bodies of Central American migrants have become commodities in the economies of violence and humanitarian aid. These occurrences are not accidents—they must be understood as the result of structural, state, and local economies of violence and inequality.

Despite the risks, many migrants make it across the border alive, but often—because of severe injuries caused by the journey—they need emergency medical care. The close relationship between securitization of the border and increased number of trauma patients is illustrated by the following detail: *Nogales International* reported that when in 2011 the government doubled the height of the border fence in the city, the number of times fire department ambulances transported someone from the border spiked (Prendergast 2013). In 2015 and 2016, the Mexican Consulate registered 125 Mexican nationals hospitalized in Tucson: most of them for fractures caused by falling off the border wall, while other reasons for hospitalization included dehydration, injuries to the feet (blisters, cuts), and drinking contaminated water.[3] The consulate also registered bites by poisonous animals, spontaneous abortions due to severe dehydration, people swept away by arroyos during the rains, sexual abuse by human traffickers, and ingestion of cactus. The numbers may seem low, but that is because the consulate only learns about a patient when either the Border Patrol or the hospital lets them know. On the other side of the border, the Juan Bosco migrant shelter in Nogales, Sonora, accepted thirty injured people in June 2015 alone (Echavarri 2015). That year the consulate and the migrant shelter both reported an increase in serious injuries along the fence. Ricardo Pineda, the Mexican consul in Tucson, said that they were seeing more migrants in need of medical attention from falling off the border fence than from crossing the desert. Most of them were women with fractures to their feet, ankles, or legs. Gilda Felix, the director of Juan Bosco shelter, told the press: "They think it's easier than walking for days in the desert but it's not. . . . It's the same crossing through the wall or through the desert, both difficult and dangerous" (Echavarri 2015).

To reduce the number of deaths the government created the Border Patrol Search, Trauma, and Rescue Unit (BORSTAR). Yet the role of BORSTAR is rather controversial because at other times border enforcement agents are the ones responsible for injuring migrants (Isacson, Meyer, and Davis 2013; Martínez, Slack, and Heyman 2013). To mitigate the deadly effects of security policies, humanitarian organizations such as Humane Borders, Tucson Samaritans, and No More Deaths, among others, took on the task of rescuing unauthorized migrants and providing them first aid (Magaña 2008). Volunteers build water stations stocked with food, clothing, and first-aid kits and set up medical camps. They also patrol the desert on foot and in vehicles in search for migrants who need help. In situations when their condition is critical—for example, when border crossers have altered mental status, difficulty breathing, or snake bites—volunteers try to persuade migrants to allow them to call 911 and transfer them to local medical facilities. Law enforcement officers at Arizona's ports of entry also have prosecutorial discretion, which enables them to consider the person's condition and use humanitarian parole to temporarily admit immigrants for health reasons, even when the patients do not have a passport and a visa.

But none of them—neither the Border Patrol agents, nor immigration officers at the ports of entry, nor humanitarian aid volunteers—have the indiscriminate provision of prehospital medical services as the official mandate of their job. In southern Arizona, this task belongs to local emergency responders. Ethical framework that underlies the principles of health care distinguishes emergency responders from Border Patrol agents, who, even when trained in first aid, are primarily concerned with enforcing the law. Their affiliation with local city or county governments also sets them apart from humanitarian volunteers who are not accountable to state agencies. How do these public service employees negotiate their seemingly contradictory functions of being part of the state apparatus, which renders invisible the victims of security policies and tactical infrastructure, while at the same time mandated to rescue those injured by government policies?

FIREFIGHTERS AS STATE ACTORS

Emergency responders have a pragmatic, hazard-oriented disposition toward the border region, which has been sensationalized and politicized in national public discourses. The labor of structure and wildland firefighting hinges on competence—practical types of knowledge, the know-how of the city or the country, acquired through repeated encounters with the dangers of the local topography (Desmond 2007). Previously called "smoke eaters" and associated with untamed bravery, firefighters have evolved into a highly trained all-hazards response task force, dispatched to vehicle collisions, confined space rescue operations, floods, and other incidents. In the 1970s, fire departments across the United States started providing prehospital medical services to the critically ill and injured in their communities. Firefighters are now routinely certified as EMTs, and are increasingly choosing to obtain a paramedic's license. In southern Arizona, even small fire departments operate Advanced Life Support ambulances, equipped with cardiac monitors and medications, and are getting more calls for health emergencies than for other types of incidents. Today fire and rescue squads are the embodiment of what historian Mark Tebeau (2003, 287) described as "the melding of men and technology into an efficient, lifesaving machine."

Fire departments have also changed their traditionally local orientation and adjusted to the demands placed on first responders by the national political milieu. As municipal service providers, they have historically played an important role in local city governance, their unions supporting candidates in mayoral and city council elections. Their significance didn't reach much further than the boundaries of the neighborhood where they served and where they knew the residents, yet now firefighters have been placed on the front lines of the federal state and its security mission. Their role in responding to 9/11 attacks, when 343 firefighters died under the collapsing towers in New York City, has solidified their symbolic status as "gallant warriors" and national heroes in the "war on terror" (Donahue 2011; Dowler 2002; Rothenbuhler 2005) and justified their co-optation into national preparedness and homeland security structures. Politically and administratively, fire and rescue services across the United States have been incorporated into the system of federal emergency management, which falls under the purview of the Department of Homeland Security. As their mandate expanded to include incidents involving all threats and hazards, firefighters have been trained to effectively respond to an open-ended list of emergencies from hazardous industrial waste spills to terror attacks involving biological, chemical, radiological, and other weapons of mass destruction, to epidemic infectious disease. They regularly participate in exercises and drills that prepare them to deal with these and other emergent threats to national and global security (see Collier and Lakoff 2008; Fosher 2009; Lakoff 2007; Masco 2014).

Yet the routine work of firefighters and paramedics rarely calls for such large-scale mobilization. Daily, they respond to 911 calls within their local jurisdictions, helping people in the most vulnerable situations, where their everyday practices are nonetheless interlaced with security politics. Firefighters work under conditions of increased anxieties in their communities and amidst residents' concerns that locally financed rescue services are being diverted to address the consequences of federal security enforcement (Lovett 2012; Prendergast 2013). Nowhere is this more visible than on the U.S.-Mexico border. Here, an already difficult physical terrain—the desert with steep crevices, abandoned mine shafts, extreme temperature changes, toxic plants, and poisonous animals—is made even more threatening by security tactics aimed at curbing undocumented migration and drug trafficking. Many of the emergencies local firefighters and paramedics respond to are the result of the life-threatening combination of the legal grid imposed on the region's physical topography. Witnessing the impacts of the enhanced border security regime on the health and well-being of U.S. and Mexican border residents and migrants alike, firefighters wrestle with the contradictions they experience as both humanitarian rescuers and uniformed state authorities. Emergency responders work in the splintered space of what Pierre Bourdieu (2014) called the "bureaucratic field," where "the left hand" of the state (in charge of social functions, such as public education, health, housing, welfare) is remediating the negative effects resulting from the actions of "the right hand" (enforcing the economic discipline and social order—the police, the courts, the prison)—in this case, border militarization. As fire and emergency medical services become ever more tightly integrated into the national preparedness and homeland security apparatus, and invested with political and symbolic functions of state authority, more and more first responders are finding themselves caught between border enforcement and social-humanitarian policies.

While unauthorized migrants who work in the United States may try to avoid interacting with health care providers out of fear of being detained and deported (Holmes 2013; Horton 2016), this is usually not an option for unauthorized migrants who become critically ill or injured while crossing the border. The burden of ethical and legal action then falls on emergency responders who, like other street-level bureaucrats such as police officers and social workers, wield considerable discretion in the day-to-day implementation of public programs (Lipsky 1980). The Emergency Medical Treatment and Active Labor Act of 1986 requires health care providers to treat anyone who needs emergency medical care regardless of income or immigration status. Fire departments follow medical protocols that outline what mechanisms of injury and what signs and symptoms warrant transporting patients by air to the nearest trauma center in Tucson. A patient's legal status in the country has no place in medical decision charts. Yet, as research in different social settings has shown, relationships between laws, policies, and medical ethics are often incongruous, making the interactions between frontline health care personnel and their "illegal" patients fraught with tension (e.g., Castañeda 2011; Chavez 2012; Heyman, Núñez, and Talavera 2009; Marrow 2012; Rosenthal 2007; Willen 2007).

In recent years, the conflation between prehospital medical care and immigration enforcement has become a major issue for firefighters who rescue unauthorized migrants in southern Arizona. Due to lack of federal mechanisms to compensate taxpayer-funded fire departments for providing treatment and transport to unauthorized migrants, emergency responders have been reporting these patients to the Border Patrol, which forces the agency to assume at least partial responsibility for the costs of medications and other supplies used to rescue, treat, and transport undocumented patients (see Jusionyte 2018). But emergency responders are divided on the issue. "The guys, from the captain down, wanna help people. That's our goal," a thirty-year veteran in the Nogales Fire Department told me. "We are not Border Patrol. Since he's on this side of the fence, wherever it is, we had been told to treat that patient. With that issue [referring the patient to the Border Patrol], you are making the EMS [emergency medical services] people become involved with immigration enforcement." In the end, humanitarian logic triumphs over policy. The same firefighter said that sometimes they had to circumvent the rules and make a "moral decision": "We've gone out to places where people were in extremely bad shape and taken medical custody of them, knowing that I should have called the Border Patrol before. Like we say here, if I'm gonna mess up, I'm gonna mess up to the good side. When that patient is walking home or something and they say: How come you didn't call the Border Patrol . . . ? I'll say: Well, you know what? Sue me."

The border zone has been called the "Constitution free zone," where the area's very proximity to the international boundary breeds concerns over security, which in turn justifies bending the law (Dorsey and Díaz-Barriga 2015). More and more often local fire departments are not even contacted to provide emergency medical services to injured border crossers. In 2015, ACLU criticized southern Arizona's Santa Cruz and Pima Counties—where Nogales and Arivaca are located—for violating the Equal Protection Clause of the Fourteenth Amendment when they found that the sheriffs' departments "selectively referred" 911 calls from migrants in distress directly to the Border Patrol, bypassing local first responders (Trevizo 2015a).

THE FENCE: AMPUTATIONS AND FRACTURES

"When it used to be the old fence, people would cross, go in and out. Not a big thing." Having worked for the Nogales Fire Department since 1985, Assistant Chief William Sanchez said that until the 1990s unauthorized crossing was very common. He, like many of those who work in the fire service, is a local of the town, where over 90 percent of the population is Hispanic and where the common language in all but government business is Spanish. Most of the residents in Nogales have family on both sides of the border and call the sister cities of Nogales, Arizona, and Nogales, Sonora, "Ambos Nogales." Founded in the 1890s, the Nogales Fire Department employs forty-two shift workers, at least three of whom began their career as volunteer firefighters on the other side of the border, in Mexico. Over the years, they have experienced changes to border infrastructure as residents of these towns first and later as emergency responders. "When we were kids, we used to cut through the fence and go buy bread and stuff over there [in Mexico] and then come back," one captain told me. Another firefighter reminisced about a man on a bicycle who would bring lemons and cheese from Nogales, Sonora, to sell at the fire station in Nogales, Arizona. The fence was there, but it didn't mean much to anybody.

It was not until the mid-1990s that a metal wall was erected to divide Ambos Nogales. This new barrier was made from steel panels that the U.S.

military had originally used as portable landing mats for Hercules cargo planes and Huey helicopters during the Vietnam War. Even the U.S. Army Corps of Engineers, the ones who designed the solid corrugated steel panels known as M8A1s, acknowledged the flaws of their construction: the landing mats had rough edges that frequently ripped the tires of heavy aircraft (Hattam 2016). By the end of the war the military had replaced them with aluminum mats, relegating M8A1s for taxiways and parking lots. After Vietnam, landing mats were easily repurposed for other ends. Measuring 12 feet long, 20 inches wide, and a quarter-inch thick, and weighing 147 pounds, the panels became "army surplus." They were subsequently redeployed to the U.S. Southwest border. Each mile of fence required 3,080 metal sheets. By 2006, they had been used to build over 60 miles of border fence in California, Arizona, and Texas. In Nogales, the new rusty steel barrier extended to 2.8 miles; depending on the location, it was 8–12 feet high and had an anti-climb guard (McGuire 2013, 472).

When the landing mat wall was erected in Nogales, emergency responders were regularly called to help unauthorized border crossers who had been injured while trying to scale the barrier separating them from the jobs on construction sites or agricultural fields in the north. The same sharp edges that damaged the tires of the military fleet in Vietnam left some migrants with large gashes, amputated limbs, and degloving injuries. Alex Flores, who has worked for the Nogales Fire Department since the mid-1990s, recalls:

> When they [border crossers] were climbing down, they would slip and the hands would get stuck up here, so they would get their fingers cut off. . . . Everything would get caught up here because it was sharp. They [authorities] say they weren't, but I think they were made intentionally like that to deter people from coming over. So people would get their fingers cut off, and they would land on this side, and the finger parts would land on the other side, usually, or they would get lost between the plates, so we never could get them out. [In] some places they used to have cuts on the bottom [of the fence] for the water to go through with grates on it. You could still see across and you could see the fingers . . . on the other side of the border, and the people were over here. Sometimes we would reach over and grab the body part, bring it over and put it on ice. It used to happen a lot.

In 2011, the aesthetically displeasing landing mat wall was replaced by a sturdier and taller bollard-style barrier. Constructed of interconnected steel tubes extending up to 20 feet above the ground and 10 feet below the surface, this fence was designed to act as a more effective deterrent against climbing over or digging under (Stephenson 2011). The different design of the barrier

Figure 3.3   U.S. side of the border: sharp rocks lining the bottom of the barrier between Nogales, Arizona, and Nogales, Sonora. Photograph by author, October 2016.

produced different types of injuries. While the earlier version, made of corrugated sheet metal, caused gashes and amputations, the present barrier is difficult to hold on to and migrants often fall down. A surgeon at the trauma center in Tucson, who has treated many injured border crossers, explained in an interview in 2015: "In certain areas the fence is up to 20-30 feet high. A fall from that height can be pretty serious. Very frequently we see patients with orthopedic injuries. Ankle fractures are very common, tib-fib—or lower extremity—fractures, and spinal fractures." He added: "It's a pattern of injury. When someone falls and lands on their feet, the energy is transferred from the feet all the way to the spine."

Some stretches of the present wall are more perilous than others. There is an offset landing with cement and rocks, where the most dramatic injuries occur. "That's probably about a four to five feet area, like a sidewalk, but with rocks sticking out from it," a paramedic in Nogales once described it to me (see Figure 3.3). "What other reason are these there for?" another firefighter asked rhetorically. "They are there to injure people so that they couldn't run from the Border Patrol." These firefighters knew from experience, having responded to help numerous patients with orthopedic, spinal, and head trauma on that small piece of land right next to the CBP parking lot. "We had people that landed on their head and died," one of them said. In February 2012, a forty-four-year-old man from Oaxaca, Mexico, died on the west side of Nogales when he sustained head and neck injuries (Pineda 2016). Two years later, in March 2014, a forty-one-year-old man from El Salvador died from head trauma after falling from the border fence near the end of Short Street (Pineda 2016). In 2016, the Nogales Police Department was investigating the death of a thirty-two-year-old woman from Juchitepec in the State of Mexico, whose body was found near the border fence in the east of Nogales. She, too, had fatal injuries after possibly falling off the fence, reported the police. Security buildup on the border was largely based on weaponizing the already difficult physical terrain. To emergency responders the causation was obvious: they did not hesitate to implicate the agency in deliberately altering the landscape to cause serious injuries to those who did not have the required documents allowing them to cross through the designated port of entry.

THE ROAD: HIGH-SPEED CHASES AND ROLLOVERS

Those deterred by the fence—as the most obvious form and spectacular operationalization of security aesthetics—cross through what the Border Patrol's strategic plan refers to as "hostile terrain." The desert may seem less harmful, but its appearance is deceptive. Journalists, scholars, and human rights activists have called the Sonoran Desert "the killing fields" and "a neoliberal oven" (see Rosas 2012). Luis Alberto Urrea (2004) warned about the cunning character of this lethal topography, noting "the deadly bite" lurking "behind the greeting-card sunrises." Here, nature functions as an extension of tactical infrastructure, performing the role of law enforcement by subjecting unauthorized border crossers to injury.

Although emergency responders from Nogales are also dispatched to rescues in the hills and canyons outside of town, it is the rural fire departments that carry the heaviest burden of treating and transporting unauthorized migrants who get hurt in the desert. In 2015, I conducted fieldwork with firefighters in Arivaca, an unincorporated community of about seven hundred residents located 11 miles north of the border. It is on a popular transit route through the desert between Nogales and Sasabe, used by undocumented migrants and drug smugglers alike. Arivaca Volunteer Fire Department, which was founded in 1986 and became a fire district in 2009, has two emergency medical responders per shift covering a territory of 612 square miles. In 2015, the department responded to 192 calls for emergency medical services, fire, welfare, and other situations; 24 of those runs involved a patient in the custody of the Border Patrol.[4]

Tangye Beckham—firefighter, paramedic, and the district's interim fire chief, who has lived in Arivaca for most of her life—said: "They are traveling at night and if you don't know the terrain, I wouldn't walk out here at night, but they do. Because they figure they are undetected. They fall off cliffs or they trip over rocks. The terrain is very rough." Emergency responders are routinely called to rescue migrants who fall into abandoned mine shafts, twist their ankles on the rocks, or lose a lot of fluids during prolonged exposure to extreme heat. Most of them need treatment for dehydration, which—after days of heat exposure—can be severe and cause permanent damage to the kidneys. Border Patrol agents often find injured migrants in locations that are remote and difficult to access, miles off the paved road, so it can take an hour or more until emergency responders reach them and begin treatment. Once the patient is in the ambulance, the drive to the closest hospital in Tucson takes another hour. When the life of the patient is in danger, emergency responders call rescue helicopters, which can cover the same distance in less than twenty minutes.

Before the checkpoints were permanently installed on both roads connecting Arivaca to the rest of the country—one at the entrance of Interstate 19 in Amado, the other on State Route 286 north of Sasabe—the Arivaca Volunteer Fire Department frequently responded to vehicle rollovers. An EMT I interviewed in 2015 told me about the "car wreck phase" in the late 1990s and early 2000s, when the Border Patrol chased vehicles carrying unauthorized migrants "packed like sardines." Once he was the first responder to arrive on scene with seventeen patients. He described the situation:

> There's been people apneic and pulseless, and, assessing the patients, I knew there was no helping them. There were some people that had broken bones, but it wasn't life threatening, so I would go on to the next patient. . . . There were people who had problems with breathing or were bleeding really bad and I would attempt to stop the bleeding and make sure they have a clear airway and make sure . . . that somebody was holding C-spine. . . . I've splinted broken femurs, I've splinted arms using a stick. We used what we had. Duct tape. Cardboard.

Roadside crosses, marking the sites where deadly accidents took place, dot the highways of southern Arizona. Emergency responders in Tubac, Sonoita, and Nogales suburban fire districts told me similar stories. Throughout the "car wreck phase," local firefighters responded to multiple vehicle rollovers, often involving pickup trucks and vans sometimes carrying dozens of unauthorized migrants, and they consistently told me that many of these deadly accidents happened as a result of pursuits on roads that have dangerous curves, often at night. Carmen Hernandez, who at the time worked as an EMT in Tubac, recalled an incident on June 6, 2009, when a Ford Excursion, carrying twenty-four people, rolled on State Route 82 east of Sonoita, and eleven unauthorized migrants were killed: "I was brand new. I remember getting off the ambulance and it was like a war zone. Bodies everywhere. . . . The first patient I remember seeing was a fourteen-year-old. . . . Then, as you start walking, there were head injuries, there was brain matter on the ground. One of the patients, he was a DOA [dead on arrival], was under Border Patrol jeep."

Despite rollovers being a topic regularly covered in the local press, often under sensationalized headlines (e.g., "13 from 'Deep in Mexico' Hurt in Arivaca Rollover," *Tucson Citizen*, February 22, 2003; "1 Dead, 7 Critical in Entrants' Crash," *Arizona Daily Star*, January 11, 2005), this incident attracted unprecedented media attention. Even though one of the survivors, a Mexican national, said a Border Patrol vehicle had been following the SUV, which accelerated and, due to the oversize load, blew a rear tire and rolled multiple times, causing most of the passengers to be ejected, officials denied that the SUV was being pursued. The investigation, led by the Arizona Department of Public Safety, focused on identifying the driver, who could have faced charges for multiple homicide (Caesar 2009). But since the driver turned out to be among the dead, the U.S. Attorney's Office convicted four other men for their part in the migrant-smuggling operation based out of Cananea, Sonora. One of them, thirty-seven-year-old Oscar Garay-Mariscal, who received $500 for his role as a "trail scout" and spent nine days in a coma after the accident, was sentenced to sixty-five months in federal prison (J. B. Miller 2011). Indexical links that hinted to larger forces and institutional responsibilities behind this and other tragic events have not been pursued.

INTENTIONAL ACCIDENTS

Descriptions of injuries that firefighters share with each other are often graphic and gory—fingers amputated by the rustic metal fence, brain matter scattered on the asphalt after a vehicle crash—but these details are salient. In the depoliticized space of the firehouse, recounting accidents is the vernacular through which they engage in social critique. As municipal service providers, fire departments and firefighter unions have long played an important role in local governance, supporting candidates in mayoral and city council elections. But the rank and file usually stay away from discussing national politics, particularly polarizing issues. Firefighters have to rely on each other: in emergency situations their lives are literally in the hands of their peers. Hence, by the unwritten rules of the firehouse, any topic that could splinter this brotherhood is a taboo. When emergency responders tell stories about trauma and rescue, they don't assign blame, but these narratives form a record that can be used to reconstruct the chain of events leading to the accident and assign guilt. Sometimes the stories point to individual responsibility; other times they hint at policy failures. Where political discourse is limited, their narrow focus on the injured body is the only acceptable means that firefighters and paramedics have to express disagreement with government actions. In this chapter, the patterns of injuries they observed became ethnographic and analytic cues—forensic traces—of state violence directed at unauthorized migrants.

In September 1966, the National Academy of Sciences and the National Research Council published a document that laid the foundation of emergency medical services in the United States: it was called *Accidental Death and Disability: The Neglected Disease of Modern Society*. The report emphasized the "accidental" nature of trauma-related injuries and deaths and lamented that "the human suffering and financial loss from preventable accidental death constitute a public health problem second only to the ravages of ancient plagues or world wars" (p. 8). To this day, the mandate of prehospital trauma management in Nogales, Arivaca, and other fire departments across the United States stems from this document. But what constitutes an accident? An accident is "an unfortunate eventuality, an incident that happens unexpectedly and unintentionally, resulting in damage" (*Oxford English Dictionary*, 2nd ed., s.v. "accident"). In Aristotelian thought, it signifies a property or quality that is not essential to a substance or object. However, as Paul Virilio (2007, 10) noted, "WHAT CROPS UP (*accidens*) is a sort of analysis, a technoanalysis of WHAT IS BENEATH (*substare*) any knowledge." To invent the ship is to invent the shipwreck; to invent the train is to invent the derailment; to invent the automobile is to produce the pileup on the highway. In his critique of new technologies and scientific progress, Virilio revisits Aristotle's ideas and writes that "the accident reveals the substance." Accidents are programmed into the products of modernity. We can see this in forensic accident investigations, which challenge the fortuitous nature of vehicle collisions and airplane crashes. The scientific discovery of the incident's chain of causation allows moral and legal responsibility to be assigned, and "the accident as such ceases to be" (Siegel 2014, 20).

Migrant injuries on the U.S.-Mexico border have never been accidental— they are not chance occurrences or contingencies. But unlike shipwrecks or automobile pileups, which happen without an intended cause, border trauma is deliberate. It is calculated and produced by those who deploy the security apparatus as the means of enacting the policy of "prevention through deterrence." The Border Patrol explicitly calls the fence part of its "tactical infrastructure" with operational goal to give them advantage over those who disregard the blunt message: no trespassing. A broken ankle or an amputated finger become proof of illegal entry—a civil offense. But crossing the border without authorization, through a clandestine passage, is a rather mild violation of the law, which precedes and substitutes for a more serious one: suspected drug trafficking—a criminal offense. When an accident is treated as a potential crime, the state assumes the right to exercise force against the victim-criminal. In her analysis of car accidents in postapartheid South Africa, Rosalind Morris (2010, 612) argues that "the state opens a space to exercise force" not by making crimes look like mere accidents, but by representing the accident as a possible crime. The injured migrant is always already implicated as a criminal. She stands in for the drug traffickers and the "murderers and rapists" that conjure up fear in the national political rhetoric.

This line of argument is important, but it is limited to discourse. This chapter urges readers to consider the infrastructure itself—the design and textures of security aesthetics that result in specific patterns of trauma—as a form of state violence and an inherent crime. Architecture theorist Eyal Weizman (2014, 16) describes built environments as "composite assemblies of structures, spaces, infrastructure, services, and technologies with the capacity to act and interact with their surroundings and shape events around them. They structure and condition rather than simply frame human action, they actively—sometimes violently—shape incidents and events." They can thus be used to reveal how states and private corporations commit crimes in the routine of governing their subjects while at the same time erasing the visible traces of their transgressions. This approach "turns space into evidence, but also into the medium in which different types of evidence come together and into relation with each other" (Weizman 2014, 19). Road accidents and traumatic falls are programmed into the built environment. Firefighters follow the cracks in urban infrastructures that threaten life and rescue those who trip and fall, in predictable—because intentional, therefore preventable—patterns. Rescue is a quintessentially spatial task, unfolding on landscapes that cripple trespassing bodies in ways that may hinder their survival: deplete them of oxygen, puncture their blood vessels, cut their spinal cords. Emergency responders study the relationship between spatial forms—physical terrain, logistical landscapes, buildings—and the types of incidents and injuries they produce. They practice using hydraulic tools to extricate bodies from mangled vehicles on the highway, and secure patients with potential back and neck injuries to the backboard before lifting them into the ambulance.

By aestheticizing its security operations, the state obfuscates its double imperative—to wound and to care—placing emergency responders in a seemingly contradictory position. In Nogales, Arivaca, and other fire departments across southern Arizona, firefighters are dispatched to incidents caused by deliberate modifications of the environment in the name of security. Not only is emergency routine on the border, but accidents are purposeful. They are not due to an error—the malfunctioning of the security apparatus. Migrant injuries are intended outcomes. Their patterns signal the role of the state in deploying tactical infrastructure. Unlike in Cold War Berlin, where those who scaled the wall escaping East Germany became heroes in the West, the political figure of the border crosser has lost its public appeal. Mexican, Honduran, and other Latin American bodies don't signify the same quest for freedom. Instead, they are seen as victims, at best; at worst, they are portrayed as vectors of criminality, as sources of threat. Either way, the wounded would tarnish the security aesthetics of the "big, beautiful wall," and, as such, are rendered invisible to all but those who are mandated to bandage their injured limbs.

NOTES

This is an updated version of an article that first appeared *in American Anthropologist* 120, no. 1, as "Called to 'Ankle Alley': Migrant Injuries and Emergency Medical Services on the U.S.-Mexico Border." I am grateful to D. Asher Ghertner, Daniel M. Goldstein, Hudson McFann, and two anonymous reviewers for comments that helped me revise it for inclusion as a chapter in the current volume.

1   In southern Arizona, many municipal and county fire departments also provide public ambulance services. In Nogales, up to 90 percent of the calls firefighters respond to each year are for medical emergencies. Considering this trend, all firefighters are required to be certified as emergency medical technicians or paramedics. The situation is similar in neighboring jurisdictions.

2   While 212 miles have some form of fencing, including Normandy-style anti-vehicle barriers, the remaining 50 miles have natural barriers—mountains and deserts.

3   Data provided by the Consulado de México in Tucson, Arizona, February 16, 2017.

4   Information obtained from the Arivaca Fire District through a public records request, May 9, 2017.

REFERENCES

Blust, Kendal. 2016. "Deaths per 10,000 Border Crossers Are up 5 Times from a Decade Ago." *Arizona Daily Star*, May 21.

Bourdieu, Pierre. 2014. *On the State: Lectures at the Collège de France, 1989-1992.* Cambridge: Polity Press.

"WE ALL HAVE THE SAME RED BLOOD"

Caesar, Stephen. 2009. "Rollover Kills 8 in SUV Near Sonoita." *Arizona Daily Star*, June 8.

Castañeda, Heide. 2011. "Medical Humanitarianism and Physicians' Organized Efforts to Provide Aid to Unauthorized Migrants in Germany." *Human Organization* 70, no. 1: 1–10.

Chavez, Leo R. 2012. "Undocumented Immigrants and Their Use of Medical Services in Orange County, California." *Social Science and Medicine* 74, no. 6: 887–893.

Collier, Stephen J., and Andrew Lakoff. 2008. "The Vulnerability of Vital Systems: How 'Critical Infrastructure' Became a Security Problem." In *Securing "the Homeland": Critical Infrastructure, Risk and (In)Security*, edited by M. D. Cavelty and K. S. Kristensen, 17–39. New York: Routledge.

Cornelius, Wayne A. 2001. "Death at the Border: Efficacy and Unintended Consequences of US Immigration Control Policy." *Population and Development Review* 27, no. 4: 661–685.

De León, Jason. 2012. "'Better to Be Hot Than Caught': Excavating the Conflicting Roles of Migrant Material Culture." *American Anthropologist* 114, no. 3: 477–495.

———. 2015. *The Land of Open Graves: Living and Dying on the Migrant Trail*. Oakland: University of California Press.

Desmond, Matthew. 2007. *On the Fireline: Living and Dying with Wildland Firefighters*. Chicago: University of Chicago Press.

Donahue, Katherine C. 2011. "What Are Heroes For? Commemoration and the Creation of Heroes after September 11." *Anthropology News* 52, no. 6: 6.

Dorsey, Margaret E., and Miguel Díaz-Barriga. 2015. "The Constitution Free Zone in the United States: Law and Life in a State of Carcelment." *PoLAR: Political and Legal Anthropology Review* 38: 204–225.

Doty, Roxanne Lynn. 2011. "Bare Life: Border-Crossing Deaths and Spaces of Moral Alibi." *Environment and Planning D: Society and Space* 29, no. 4: 599–612.

Dowler, Lorraine. 2002. "Women on the Frontlines: Rethinking War Narratives Post 9/11." *GeoJournal* 58, nos. 2–3: 159–165.

Dunn, Timothy J. 1996. *The Militarization of the U.S.-Mexico Border, 1978–1992: Low-Intensity Conflict Doctrine Comes Home*. Austin: CMAS Books, University of Texas at Austin.

Echavarri, Fernanda. 2015. "More Immigrants Injured Falling from Border Fence." *Arizona Public Media*, June 30.

Evangelista-Ysasaga, Michael. 2017. Interview by David Greene. *Morning Edition*. NPR. March 29. https://www.npr.org/2017/03/29/521884308/potential-u-s-mexico-wall-builder-has-family-in-the-u-s-illegally.

Fassin, Didier. 2012. *Humanitarian Reason: A Moral History of the Present*. Berkeley: University of California Press.

Fosher, Kerry B. 2009. *Under Construction: Making Homeland Security at the Local Level*. Chicago: University of Chicago Press.

Haddal, Chad C., Yule Kim, and Michael John Garcia. 2009. *Border Security: Barriers along the U.S. International Border*. Congressional Research Service Report to Congress, March 16.

Hattam, Victoria. 2016. "Imperial Designs: Remembering Vietnam at the U.S.-Mexico Border Wall." *Memory Studies* 9, no. 1: 27–47.

Heyman, Josiah McC, Guillermina G. Núñez, and Victor Talavera. 2009. "Healthcare Access and Barriers for Unauthorized Immigrants in El Paso County, Texas." *Family and Community Health* 32, no. 1: 4–21.

Holmes, Seth M. 2013. *Fresh Fruit, Broken Bodies: Migrant Farmworkers in the United States.* Berkeley: University of California Press.

Horton, Sarah B. 2016. *They Leave Their Kidneys in the Fields: Illness, Injury, and "Illegality" among U.S. Farmworkers.* Berkeley: University of California Press.

Infante, César, Alvaro J. Idrovo, Mario S. Sánchez-Domínguez, Stéphane Vinhas, and Tonatiuh González-Vázquez. 2012. "Violence Committed against Migrants in Transit: Experiences on the Northern Mexican Border." *Journal of Immigrant Minority Health* 14, no. 1: 449–459.

Isacson, Adam, Maureen Meyer, and Ashley Davis. 2013. *Border Security and Migration: A Report from Arizona.* Washington, DC: Washington Office on Latin America, December 5.

Jimenez, Maria. 2009. *Humanitarian Crisis: Migrant Deaths at the U.S.-Mexico Border.* San Francisco: American Civil Liberties Union of San Diego and Imperial Counties/ Mexico's National Commission of Human Rights.

Jusionyte, Ieva. 2018. *Threshold: Emergency Responders on the U.S.-Mexico Border.* Oakland: University of California Press.

Lakoff, Andrew. 2007. "Preparing for the Next Emergency." *Public Culture* 19, no. 2: 247–271.

Lipsky, Michael. 1980. *Street-Level Bureaucracy: Dilemmas of the Individual in Public Services.* New York: Russell Sage Foundation.

Lovett, Ian. 2012. "Border Cities Are Burdened with Calls for Help." *New York Times,* August 26, A16.

Magaña, Rocío. 2008. "Bodies on the Line: Life, Death, and Authority on the Arizona-Mexico Border." PhD diss., University of Chicago.

Marrow, Helen B. 2012. "Deserving to a Point: Unauthorized Immigrants in San Francisco's Universal Access Healthcare Model." *Social Science and Medicine* 74, no. 6: 846–854.

Martínez, Daniel, Jeremy Slack, and Josiah McC Heyman. 2013. "Part I: Migrant Mistreatment while in U.S. Custody." In *Bordering on Criminal: The Routine Abuse of Migrants in the Removal System.* Washington, DC: Immigration Policy Center.

Masco, Joseph. 2014. *The Theater of Operations: National Security Affect from the Cold War to the War on Terror.* Durham, NC: Duke University Press.

Mbembe, Achille. 2003. "Necropolitics." *Public Culture* 15, no. 1: 11–40.

McGuire, Randall H. 2013. "Steel Walls and Picket Fences: Rematerializing the U.S.-Mexican Border in Ambos Nogales." *American Anthropologist* 115, no. 3: 466–480.

Miller, J. B. 2011. "Final Defendant Sentenced in Case of SUV Rollover That Killed 11 People." *Nogales International,* September 27.

Miller, Todd, and Gabriel M. Schivone. 2015. "Gaza in Arizona: The Secret Militarization of the U.S.-Mexico Border." Salon.com, February 1. https://www.salon

.com/2015/02/01/gaza_in_arizona_the_secret_militarization_of_the_u_s_mexico
_border_partner.

Montoya, Aaliyah. 2016. "Border Patrol Works to Combat Advanced Activity." *Douglas Dispatch*, February 16.

Morris, Rosalind C. 2010. "Accidental Histories, Post-Historical Practice? Re-Reading *Body of Power, Spirit of Resistance* in the Actuarial Age." *Anthropological Quarterly* 83, no 3: 581–624.

National Academy of Sciences and National Research Council. 1966. *Accidental Death and Disability: The Neglected Disease of Modern Society*. Washington. DC: National Academies Press.

Nevins, Joseph. 2010. *Operation Gatekeeper and Beyond: The War on "Illegals" and the Remaking of the U.S.-Mexico Boundary*. New York: Routledge.

Pineda, Paulina. 2016. "Woman Dies after Apparent Fall from Border Fence." *Nogales International*, June 21.

Prendergast, Curt. 2013. "Border Ambulance Leaving City with $250k in Unpaid Bills." *Nogales International*, October 25.

Rosas, Gilberto. 2012. *Barrio Libre: Criminalizing States and Delinquent Refusals of the New Frontier*. Durham, NC: Duke University Press.

Rosenthal, Anat. 2007. "Battling for Survival, Battling for Moral Clarity: 'Illegality' and Illness in the Everyday Struggles of Undocumented HIV+ Women Migrant Workers in Tel Aviv." *International Migration* 45, no. 3: 134–156.

Rothenbuhler, Eric. 2005. "Ground Zero, the Firemen, and the Symbolics of Touch on 9/11 and After." In *Media Anthropology*, edited by Eric W. Rothenbuhler and Mihai Coman, 176–187. Thousand Oaks, CA: SAGE.

Siegel, Greg. 2014. *Forensic Media: Reconstructing Accidents in Accelerated Modernity*. Durham, NC: Duke University Press.

Slack, Jeremy, and Howard Campbell. 2016. "On Narco-Coyotaje: Illicit Regimes and Their Impacts on the U.S.-Mexico Border." *Antipode* 48: 1380–1399.

Slack, Jeremy, and Scott Whiteford. 2011. "Violence and Migration on the Arizona-Sonora Border." *Human Organization* 70, no. 1: 11–21.

Stephenson, Hank. 2011. "Nogales Border-Fence Revamp Under Way." *Nogales International*, February 14.

Tebeau, Mark. 2003. *Eating Smoke: Fire in Urban America, 1800–1950*. Baltimore: Johns Hopkins University Press.

Trevizo, Perla. 2015a. "ACLU, Faith Leaders: Don't Refer 911 Calls to Border Patrol." *Arizona Daily Star*, May 28.

——. 2015b. "Border Apprehensions at 'Unheard of' Lows." *Arizona Daily Star*, September 5.

——. 2015c. "Officials: Past Border Tech Efforts Failed, but This One Won't." *Arizona Daily Star*, December 26.

Urrea, Luis Alberto. 2004. *The Devil's Highway: A True Story*. New York: Little, Brown.

U.S. Border Patrol. 1994. *Border Patrol Strategic Plan, 1994 and Beyond*. Washington, DC: U.S. Border Patrol, July.

U.S. Customs and Border Protection. 2012. "Facilities Management & Engineering (FM&E) Tactical Infrastructure." February 29. https://www.dhs.gov/xlibrary/assets /mgmt/cbp-fmetacticalinfrastructure2012.pdf.

———. 2017. "Solid Concrete Border Wall RFP." Solicitation No. HSBP1017R0022, March 17. https://www.fbo.gov/?s=opportunity&mode=form&id=151d4eaab6927f4e 2d6d396d084c23f1&tab=core&_cview=1.

Virilio, Paul. 2007. *The Original Accident*. Cambridge: Polity.

Vogt, Wendy A. 2013. "Crossing Mexico: Structural Violence and the Commodification of Undocumented Central American Migrants." *American Ethnologist* 40, no. 4: 764–780.

Weizman, Eyal. 2014. "Introduction: Forensis." In *Forensis: The Architecture of Public Truth*, 9–32. Berlin: Sternberg Press.

Willen, Sarah S. 2007. "Toward a Critical Phenomenology of 'Illegality': State Power, Criminalization, and Abjectivity among Undocumented Migrant Workers in Tel Aviv, Israel." *International Migration* 45, no. 3: 8–38.

4

Fugitive Horizons and the Arts of Security in Honduras

Jon Horne Carter

In 2014 a young Harvard alum named Octavio Sánchez brought to the president of Honduras a radical solution to the problems of corruption and insecurity plaguing the country. Sánchez was an advocate for charter city developments in Honduras, which he touted as a chance to rebuild the country from the inside out. The idea was to invite corporations to develop regions of the country as autonomous spaces, where corporations would create their own legal systems, educational standards, police forces, and so on. If they succeeded, he argued, the Honduran state would be forced to catch up.

It was, in fact, an idea he was reviving. Charter cities had been introduced several years before, as part of a broad initiative outlined by Paul Romer, an economics professor at New York University. Romer had written extensively on free-trade zones and economic liberalism, and saw charter cities as the next frontier of development in countries where corruption and graft often rendered institutions and government ineffective. Romer proposed that private companies, foreign or domestic, would be invited to invest in developing economic centers across a given country, which would be dedicated to manufacturing, finance, shipping, or other industries. In return for their investment, corporate boards would govern these areas autonomously. Inside these "Special Economic Development Regions" (Regiones Especiales de Desarollo [RED]) in Honduras, for example, private companies would write their own laws, contract their own police force, and maintain their own systems of justice, education, accounting, and taxation. It was presumed that corporate management and administrative strategies from abroad would be stronger and more accountable than those of the Honduran state. In turn these would create pockets of stability in a country that was still reeling from the coup against President Manuel Zelaya in 2009, and serve as economic engines for the country at large. Legislation to create RED was passed and then overturned by the Honduran Constitutional Court, which cited these extraterritorial spaces as a threat to state sovereignty. Then, four of the five judges behind the ruling were sacked by congressional order and replaced by judges who passed the amendment a second time.

The removal and appointment of justices was widely regarded as an assault on the judicial branch of government. It seemed to highlight the institutional instability that was the basis for charter cities in the first place, and plans for charter cities stalled until Sánchez emerged as a new face for the movement. And in the aftermath of the initial scandal, he framed his vision differently. The promise of charter cities was not only economic development. Economic development was only the beginning. Charter cities would counteract the ills of the present, the institutional decay, purges of the entire national police force, expansion of violent organized crime groups nationwide, and the climbing levels of impunity, by opening Honduras to competing systems of justice. The independent legal systems and police forces implemented by investors, Sánchez argued, would be superior to those of the state itself, and rebuild the country from the inside out. "If we are able to create a system that works," he said, "this will become the most revolutionary process in the history of Latin America. And if we have to bring justice from outside, we will" (Mackey 2014). Sánchez was clear: charter cities were different from gated communities. These were not just more exclusive enclaves of the rich, with walls and guarded entrances. They were to be cities of the working classes, and invited collective, rather than exclusive, speculation on a future Honduras. But the spirit of that invitation contrasted sharply with the daily realities of most Hondurans, more than 50 percent of whom live in poverty. Across the barrios of the Honduran capital, Tegucigalpa, Sánchez's bold promises and rudimentary computer models simply fell flat. The idea was widely criticized as a graft benefiting the country's elite business people and their contacts in the murky world of global finance. From the perspective of the urban poor, the promise of security was not dissimilar to that of other commodities marketed widely but accessible only to middle and upper classes, whether brand new automobiles or vacations on Caribbean islands. Amidst widespread skepticism toward the plan, a second amendment was passed to change the designation of RED to "Zone for Employment and Economic Development" (Zonas de Empleo y Desarollo Económico [ZEDE]), and the first charter city experiment was initiated on the island of Amapala in southern Honduras.

The charter city debate in Honduras is divisive because it highlights a divergent sense of what security is and how one might establish it—whether for oneself or for Honduras as a whole. The majority of Hondurans who would work in the assembly plants of the ZEDE already recognize the destabilizing effects of unchecked corporate power and extreme forms of economic liberalism on their daily lives. And while these have been expanded steadily since the early 1990s, the urban poor have been learning to live and cope with escalating insecurity, from currency devaluations to falling wages. Enormous disparities in power and wealth exist alongside hulking informal economies, which supplement an increasingly restrictive world of service and information jobs. In Central America the flow of illegal drugs toward U.S. markets during this same period has resulted in the strengthening of cartels and para-state groups, against which politicians and military forces promise the restoration of law and order. But how does one define "security" in places where the state is not the sole or dominant arbiter of power? Particularly in places where criminal gangs, drug cartels, and transnational corporations all vie for power, or where they do not exist in clear opposition to the state?

In this chapter I draw from fieldwork in several working-class neighborhoods on the outskirts of Tegucigalpa, Honduras, where state security forces and powerful street gangs battle for control. These are barrios where policing is often viewed as a double-edged sword, in some sense essential to restraining criminal activity but also mired in a long history of betraying public trust and undermining the law police are tasked to protect. Here any effort by the state to create a shared sense of how security might look and feel is complicated by the permeable boundaries between state and criminal groups. And as such, the performance of security by the state sets the stage for a counterperformance. For years this counterperformance was the province of gangs themselves, who tattooed their bodies in defiance of state violence. But more recently, after more than a decade of authoritarian policing, it is not in the flamboyant revolt of gang life but in the subtle gestures of everyday survival that the counterperformance to state security work is found. I am thinking of the generation of youth that has come of age during the 2000s and the escalation of the war on gangs in northern Central America, surrounded by mortal danger. For those young people and their families, it is subtlety and restraint that is often the difference between life and death. In this chapter I will outline an attunement to the dangers of the present in Honduras and the subtle strategies of avoiding them. Outside of what D. Asher Ghertner, Hudson McFann, and Daniel M. Goldstein (this volume) describe as "building fortresses," I am interested in the notions of "screening threats" and "calibrating vulnerabilities" as these are writ small into the habits and dispositions of a community bound by its own sense of what security means.

SENSES OF SECURITY

In 2014 while Oscar Sánchez was courting political support for the charter city initiative, I sat with my friend Vanesa in her tiny, plank-wood house in barrio Los Pinos, on the edge of Tegucigalpa.[1] We were in front of the television with her two daughters, watching the footage of child migrants crossing the U.S. border as CNN commentators debated whether this was a humanitarian crisis or criminal entry into the country. In zones of the city where gang violence suffocates daily life as it does in Vanesa's, fleeing the country and heading across México on foot is a common strategy for survival. Vanesa was worried that her two sons would leave for the United States as well. Many of the neighbors' children had also gone, some leaving in the middle of the night. That was because, Vanesa said, a mother would always protest and break down. But the children have so few options, they have to leave. So they vanish and call from the United States when they arrive.

It had been difficult to keep the children hopeful, she said. After her eldest son was hit by a bus and killed during street demonstrations against the ousting of President Zelaya, the driver had escaped arrest, and the other siblings mourned his loss as the country descended into institutional gridlock, public demonstrations, and police repression. After five years of street protests, the police squadrons in thick, black armor, with their teargas cannons and shields, had lost much of the potential to shock they wielded over civilians just after the coup. Armored police were an everyday sight, and with the discarded protest signs, teargas canisters, and political graffiti scrawled across the walls downtown, they merged with the material reality of the post-coup city poised for deeper destabilization. Opposition to the coup brought together activists from a variety of social movements as a coalition calling itself La Resistencia, a name which linked political protest with the resilience required of all Hondurans exposed to sustained military repression, emergency policing, and everyday violence from street gangs and organized criminal groups. As state forces regulated public space across the city with foot patrols and checkpoints, cataloging civilian identities through mobile software, gang violence in marginal barrios escalated as well, leaving many to wonder where security might be found at all.

These divergent notions of security invite us to consider the dual elements of what Jacques Rancière (2009) calls a "community of sense." For Rancière the community of sense is premised upon shared criteria of judgment and interpretation which, being consistent across a social field, affirm states of belonging or nonbelonging. Clearly some communities of sense emerge as normative across time, codified into custom and law. But, as Ghertner et al. (this volume) point out, these are always coeval with the multiplicity of lived experiences unfolding elsewhere that cohere as communities of their own. Vanesa and Sánchez, for example, each ask in their own ways how security might look or feel in contemporary Honduras, indicating quite different "terms of sensibility" (Ghertner 2015, 127) at work. Among Vanesa and her neighbors, the promises of a charter city generated more suspicion than excitement. And I think it is necessary to emphasize here that such suspicion is more than a cynical response to the inevitability of graft and corruption in modern state life. Thinking with Rancière, I would suggest that it is at the heart of a sensibility shared across many of the poor barrios of Tegucigalpa where socioeconomic precarity and militarized policing have become mutually reinforcing. We might think of suspicion, then, as a cultivation of preparedness which, in Vanesa's case, establishes at least minimal stability for herself and her family, where the state is no longer trusted. Such suspicion is but one element of the emergent subjectivities of crisis in Honduras that I would like to explore here.

But before going further let me step back and think historically about the shifting sensibilities of danger in urban spaces, such as Tegucigalpa, since countries in northern Central America began scapegoating gangs for a host of national problems in the early 2000s. Gang members were easily caricatured as both a moral and existential threat, and made the trojan horse by which militarized policing was established as the norm across the first decade of the twenty-first century. It is helpful here to think of this transition in the aesthetics of power, as Jean and John Comaroff (2016) have suggested, as a response to the failed materialization of the Foucauldian biopolitical telos, and its utopia of administered society, by the end of the twentieth century. In turn this failure generates new spectacles and condensations of state power, often targeting petty crime and everyday vectors of insecurity. "Where governance is seriously compromised," they write, "law enforcement may provide a privileged site for staging efforts—the double entendre is crucial here—to summon the active presence of the state into being . . . to produce both rulers and subjects who recognize its legitimacy" (Comaroff and Comaroff 2004, 809). The threat of the "gang member" emerges in northern Central America in the wake of the Cold War, when state leadership shifted from military to civilian leadership, and the politics of authoritarian nationalism shifted to free market liberalism. By the late 1990s in Honduras, agrarian producers were displaced by an influx of cheap, global commodities. Many migrated to cities like Tegucigalpa and San

Pedro Sula and squatted on unoccupied terrain at the urban periphery, establishing the sprawling residential swaths of today's urban poor.

On the urban periphery a new generation of youth came of age to find themselves geographically isolated from the city at large, and at a distance from economic and educational opportunities. The children of poor families circulated the city, for fun or seeking odd jobs, and became the subject of a wave of sociological studies that put a name to the phenomenon as the child "at risk," each of which could become threatening if those behaviors congealed into the figure of the *delincuente*. This newly threatening figure was typified by the children who banded together in small gangs, whose embrace of risk and danger fascinated as much as it concerned the wider public. Writing on violence and the postwar setting in El Salvador, Moodie (2006) describes the passage from the postwar to the free market era in which the "value of death" shifted across the 1990s, from one associated with martyrdom and political action to one of assumed risk. Daily accidents, harm, and death became naturalized elements of the free market setting. Likewise the clearing of homeless or nomadic groups of adolescents from public spaces was considered essential to investment in business districts downtown, and by the early 2000s the number of reported violations against youth by police and private security officers had risen to reach international infamy (Jahangir 2002). The impacts of free trade, international debt, and structural adjustment programs, combined with narco-trafficking cartels moving cocaine north to the United States, formed a crucible of instability and volatility in which the lives of poor youth were suspended. The term *seguridad ciudadana*, or public safety, became a refrain of activists and politicians seeking to balance the welfare of a vast demographic of young people while also responding to a public that demanded protection from urban crime closely associated with them.

Returning to Rancière, this heightened anxiety around the figure of the delincuente and gang member in the early 2000s evinces a gathering consensus about the aesthetics of security and danger. And as such, we might then begin to think of gang life differently, in the vein of what Rancière (2010, 139) calls "dissensus," which "breaks with the sensory self-evidence of the 'natural' order that destines specific individuals and groups to occupy positions of rule or of being ruled, assigning them to private or public lives, pinning them down to a certain time and space, to specific 'bodies,' that is to specific ways of being, seeing, and saying." Tens of thousands of gang members across northern Central America were extensively tattooing their upper body and faces in the early 2000s, covering them with gang insignia, spiderwebs, satanic horns, skulls, and demons. Gang tattooing reclaimed the body from dehumanizing processes of economic and state violence. Their bodies were both desecrated and venerated, hideous and beautiful, snaring the eye while inciting fear. In this sense they performed a dramatic reorientation of the gang member's body as it existed in the prevailing community of sense.

Today, more than a decade later, these gangs are criminal mafias that function as part of the broader organized crime groups, and it is not my goal to romanticize them here. But I do think it is vital to look back at their emergence and the importance of sacralizing a physical body that was under siege. Elsewhere I describe as "gothic sovereignty" the aesthetic play of inversions in communities outside of the law that operate in conscious and open antagonism with official institutions whose legitimacy is undermined by corruption (Carter 2014). Tracking the aesthetic shifts in the sensible widens the interpretive field of what Goldstein (2010, 489) calls "critical security anthropology," in which security, a tool within the manifold tactics of governmentality, "calls on the power of fear to fill the ruptures that the crises and contradictions of neoliberalism have engendered." Herein, it is through the aesthetic consensus that "fear" moves from an emotion to a consolidated, politicized affect.

The irruption of the gangs' seductive and transgressive aesthetic did not directly confront state force on its own terms, but disordered the semiotics of the body targeted in a state of exceptionality (Agamben 1995). The Mano Dura (strong hand) campaigns initiated in the early 2000s, however, transformed the aesthetics of everyday policing in turn. Mano Dura campaigns broadened police powers in El Salvador, Guatemala, and Honduras, to eliminate street gangs and lower surging crime rates in major cities. In Honduras Mano Dura legislation allowed for the detention of suspects for gathering on street corners in small groups, or on the basis of a single tattoo. Platoons wearing black masks and camouflage tactical gear stormed through the urban barrios. While the state struggled with public trust and institutional integrity, Mano Dura theatricalized security as an ordering force, a range of practices on display, ever ready to stage itself as the dominant semiotic register of public life. Gang aesthetics, on the other hand, covered the body with a tattoo-shell of images and symbols, training the senses of the subject, and of the onlooker, that the threat of violence would come from "security" itself.

THIN BLUE LINE

When I arrived back to Tegucigalpa in 2017, friends insisted that I should stay in a hotel downtown because safety in Los Pinos had deteriorated so badly. Don't worry, they said, the most expensive hotels were slashing prices. Tourism and corporate travel had fallen off dramatically in recent years when Honduras had been named, repeatedly, as one of the most violent countries in the world. By nightfall I was shocked to find nearly every restaurant closed in the once-bustling hub surrounding the hotel district, and the next morning, as I walked to the central plaza, Cervantes Avenue—lined with bookstores, human rights offices, and souvenir shops, the cultural heart of downtown—was hardly recognizable. Storefront signs had been removed and many businesses appeared to be permanently closed. All of this had happened within one year.

I went to see my friend Reina, whose souvenir shop has been nearby since the early 1990s. The storefront was locked. She was inside sipping coffee in a T-shirt and sweatpants. "I never open the store these days," she said, pointing to what little remained of her inventory. "It happened so quickly . . . one afternoon three young men came here and walked right inside, said we had to pay them extortion money," she said. "After they left I felt dizzy," she said. "You know what it means, if they are here extorting me? If they are here, they control the whole city. They aren't afraid of anyone." In 2013, the Honduran Bureau of Business and Industry estimated that more than one thousand businesses had closed due to extortion, from nightclubs to haberdasheries, restaurants, and beauty salons (Associated Press 2013). Rather than report extortion to the police, most owners closed indefinitely for their own safety. Over the last decade, three attempts to purge the national police of criminal actors seem to have had little impact, though they succeeded in drawing attention to the depth of the problem by exposing a number of high- and low-ranking officials. A commission initiated in April 2016 demanded the investigation of five hundred officers alleged of criminal activity, and eighty-one officials and police connected with gang organizations. As the barrier separating criminal gangs and state police blurs, the circulation of uniforms into nonpolice groups has made police impersonation a common occurrence. The national police tried to ensure their appearance could not be falsified by implanting computer chips into new uniforms, which could be scanned to identify the officer to whom the uniform was assigned (see Figure 4.1). I asked Reina what she thought of it. "How will I scan somebody's uniform, if the officer shows up here?" Reina asks. "This used to be a problem you had in the barrios way out there, far away. This street, we are businesses that have been here for over fifty years. Many of these belong to respected families. And all of us here take care of each other. If you had a problem with a thief or a drunkard, you could call the police. Well, look at it here now. We have no one left to call."

Much as the state is compelled to address the closing gap separating institutions of law enforcement and powerful criminal entities, which threaten to establish a simultaneity between governance and criminal predation, it is

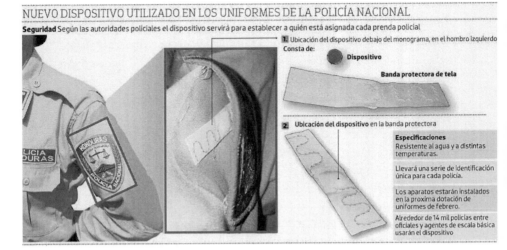

Figure 4.1 This illustration, from *El Heraldo* newspaper in Tegucigalpa, depicts microchip technology added to police uniforms to combat officer impersonation and to assure the public that police institutions can police themselves.

the less dramatic work carried on by witnesses, victims, and bystanders to this conflict that holds together the social worlds of a majority of Hondurans. These arts of survival include a range of skills and strategies that emerge mimetically with failing institutions, an aesthetic labor as much as gang tattoos or the slick armor shielding special forces police. The difference, however, is that within the multiple communities of sense operating in Tegucigalpa at a given time, arts of survival seek illegibility.

By the end of last decade, one of the impacts of Mano Dura policing was, ironically, significant infiltration of police units by gangs and criminal groups. National police in Honduras pushed for experiments in community policing that were successful in stemming corruption in Mexico City, Chicago, Paris, and elsewhere (Muller 2010). Instead of rotation between precincts, the idea is that officers are assigned to a single district where they are expected to cultivate local relationships and build trust over time. Before the experiments began in the district where Los Pinos is located, police scheduled an "open dialogue" at the local community center. On the morning of the meeting, a gleaming bus with tinted windows rounded the corner and parked on the dirt streets. No fewer than fifty police cadets stepped out and filed into the community center.

It was a weekday morning and most of the men from Los Pinos were either at work or out looking for it, and I arrived to find the community center largely empty except the first two rows of chairs taken up entirely by elderly women from the neighborhood. The meeting began with a long statement by the head of the local police precinct, describing what community policing was and what problems it sought to address. It was essential, he said, that community members take courage, speak up, and report to the police what they knew about gangs and drug traffickers. To withhold information, because one was afraid of retaliation, was to protect criminals and keep police from doing their jobs. In the front row of the auditorium a woman stood in objection, insisting the officer knew very well why no one reports local crimes. He winced melodramatically and told her not to insinuate that police were complicit in criminal activities. Another woman interrupted, saying that if their precinct was not involved with gangs, they were nonetheless powerless to protect anyone. After a few moments the officer lashed out at the front row, ordering them to sit, and then made a vulgar comment to other police on the stage. There was an uproar of cross talk and shouting, and within minutes the officers waved their arms and went back to the bus. The meeting was over.

123

What was most notable however was the total absence of community members who regularly griped about corruption in the local precinct. Some were at work, but most were at home. They simply would not make themselves visible to the police, as critics of police work or as informers from the neighborhood. There were too many eyes watching, a friend told me later. But the frustration and distrust that ran through this meeting was typical of others I attended elsewhere. Instead of resolving deep distrust of the police, the public dialogues attempted to stage an encounter between two articulations of security in Tegucigalpa: one official, premised on judgments that demonstrated a readiness to criminalize barrio residents; and the other local, fugitive to the criminalizing gaze of the police. What Goldstein (2005) describes as "flexible" justice in Bolivia, in which the relationship between the subject and the law is reconfigured through familiar inner principles of neoliberal subjectivity, begins with a lack of security. But the heavy silence between the community and police in Los Pinos is the result of an impasse, in which it is *not* possible to act. Here the understaffing of police units, lack of resources, and inadequate salaries run into the challenges of confronting massive criminal networks that put both authorities and civilians in impossible positions. Police demanded that community members come forward, even when it was unlikely that they could protect them, and everyday street-smarts of community members became an object of suspicion, a possible threat. As neighbors are mined as informers, the

Figure 4.2   This image, of the Military Police of Public Order, frames the aesthetic dimensions of emergency power as an object of photographic composition.

need for deflection and secrecy grows exponentially. Here, "community polic-ing" reverses itself.

The era of Mano Dura policy came to an end, not under the weight of its widely documented failures to reduce violence and crime, but as one emergency engulfed another in the 2009 coup against Zelaya (Mejía 2007). Efforts to purge the police force of criminal elements were put on hold as mass protests and civil mobilization against the coup were met with police and military repression, live ammunition, and curfews. Upheaval contin-ued through elections six months later that placed conservative candidate Porfirio Lobo in the office of president. The Lobo administration escalated repression against journalists and protesters around the country such that within months the country was the "murder capital of the world" (Robles 2012). Across the first years of Lobo's presidency the disappearance and as-sassination of protesters, labor leaders, journalists, lawyers, and then the as-sassinations of the national antidrug czar and his personal lawyer, sparked outrage, which by 2012 drew condemnation from the U.S. Department of State. U.S. aid to Honduras was suspended, with the specific aim of shaming its police institutions.

Under Lobo the national police had undergone its first post–Mano Dura transition, which integrated the military and civil police into a hybrid force, the Intelligence Troop and Special Security Response Groups. In 2013, the Lobo administration then founded the Military Police of Public Order (Policía Militar del Orden Público [PMOP]), whose official purpose was to take back gang-controlled zones of the city and to dismantle organized criminal rackets. These were the familiar goals of Mano Dura campaigns, but the PMOP's highly stylized uniforms seemed to inaugurate a new era in law enforcement (see Figure 4.2). The PMOP were dressed in slick black suits, covered in black armor, their faces entirely covered by black masks, goggles, and black helmets, making it impossible to discern one officer from another. Their deployment was followed by a spike in formal complaints of police abuse. Meanwhile the national police were on strike, demanding better work conditions, salary, hours of downtime, and proper compensation, all of which highlighted the structural conditions by which bribes and corruption became ubiquitous. And as collusion between police and gangs drove communities away from the aesthetic consensus surrounding traditional law enforcement practices, the stylization of the PMOP introduced a faceless and dehumanized surface upon which state power could be visualized as an indiscriminate force before which any subject was a potential criminal.

SCREENING THREATS

Vanesa's husband, Jorge, called to tell me that Adner, their neighbor, had been deported from the United States and had just arrived home. I've known Adner, twenty years old at the time of this writing, since he was just a few years old. I wanted to talk to him about his journey through México and across the U.S. border. For the previous four months we had been talking over the payphone in an Arizona prison, where the air conditioning was so extreme he caught the flu multiple times. It had been extremely difficult, but he was back now.

As I left downtown the driver of the taxi apologetically asked for additional fare. There were PMOP and gang checkpoints across the southern rim of the city where we were headed. I'd have to pay them, if we were stopped, but it would be better if he handled it all. "They weren't out this morning, but they're still watching," he said.

When we arrived, Jorge was standing on the side of the paved road, outside an internet café that he manages. He was a gang intervention expert in the 1990s when I first met him, but pulled back when local gangs joined national cartel groups. He was skeptical that we would be able to see Adner at all. We'd have to wait until he got in touch with us; seeking him out would be improper.

It was common for gangs and extortionists to target recently arrived deportees, who they suspected of maintaining bank accounts in the U.S. After extorting money from them, gangs grilled deportees to expose any competency in conversational English. Deportees were then used to expand extortion to English-speaking persons in the United States, who would wire money to Honduras to buy a loved one's protection. Extortion cast a wide net, and anyone with skills was dragged in. "We shouldn't bother him," Jorge said. "Right now he needs to be invisible. If he's smart he's lying to everyone."

"Lying?" I asked.

"He needs to be smart. He's been gone a while and people that live in the U.S. lose touch with how things are here."

We called his cell number, at the agreed time, and there was no answer. "That's good," Jorge said. "Right now, the way it is here, I feel uncomfortable asking anyone to talk about going *mojado* [pursuing undocumented migration]." As we waited to hear from Adner, Jorge went on about the importance of never telling the truth. When extortion rackets were so extensive, this was the only way to keep yourself and those around you safe.

Julian Pitt-Rivers wrote the first ethnographic treatment of secrecy in his book about a Spanish mountain village during the Franco era, titled *The People of the Sierra* (1954). As Michael Taussig (1999) recounts, Pitt-Rivers chose the town because it was the epicenter of agrarian anarchism in Spain, but during Franco's dictatorship no open discussion of anarchism was possible. Only long after the fact, in the 1971 preface to the second edition, did Pitt-Rivers acknowledge that this study of the social life in a village is also a study of secrecy. The book was his rebuttal to the notion that concealment in social life was furtive or disingenuous. He reflects on the techniques and expressions of secrecy within his local friendships and the ambiguous registers of intimacy that animate *confianza*, or trust. Secrecy and dissimulation animated solidarity rather than undermining it. He describes Andalusians as "the most accomplished liars I have ever encountered," who knew exactly when to level the truth and when to withdraw it, all the while, he writes, learning exact control of their facial expressions from a young age, as masters of artifice (quoted in Taussig 1999, 59–60).

More recently and in the postwar context of Guatemala, Diane Nelson (2009) examines the many forms of self-preservation required when one is surrounded by weakened state institutions and violence. Writing on *engaño*, or duplicity, she states that "the sense that the world available to our senses has another face behind it (becomes) a site of intense affective and hermeneutic investment in the aftermaths and ongoing experiences of war and violence"

(Nelson 2009, xv). Engaño, then, is a form of suspicion suffusing subjectivity and sociality, which derives, especially in the context of war and its aftermath, from the fragility of historical knowledge as a contested site and the uncertainty of daily life where the scars of conflict lay open still. In thinking through the process by which her fieldwork during the civil war connected her with communities in which clandestinity was a matter of life and death, Nelson describes her initial naivete but growing awareness of the spoken and embodied "counterstrategies" developed to survive counterinsurgency, spying, and state terror. Engaño operates on the surface of social life, as a field of fictive invention channeling and directing the other away from vulnerability.

Critical security studies might take inspiration from Nelson's sustained attention to engaño and her methodological agility, nimble enough to work with the very ambiguity of the informant as an autonomous entity, not to be dispelled by the positivist impulse. Engaño emerges on that surface layer of the social where the state of emergency and vulnerability interface, and it becomes possible to treat techniques of "ethnographic refusal" as the very object of ethnographic inquiry rather than its negation. Audra Simpson (2014) writes eloquently on refusal in her work on the Iroquois politics of recognition in settler-colonial states, asking how ethnographers can attune both their sensibilities and their scholarly production to the fugitive expressions that circulate across the bodies and cultural worlds of the targeted and the vulnerable. In this manner the study of power in its biopolitical permutations is not reduced to the narrative or testimonial of the subject victimized by it, but instead engages those counterstrategies, in Nelson's terms, which engender ambiguity of the expected while becoming forms and styles that we can recognize as "arti-factual."

When Adner finally texted Jorge's phone, we were looking through the window of his internet café, watching the PMOP assemble a checkpoint. "Adner says come now," Jorge said. We walked to Adner's mother's house at the bottom of the barrio. Storm clouds gathered and it looked like rain. His sister answered the door, cautiously, as their house is on the border of two gang territories and thus doubly at risk for extortion. Inside it was dark and hot. A television blared in the center room. His sister pointed to an open door at the end of the house and inside we found Adner sitting cross-legged on his bed. He leapt up to shake our hands. As Jorge made small talk, Adner peeped out the window. He seemed jumpy and distracted. Jorge asked how long he planned to stay inside the house without leaving. He smiled and shrugged. "There's not much to do outside anyway," he said.

As the small talk continued, raindrops fell one at a time on the corrugated metal roof. A breeze whisked through the house, drying the sweat on our bodies. Then sheets of rain were pounding down, and we could hardly hear anything else. Adner leaned forward and gestured for me to turn on the recorder. "Now we can talk," he said, smiling for the first time.

He reached into a bag and handed us his deportation papers. I thought they would be a bad memory, but he handed them to us with obvious pride. "Once you have these, you know how all of it works," he said.

"All what?" I asked.

"Going north," he said. Adner had been part of the wave of youth who fled the country in 2014, many of whom were minors, as was he at the time. Vanesa and I had watched on television that afternoon with her daughters as Obama delivered a press conference to declare what was happening a "humanitarian situation." It certainly was that, though Adner and others found power in flight. He and his friends found solidarity in staying low-key and out of sight, in moving across thousands of miles of unfamiliar terrain, and clinging to the top of Mexican cargo trains before hiking into the Sonoran Desert dodging surveillance technologies, police, and vigilantes. Adner was waiting for a friend in North Carolina to wire him money, which he planned to use to go again, but until he got the call that the money was delivered, he wouldn't leave the house. He searched for WiFi with his cell phone and downloaded infographics detailing border security up to the minute. We laughed at memes making fun of Mexican police. He had a sense of how to get there—and what to do if he was caught.

That afternoon when Jorge and I said goodbye to Adner, we walked back to the house he and Vanesa have lived in for the last few years, on the bank of a contaminated river that marks the boundary between their barrio and another. Vanesa tells us that her nephew, Antonio, was caught in Texas. Jorge looked at the ground and lit a cigarette. She asks about our visit with Adner, but then returns to Antonio. Her sister called, wailing, the morning she realized he had gone. He had vanished in the middle of the night like so many others.

"Really, do people in your country think we are irresponsible parents?" she asked, looking at me. "We don't want our kids to get lost in Arizona, in the desert. We know it's dangerous. But here our kids sit in the house like it's prison." Vanesa's daughter Ana looked up, putting her phone down. She is nineteen, her hair put up in braids that her sister had been weaving all afternoon.

"They say that when the migrants get to the U.S. that the police think they're criminals. Like gang members," she said. I told her that was true. "But that's not right because they leave Honduras *because* they aren't criminals. But in the U.S. they say they are criminals."

"Some say that," I replied.

"But they should know that in this country right now we can't trust anybody. Police, gangs—it doesn't matter. If they know who you are, they can make you get involved with them. You don't have a choice. They make you kill or use drugs, and turn you into people like them. Here it doesn't matter what you want to do with your life, they will *make* you a criminal."

"So how do you stay safe?" I asked.

"All you can do is be careful," she said. "You have to trust in god. But sometimes things happen and you just run. Like Antonio. Everyone thinks about it. All the kids around here talk about it." We sat in silence for a moment, and then she was back to her phone, head down and pecking at the keyboard, communicating with friends who were also locked inside their homes, a few streets up the hill. Vanesa chuckled at Ana's distractedness.

"These kids are accustomed to all this now," Vanesa said. "It's what they know."

CALIBRATING VULNERABILITIES

Computing engineer Steve Mann's (Mann, Nolan, and Wellman 2003) notion of "sousveillance" takes the position of the subject of surveillance and imagines its power to "look back" at authority from a position outside of power. In her recent book on the surveillance of Blackness, Simone Browne (2015) extends Mann's notion of sousveillance to ask about self-defense in communities subjected to systematic repression and surveillance, and to imagine a continuum of counterstrategies to hegemony. For Browne (2015, 21), "dark sousveillance" are those tactics and techniques of disruption that "chart(s) possibilities and coordinates modes of responding to, challenging, and confronting a surveillance that was almost all-encompassing." In the context of Honduras, we might imagine such inverse-panoptic refractions as emerging from new communities of sense, in which acts of flight, camouflage, evasion, or becoming-illegible are grounded in ways of knowing that are particular to the most troubled geographies of late liberalism.

But to look at Jorge in comparison with the younger generation, and their adaptation to imperceptibility and flight, he's a bit more old-school. In certain moments I catch him thinking that one day these complex and interlocking crises will pass. For him, the future still holds. All there is to do is to navigate the present. At the end of my visit to Tegucigalpa I made a final trip to see Jorge and Vanesa. I find Jorge in the door of the internet café, watching the PMOP as they stop vehicles and ask for legal documents. "And see this is why," he began immediately, "we nicknamed the president Juan Robando [i.e., "thieving"], instead of Juan Orlando." He stood with a group of taxi drivers who watched the checkpoint with a studied disinterest, though each of them considered it a legal form of robbery. When Juan Orlando Hernández became president in 2014 he had increased deployments of the PMOP, despite the many legal cases pending against them for false arrests and abuses. At a time when economic migration out of the country was higher than it had ever been in history, Orlando had expanded the PMOP budget by raising taxes. "He's got a military background," Jorge said, "and so he's going to make us pay for [the PMOP] to be sent into the streets, where they just continue robbing us like this. They're supposed to be fighting the extortionists," he said, pointing at the checkpoint. "But anytime they come here, everyone shuts down their businesses for the day. These guys are aggressive. We don't want to be harassed. So whether it's gangs or the police, we lose money either way."

Jorge walked inside his shop and he looked at the checkpoint through the window. He turned on one of the computers. Suddenly on the screen appeared live security footage from a camera hung from the roof outside (see Figure 4.3). I watched it in astonishment. "The police think the camera is there to watch for thieves, or in case gang members show up," he said. "But on days when they are here collecting fines from humble people as we come and go from our neighborhood, we have to treat them like criminals too." We watched out the window as money exchanged hands between police and drivers. But, I asked him, hasn't corruption of this kind always been something of a norm around Tegucigalpa? Didn't most underpaid police take bribes to offset their stagnant wages?

"No, out here now, it's all one thing," he said. "Gangs and police, working together. While they set up the checkpoint here, over the hill in another neighborhood, the gangs are collecting extortion. Gangs and police are never in the same place at the same time. Later, when the gangs shoot somebody because they won't pay extortion, the police go over there. If they take somebody to jail for it, they let them out by the morning. That's how it is!"

"What are you going to do with these recordings?" I asked. "Would you give them to one of the NGOs as part of police corruption investigations?"

He laughed. "No way . . . those cases take years to go through the courts. If they find out it was you, then your family gets threats and you end up having to leave the country. No, what I'm doing here is making a community record." He clicked on a folder in the computer's hard drive. Inside were more than twenty surveillance videos shot from the camera outside of similar police operations. "I'm just telling you. Only you and a couple of people know about it. But one day, whenever things change, I'm going to donate all of this, all these recordings to the national archives. Anthropologists and people who come from abroad and want to study what happened, how things worked in

Figure 4.3 The security camera of a local business in Tegucigalpa. Photograph by author, July 2014.

Honduras—all of them can watch it and see with their own eyes what it was like." And with that, Oscar Sánchez was no longer the only person with a utopia in mind. For Jorge, every act of witnessing refined a sense of what kind of justice might one day redeem the present. In the meantime, survival was so many little things: a vacant stare, a fabricated story, an imperceptible gesture, or a sense of when to disappear.

THEORIZING SECURE WORLDS

The provenance of security in fragile and emergency-prone states, stretched to the limits by informal and illicit economies and institutional disinvestment, can be a varied field of ideas and solutions, where the "sense" of security is uneven and often contradictory. Each solution—whether charter cities, tattoo-bedecked gang families, police in futuristic black armor, undocumented teenaged migrants, or stalwart citizens repurposing their surveillance cameras to record security itself—hints at a horizon of possibility, harnessed or held by a constituency for whom security has particular meanings and ends. In this field of play, communities of the Tegucigalpa cityscape build a shared attunement (Stewart 2011) in which the city and its sensibility come together and produce worlds where life must and does endure. Some of these worlds attempt to retain their monolithic status, deploying armored brigades and security utopias for the wealthiest classes, while others cultivate subtle tactics that ensure those powers, and the vision of the future that depends on them, are never absolute. For critical ethnographies of security, these fugitive signs and sensibilities map the future of political communities, making sure they remain open, even after they have been "proofed."

NOTE

1   All names used in this essay are pseudonyms.

REFERENCES

Agamben, Giorgio. 1995. *Homo Sacer: Sovereign Power and Bare Life*. Stanford, CA: Stanford University Press.

Associated Press. 2013. "Congreso nacional aprueba dicreto que crea la Policía Militar." *Proceso*, August 22. http://www.proceso.hn/component/k2/item/16204.html.

Browne, Simone. 2015. *Dark Matters: On the Surveillance of Blackness*. Durham, NC: Duke University Press.

Carter, Jon. 2014. "Gothic Sovereignty: Gangs and Criminal Community in a Honduran Prison." *South Atlantic Quarterly* 113, no. 3: 475–502.

Comaroff, Jean, and John Comaroff. 2004. "Criminal Obsessions, After Foucault: Postcoloniality, Policing, and the Metaphysics of Disorder." *Critical Inquiry* 30, no. 4: 800–824.

———. 2016. *The Truth about Crime: Sovereignty, Knowledge, Social Order*. Chicago: University of Chicago Press.

Ghertner, D. Asher. 2015. *Rule by Aesthetics: World-Class City Making in Delhi*. New York: Oxford University Press.

Goldstein, Daniel M. 2005. "Flexible Justice: Neoliberal Violence and 'Self-Help' Security in Bolivia." *Critique of Anthropology* 25, no. 4: 389–411.

———. 2010. "Toward a Critical Anthropology of Security." *Current Anthropology* 51, no. 4: 487–517.

Jahangir, Asma. 2002. *Report of the Special Rapporteur on Extrajudicial, Summary or Arbitrary Executions: Mission to Honduras*. Geneva, Switzerland: United Nations Commission on Human Rights.

Mackey, Danielle Marie. 2014. "'I've Seen All Sorts of Horrific Things in My Time. But None as Detrimental to the Country as This: US Conservatives Are About to Run a Dangerous Economic Experiment in Honduras." *New Republic*, December 14. https://newrepublic.com/article/120559/ive-seen-sorts-horrific-things-time-none-detrimental-country-this.

Mann, Steve, Jason Nolan, and Barry Wellman. 2003. "Sousveillance: Inventing and Using Wearable Computing Devices for Data Collection in Surveillance Environments." *Surveillance and Society* 1, no. 3: 331–355.

Mejía, Thelma. 2007. "In Tegucigalpa, the Iron Fist Fails." NACLA *Report on the Americas* 40, no. 4: 26–29, 47.

Moodie, Ellen. 2006. "Microbus Crashes and Coca-Cola Cash: The Value of Death in 'Free-Market' El Salvador." *American Ethnologist* 33, no. 1: 63–80.

Muller, Michael-Markus. 2010. "Community Policing in Latin America: Lessons from Mexico City." *European Review of Latin American and Caribbean Studies* 88: 21–37.

Nelson, Diane. 2009. *Reckoning: The Ends of War in Guatemala*. Durham, NC: Duke University Press.

Pitt-Rivers, Julian. 1954. *The People of the Sierra*. London: Weidenfeld and Nicolson.

———. 1971. *The People of the Sierra*. 2nd ed. Chicago: University of Chicago Press.

Rancière, Jacques. 2009. "Contemporary Art and the Politics of Aesthetics." In *Communities of Sense: Rethinking Aesthetics and Politics*, edited by Beth Hinderliter, Vared Maimon, Jaleh Mansoor, and Seth McCormick, 31–50. Durham, NC: Duke University Press.

———. 2010. *Dissensus: On Politics and Aesthetics*. Edited and translated by Steven Corcoran. London: Bloomsbury Press.

Robles, Frances. 2012. "Honduras Becomes Murder Capital of the World." *Miami Herald*, January 23. http://www.miamiherald.com/latest-news/article1939373.html.

Simpson, Audra. 2014. *Mohawk Interruptus: Political Life across the Borders of Settler States*. Durham, NC: Duke University Press.

Stewart, Kathleen. 2011. "Atmospheric Attunements." *Environment and Planning D: Society and Space* 29, no. 3: 445–453.

Taussig, Michael. 1999. *Defacement: Public Secrecy and the Labor of the Negative*. Stanford, CA: Stanford University Press.

5

Security Aesthetics and Political Community Formation in Kingston, Jamaica

Rivke Jaffe

To those unfamiliar with Downtown Kingston, its inner-city neighborhoods—gang territory where criminal "dons" are in charge—often appear to be chaotic, dangerous, and lawless areas. If outsiders cannot avoid traveling through such neighborhoods, they drive through as quickly as possible, to escape having to interact with residents. However, precisely to prevent ill-intentioned strangers from speeding through and committing drive-by shootings, residents have removed the drain covers at the intersections of the streets. The deep trenches this creates force cars to slow down, allowing strategically placed observers to check out any outsiders entering the neighborhood. Elsewhere, artful arrangements of urban debris—an old fridge, a burned-out car chassis—serve a similar purpose. In addition to having to navigate these improvised speed bumps, unfamiliar drivers are bewildered by the many one-way streets. Cars will turn down one of the many narrow streets without traffic signs, only to find themselves forced to reverse in the face of an oncoming vehicle.

My first visit to the inner-city neighborhood of Brick Town, in 2010, was to meet Roger, a close relative of the General, the neighborhood's former don.[1] I had no car at the time, but my former student Joshua, who worked at a government agency nearby in Downtown Kingston, was willing to give me a ride. While he wanted to help me, Joshua was scared to drive to the neighborhood alone as he had never been there before, so he chartered Flynn, a coworker who lived in an adjacent inner-city area, to join us as an "escort." Joshua's nervousness was contagious, and I also began to feel a little jittery as we stepped into his expensive Honda. Flynn indicated the direction Joshua should drive, away from the busy market area. We moved through narrow, potholed streets and past dilapidated housing covered with graffiti referencing the General (who had been in jail for several years) and his son, and the political party with which they were aligned. Joshua drove just a little too quickly, and I tried to convince him to slow down as I studied a map of Kingston, attempting to figure out which streets were one-way and which were not. Flynn chuckled at my concern with how the government had designated a street: "Dem nuh observe one-way inna dis ya part a di world [They do not observe one-way in this part of the world]," he commented drily.

His depiction of the area as anarchic put me in mind of my first fieldwork in Jamaica, in 2000, when my overwhelming impression of the city was one of disorder. After three months in Kingston, I felt a physical relief as my plane landed in the Netherlands and the neat, orderly grid of the Dutch agricultural landscape came into view. While I had enjoyed my fieldwork, I experienced Jamaica's urban sensorium as chaotic and disorienting—its streets packed with people, cars, handcarts, goats, and lined with hand-painted stalls and signs advertising all manner of goods; people shouting at each other over the loud music blaring from vehicles, stores, and CD vendors' speakers; the smells of exhaust fumes, rotting garbage, and barbecued meat; my movements through its dust and heat on foot, or in crowded minibuses and route taxis pressed up against other sweaty passengers.

As I returned over the years that followed, and as my access expanded to areas only accessible by private car, I discovered, first, that Kingston also included many middle-class spaces with a style resembling the "orderly" aesthetics I had projected onto Dutch landscapes. More importantly perhaps, I realized that the public spaces of Downtown Kingston were actually organized in a very tight and controlled fashion. The underlying social and political logic of these low-income areas, as well as the orderly colonial grid plan that Downtown streets follow, were not evident to me initially, distracted as I was by what I perceived as chaos and disorder. It took me a significant period of time to be able to recognize the order according to which these streets operated.

To many wealthier Kingstonians, life in inner-city neighborhoods has a similarly foreign quality, and Flynn's remark on one-way resonates with their sense of Downtown Kingston as a chaotic area where national laws do not apply. However, inner-city residents *do* take the official one-way traffic rules seriously. Precisely because the traffic signs are generally unclear, when unfamiliar drivers accidentally turn down a street in the wrong direction, people on the sidewalk will immediately call out and signal for them to reverse: "One-way!

One-way! Turn back!" Belying Flynn's comment, and counter to popular opinion, residents invest considerable energy in correcting transgressions. Areas such as Brick Town are by no means lawless—their social life operates according to strong norms of appropriate behavior, including rules about who can go where. They are characterized by a system of order in which dons play a central role, but which often complements rather than clashes with state law (Jaffe 2013).

This don-based system of order, which sets norms for public conduct and guides urban mobilities, should be understood in relation to a politics of aesthetics. The formation of political communities around dons and their neighborhood territories is intimately connected to the emotional and ethical work that a range of popular culture texts, images, sounds, and performative practices do within specific urban spaces (Jaffe 2012a). In the context of urban Jamaica, with its extremely high rates of violent crime, this order and this aesthetics relate directly to issues of security. The various aesthetic forms that outsiders associate with violence and poverty, such as political and gang graffiti, or potholed roads without drain covers, may in fact be key interventions in producing a bordered space of safety for residents.

In this chapter, I approach security aesthetics as inherent to the production and reproduction of social difference. Specific security signs, buildings, technologies, and arrangements of bodies interpellate and move people in different ways, reinforcing existing forms of differentiated citizenship or delineating new forms of political community. Understanding the connection between urban security aesthetics and processes of subject formation requires an attentiveness to the entanglement of aesthetic forms with their material surroundings, including the built environment of cities. I understand Jamaica—a country with high levels of violent crime that is divided along lines of skin color, class, and political affiliation—as characterized by multiple regimes of security aesthetics.

In what follows, I compare and contrast the "Downtown security aesthetics" that speaks to inner-city residents in neighborhoods ruled by dons and the "Uptown security aesthetics" that makes wealthier Kingstonians who reside in the city's elite districts feel safe. I explore how these regimes both connect and separate different urban populations and territories: in discussing these different aesthetic regimes, I aim to show that they are not entirely separate and can exist simultaneously in one area. Rather than comparing different parts of the city, I concentrate on social spaces within Downtown neighborhoods such as Brick Town to examine what makes differently positioned people feel safe there and, conversely, how these feelings of safety are central to community formation.

I explore these security aesthetic regimes based on extensive ethnographic fieldwork conducted over multiple periods. In developing my analysis of

Downtown security aesthetics, I draw primarily on a long-term research project on donmanship that involved fieldwork in Brick Town, concentrated mainly in the period 2010–2013 but with follow-up visits in more recent years. My discussion of Uptown security aesthetics draws on my friendships and professional interactions with middle-class Jamaicans developed in the context of multiple research projects, and more generally on my experiences of living and working in different middle-class areas of Kingston from 2006.

Based on these different fieldwork experiences, the rest of this chapter examines the role of security aesthetics in both reproducing and realigning difference, through its shaping of communities of sense (Rancière 2006). The first section connects philosophical and anthropological work on the politics of aesthetics to considerations of spatiality and materiality, in order to develop a more emplaced understanding of the relations between aesthetic forms, bodies, and politics. The next section provides background to Kingston's sociospatial divisions and the pluralization of security. This is followed by a discussion of differentiated security aesthetics and political community formation in Downtown Kingston, with the concluding section proposing that the approach elaborated in this chapter can help us understand the role of the senses in shaping political geographies.

EMPLACING THE POLITICS OF AESTHETICS

Following the interpretation put forward by D. Asher Ghertner, Hudson McFann, and Daniel M. Goldstein (this volume), I understand aesthetics broadly as the domain of sense perception; my analysis of security aesthetics concentrates on how security and insecurity are *sensed* through bodily engagements with the urban environment. Safety is something that is felt in a corporeal way as people move through urban space: security and insecurity, apprehension and reassurance, are bodily sensations that are produced in response to a range of aesthetic forms, from architectural and design elements to gang graffiti and armed response signs. Certain markers on the urban landscape work, intentionally or unintentionally, to generate feelings of comfort and a sense of belonging, while others elicit fear and sensations of being out of place. These affective responses to aesthetics are embodied and emplaced, and as such these sensations are not distributed uniformly across the urban population. By enabling a shared way of sensing the world, aesthetic forms are central to the formation of subjects and communities, a process that is highly political—especially when connected to security.

The political role of aesthetics has been outlined incisively by philosopher Jacques Rancière (2006, 2010), whose concept of "the distribution of the sensible" (*le partage du sensible*) emphasizes the role of art in organizing what is visible, audible, conceivable, and speakable. This attunement of sensory perception toward a shared norm—the production of what Rancière calls "consensus," or "sensing together"—is central to processes of subjectivation and the inscription of community. Any sociopolitical order, he argues, is supported by a perceptual and conceptual regime, which structures how people feel and know that an order is normal, natural, and proper. Understanding not only why sociopolitical orders persist, but also how they come to be challenged, requires attending to both consensus and dissensus, the crafting and the disruption of a shared sense experience (see also Panagia 2009).

A number of anthropologists have begun to explore ethnographically how the relations between politics, aesthetics, and sensory perception take shape in lived experience and everyday life. This anthropological work also seeks to understand empirically how the political imagination takes on a material form, critiquing Benedict Anderson's (1991) concept of imagined communities for privileging semiotics and neglecting the role of embodiment and the senses. In their work on sensory citizenship, for instance, Susanna Trnka, Christine Dureau, and Julie Park (2013) highlight the significance of the embodied sensing of the world in the formation of political subjects and communities. They suggest that sensory differentiation is central in the processes of inclusion and exclusion that structure the boundaries of citizenship: our experience of social sameness and difference works through emotionally loaded senses of vision, hearing, smell, and so on. In her work on the nexus between media, religion, and community, Birgit Meyer (2009) argues similarly for a sensorial turn in our understanding of the political imagination, but places a more explicit emphasis on the role of materiality. She emphasizes that for the imagination to be experienced as real in an embodied fashion it must be made material, arguing that "more attention needs to be paid to the role played by things, media and the body in actual processes of community making" (Meyer 2009, 6). By focusing on the religious mediation of community, Meyer's work also deliberately focuses on what she calls "aesthetic formations" beyond the nation-state and democratic politics.

While these ethnographers hint at the role of space and the built environment in these sensory processes, their engagement with the emplacement of embodied experience has tended to be limited. In my analysis of Jamaica's security aesthetics, I focus on the role of both materiality and spatiality in producing politico-aesthetic order. This chapter focuses not so much on the built environment per se, as on the "material-affective encounters" that the editors of this volume highlight, and on the geographies of these encounters.

My analysis concentrates on sensorial engagements with urban surroundings, including prominently, but also going beyond, the city's built forms. Through an analysis of visual markers such as graffiti and urban debris, but also of other, less bounded sensorial stimuli (such as smells, temperatures, and exposure to different types of bodies), I seek to understand how these aesthetic forms shape different securitized communities of sense, but also *where*. In this sense, the chapter highlights the geographical dimension of two of the modalities set out by Ghertner et al. (this volume): it analyzes how sociospatially distinct forms of calibrating vulnerabilities, of socially regulating assessments of risk, intersect with elements of urban fortressing, those "interventions in built form [that] deploy visual and other sensory signals to fashion aesthetic norms about how security looks, sounds, and feels."

By attending to urban space and its differentiation, I also hope to shift analyses of political sense-making away from the privileged territory of the nation-state and toward forms of political geography that emerge within nations and beyond the direct control of state. In the next section, I explore the sensorial politics of difference within don-controlled inner-city "garrisons." I analyze how Downtown and Uptown Kingstonians experience safety within these spaces and consider the differentiation of security aesthetics in relation to the formation of distinct political communities. Rather than associating these aesthetic regimes only, or primarily, with feelings of fear and a sensory attunement to threat, I emphasize their function in generating positive sensations of safety, comfort, and familiarity.

SPATIALIZED DIFFERENCE AND SEGMENTED SECURITY IN KINGSTON

As my reference to Uptown and Downtown Kingston suggests, this broad binary is a central type of urban imaginary that spatializes urban difference along lines of class as well as skin color (see Map 5.1). While urban life encompasses more types of sociospatial order than these two realms alone, these realms reflect a form of division that is central to the lived experience of urban residents (Carnegie 2017). Roughly speaking, Uptown is associated with wealthier "brown" Jamaicans of mixed or ethnic-minority descent, while Downtown is understood as the part of the city where impoverished "black" African-Jamaicans live. While analyses of census data indicate that Kingston's residential segregation along lines of skin color decreased significantly during the twentieth century (Clarke 2006), in my experience many residents from a range of social backgrounds narrate Kingston in terms of a combination of class and skin color mapped onto a largely bipolar sociospatial structure. The ethnoracial categories of brown and black are not strictly phenotypical,

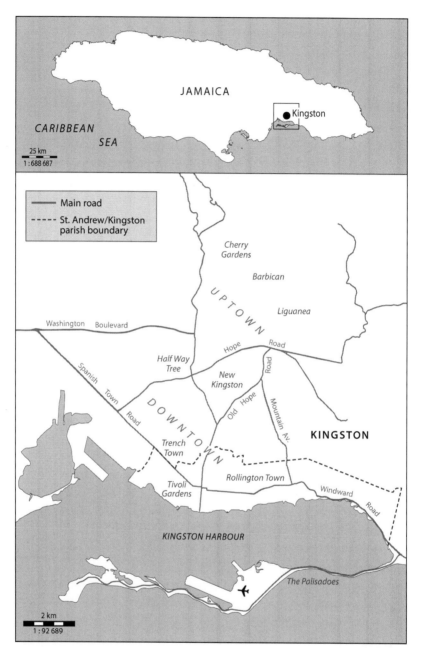

Map 5.1   Map of Kingston. Created by Rowan Arundel, based on map from Jaffe (2012b).

but coproduced with class and urban space, with geographical designations—Downtown, or "inner-city"—used as adjectives that are taken to self-evidently mean lower-class and black. These dichotomous frames shape differential readings of bodies across the urban landscape, based not only on skin color and class markers (such as clothing and speech) but also on their spatial location (Jaffe 2016).

Within Downtown Kingston, residents differentiate between neighborhoods based on their political affiliation to either the Jamaica Labour Party (JLP) or the People's National Party (PNP). In the Cold War context of the decades following Jamaica's independence in 1962, both parties concentrated low-income supporters in so-called political garrisons in Kingston's inner-city areas. Through a system known as garrison politics, they supplied local leaders—who later became known as dons—with money and weapons in order to defend and expand their political turf, resulting in hundreds of deaths due to electoral violence (Sives 2010). While recent elections have been largely peaceful, Downtown Kingston's neighborhoods remain divided by a deeply felt "political tribalism," and the dons who lead these areas have largely maintained their party-political affiliation, even if much of their income now comes from extralegal activities rather than from politicians.

These sociospatial differentiations are often connected to safety, and residents use levels of violence and crime to distinguish both between Uptown and Downtown, and between different garrisons or "ghettos." Media representations of Downtown Kingston depict inner-city areas as highly dangerous; both the daily newspapers and the televised news are a constant stream of brutal homicides, armed robberies, and police killings. Indeed, such violence is sadly commonplace. Yet many inner-city residents do not necessarily move about anxiously, in permanent fear of crime, of the don, or of the police. In my research on donmanship, residents of Brick Town and other inner-city neighborhoods often stressed the role of a strong don in guaranteeing security, and particularly in preventing theft, rape, and murder. The widespread legitimacy of the most successful dons has relied on the capacity to "set the order," to establish social norms and to punish transgressions swiftly and effectively, whether through violent retribution or through banishment (see also Charles and Beckford 2012). In contrast, neighborhoods without an effective don may suffer from higher rates of crimes, perpetrated by both locals and outsiders.

Inner-city residents often do not move easily outside their own neighborhood—while they may feel safe in their own community, they are often more fearful of entering other low-income areas. The historical legacy of political tribalism and more recent gang conflict is a fragmentation of Downtown between JLP and PNP neighborhoods, run by rival dons, and residents venturing into adjacent neighborhoods even for social visits may be misrecognized as hostile strangers. A different set of anxieties limits the movements of inner-city residents to and in Uptown Kingston, where the un-familiar aesthetic order of upscale spaces of work, leisure, and consumption—their air-conditioned chill, their specific norms of acceptable appearances, and proper intensities of sound—often elicits a physical sensation of being out of place. The urban poor know that their presence in wealthier areas is often construed as a security threat, and a fear of being humiliated in encounters with security guards, salespeople, or snooty office workers accompanies many people when they leave the familiarity of Downtown.

Like Downtown residents, Uptown residents generally do not rely primar-ily on the police for their security needs (see Jaffe 2012b). Rather, many wealth-ier Kingstonians have turned to private security companies, retreating behind walls and into gated communities protected by armed security guards. As in many other segregated cities (see, e.g., Caldeira 2000), public space, poverty, and danger are easily conflated, and fear of crime leads many Uptown residents to retreat into highly secured, privatized spaces. Many of them rarely venture into Kingston's public spaces, moving swiftly between fortified enclaves of residence, work, and leisure in tightly locked SUVs that are protected from theft and carjacking by vehicle tracking systems. Stories abound of husbands prohibiting their wives from venturing "below Crossroads" (roughly south of New Kingston, shown on Map 5.1), and Jamaicans of all class backgrounds con-stantly expressed surprise at my working in inner-city neighborhoods.

Yet there are certain public spaces in Downtown, at certain times, that Uptown Kingstonians do frequent, including two specific social and physical spaces: the market and the street dance.[2] In what follows, I concentrate on the aesthetic formation of safety and political community in inner-city areas such as Brick Town, starting with a discussion of the features and effects of Down-town security aesthetics that work through the larger space of the neighbor-hood, followed by a consideration of the smaller, more specific time-spaces within which Uptown security aesthetics are mobilized.

DOWNTOWN SECURITY AESTHETICS

The same aesthetic features of garrisons or ghettos that make outsiders feel unsafe may be central to residents' feelings of security. The sights, sounds, and other sensations that Uptown Kingstonians have learned to read as *chaka-chaka* (messy, disorganized), and that they associate both discursively and extralin-guistically with poverty and violence, are central to the don-based sociopolitical order that is often the most effective security system available to residents. While the visual aesthetic that dons mobilize is not a style characterized by smooth lines, grids, or materials, their shaping of the landscape is not haphazard or chaotic. The drain covers that are removed, the potholes, and the informal speed bumps do not necessarily elicit a sensation of neglect. Rather, they are recognized as deliberate interventions (or noninterventions) in the cityscape that realize the slow movement of vehicles. The burly men hanging out on the corner, some blocking the streets with their cars, are not potential robbers, but are actively engaged in surveilling all passersby and repelling unwelcome intruders—the feelings of protection they provide is analogous to that of uniformed guards, gates, and security cameras in elite areas.

For Uptown Kingstonians, the ubiquitous murals of deceased dons and political and gang graffiti may contribute to a "ghetto look" associated with poverty and violence. This is a "look" not altogether dissimilar from the aesthetic regime used in New Delhi to evaluate whether a space is a "slum" or not (Ghertner 2015), or from the visual signs of disrepair and alleged danger targeted by "broken windows" policies in U.S. cities. To local residents, however, these murals and inscriptions both mark important public sites within the neighborhood and visually assert place-based genealogies of power and protection. The murals depicted in Figure 5.1, for instance, mark out a genealogy of local leadership within the neighborhood, of different deceased leaders of a criminal organization with close historical connections to the PNP. Not coincidentally, this wall of fame is situated along a street associated with the birth of this political party, rooting this leadership in national political history. The men in these portraits gaze directly at passersby, some smiling, some stern, all everyday reminders to residents of who is watching over them. Like other important political portraits, the murals of the most important leaders are cared for and restored if necessary. Such visual updates often entail repainting dons' features in fresh detail, but may also involve a modernization of their clothes or jewelry to reflect more recent fashion. Maintaining the artworks is a way of ensuring that the memory of these leaders does not erode.[3]

To many inner-city residents, such visual interventions in the urban landscape combine to produce a "security atmosphere," a set of material-affective relations that is atmospherically immersive and lies in between bodies, objects, and material spaces (Adey 2014; cf. Ben Anderson 2009). In this context, this enveloping spatiality can produce a sense of intimacy and comfort, of being watched over and protected, even while these responses to surveillance may coexist with more ambiguous affective impacts, such as wariness and tension. As Darren Ellis, Ian Tucker, and David Harper (2013) note, the affective

Figure 5.1 Commemorative murals. Photograph by author.

atmospheres of surveillance work at the edges of consciousness, with the system of surveillance remaining almost but not quite unnoticed, the feelings it produces not directly qualified or registered through linguistic representation.

The material interventions effected by dons tend to be connected to the system of garrison politics—in PNP areas such as Brick Town, especially during election times, the color orange will be in evidence on walls, in flags, or in people's dress, while JLP areas shade green (see Figure 5.2). As residents are socialized into political partisanship, the colors, hand signals, and sounds of the political party generate positive sensations. Sharon, a resident of a PNP-affiliated community in Central Kingston where I did previous fieldwork, described the affective experience of the singing of the party anthem at political rallies: "When they play the party anthem, shivers just run down your spine. You put your hand over your heart and everyone is singing . . . it's so beautiful!" Sharon and two of her friends demonstrated this by singing the first lines of the PNP anthem, "Jamaica Arise." Such experiences underline the potential of music to produce political subjectivities through emotional impact and bodily sensation. Like party anthems, party colors, logos, and hand signs can

Figure 5.2 "PNP ZONE," political graffiti. Photograph by author.

come to work in a precognitive fashion to produce sensations of affinity, intimacy, and familiarity. Together, the aesthetic forms related to dons and partisan politics combine to form a style of "garrison aesthetics," a set of sensory relations to the material environment not entirely dissimilar to those of the military base to which the term originally referred.

Our bodily responses to specific aesthetic forms are learned; our senses need to be attuned along specific distributions. Downtown security aesthetics is not only embedded in the general landscape of the neighborhood streets and the people and objects that fill them, it also relies on a constant, often subconscious monitoring of the neighborhood atmosphere. Feeling safe in this context requires an intimate sensorial knowledge of what danger feels like. The ability to sense whether the area is "cool" or "hot" in terms of political or gang conflict, to perceive when violence is imminent, relies on a deeply embodied knowledge of which sounds, sights, and sensations one needs to attend to in order to remain safe. These sensorial skills involve glancing automatically at men's waistlines or judging the weight of a backpack slung over a teenager's shoulder to assess whether they are carrying a weapon. They involve recognizing which bodily movements tend to be followed by bloodshed; which silences indicate calm, and which indicate that gunfire might be about to erupt; which sounds are gunshots fired in celebration or warning and which are intended to kill. While residents have described these skills and sensibilities to me, my immersion has never been such that they became natural to me; I never really internalized this knowledge of where to look or what to hear as reflexes.

The regime of Downtown security aesthetics sketched here is intimately related to the system of donmanship. Interventions into the built environment, such as the improvised speed bumps described previously, work as coded elements of "fortress design," help slow down movement, and regulate access to the neighborhood. The neighborhood-level political community that can form around a don is produced aesthetically through a range of popular culture expressions that generate feelings of intimacy and generate an almost supernatural aura around these leaders (Jaffe 2012a). The shared experience of belonging to a specific sociopolitical order that these sensory skills and experiences produce—the Rancièrean consensus—connects directly to a feeling of being safe, of being protected within the bordered space of that order. The design of urban divisions, both between different Downtown neighborhoods and between Uptown and Downtown spaces, calibrates feelings of security and belonging simultaneously.

UPTOWN SECURITY AESTHETICS IN DOWNTOWN SPACES

As noted above, wealthier Kingstonians tend to eschew the Downtown area, and more generally those urban spaces marked aesthetically as poor and dangerous by their "messy" visual order, and by their intensities of heat, smell, and noise. Yet under certain circumstances, middle-class Jamaicans do leave the safety of Uptown to seek out precisely these spaces of poverty and crime. How can we explain these visits? What motivates Uptown residents to leave their zone of comfort, and how can a focus on sociospatially differentiated security aesthetics help understand what makes such transgressions of established class and color boundaries possible?

I suggest we can understand the motivations in the context of larger shifts in Jamaican cultural politics. Articulations of ethnonational belonging and cultural authenticity have shifted from a model of "Creole multiracial nationalism," embodied by brown Jamaicans and with a state-led emphasis on folk traditions in rural areas, toward one of "modern Blackness" (Thomas 2004). This latter framing, fed by a range of national and international influences, privileges Blackness as the basis for national belonging and re-roots the site of cultural authenticity in the urban space of the "ghetto." In this context, as brown middle-class claims to cultural citizenship became less self-evident, performances of Jamaicanness have increasingly come to involve the embrace of aesthetic expressions of Blackness. This is discernible in the new middle-class enthusiasm for consuming certain elements of Rastafari culture, previously spurned as a dirty and disreputable form of Blackness (Jaffe 2010). In addition, I suggest that, whereas claiming some level of familiarity with Kingston's ghetto spaces might have been a threat to middle-class status a few decades ago, it has now become a distinct element in performances of national belonging, pursued by some, if certainly not all, segments of the urban middle class. Two specific time-spaces that enable such performances are the Downtown street market early on Saturday mornings, and various inner-city street dances held late at night. While Uptown visitors would not seriously entertain the idea of living in Downtown Kingston—it would never be a space of home—this part of the city has become more viable as an occasional space of consumption and leisure.

Given the fact that Downtown does remain associated, both discursively and statistically, with much higher levels of violent crime than other parts of Kingston, how do Uptown residents balance a desire to be there with their fear of being victimized? What allows their general sense of insecurity to be temporarily suspended? I suggest that those wealthier Jamaicans who do visit Downtown seek out temporally bounded places that are characterized by the presence of Uptown security aesthetics. This classed aesthetics relies on a mix of sensory stimuli associated with the order and safety of the city's wealthier areas. In short, the insecurity that Uptown visitors to inner-city neighborhoods experience is mitigated when certain material-affective encounters with the urban environment that are associated with danger—heat, noise, smells, the lack of a linear visual order—are diminished or modified.

Quite a few older Uptown residents and some younger professional couples make a point to do their weekly produce shopping in the Downtown open-air market. Middle-class status is generally tied up with specific, sanitized spaces of consumption. The supermarket plays a particularly important role in this regard; it is a symbolic site of formal fixed prices, gleaming aisles and shopping trolleys piled high with imported goods that many inner-city residents spoke about to me in terms of both inaccessibility and yearning. Yet a certain "rootsiness" can be achieved by complementing supermarket shopping with trips to the market for fresh local produce, maintaining a relationship with "your vendor," and performing a type of streetwiseness that involves bartering to get the freshest goods for the best price. Various Uptown people of my acquaintance frequented the Downtown market, but all of them went there only very early on Saturday mornings, usually around 5 or 6 A.M. This timing is not coincidental, as it is associated with a very different market aesthetics than other times of the day or week.

One important feature is the coolness of the early morning market. Heat is not conducive to a middle-class status, as it is incompatible with middle-class hairstyles and professional dress codes. More generally, heat (or "hotness") is associated with public space (in contrast with the air-conditioned temperature of middle-class private space), and consequently equated with poverty, crime, and an overall reputation of "volatility." Due to its higher altitude and a greater prevalence of greenery, Uptown neighborhoods tend to be physically cooler than Downtown, but the "hot" reputation of the poorer areas refers to both temperature and alleged temperament. The cooler temperature of the early morning market has other sensory implications. Toward the end of the day, the market tends to smell strongly of squashed and rotting vegetables that have been baking in the sun, of decreasingly fresh fish and meat, of garbage accumulating in the gutters, and of buses, cars, and loaded handcarts inching through the packed streets. Both the heat of the sun and the throngs of people jostling past the stalls make for a sweatier, more intimate tactile experience. In contrast, at 6 A.M., the market presents an orderly visual appearance, with the produce still displayed in neat stacks, looking and smelling fresh. The streets are largely free of litter, and the limited number of shoppers at that hour means the noise level and the measure of physical contact are not very intense. Within the general context of Downtown, these features combine to present a very calm sensory landscape, certainly for a market district. To the extent that this is possible, this is a version of Downtown that approximates the aesthetics of Uptown, while maintaining the "authentic" aesthetics of poverty and informality.

Younger middle-class people may not be as invested in shopping at the street market. Their visits to Downtown are more likely to be in the context of dancehall and reggae parties, both directly associated with inner-city areas. For these visitors (many of whom are university students), participating in the dancehall and reggae music scenes is a way of feeling closer to an "authentic" form of national culture (Pereira Martins 2009). Specific street dances have tended to be popular among the Uptown crowd, including Passa Passa, a weekly Wednesday night dance that was held in the West Kingston JLP garrison of Tivoli Gardens until 2010, and Ole Hits, a Sunday night dance in Rae Town, a PNP neighborhood in Central Kingston. As Donna Hope (2006, 128) notes, the dance is a site that "temporally connects the 'uptown' middle classes with their 'downtown' inner-city counterparts within spaces that are considered dangerous and volatile, particularly because they are peopled by Kingston's urban poor." What aesthetic adaptations are necessary to suspend the sense of danger?

While the dark of the night would generally contribute to the menacing character of an inner-city space, like the early morning market the timing of the dance means that the experience is much cooler than during the day. Somewhat older visitors prefer to attend Ole Hits, which favors classic roots reggae, a genre associated less with violence than dancehall. Yet at all street parties the booming music and crowds of partygoers create an intense atmosphere, even if Uptown visitors often maintain a bit of a distance to the sensory heart of the party, remaining on the fringes of the most heated dancing. But it is precisely what Julian Henriques (2010) identifies as dancehall's "vibrations of affect" that literally force Uptown and Downtown to move to the same frequency, enabling an embodied consensus that temporarily transcends class and ethnoracial boundaries.

In addition to the minor adaptions of environmental intensities of heat and sound in the specific time-spaces of the early morning market or the late-night dance, another form of aesthetics that is perhaps less explored resides in the bodies of people. An important visual and sonic sensory stimulus for feeling safe resides in the presence of other Uptown Kingstonians, their social position obvious through a combination of features including skin color, clothing, hairstyle, speech, and physical bearing. While crowds of poor people are easily construed as an indication of insecurity, the presence of others who look and sound like you is an essential part of Uptown security aesthetics. Like the marketplace early on a Saturday morning, the sight of other brown people and the sound of their similar accents form a critical aesthetic element. However, another category of strangers also contributes to a feeling of safety among "native outsiders": the tourists—mainly Japanese but sometimes European or North American—who frequent Downtown dancehall parties with much less trepidation than many middle-class Jamaicans. The presence of these lighter-skinned (if not always white) dancehall fans also works in a reassuring fashion, as there is a widely shared national concern with shielding tourists from Jamaica's violence. This aesthetic function of emplaced human bodies connects to work by Arun Saldanha (2007) on what he calls the viscosity of race, the material-affective process by which bodies with specific phenotypes (complicated by dress, behavior, and context) gather and stick together within certain spaces.

In the market and at the dance, a specific blend of sensory presences, absences, and intensities allows an approximation of Uptown security aesthetics. This remains a thin veneer that stands in delicate balance with the dominant aesthetics of poverty and violence that generates feelings of insecurity as well as cultural authenticity. Uptown visitors' different perceptual attunement means they may not notice those features that make local residents feel safe, nor do they recognize the indications of potential violence—their always fragile sense of security depends in part on a perceptual naiveté. My own perhaps more robust sense of comfort and safety in these same areas is similarly bolstered by my underdeveloped radar for conflict.

Yet what actually keeps outsiders safe is in many cases the order maintained by a don. This was certainly the case with Passa Passa, with Tivoli Gardens run under "One Order" of Christopher "Dudus" Coke, Jamaica's most influential don until his extradition to the United States in 2010, whose rules included a prohibition on violence against outsiders in his community. Similarly, the central marketplace has long been tightly run by, and divided between, dons from the two adjacent garrisons, who organized a system of security and hygiene while charging vendors with "market fees." Even as the aesthetic interventions that dons make may be either imperceptible to outsiders, or perceived as part of what makes a neighborhood feel dangerous, it may well be precisely this system that prevents visitors from harm. This balance of perceiving and not perceiving, of recognizing and misrecognizing different aesthetic forms, allows Uptown Jamaicans to visit inner-city neighborhoods and feel physically and emotionally closer to the political community of the nation, while remaining largely oblivious of the don-led political community that is central to shaping these areas.

TOWARD A POLITICAL GEOGRAPHY OF SENSATION

How do political powers mobilize aesthetic means to simultaneously produce a sense of security and a sense of community? As Ghertner et al. (this volume) outline, security aesthetics can be analyzed as a governmental modality, a way of managing social and political life that works through inclusion and exclusion of subjects from a political community of sense. In Kingston's inner-city areas, dons draw on the politics of aesthetics to create among residents what we could read in Rancière's terms as a perceptual consensus—the shared attunement of the senses is central to the formations of political subjectivities around donmanship. They realize informal, apparently "disorderly" visual and infrastructural interventions into the built environment that act as forms of fortressing, expressing a specific security-cum-political order.

Yet the dons' neighborhood work is not the only "calibration of vulnerabilities" at work in Kingston. The city and its Downtown areas encompass multiple, overlapping regimes of security aesthetics, through which risks are imagined and affectively experienced in different ways by differently situated subjects. The fortressing intent of dons' "designs" is visible to some, but not to others; these interventions lie somewhere in the middle of the "spectrum of visible security," articulating an "aesthetic paradox" (Coaffee, O'Hare, and Hawkesworth 2009) that is crucial to allowing the copresence of normally segregated publics.

Despite a widespread fear of Downtown Kingston among wealthier Jamaicans, they feel relatively safe there under certain circumstances. In efforts to reaffirm their belonging to a different community of sense, that of the Jamaican nation, they seek out some of these same areas—I have suggested that the early morning market and the street dance work as learned time-spaces where dangerous authenticity can be experienced safely through the approximation of an Uptown security aesthetics of sensory order. Here too, being able to inhabit public space while feeling comfortable and safe is central to feelings of political belonging (cf. Noble 2005), even if the political community in question is not coterminous with that of inner-city residents. Uptown and Downtown Kingstonians can occupy the same material surroundings simultaneously, but be subject to distinct processes of aesthetic interpellation.

Can these different aesthetic regimes—tightly connected to both security and political belonging—coexist without bleeding into each other? How much of an Uptown aesthetic regime do outsiders bring with them when they visit Downtown? How much of it do they lose? What residues might they leave behind? One preliminary answer might lie in current police attempts to "dismantle the garrison" and diminish the power of dons by harnessing the power of aesthetics. A clear attempt at creating dissensus among inner-city residents is the police's "gang mural removal" campaign, during which don murals or texts referencing dons were painted over in "constabulary blue" (see Figures 5.3–5.5). The building in Tivoli Gardens that had functioned as Dudus's former headquarters was similarly taken over by the police and repainted in blue and white in the same style as Jamaica's other police stations. Such interventions in the built environment are evident efforts to disrupt the dominant aesthetic, political, and security regime.

In this chapter, I have sought to elaborate how differently positioned residents experience this sensory belonging and nonbelonging in an emplaced and embodied fashion, within a violent and divided cityscape. This elaboration is a preliminary move to develop a political geography of sensation: a spatially

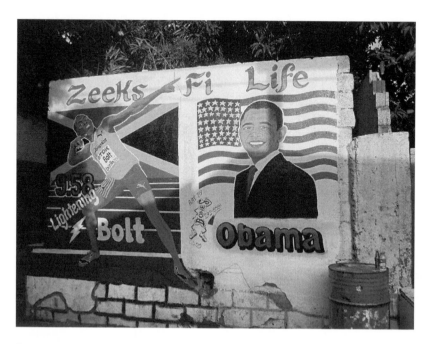

Figure 5.3 Mural celebrating neighborhood don "Zeeks," reading "Zeeks Fi [For] Life." Photograph by author.

Figure 5.4 "Zeeks Fi Life" mural, painted over. Photograph by Tracian Meikle.

Figure 5.5   Painted-over mural. Photograph by Tracian Meikle.

sensitive way of understanding how different aesthetic forms work to delineate multiple political communities, through their elicitation of emplaced experiences of fear, comfort, and longing that connect the scales of the street, the neighborhood, the city, and the nation.

NOTES

1   All names of persons used in this article are pseudonyms, as is the name of the neighborhood "Brick Town."
2   Other, slightly less porous public spaces might include museums and art galleries and certain government buildings in Downtown Kingston, as well as specific events, such as charity runs. In contrast to the market and the street dance, however, these spaces and events tend to be "made safe" by private security guards.
3   My visual analysis of these artworks is closely informed by research done by Tracian Meikle, whose forthcoming dissertation provides a detailed ethnographic and aesthetic analysis of such memorial murals.

REFERENCES

Adey, Peter. 2014. "Security Atmospheres or the Crystallisation of Worlds." *Environment and Planning D: Society and Space* 32, no. 5: 834–851.

Anderson, Ben. 2009. "Affective Atmospheres." *Emotion, Space and Society* 2, no. 2: 77–81.

Anderson, Benedict. 1991. *Imagined Communities: Reflections on the Origin and Spread of Nationalism.* Rev. ed. London: Verso.

Caldeira, Teresa. 2000. *City of Walls: Crime, Segregation and Citizenship in São Paulo.* Berkeley: University of California Press.

Carnegie, Charles V. 2017. "How Did There Come to Be a 'New Kingston'?" *Small Axe* 21, no. 3: 138–151.

Charles, Christopher, and Orville Beckford. 2012. "The Informal Justice System in Garrison Constituencies." *Social and Economic Studies* 61, no. 2: 51–72.

Clarke, Colin G. 2006. *Decolonizing the Colonial City: Urbanization and Stratification in Kingston, Jamaica.* Oxford: Oxford University Press.

Coaffee, Jon, Paul O'Hare, and Marian Hawkesworth. 2009. "The Visibility of (In)Security: The Aesthetics of Planning Urban Defenses against Terrorism." *Security Dialogue* 40, nos. 4–5: 489–511.

Ellis, Darren, Ian Tucker, and David Harper. 2013. "The Affective Atmospheres of Surveillance." *Theory and Psychology* 23, no. 6: 716–731.

Ghertner, D. Asher. 2015. *Rule by Aesthetics: World-Class City Making in Delhi.* New York: Oxford University Press.

Henriques, Julian. 2010. "The Vibrations of Affect and Their Propagation on a Night Out on Kingston's Dancehall Scene." *Body and Society* 16, no. 1: 57–89.

Hope, Donna P. 2006. "Passa Passa: Interrogating Cultural Hybridities in Jamaican Dancehall." *Small Axe* 10, no. 3: 125–139.

Jaffe, Rivke. 2010. "Ital Chic: Rastafari, Resistance and the Politics of Consumption in Jamaica." *Small Axe* 14, no. 1: 30–45.

———. 2012a. "The Popular Culture of Illegality: Crime and the Politics of Aesthetics in Urban Jamaica." *Anthropological Quarterly* 85, no. 1: 79–102.

———. 2012b. "Criminal Dons and Extralegal Security Privatization in Downtown Kingston, Jamaica." *Singapore Journal of Tropical Geography* 33, no. 2: 184–197.

———. 2013. "The Hybrid State: Crime and Citizenship in Urban Jamaica." *American Ethnologist* 40, no. 4: 734–748.

———. 2016. *Concrete Jungles: Urban Pollution and the Politics of Difference in the Caribbean.* New York: Oxford University Press.

Meyer, Birgit. 2009. "From Imagined Communities to Aesthetic Formations: Religious Mediations, Sensational Forms, and Styles of Binding." In *Aesthetic Formations: Media, Religion, and the Senses,* edited by Birgit Meyer, 1–28. Dordrecht: Springer.

Noble, Greg. 2005. "The Discomfort of Strangers: Racism, Incivility and Ontological Security in a Relaxed and Comfortable Nation." *Journal of Intercultural Studies* 26, nos. 1–2: 107–120.

Panagia, Davide. 2009. *The Political Life of Sensation*. Durham, NC: Duke University Press.

Pereira Martins, Sanne. 2009. "Uptown Top Ranking: Negotiating Middle-Class Masculinity and Sexuality in Kingston, Jamaica." MA thesis, Leiden University.

Rancière, Jacques. 2006. *The Politics of Aesthetics: The Distribution of the Sensible*. London: Continuum.

———. 2010. *Dissensus: On Politics and Aesthetics*. London: Continuum.

Saldanha, Arun. 2007. *Psychedelic White: Goa Trance and the Viscosity of Race*. Minneapolis: University of Minnesota Press.

Sives, Amanda. 2010. *Elections, Violence and the Democratic Process in Jamaica, 1944–2007*. Kingston, Jamaica: Ian Randle Publishers.

Thomas, Deborah. 2004. *Modern Blackness: Nationalism, Globalization and the Politics of Blackness in Jamaica*. Durham, NC: Duke University Press.

Trnka, Susanna, Christine Dureau, and Julie Park. 2013. "Introduction: Senses and Citizenships." In *Senses and Citizenships: Embodying Political Life*, edited by Susanna Trnka, Christine Dureau, and Julie Park, 1–32. London: Routledge.

AESTHETICS AND COMMUNITY FORMATION

6

Staging Safety in Brooklyn's Real Estate

Zaire Z. Dinzey-Flores
and Alexandra Demshock

During the winter of 2005, the popular leftist Brooklyn magazine *Stay Free!* ran a satirical flip cover for *American Gentrifier* (Hearst 2005; see Figure 6.1). The spread features a staged portrait of a white, heteronormative couple. The man, later described as an "emasculated Park Slope husband," sports a Baby-Björn carrier with a white infant inside. Hovering over the young family are explicit headlines detailing the "preoccupations" of potential Brooklyn gentrifiers, among them "BED STY: STILL TOO BLACK?" and "10 VIOLENT CRIMES YOU CAN LIVE WITH." The headlines depict two frequently codified concerns of neighborhoods in the early stages of gentrification: the demographic composition of the neighborhood (". . . TOO BLACK?") and the question of safety or concomitant violence that new, presumed white residents would have to contend with in these spaces. The images and text of the cover reveal something of the relationship between Blackness and insecurity or, alternatively, whiteness and safety that has characterized conversations about the American city for generations.

The black "Bed-Sty" alluded to on the *American Gentrifier* cover is located in central Brooklyn. Formally known as Bedford-Stuyvesant and colloquially called Bed-Stuy (rhymes with "buy"), the neighborhood would eventually, in the mid-to-late twentieth century, become home to one of the highest concentrations of black residents in the United States. The popular imaginary surrounding Bed-Stuy would also become synonymous with the image of the "dark ghetto," a lightning rod for the fears of the whiter and wealthier U.S. population (Clark 1965). The racial segregation, poverty, and urban disenfranchisement that intensified in the 1970s and 1980s marked Bed-Stuy as a black

Figure 6.1 *American Gentrifier*, the flip cover of the winter 2005 issue of *Stay Free!* magazine.

dystopia, a "scary" neighborhood, with stretches referred to as "Vietnam." The unsafe, black "Do or Die" Bed-Stuy has been elaborated through the historical layering of negative significations that have resulted in what economist Glenn Loury (2002) would call "spoiled collective identity" or the "racial stigma" of the "Black ghetto."

From Great Migration–era blockbusting and redlining to an onslaught of subprime lending that began in the 1990s (Botein 2013; Wilder 2000), the machinations of the real estate industry intimately tangled with processes of neighborhood racialization and played an important role in rendering Bed-Stuy an unthinkable geography for a white family to call home. And yet, although still predominantly black, its demographics have been dramatically shifting since the turn of the twenty-first century, characterized by sharp increases in both real estate values and the proportion of white residents, particularly in the wake of the 2008 financial meltdown and recession. Attracted by Bed-Stuy's ample supply of architecturally significant historic brownstones and by comparatively more affordable housing than Manhattan, an influx of new residents grew the white population from less than 1 percent in 1990 to 15 percent by 2010 (Gregor 2014). From the scary center of black Brooklyn to one of New York's coolest places for white people, the image of Bed-Stuy has undergone a radical change in the past decade. This chapter asks how Bed-Stuy became safe, not scary, and even cool. How is the layering of decades of negative spatial significations undone and rebranded? Given its hand in the production of the neighborhood's disinvestment, what role do the narrations of the real estate industry play in this reinvention?

"DO OR DIE" BED-STUY: THE INVENTION OF A "GHETTO"

"Sometimes it seems there is no Bedford-Stuyvesant in Brooklyn, not the way there is a Greenwich Village in Manhattan or a Middle Village in Queens," a 1985 *New York Times* article opened (Douglas 1985, B1). Its borders and boundaries, the reporter claimed, were porous and shifting, and it was rather a place "defined not by geography but by social pathology and race" (Douglas 1985, B1). The "first" black Bed-Stuy was a small community of freedmen known as Weeksville buried beneath a stampede of brownstone development that coincided with the construction of the Brooklyn Bridge in the 1880s. But that black Bed-Stuy was short lived. In fact, the two neighborhoods, Bedford and Stuyvesant Heights, that would evolve into the hyphenated moniker just before the Great Depression housed mostly well-to-do white Anglo and European immigrant homeowners. In 1920, the area was home to roughly 45,000, mostly white, residents (Charles 2010). Following the construction of the subway line between Harlem and Bedford in 1936, many black people left overcrowded upper Manhattan for more readily available housing in Bedford-Stuyvesant, while foreign-born black people simultaneously immigrated there from the Caribbean and Africa. Just as black New Yorkers made entry into the formerly white Bed-Stuy, an accelerated stream of African American migrants from the South also began to settle there. The neighborhood had attracted 65,000 black residents by 1940 (Charles 2010). By the mid-1980s, the neighborhood had become the second largest black community in the country, only surpassed by Chicago's sprawling South Side. Bed-Stuy, more important than its precise location on the map, had become "synonymous with black and has remained so ever since" (Massood 2001, 267).

During this critical juncture of racial succession, the Home Owners' Loan Corporation, created in 1933 to ease the Depression's blows, developed a set of Residential Security Maps for mortgage underwriting to classify neighborhoods based on the perceived risk of lending there (Badger 2017). Bed-Stuy, deemed a leader in "colored infiltration," received the lowest security rating (D) designated with a red line around the neighborhood, thus making it a zone within which virtually no formal mortgage lending would occur for decades—a pattern of disinvestment that itself underwrote the neighborhood's reputation as a segregated "ghetto" (Wilder 2000). These security maps "put the imprimatur of the federal government behind the proposition that the presence of some human beings was harmful" (Wilder 2000, 186). In an August 2017 *New York Times* article about the maps' enduring national effects, Bed-Stuy is offered up as a landmark case in the history of racially exclusionary finance and disinvestment that defined the redlining crisis (Badger 2017). As neglect intensified, so did crime, and "a causal connection between color and decay," between Bed-Stuy and "muggings by the 'sunburnt elements' and biological thieves alleged to be infiltrating," became naturalized (Wilder 2000, 197–198).

· Due to heightened racial stigma, real and perceived increases in crime, and the absence of residential financing, white Bed-Stuy residents fled in droves to New York's new suburbs, with over a half million departing from Brooklyn between 1950 and 1970, as roughly twenty thousand nonwhite arrivals took their place each year (Wilder 2000, 212). White residents still accounted for more than half of the neighborhood's population at midcentury, but twenty years later, as the second Great Migration began to taper, Bed-Stuy had become 84 percent black and had developed into the most overcrowded community in New York, with 450,000 people in 653 residential blocks (Davies 2013, 744; Manoni 1973). In 1966, its reputation as a blighted area drew Senator Robert F. Kennedy to take a walking tour of the neighborhood, exposing him and, in turn, the nation, to its "run-down housing, piles of refuse, abandoned buildings, and filthy streets" (Davies 2013, 736). A young Bed-Stuy homeowner in 1974 explained the tendency of crimes all over Brooklyn to be misattributed to his neighborhood: "To the outside world . . . all of Brooklyn is 'Bed-Stuy'" (quoted in Rejnis 1974, 1).

Bedford-Stuyvesant's markedness as the borough's literal dark center and its prominent position in pop cultural artifacts produced a slippage between significations of the neighborhood and that of Brooklyn more broadly. When rapper Jay-Z (1998) speaks of "Bed-Stuy, Brook-nam" taking on the world, his community becomes shorthand for (inextricably) black-and-dangerous-Brooklyn as a whole, in spite of the borough's (and even Bed-Stuy's) vastness and variability.

The Bed-Stuy conflated with a Brooklyn steeped in crack cocaine and murder in the 1980s and 1990s would undergo a major transformation—but not wholesale disappearance—in the new millennium. A black real estate agent working in the area recounted to coauthor Dinzey-Flores during neighborhood fieldwork an interaction between a young, white European woman and a young, white American man that he had overheard while sitting in a first-class seat on a flight abroad: the man told the woman that he was from New York, upon which the woman excitedly shared with him her fascination with Brooklyn. The man, a Manhattanite, was stunned as the woman made a quick transition from aspiring to visit not only Brooklyn, but more specifically "cool" Bed-Stuy. By the second decade of the twenty-first century, the narratives imbricating threat and Blackness have become pasteurized into hip versions that increasing numbers of middle-class white people find attractive. Different from Derek Hyra's (2017, 89) notion that white gentrifiers seek the thrill of proximity to urban danger by "living *The Wire*," this tamed version represents what Dinzey-Flores (unpublished) terms an "allayed whiteness": "embracing blackness in a new form . . . a twenty-first-century brand of whiteness configured with a particular appreciation of blackness and a constricted version of its spatial manifestations." Blackness repackaged into a trendy, edgy, and consumable form then displaces the significations of danger while still, by default, attributing safety to whiteness.

STAGING SAFETY

In order for Bed-Stuy to transform into a place suitable for the white *American Gentrifier* family of three, its *cool* must evolve into *safe*. In a cognitive sociological analysis of the concepts, Ruth Simpson (1996, 549) explains that "perceptions of safety and danger are 'intersubjective'—products of social construction, collective agreement, and socialization." As the unmarked signifier in the lexical pair, safety is defined as "the absence of danger," itself often a set of "inconsistent and ambiguous clues" derived from one's surroundings (Simpson 1996, 549). The instability of safety as an analytic category simultaneously presents challenges for studying the social production of symbolic safety while suggesting that those who have a stake in a shared perception of safe places are tasked with cultivating perceptions of safety and combating narratives of danger. As Wayne Brekhus (1998, 35, 44) explains, studying what is often unarticulated, unattended to, and understood to be "epistemologically unproblematic" can be difficult and requires the outlining of the unmarked phenomenon's "negative spaces."

As Simpson (1996, 551) puts it, "Perceiving any object as safe requires ignoring the potential for harm. While perceiving danger can sometimes be a simple matter of observation, perceiving safety necessarily involves rationalization," or engagement in discursive and spatial interventions into landscapes and their representations, a process that coauthor Demshock (unpublished) calls "the safety project." The markers and built manifestations of safety and danger are always social and require active maintenance and reproduction. Thus, safety's social unmarkedness necessitates that real estate professionals and homeowners highlight aesthetics, signs, and discourses of security in order for a community to maintain its reputation as a safe place and for the homes in it to retain, or even increase, their symbolic value of safety.

The real estate industry, a collaborator in perpetuating negative neighborhood stigmas through participation in activities such as redlining, slum clearance, urban renewal, and eminent domain (Connolly 2014; Gotham 2002; Satter 2009; Schafran and Wegmann 2012), now uses its power and influence in these same communities to undo the narratives of danger and blight they helped to create. At the height of the discriminatory lending that preceded the Fair Housing Act of 1968, the National Association of Realtors, through its professional code, mandated that its members restrict buyers and renters "of any race or nationality, or any individual, whose presence will clearly be detrimental to property values" in white communities (Laurenti 1960, 17). Christopher Mele (2000, 192), for example, notes how real estate professionals in New York's Lower East Side systematically encouraged disinvestment and later abandonment by promoting capital withdrawal through planned neglect and deliberate property depreciation via the absence of repair and maintenance and later through "arson-for-profit." Now, in the context of twenty-first-century redevelopment, real estate agents instead serve as important orators of safety narratives through interactions with clients, property listings, area tours, and neighborhood reports. In an era of globalized gentrification (Smith 2002), frontline real estate workers are central to rescripting crime-ridden neighborhood "stigmata" (Goffman 1963) in service of inflating property value.

How and by what built environmental and discursive mechanisms, then, does real estate move in the opposite direction, rolling back the negative ascriptions that it collaborated in deploying for decades? Here, we examine how the real estate industry participates in making a neighborhood previously labeled dangerous and insecure safe for wealthier investors and residents. What is safety, as elaborated by real estate? How is safety staged?

In order to investigate the staging of safety in Bedford-Stuyvesant, we study closely its production by real estate companies. Mark Lane, Michael Seiler, and Vicky Seiler (2015, 21, emphasis added) describe staging as "the process where a seller uses furnishings and decorations arranged in the *most universally appealing* way in the hopes of attracting the greatest number of potential buyers and thus receiving the highest possible offer price." Pat Esswein (2012, 67) elaborates: "Stagers declutter if you haven't, rearrange furniture to improve traffic flow and create a sense of spaciousness, and make sure your décor doesn't shout your personal tastes." While there is little research on the real effects of staging, Lane et al.'s (2015, 31) work shows that staging informs buyer opinion more than price: "We find that furniture quality and color choices do not appear to have a significant effect on the actual revealed market value of the property, but they do have a strong impact on the perceived livability and overall impression of the home." In other words, a potential buyer is more likely to make an offer or give positive feedback about a property when it is professionally staged. Staging in the sphere of real estate has been restricted to the treatment of interior spaces, yet we argue here that the act of organizing appearances to modify the opinions and "perceived livability" of a space can apply as much to neighborhoods as individual properties. If, in a home, interior staging takes place through narrations of a property's history and special features, decluttering, strategic lighting, and neutral furnishings, neighborhood staging takes place through the graphic presentation of favorable crime trends, narratives of neighborhood renaissance, pictures of trendy and buzzing streets, the projection of a healthy relationship between home and community, and the invocation of pop-cultural cachet. Such discursive and aesthetic staging, in home and neighborhood, informs symbolic understandings of how safety is to be read into a place.

We examine the production of safety in gentrifying Brooklyn via a set of "safety furnishings"—that is, the spatial, visual, and narrative elements, the furniture and décor, that in a neighborhood, as in an individual home, are rearranged to produce the perception of safety. We specifically consider the racial codes implicit in what are considered "universally appealing" stages by conducting content and narrative analysis of two types of data to develop a critical reading of safety staging: (1) the graphic and textual materials contained in property listings, and (2) neighborhood profiles produced and circulated by real estate companies.

We specifically analyzed property listings of one- to three-family homes for sale in four Brooklyn neighborhoods in spring of 2017. A popular real estate search engine published the listings. To provide a historical view, we compared these listings with those collected approximately two years earlier from a luxury regional real estate company. In total, we analyzed 139 property listings, including a total of eighty-two Bedford-Stuyvesant listings.[1] For comparative purposes, we analyzed listings in the demographically stable Brooklyn neighborhoods of Park Slope (thirty-nine listings), Downtown Brooklyn (four listings), and Brooklyn Heights (fourteen listings). While these other three neighborhoods have undergone gentrification in the past, they have been considered "good" neighborhoods in the real estate world for more than a decade, and for as long as twenty-five years in the case of Park Slope.

Realtors typically pack property listings with details that semiotically elaborate the home and the neighborhood. The average listing includes the property address, the list price, the number of bedrooms and bathrooms, square footage, exterior and interior photographs, and a narrative description of the property. For example, one such property listing for a brownstone in Bed-Stuy, initially listed for $3.35 million in September 2016, opens with a description of the property as "the most beautiful brownstone renovation on the market today" and gestures toward its location directly in the projected path of Brooklyn's gentrification storm, on "the cusp of Bedford Stuyvesant and Clinton Hill." Interior descriptions complement the cognitive map, which further emphasize its placement in historic Brownstone Brooklyn: "This quintessential Brooklyn home retains its original character," boasts the listing. It further emphasizes the property location's comfortable distance from the physical and sensorial hardships of "Do or Die Bed-Stuy": "For maximum occupant comfort, each floor is equipped with a security panel as well as a Nest thermostat."

In our analysis, we concentrate on such narrative descriptions and examine neighborhood descriptions of Bedford-Stuyvesant offered by five prominent real estate companies. Brokerages often provide general neighborhood profiles to provide guidance for potential buyers. We suggest that neighborhood staging takes place in property listings and in these neighborhood profiles, which often include photographs and videos that highlight the contextual packaging on which the property listings rest.

THE FURNISHINGS OF SAFETY

Real estate narratives serve as a powerful tool for constructing safety by establishing consistent sensory clues for determining a property's relative security and its prospective buyers' potential to be isolated from signs of danger (see Zeiderman, this volume). Opposite in substance but similar in form to "nuisance talk" (Ghertner 2015, 79) and "the talk of crime" (Caldeira 2000), which variously emphasize and deride the perceived disorder and unruliness associated with ungentrified urban areas, these narratives furnish safety through what we argue are six aesthetic strategies, which we inductively gleaned from the listings we analyzed: (1) designing glass-house bubbles, (2) picturing quietness, (3) creating prefabricated escape hatches, (4) technologizing aesthetics of security, (5) narratively renovating the neighborhood, and (6) applying scientific objectivity. We detail each of these strategies below, quoting directly from listings to demonstrate the performative staging of safety built up through each.

Designing Glass-House Bubbles

The listings in Bed-Stuy exhibit a persistent use of adjectives that point to expansive interiors: "vast," "open," "dramatic," "lofty." These interiors are always light filled, with copious and large "floor-to-ceiling" windows and doors "offering expansive and leafy views"; a transparent large bubble from which buyers can experience the "vastness" of the outside while staying "comfortably" and securely inside. These "bubbles" continue from the interiors of the home—the living room, the great master bedrooms, the "imposing size of bathrooms" that make you "think you are not in an urban townhouse"—to private exteriors. Inside and outside, in "private terraces," "secret gardens," and "enclosed backyards," potential buyers read the promise of "relaxing in privacy of leafy trees."

Like skilled craftsmen who blow bubbles into molten glass for artistic effect, realtors blow glass bubbles narratively to imagine a secluded and magnified expansiveness that centralizes the features of the property and offers potential residents an "oasis," a "city retreat," or an "immaculate back garden retreat." Bubbled up, these Bed-Stuy properties float away from their surroundings, offering, as one listing put it, "resource[s] [the] urban dweller will always need more of": "space," "comfort," and "warmth," which oppose or narratively isolate any association with potential lingering dangers of the neighborhood. Even though it is the home that is bubbled up and isolated, the effect—amplified through photographs emphasizing visual command over, but in clear separation from, exteriors—is that it is the outside world that is frozen.

One could argue that the same focus on spacious interiors, massive windows, and light-filled rooms is standard for real estate listings more generally. After all, darkness carries a plethora of negative connotations. Yet, the expansiveness of the interiors in Park Slope, Brooklyn Heights, and Downtown Brooklyn—neighborhoods that market consensus has deemed established and white—was hardly connected narratively to privacy. Dramatic windows were not articulated as barriers, but more as places from which to admire or take in the outside. From these light-filled "windows on the world," the imagined homeowner of a Brooklyn Heights property has her own private view of the Manhattan skyline and the Promenade, in contrast to an amorphous immediate environment of "gardens" and "trees" more typical of Bed-Stuy listings.

Thus, the big interiors with large windows open up the world rather than confine it to the home property, which is the case in the Bed-Stuy descriptions, where public space is implied as black and unsafe. Unlike the idea and articulation of suburbia as part of a tree-laden landscape where the comforts of the property extend into the surroundings, the promise of trees, "lush gardens," and greenery is "safely" contained in the immediacy of the home. For example, one Bed-Stuy listing encourages sitting by a "massive apple tree for [a] lazy afternoon of reading." The green, light-filled property boundary between the home and the neighborhood, thus, is enforced; it creates a reflection or introspective disposition rather than an open field of vision, much as bubbled glass clouds the view of what is beyond.

Picturing Quietness

In Bed-Stuy property listings, the neighborhood is silent. There are "quiet," "tree-lined streets," with "not a lot of traffic." Here, the house, not the people, is "nestled in gorgeous tree-lined" or "bucolic" blocks. Quiet is expressed as a static image, devoid of people and activity close to the home base. The sounds of the street have long been part of the way in which good neighborhoods are sonically distinguished from bad neighborhoods. Safety is evoked in silence. Characterizations of suburban safety, for example, "emphasize environmental features of peacefulness, through evocative place names, greenery, relative quiet . . . historic signifiers, rural settings, rolling hills . . . well-kept trees, bushes, and lawns, flowers and welcome mats . . . immunizing features and preventative agents against the forces of evil" (Wallace 2008, 400–401). Brooklyn real estate companies communicate quietness through images of lush vegetation, visually differentiating the hush of a white nature from the noise of a black street. Listings and neighborhood descriptions alike center the urban tree as the primary symbol of tranquility in Bed-Stuy. One listing celebrates Bed-Stuy as home to the "Greenest Block in Brooklyn." Nearly all the profiles analyzed featured at least one very still photo of a Bed-Stuy block— brownstones flanked by full, summer foliage. Even images of busy sidewalk cafés—paying customers at tables, not idle interlopers perched on stoops— convey an air of residential hush meant to suggest a nonthreatening and secure environment.

But the association of safety and silence is not universal, as scholarship and policy in environmental design has tended to emphasize (Brantingham and Brantingham 1993; Lévy-Leboyer and Naturel 1991). Residential calm can be acceptably punctuated but not wholly disrupted by the din of cultural events and upscale bars, but *noise* is a racialized sonic phenomenon. Black and brown families are noticeably absent from real estate websites' photographs of Bed-Stuy. They, we can presume, represent a source of unwelcome clamor that agents edit out of the auditory landscape of the neighborhood. Indeed, as Jennifer Lynn Stoever (2016, 2) notes, both sound and listening are racial phenomena: "White Americans often feel entitled to respect for their sensibilities, sensitivities, and tastes, and to their implicit, sometimes violent, control over the soundscape of an ostensibly 'free,' 'open,' and 'public' space." Bed-Stuy real estate listings, clearly attentive to the sensory preferences and auditory sensibilities of would-be gentrifiers, seek to picture quiet so that homeowners can imagine their sound (or silence) as being that which is heard.

Creating Prefabricated Escape Hatches

While these listings create a bubble from the immediate neighborhood, they also create what we call "prefabricated escape hatches" that promise the ability to "speedily" and "swiftly" get from the house to the "established" white-scape of Manhattan through a closely located subway. All listings in Bed-Stuy refer to the good and accessible transportation that will have you in Manhattan in "20 minutes." The listings reliably index a twenty-minute commute time, and the referent is always Manhattan (except in one case we observed, which was in Downtown Brooklyn). We characterize this mechanism as prefabricated because of its use across all properties, regardless of a listed property's actual distance from the train.

Bedford-Stuyvesant is in the shape of a triangle, with three possible primary train lines: the J/Z, the A/C, and the G trains. While there are properties that are very close to the trains, many require more than ten-minute walks or bus rides to the nearest station. And while the commute to lower Manhattan is generally short on these lines, it varies depending on whether one takes a local or express train. Furthermore, all listings boasted easy and quick accessibility to the trains, not recognizing the wide swath of commuting experiences in the neighborhood depending on house location. The importance of accessibility to Manhattan emphasizes how this neighborhood becomes attractive and safe to the degree that transportation can make the distance effaceable. Transportation offers a levitation device that whisks you from house bubble to Manhattan. Bed-Stuy, despite its former reputation as the dark ghetto, a world apart, is now within striking distance of Manhattan.

In contrast, the listings in Park Slope, Downtown Brooklyn, and Brooklyn Heights hardly cared to mention the subway. A handful of listings mentioned the subway was "close," generally not specifying the station, train, or time to anywhere. Instead, prospective residents were informed of the properties' location in "the heart of everything this thriving neighborhood has to offer."

Technologizing Aesthetics of Security

Safety was explicitly messaged in references to security systems: "security cameras," "control 4 smart system with state of the art security," "work-space and command center where the multi-camera high tech security system can be monitored," "smart home features," "ADT security system," "fence around property for privacy." Security and surveillance features—laden with physical, aesthetic, and technological value—invoke safety and insinuate a threat outside, which, in turn, reaffirms their utility and the need for their presence. In a neighborhood often unfamiliar to potential buyers and thus subject to stereotypes and preconceptions used to justify pointed security measures, these technologies promise buyers complete control and a means to futureproof themselves: they can "navigate or remotely monitor the entire house with ease and comfort" or enjoy the "same level of security, comfort, and quality" implied in more familiar neighborhoods. Threat, insecurity, and fear are housed in "secure" warm language that confers power and control on the owner and belies the very environment of danger to which it alludes. Technological advancement and modernity are locked in the formulation of these security technologies, highlighting the centrality of the latest residential design aesthetics to the consolidation of a sense of security and a techno-aesthetic feeling of pleasure in control and enjoyment in use.

Most Bed-Stuy listings obscure the explicit *securing* component of the modern security systems designed to insulate owners from implicit dangers. They do so by employing the softer language of luxury, amenity, and comfort these systems are said to provide. This sleight of hand can be seen in the juxtaposition of the security panel and Nest smart thermostat in one of the listings. As in the "Control 4 System" mentioned in one listing, these technologies promise to "make your home the smartest in the block," with "everything working together to create a more comfortable, convenient, and enjoyable home" (Knightsgate, n.d.). These technologies offer simultaneous and networked "product solutions" to "entertainment," "smart lighting," "comfort and convenience," "safety and security." In this way, security and a sense of safety are devised in a web of home amenities that not only ease the inhabitants' management and experience of the home, but also enhance the sense of power of the home's occupants while responding to modernist consumerist aspirations evidenced in the latest gadgets. Security is smart, and Bed-Stuy has smart homes, defined by a techno-aesthetic that implies user appreciation through engagement and control rather than contemplation. The pleasure of life in Bed-Stuy, aestheticized security technologies seem to suggest, comes not from reflecting on the neighborhood or mere observation, but from the making of the home and the interactive exercise of security practice. Own and command a home/neighborhood; don't just dwell in it.

The warm, fuzzy focus of these security techniques is not incidental. Realtors are selling a neighborhood with a past—a stigmatized past that they helped produce—which they now have to manage. Propagated through the evening news and, later, a litany of New York City–based crime dramas, Bed-Stuy entered the new millennium with an enduring profile of violence, drug addiction, and unemployment, dragging the symbolic and institutional weight of the 1970s heroin epidemic, the crack cocaine frenzy of the 1980s, and the murderous years of the early 1990s. To emphasize the hard edges of security technologies with words like "surveillance" and "safety" would make that history too explicit, indexing a threatening outside. Instead, the features and furnishings of the home as technologically advanced and equipped with mechanisms that cultivate a sense of control and comfort assuage possible safety concerns while avoiding direct reference to any insecurity or safety deficiency in the neighborhood. This is the difference between bulletproof glass and an inconspicuous surveillance camera—the latter communicates the same sense of added security without underscoring the threat (in this case, live ammunition). In contrast, in Park Slope, Brooklyn Heights, and Downtown Brooklyn listings, reference to security was absent from any invocation of modern amenities. Technology here rested strictly in comfort, and security was removed from the technological attributes of the desirable properties.

Narratively Renovating the Neighborhood

The real estate listings and neighborhood profiles are strategic in their presentation of the neighborhoods and reveal an awareness of the resignifications that selling property in the neighborhood requires. The property listings offer limited information on Bedford-Stuyvesant. But the succinct message, reinforced by the neighborhood summaries, is clear: it is "historic," with beautifully preserved "Gothic, Victorian and Romanesque" architecture, and it is "growing and rapidly appreciating," "burgeoning," "ever so scenic," "vibrant," with more and more restaurants and coffee shops opening every day. A good number of listings name the relevant (new) businesses, strictly confined to leisure sites and spaces of consumption—parks, restaurants, and coffee shops. Some listings even offer the names of restaurants and coffee shops that are soon-to-open amenities. The sense is of a neighborhood that will eventually (if not yet) deliver everything the homeowner desires. Be a part, one listing pleads, of "Brooklyn's dynamic, evolving cultural ecosystem," while another contends that it is "not up and coming, this neighborhood arrived and shines." Still another states that there has "never been a better time to live and play in this neighborhood." The tone is urgent, with a hint of persuasion. Like these listings, the brokerages' Bed-Stuy profiles foreground the neighborhood's long historical roots, situating the architecture and the "historic brownstones" with "highly ornamental detailing" and "classical architectural elements" in its seventeenth-century Dutch origins. A contemporary community garden is said to help preserve the area's agricultural heritage. The listings rewrite the neighborhood into popular culture through references to its gritty yet distant past, now recast in glossy packaging: Billy Joel's song "You May Be Right" (1980) (boasting of his bravery, he sings, "I walked through Bedford-Stuy alone"), Spike Lee's homage to boiling racial tensions on a hot summer's day in *Do the Right Thing* (Lee 1989), and Chris Rock's comedic reflections on his impoverished childhood in *Everybody Hates Chris* (2005–2006). These consumable depictions are presumed to be universally cool, while simultaneously pointing out long traditions of homeownership and recent gentrification.

Brief and thematically narrow narratives limit the neighborhood's history and realities to those that are amenable to preserving the glass bubble, while recognizing the need to foreground the neighborhood's history. The brevity exposes, if subtly, all apprehension. Here, what remains unsaid can reverberate as loudly as what is said. The delicately calibrated message, unlike that of the so-called stable neighborhoods, is that Bed-Stuy and its properties are being "renovated." In contrast, in Park Slope, Brooklyn Heights, and Downtown Brooklyn, homes are "restored" into their standard and essential form.

The racial significations are encoded in the language of renovation. Renovating a property or a neighborhood implies improvement and departure, a metaphorical rescue or overcoming from historical form and memories. A renovation is always aspirational, a presumed improvement or overcoming of an earlier stage or period of loss, but also always incomplete and underway. Restoration, in contrast, suggests a return to a former glory. In the practice of restoration, safety is already realized. It must simply be pulled out of the drawer, polished, and spruced up. In the practice of renovation, safety must be sought and persistently defended—it is a project in which one is invited to partake as an active agent of improvement, not just for oneself, but for a neighborhood and even community.

Applying Scientific Objectivity

Realtors also stage safety by providing addenda to their property listings, where potential buyers can do their own "objective" analysis of crime in the neighborhood. Riddled with pie charts, bar graphs, tables, and maps, these visual aids provide statistics on the neighborhood. And it is in these that we find the only direct treatment of crime, tucked at the bottom of the page, after a statistical gallery of population, demographic, employment, and educational data. What is reported is the *risk* of crime—that is, not the number of incidents reported, but rather the odds of crime being committed against property or person when compared with other zip codes. The presentation invokes a scientific rationality by offering a set of assurances about the accuracy of the data that include explanations of the sources of the numbers and a contextual description of the wider pattern of higher (not high) crime rates found in cities as compared with suburbs. The narrative presented supplements the credibility of implicitly subjective judgments by realtors when promoting a safe and "desirable" property within an "improving," but not crime-free, neighborhood.

The scientific objectivity of the presentation is mediated rhetorically and visually, even as interpretive doubts are recast in the data. At the bottom of the report, the real estate brokerage offers a caveat about the information presented, asserting that "all information presented on this web page is deemed reliable but is not guaranteed and should be independently verified by the users of this site."

Realtors have also used maps to convey an objective treatment of crime and safety. Real estate websites like Trulia (www.trulia.com) plot home listings on crime maps with the areas shaded red indicating the highest level of aggregate crime. Sorted into blocks, the red areas are deemed less safe. Evoking the residential security maps that produced redlined neighborhoods in the past, these maps fade away (become less red) from gentrifying neighborhoods. This fading-away marks these neighborhoods as formerly dangerous and in the process of improving. They do the work of staging safety objectively, as the encroaching yellow and green shading promises value appreciation (Lynch and Rasmussen 2001; Peterson and Krivo 2012; Tita, Petras, and Greenbaum 2006).

Aurora Wallace (2008, 6) describes the maps as representations of crime "congealed into a set of images that renders the space in which it occurs governable, while also providing a set of tools to the private citizen with which to gauge, and ultimately take responsibility for, their own personal safety." Her analysis points to the climate of responsibilization taking hold in the twenty-first century, in which the state seeks to "mobilise the 'active citizen'" to manage one's own basic needs, including taking steps to avoid crime dangers rather than addressing the root causes of crime (McCahill 1998, 55). Thus, "individual citizens now have the burden of using new media technology," like real estate crime maps, "to supply information for protection against danger," but also for the cultivation of symbolic safety in order to increase and maintain property values (Wallace 2008, 7). These "scientific" tools establish a cartography of safety that extends from the interior of the home to the outside, charting a secure geography reliably attainable by the resident.

SAFETY'S PROMISE OF INEQUALITY

As realtors stage safety, they signal Bedford-Stuyvesant as a prime site for development. These articulations of safety are not neutral in their invocation of the prized, racialized lifestyles that are attached to safety. Conversely, the fading red lines of Bed-Stuy represent displacements and (in)voluntary relocations of the historically black community. Absent from the neighborhood's stage are the people. The safe properties are sold as depersonalized, their built environments solely humanizing the (white) buyer seeking his/her own comfort, safety, privacy, and sound investment. If we consider the context in which safety is staged and the ensuing technologies, it is evident that selling Bedford-Stuyvesant also drives racial and class-based segregation in ways that mirror the redlining of the twentieth century. Staging rewards safe, "green" areas with additional investment and development while further marginalizing the "redlined" areas on crime maps by diverting prospective buyers and driving down prices such that the community's least privileged residents become relegated to those sections (Wallace 2008, 21; Xie and McDowall 2010). Safety staging simultaneously foregrounds bourgeois aesthetics while distancing the alleged safe place from *there*, the dangerous—darker, poorer, urban—places marked by their ubiquity in crime news, drawing boundaries between the safe space of their property and the distinctly separate locations where crime belongs or makes sense. The imperative that criminalizes Blackness and poverty and, in turn, landscapes the city to meet the demands of capital accumulation and middle-class mortgage payments, feeds off a staging of safety (Muhammad 2010; Wacquant 2001a, 2001b). The furnishings that stage safety circulate with technologies that stand in for the cartographic practice of redlining in a real estate world where safety becomes a proxy for whiteness and wealth. Blackness—physically and symbolically—and its attachment to criminality are solidly cemented *behind* the stage, relegated to dangerous "personal décor" that detrimentally affects the opinion of the properties and the neighborhood, unseen and unstated, with little to no value.

NOTE

1   Of the twenty-seven listings from the luxury real estate company from November 2014 to April 2015, seventeen listings were in Bed-Stuy, seven in Park Slope, two in Downtown Brooklyn, and one in Brooklyn Heights. Of the 112 listings sampled from the real estate search engine between March and April 2017, sixty-five describe properties in Bed-Stuy, thirty-two in Park Slope, two in Downtown Brooklyn, and fourteen in Brooklyn Heights.

REFERENCES

Badger, Emily. 2017. "How Redlining's Racist Effects Lasted for Decades." *New York Times*, August 24.

Botein, Hilary. 2013. "From Red-Lining to Subprime Lending: How Neighborhood Narratives Mask Financial Distress in Bedford-Stuyvesant, Brooklyn." *Housing Policy Debate* 23, no. 4: 714–737.

Brantingham, Patricia, and Paul Brantingham. 1993. "Nodes, Paths and Edges: Considerations on the Complexity of Crime and the Physical Environment." *Journal of Environmental Psychology* 13, no. 1: 3–28.

Brekhus, Wayne. 1998. "A Sociology of the Unmarked: Redirecting Our Focus." *Sociological Theory* 16, no. 1: 34–51.

Caldeira, Teresa P. R. 2000. *City of Walls: Crime, Segregation, and Citizenship in São Paulo.* Berkeley: University of California Press.

Charles, Mario A. 2010. "Bedford-Stuyvesant." In *The Encyclopedia of New York City*, edited by Kenneth Jackson, Lisa Keller, and Nancy Flood, 109–110. New Haven, CT: Yale University Press.

Clark, Kenneth. 1965. *Dark Ghetto: Dilemmas of Social Power.* New York: Harper and Row.

Connolly, Nathan D. B. 2014. *A World More Concrete: Real Estate and the Remaking of Jim Crow South Florida.* Chicago: University of Chicago Press.

Davies, Tom Adam. 2013. "Black Power in Action: The Bedford-Stuyvesant Restoration Corporation, Robert F. Kennedy, and the Politics of the Urban Crisis." *Journal of American History* 100, no. 3: 736–760.

Demshock, Alex. Unpublished. "The Safety Project: Real Estate Value, the Construction of Safety, and the Persistence of Housing Inequality."

Dinzey-Flores, Zaire Z. Unpublished. "Allayed Whiteness and the Racial Aesthetics of Expensive Brooklyn." Working paper, Department of Sociology, Rutgers University, last modified May 11, 2018.

Douglas, Carlyle. 1985. "In Brooklyn's Bedford-Stuyvesant, Glimmers of Resurgence Are Visible." *New York Times*, April 19.

Esswein, Pat Mertz. 2012. "How to Sell Your Home Fast." *Kiplinger's Personal Finance* 66, no. 5: 65–68.

Ghertner, D. Asher. 2015. *Rule by Aesthetics: World-Class City Making in Delhi*. New York: Oxford University Press.

Goffman, Erving. 1963. *Stigma: Notes on the Management of Spoiled Identity*. Englewood Cliffs, NJ: Prentice-Hall.

Gotham, Kevin Fox. 2002. *Race, Real Estate, and Urban Development: The Kansas City Experience, 1900–2000*. Albany: State University of New York Press.

Gregor, Alison. 2014. "Bedford-Stuyvesant: Diverse and Changing." *New York Times*, July 9.

Hearst, Andrew. 2005. "American Gentrifier." *Andrew Hearst Blog*, January 12. Accessed April 12, 2017. http://andrewhearst.com/blog/2005/01/american_gentrifier.

Hyra, Derek. 2017. *Race, Class, and Politics in the Cappuccino City*. Chicago: University of Chicago Press.

Jay-Z. 1998. "Money, Cash, Hoes." By Shawn Carter, Earl Simmons, and Kasseem Dean. Track 6 on *Vol. 2 . . . Hard Knock Life*. Roc-a-Fella Records and Def Jam Recordings.

Joel, Billy. 1980. "You May Be Right." By Billy Joel and Phil Ramone. Track 1 on Billy Joel, *Glass Houses*. Columbia Records.

Knightsgate. n.d. "Control 4." Accessed April 10, 2017. http://www.knightsgateuk.com /control-4.

Lane, Mark, Michael Seiler, and Vicky Seiler. 2015. "The Impact of Staging Conditions on Residential Real Estate Demand." *Journal of Housing Research* 24, no. 1: 21–36.

Laurenti, Luigi. 1960. *Property Values and Race: Studies in Seven Cities*. Berkeley: University of California Press.

Lee, Spike, dir. 1989. *Do the Right Thing*. 40 Acres and a Mule Filmworks. Los Angeles: Universal Pictures.

Lévy-Leboyer, Claude, and Véronique Naturel. 1991. "Neighborhood Noise Annoyance." *Journal of Environmental Psychology* 11: 75–86.

Loury, Glenn. 2002. *The Anatomy of Racial Inequality*. Cambridge, MA: Harvard University Press.

Lynch, Allen, and David Rasmussen. 2001. "Measuring the Impact of Crime on Housing Prices." *Applied Economics* 33: 1981–1989.

Manoni, Mary H. 1973. *Bedford-Stuyvesant: The Anatomy of a Central City Community*. New York: Quadrangle.

Massood, Paula J. 2001. "Which Way to the Promised Land? Spike Lee's Clockers and the Legacy of the African American City." *African American Review* 35, no. 2: 263–279.

McCahill, Michael. 1998. "Beyond Foucault: Towards a Contemporary Theory of Surveillance." In *Surveillance, Close Circuit Television and Social Control*, edited by Clive Norris, Jade Moran, and Gary Armstrong, 41–65. Aldershot, UK: Ashgate.

Mele, Christopher. 2000. *Selling the Lower East Side: Culture, Real Estate and Resistance in New York City*. Minneapolis: University of Minnesota Press.

Muhammad, Khalil Gibran. 2010. *The Condemnation of Blackness: Race, Crime, and the Making of Modern Urban America*. Cambridge, MA: Harvard University Press.

Peterson, Ruth, and Lauren Krivo. 2012. *Divergent Social Worlds: Neighborhood Crime and the Racial-Spatial Divide*. New York: Russell Sage Foundation.

Rejnis, Ruth. 1974. "Young People Coming Home to 'Bed-Stuy.'" *New York Times*, October 20.

Rock, Chris. 2005–2006. *Everybody Hates Chris*. Aired September 2005–May 2006 on UPN.

Satter, Beryl. 2009. *Family Properties: Race, Real Estate, and the Exploitation of Black Urban America*. New York: Metropolitan Books.

Schafran, Alex, and Jake Wegmann. 2012. "Restructuring, Race, and Real Estate: Changing Home Values and the New California Metropolis, 1989–2010." *Urban Geography* 33: 630–654.

Simpson, Ruth. 1996. "Neither Clear nor Present: The Social Construction of Safety and Danger." *Sociological Forum* 11, no. 3: 549–562.

Smith, Neil. 2002. "New Globalism, New Urbanism: Gentrification as Global Urban Strategy." *Antipode* 34: 427–450.

Stoever, Jennifer Lynn. 2016. *The Sonic Color Line: Race and the Cultural Politics of Listening*. New York: New York University Press.

Tita, George, Tricia Petras, and Robert Greenbaum. 2006. "Crime and Residential Choice: A Neighborhood Level Analysis of the Impact of Crime on Housing Prices." *Journal of Quantitative Criminology* 22: 299–317.

Wacquant, Loïc. 2001a. "Deadly Symbiosis: When Ghetto and Prison Mesh." *Punishment and Society* 3, no. 1: 95–133.

———. 2001b. "The Penalization of Poverty and the Rise of Neo-Liberalism." *European Journal on Criminal Policy and Research* 9: 401–412.

Wallace, Aurora. 2008. "Things Like That Don't Happen Here: Crime, Place and Real Estate in the News." *Crime, Media, Culture* 4, no. 3: 395–409.

Wilder, Craig. 2000. *A Covenant with Color: Race and Social Power in Brooklyn*. New York: Columbia University Press.

Xie, Min, and David McDowall. 2010. "The Reproduction of Racial Inequality: How Crime Affects Housing Turnover." *Criminology* 48, no. 3: 865–896.

Z. Z. DINZEY-FLORES, A. DEMSHOCK

7

Expecting the Worst

Active-Shooter Scenario Play in American Schools

Rachel Hall

A flier titled "A Brief History of School Safety Drills" is sent home at the beginning of the fall semester to the parents of children attending public schools in an affluent school district in the Northeast. The flier informs parents that "the type and frequency have changed over the years, but the purpose of the practice of drills has always been the same: to ensure students and staff are prepared to quickly make their way to safety in the event of an emergency situation" (Capital Region BOCES 2018). While it is true that public schools in the United States have observed safety drills since the mid-twentieth century, it is not the case that the purpose of those drills has remained constant over time. The earliest such rehearsals for emergencies were fire drills and regionally specific weather drills such as tornado or earthquake drills. During the height of the Cold War, students made like Bert the Turtle in duck-and-cover drills, during which they rehearsed for nuclear war by sheltering in place under their desks. In these historical examples drawn from the twentieth century, school safety drills involved rehearsing the organized movement of students to positions of relative safety within or without the building and assuming bodily postures intended to protect against structural and corporeal vulnerabilities. But in recent years, school safety drills designed to address the threat of mass shootings emphasize aesthetic as much as, if not more than, logistical training. First implemented in response to the mass shooting at Sandy Hook Elementary School in 2012, the newest genre of school safety drills simulates the event of an armed and dangerous intruder on school grounds and often involves the participation of local law enforcement agencies, hired actors, and student volunteers.

Consider the following description of an "active-shooter" drill conducted at an elementary arts magnet school in Goose Creek, South Carolina (Thompson 2013, paras. 1–3):

> "I want to see my kids! Bang! Bang!" the man shouted as he stormed into the front office of a South Carolina elementary school and pointed a handgun at a secretary and custodian. Both went limp at the verbal gunshots, and the "shooter," a police officer taking part in a school safety drill, continued his rampage.
>
> While an assistant principal dialed 911, the gunman took aim at two students and their principal. All fell to the floor with bloody, fake wounds.
>
> "We are in lockdown," announced a woman over the public address system at Howe Hall Arts-Infused Magnet School in Goose Creek, S.C. Students and teachers hunkered silently in darkened classrooms away from closed blinds and locked doors, while police officers with rifles worked their way through hallways decorated with student art.

Using methods derived from the theater, active-shooter drills attempt to simulate, as realistically as possible, acts of gun violence on school campuses. They rely on scripting, mise-en-scène, blocking, props and makeup, as well as improvisation on the part of the students and teachers emplaced within these scenarios. The designers of these experiences understand the realist aesthetics of active-shooter drills not in terms of enhancing the play or entertainment aspects of the experience but as a means of heightening the seriousness of the play for participants so as to improve the quality of their training.

The logic of "preparedness" that undergirds these drills has it that the more closely the sensory and emotional contours of a real event can be simulated, the better prepared that community will be so as not to freak out when it actually happens to them in the future. For example, some parents in a Chicago suburb were upset to learn that Cary-Grove High School would be running an active-shooter drill in January 2013 in which someone would be shooting blanks in the hallways "in an effort to provide our teachers and students some familiarity with the sound of gunfire" (CBS News 2013). Sharon Miller, a parent who objected to the use of blanks during the drill, said, "They run fire drills all the time, but they don't run up and down the hallway with a flamethrower" (CBS News 2013). Miller's analogy provides a concise articulation of the difference between traditional school safety drills and the new paradigm in school security. In the conventional model of fire drills, the point is to practice the logistics of getting students and teachers out of the building quickly and in a calm and orderly fashion, not to impart the experience of *what it feels like* to be in a building on fire. Active-shooter scenarios simulate the unwanted event, which puts the accent on the aesthetic and sensory experience of participants.

Active-shooter drills are merely one element in a broader aesthetics of school security in the twenty-first century. First, in active-shooter scenario play, the unwanted event is understood as a problem of human performance on the part of potential victims and, consequently, requires experiential training that helps security experts and laypersons alike to calibrate local vulnerabilities. Schools hire security experts or partner with local police, who run realist simulations of mass shootings so that students and teachers might learn how to perform better under duress. Paramilitary in tone, active-shooter drills introduce uncertainty and chaos into school communities so that the members might experience something akin to the worst-case scenario and thereby inoculate themselves against the prospect of being emotionally and psychologically overwhelmed when the real thing occurs. Drills are followed by a performance review in which representatives of local law enforcement or privately contracted security companies evaluate how students and teachers performed under simulated distress. To date, active-shooter drills are mandatory in two-thirds of U.S. states.

Second, the unwanted event of a school shooting requires "target hardening," or making schools function more like fortresses, which involves well-designed architectural and landscape fixes in affluent districts and increased labor for teachers in less flush districts, who are expected to act as sentries, vigilantly monitoring the school and its grounds. What Jonathan Massey (2014) has termed "risk design" remakes the built environment of some communities in preparation for the next attack, embedding the armature for future attacks within a building's infrastructure. Elsewhere, I have described the redesign of Sandy Hook Elementary School as an example of risk design nested within resilient design (Hall 2020). "Embedded security" renders risk design invisible to children, even as it reassures adults in the know.

Third, teachers and students are asked to continuously screen the student body for threats. More specifically, they are encouraged to practice behavioral and psychological profiling of their community and report their observations and feelings to school resource officers (armed members of the local police force with an on-campus presence), so that potentially threatening students can be removed from the community *before* violence erupts. For example, a public service announcement produced by a nonprofit group called The Sandy Hook Promise dramatizes how high school students missed the killer in their midst. The ad runs the same sequence of shots twice in quick succession. The first time through, a formulaic school-year montage tells the story of a budding romance. The second time through, the ad reveals an alienated student plotting a mass shooting in the background of the young lovers, whom viewers mistook for the main characters the first time through. The tone of the ad is admonishing: if only viewers had been paying closer attention to what was clearly visible in each shot, disaster might have been averted.

This chapter focuses on the first of these approaches to school security: calibrating vulnerabilities. In what follows, I argue that active-shooter drills constitute a new, performance paradigm in school security. I describe and analyze how communities across the United States engage in active-shooter scenario play in an effort to inoculate themselves against the unwanted event of a school shooting. The chapter asks and attempts to answer the following questions: To what are we to attribute this shift in school security, from logistics to aesthetics? By what logic of governance is a live simulation of a mass killing spree on school grounds an appropriate or effective means of addressing the problem of gun violence in our society? And what cultural lessons are imparted to the students, who have no choice but to participate in the training process?

THE PERFORMANCE PARADIGM IN SCHOOL SECURITY

The performance paradigm in school security designs and runs simulations of terrifying scenarios in order to teach students and teachers how to perform better under duress. Proponents of scenario play extol the value of experiential learning. As Diana Taylor (2009, 1888–1889) observes of scenario thinking, "The basic idea, that people learn, experience, and come to terms with past and future behaviors by physically doing them, trying them on, acting them through, and acting them out—is the theory of ritual, older than Aristotle's theory of mimesis and as new as theories of mirror neurons." Preparedness training values verisimilitude. The more faithfully simulations approximate what it's like to actually be victimized by gun violence, the more prepared the students will be when the real thing occurs (see Figure 7.1).

The performance paradigm in school security began as a response to the mass shooting at Columbine High School in Colorado in 1999. At that time, most states started requiring schools to implement emergency management plans capable of dealing with disaster scenarios ranging from the traditional fire and weather events to school shooting prevention and response training

Figure 7.1   Area police bust in as students at Cuba-Rushford High School in Cuba, New York, take cover during an active-shooter drill at the school on April 4, 2013. The session was the Cuba Police Department's response to the December 2012 massacre in Newtown, Connecticut. Photograph by Bob Clark/Olean.

(Thompson 2013). The performance paradigm is firmly entrenched in a risk management framework and cues off of the professional norms of threat assessment as practiced by the Secret Service. In response to the mass shooting at Columbine, the Secret Service (in collaboration with the Department of Education) conducted the Safe School Initiative, a study of school shootings since the earliest identified event in 1974 through June 2000. The Safe School Initiative culminated in *Threat Assessment in Schools: A Guide to Managing Threatening Situations and to Creating Safe School Climates* (Fein et al. 2004). Other federal resources for retooling human behavior for the age of risk management include those provided by the Department of Homeland Security, which provides funding for and training in emergency preparedness. Through its Office of Safe and Healthy Students, the U.S. Department of Education offers resources and funding opportunities in emergency planning, ranging from managing MRSA skin infections to crisis planning. The Federal Emergency Management Association provides a toolkit of resources in its Multi-Hazard Emergency Planning for Schools course, which includes scripted exercises, drills, workshop materials, and a range of disaster scenarios.

More recently and in response to the mass shooting at Sandy Hook, the trend in school security is to implement "intruder drills." In 2013, ten states passed legislation updating policy on school security, mandating "intruder" and/or "active-shooter drills" every semester or school year. Many more states have since adopted the drills. Currently, two-thirds of U.S. public schools run the most extreme version of "intruder" drills, otherwise known as "active-shooter drills" (Moser 2016). Intruder drills range from "soft" and "hard" lockdowns (also known as reverse-evacuation or shelter-in-place drills) to "active shooter" or "code red" drills. The difference between a "soft" and "hard" lockdown is somewhat akin to the difference between a tornado watch and a tornado warning. "Soft" lockdowns imply that there is no immediate, identified threat. During a "soft" lockdown students and teachers shelter in place, while designated school safety officials sweep the school. Participants in "soft" lockdowns know that this is a drill. This is only a drill. A "hard" lockdown indicates an immediate, known threat. In other words, this is not a drill. In the case of a "hard" lockdown, all students and staff shelter in place and await the arrival of first responders.

The character of drills varies greatly from one state to another. For example, California Assembly Bill 549 mentions the promotion of school safety, but it "prioritizes mental health services and intervention services, restorative and transformative justice programs, and positive behavior interventions and support" (California Assembly Bill 549). By comparison, Alabama House Bill 91 is more aligned with the security culture of terrorism prevention. It requires the implementation of Code Red School Safety Plans. Cueing off of the color-coded Terror Alert Threat Level system implemented by the Bush administration and phased out by the Obama administration, this plan requires Alabama schools to run code red safety alert drills during the first six weeks of fall and spring semesters.

Developed in the context of a war on terror, active-shooter drills draw on the genealogy of war games. In terms of historical precedent, the closest comparison would be large-scale theatrical civil defense drills run in the United States, Britain, and Canada at the height of the Cold War. Tracy Davis (2007) provides a deft analysis of those drills as rehearsals for nuclear war. But in the post–Cold War era, the keywords are no longer "rehearsal" and "deterrence" but rather "simulation" and "preparedness," where preparedness has expanded from the domain of logistics and the material preparations associated with the bomb shelter or storm evacuation plan (i.e., stocking the pantry, putting together a first aid kit, mapping an escape route, or acquiring a generator, etc.) to the realms of human behavior and affect. The goal of active-shooter simulations is "target hardening," where the targets are human beings. Preparedness training borrows the language of target hardening from architecture. Like the built environment of the school, the people who use the space must also be hardened. Much as emergency medical technicians, police, and firefighters and members of the military currently undergo routine active-shooter training, so must members of the "education corps."

Although active-shooter drills have genealogical ties to Cold War civil defense drills, they are referred to by crisis management experts and school officials alike not in terms of the theatrical metaphor of rehearsal popular during the Cold War era—which maintains a firm distinction between practice for and performance of the main event—but rather in terms of the military and video gaming metaphors of drills and simulations—where training for and engaging in warfare are understood to exist on a continuum of sensory experience (Brady 2015). The difference between "rehearsal" and "simulation" is not merely semantic but also historical. It corresponds to the shift delineated by Brian Massumi (2005) from prevention to preemption: "Prevention corresponds to neoliberal Cold War politics. Preemption does not prevent, it effects. It induces the event, *in effect*. Rather than acting in the present to avoid an occurrence in the future, preemption brings the future into the present. It makes present the future consequences of an eventuality that may or may not occur, indifferent to its actual occurrence. The event's consequences precede it, as if it had already occurred." Preemption cues off of risk indicators. Massumi offers the example of a financial expert or cable TV host expressing anxiety about the economy. This indicator of trouble on the horizon produces widespread panic, which dramatically effects the direction of global markets. In the context of the performance paradigm of school security, preemption induces the future sensory consequences of acts of gun violence that may or may not occur.

The notion that highly realistic simulations make for more prepared students means that the designers of performed experience rely heavily on the realist conventions of fictional genres that traffic in gun violence. Scripting and enactment of active-shooter scenario play are influenced by the adult and older child participants' consumption of fictional portrayals of law-and-order and suspense genres. That is, those who have consumed TV programs and films within these media genres know what an armed intruder looks like, how he comports himself, how he negotiates the space that he is traversing, how he catches his victims unawares, how his victims shrink from him in terror or perform heroic hostage negotiations in which cooler heads prevail. School districts in Illinois, Tennessee, North Carolina, and Washington are among those that have used mock shooters to heighten the dramatic realism of the drills (Thompson 2013). In some cases, schools hire professional actors, who scream at the participants while firing blanks. Other schools have hired actors to play the role of distraught, panicked parents, who arrive at the school and attempt to physically force their way into the school in order to find their children. Still other schools have gone so far as to incorporate special effects, using makeup and fake blood to simulate gunshot wounds. For example, an Indiana school ran a shooting drill with fake blood and a body count (Goldstein 2013). While some schools have incorporated fake blood into their simulations of gun violence, the debt to fictional portrayals of gun violence goes largely unacknowledged in order to sustain the collective illusion that active-shooter scenario play soberly references an external reality of gun violence, rather than participating in the pleasures produced by fictional portrayals of gun violence.

There is a correlation between active involvement from local law enforcement agencies and the trend toward more elaborate simulations of school shootings and terrorist attacks. The dramatic tension of active-shooter simulations increases accordingly. At a drill in Hudson Falls, New York, local police officers wearing body armor and carrying unloaded guns played opposite an actor hired to portray a hostage taker (Thompson 2013). The largest and most expensive school shooter drill ever conducted was staged at Liberty Middle School in West Orange, New Jersey, in August 2013. The scenario was as follows: four gunmen enter the school and open fire. Teachers and students hide in their classrooms. The cops arrive on the scene, followed by a SWAT team. A few minutes later, fireworks exploded from a car parked in the school lot to simulate the detonation of an improvised explosive device. The script called for the school principal to be shot and killed. It also featured an actor, who played the role of a distraught parent, who was trying to get inside the school to his thirteen-year-old son as the gunmen open fire. Sergeant John Morella of the West Orange Police Department said his agency worked with state and federal authorities, and the drill was funded by the Department of Homeland Security to the tune of $140,000. Fox News (2013) reported that a video recording of the drill could be used to train law enforcement around the country to deal with similar types of events.

Private companies are also getting involved and are marketing their services as a kinder, gentler version of what local law enforcement provides. Code Red Training Associates, Inc., describes itself as a service provider to school administrators faced with the "daunting" task of implementing emergency preparedness programs. A producer of school shooter simulations, Code Red Training Associates founder Carla Holtzclaw has coordinated active shooter/terrorist simulations involving 700 to 6,500 students, educators, parents, law enforcement, fire departments, hospitals, and Office of Emergency Services. According to her biography, she has also served as an evaluator for natural disaster and bioterrorist exercises. Additionally, she has served as the principal facilitator for actual critical incident debriefings that further inform law enforcement and education professionals in the important work of school safety. The company positions its programs as moderate by comparison to programs designed by law enforcement agencies. Holtzclaw told a contributor to NBC's *Today Show* that there are three kinds of code red drills (Horn 2011). The first kind—those designed by law enforcement officers—provide "heightened anxiety training" and are "inappropriate for schools." She criticizes these drills as unacceptable and argues, "All that does is to train children (and teachers) to be fearful and feel like victims, waiting for police to rescue them." The second kind of code red drill is the SWAT approach, which encourages teachers and students to take the offensive with a potential shooter. The third kind—and best according to Holtzclaw—offers a partnership between her company and police procedures, which is focused on the needs of schools. In other words, her company's website advertises its product as unique in the market because "our Code Red Lockdown Protocols are the only Armed Intruder/Active Shooter school response program that is fully integrated with law enforcement's post-Columbine first responder procedures while focused on the realities and needs of the classroom."[1] While the company's sales pitch is that its program is just right: not too anxiety-producing or vigilante, a major component of its training program is designed unpredictability.

According to its website, "Code Red Training Associates strongly encourages schools to redesign their drills to actually practice the unpredictability of natural or man-made disasters. Initial steps should include blocking a customary evacuation route so that teachers and students have to identify and use a secondary route. A few students can be tapped on the shoulder and 'hidden' so that roll taking takes on increased importance." The company accuses the police of producing anxiety and yet its program calls for built-in uncertainty, and one of its proudest offerings is a large-scale simulation of a school shooter or terrorist attack on a school.

Whether scripted by local law enforcement officers or private companies, active-shooter simulations design uncertainty, and therefore genuine suspense, into the experience. Unannounced drills are a form of what Richard Schechner calls "dark play" (Schechner 2013, 118–119). In dark play, not all of the players know that what they are involved in is only a game or, in the parlance of school safety drills, just a simulation. In fact, the risk management logic around disaster simulation has it that the surprise element is necessary in order to come as close as possible to simulating a real event. In El Paso, Texas, one school set up a surprise lockdown simulation, meaning that students were not informed that what was happening was only a drill. The surprise drill upset some parents, who received panicked text messages from their children. The superintendent of schools defended the surprise drill, arguing that if you warn too many teachers and students ahead of time then the simulation is not effective (Goldstein 2013). In other words, the realism of the simulation refers as much, if not more, to the feelings conjured up in participants as to the look of gun violence.

There has been some acknowledgment that such drills could raise mental health issues, but only with respect to students with mental disabilities. Public School 79 in East Harlem, which serves students ranging in age from twelve to twenty-one, ran a surprise lockdown drill in December 2012, less than a week after the shooting at Sandy Hook. The drill caused alarm among teachers and students alike. One teacher dialed 911 and police officers showed up on the scene thinking that the school was under immediate threat. The *New York Times* reported that the school serves three hundred students with special needs, including those with emotional disabilities. The lockdown drill began when a woman's voice came over the school PA system saying, "'Shooter,' or 'intruder,' and 'get out, get out, lockdown.'" One staff member told the *Times* that it was hard to tell if the woman speaking was actually talking to a gunman or to teachers and students throughout the school. A spokesperson for the New York City Education Department said that they were looking into how the drill was conducted. According to the *Times*, the school's principal declined to comment (Baker and Vadukul 2012). In this case, the surprise drill prompted an investigation because the student population is coded as uniquely vulnerable to the mental effects of simulation. The same concerns are not raised on behalf of children in general.

THE STRATEGIC PERMEABILITY OF MIMETIC PLAY

I refer to active-shooter drills as "scenario play," rather than "drills" because I want to stress the aesthetic and symbolic dimensions of these performances. Thus far, the exclusive focus on the presumed instrumentality of active-shooter scenario play has enabled its broad implementation in U.S. public schools to go uncontested. Performance studies scholarship provides resources for understanding these cultural practices otherwise and in a way that opens them up to contestation. Diana Taylor's concept of the scenario, in particular, is helpful for analyzing the aesthetic dimensions of active-shooter simulations, and provides a vocabulary for talking about the conceptual and political work that they do. Taylor (2009, 1888) describes scenarios as frameworks for thinking and argues that scenarios have become "the privileged site for modeling a wide range of practices, from theatrical as-if simulations of catastrophic events such as nuclear war to hypothetical what-if setups such as a ticking bomb to acts of torture . . . to scenarios that aim to heal victims by working through trauma to conflict-resolution preparation, such as *Virtual Peace*, which trains peacekeepers in an immersive, multi-sensory game-based environment that simulates real disaster relief and conflict resolution." If scenarios are *both* frameworks for thinking *and* the privileged site for modeling all manner of events—desirable and undesirable—then scenario play simultaneously renders a particular version of reality and attempts to rework that version of reality into an alternate one.

Taylor's (2003) earlier work on scenarios is concerned with the ways in which scenarios preserve culturally specific imaginaries. The repeated reactivation of scenarios drawn from the distant past (e.g., the scenario of colonial encounter or the frontier scenario) keeps those cultural imaginaries alive and well in the present. Taylor endeavors to make room for embodied acts of historical transmission (the repertoire) alongside the enduring artifacts of what traditionally counts as historical evidence among European cultures (the archive). In this context, she describes scenarios as "culturally specific imaginaries—sets of possibilities, ways of conceiving conflict, crisis, or resolution—activated with more or less theatricality. Unlike trope, which is a figure of speech, theatricality does not rely on language to transmit a set pattern of behavior or action" (Taylor 2003, 13). Instead of privileging texts and narratives, she argues, "we could also look to scenarios as meaning-making paradigms that structure social environments, behaviors, and potential outcomes" (Taylor 2003, 28).

Perhaps most pertinent to the present discussion of scenario play, Taylor (2003, 32) writes that scenarios work through "reactivation rather than duplication" and are, therefore, "not necessarily or even primarily mimetic." This distinction makes sense in the context of Taylor's attempt to legitimate the repertoire through a theorization of embodied acts of historical transfer. The point of her project is to challenge the influence of Western colonial aesthetics and epistemologies on contemporary historiography. I agree with her assertion that scenario play is not straightforwardly mimetic—in the narrow sense of a bounded and faithful imitation of an external reality. But I want to insist that when scenario play is used to model unwanted futures, it engages mimesis in multiple and contradictory ways. A theorization of scenario play in terms of mimesis is crucial to understanding how it becomes self-justifying and, therefore, postpolitical or beyond debate. When scenario play works on the future, simulations of unwanted events are neither duplications nor reactivations of tragic historical events; rather, simulations of unwanted events are dreadful, self-propagating cultural imaginaries.

Stephen Halliwell's (2002) reconceptualization of the history of mimesis in Western art is helpful for thinking through the contradictory ways in which scenario play engages mimesis. Drawing primarily on Plato's and Aristotle's understandings of mimesis and Goethe's writings on aesthetics, Halliwell argues that mimesis is a double-faced and ambiguous concept. Debates have been organized around the polarity between outward-looking mimetic works of art and the internal organization of works of art. In the first case, art can be assessed in terms of how faithfully it renders the real. In the second case, art must be believable on its own terms and according to its internal system of rules. Halliwell encapsulates this tension in terms of competing models of mimesis, which he terms "world-reflecting" and "world-simulating." According to Halliwell, the power of mimetic works of art derives from (1) their potency as communication media that offer a compelling worldview and (2) their capacity to psychologically affect audiences. It is for this reason, he notes, that concepts of mimesis return us, again and again, to interrogations of the relationship "between the world inside and the world outside the mimetic work" (Halliwell 2002, 22). These questions are especially pressing in the case of active-shooter scenario play. It is in the language of mimesis, understood as world-reflecting, that gun-violence preparedness makes its case. The rationale for conducting these drills (over and over again) relies on a mimetic understanding of active-shooter scenario play by reference to an external reality of gun violence, which is conceptualized as a general and increasingly common social problem that is largely unavoidable. And scenario play mandates that students and teachers enter the world of the mimetic work, based on references to an external reality of gun violence, and routinely play the role of its virtual victims in the here and now.

Scenario play's two-faced relationship to mimesis—*both* world-reflecting *and* world-simulating—is exemplary of what Michel Foucault (2007, 35) termed "the apparatus of security," which corresponds to a form of governance that understands the governed within their milieu: "Security will try to plan a milieu in terms of events or series of events or possible elements, of series that will have to be regulated within a multivalent and transformable framework." In short, the milieu appears as a field of intervention from the perspective of governance. And what Taylor calls the scenario might also be called the planned (or partially scripted) milieu. It is precisely through the yoking together of two different types of mimesis, which roughly correspond to the distinction between the milieu (world-reflecting) and the planned milieu (world-simulating), that the dreadful cultural imaginaries informing active-shooter simulations become self-propagating.

For Foucault, governance within the apparatus of security must let go of moral judgments about the reality to be reworked, the better to make it function in a more desirable fashion. If the apparatus of discipline operates within spaces of enclosure and exercises judgment regarding what constitutes a good or a bad object, a desirable or undesirable behavior, the apparatus of security suspends judgment in order to understand the milieu in all of its complexity and in order to watch scenarios unfold: "What is involved is . . . standing back sufficiently so that one can grasp the point at which things are taking place, whether or not they are desirable. This means trying to grasp them at the level of their nature, or let's say—this word not having the meaning we now give it—grasping them at the level of their effective reality" (Foucault 2007, 69). If governance aspires to grasp events at the level of their effective reality, there is little room for governance to render moral or aesthetic judgments on the field to be governed. And yet, the planned milieu, or scenario, is a work of invention, if not a mimetic representation, per se.

The question of whether active-shooter scenario play is world-reflecting or world-simulating is a complicated one. The paradox of security is that it treats the unwanted event as immanent to the milieu to be governed in order to make it available to techniques of governance and yet, in so doing, renders the reality of the unwanted event indisputable: "The mechanism of security works on the basis of this reality, by trying to use it as a support and make it function, make its components function in relation to each other" (Foucault 2007, 69). Within the apparatus of security, governance accedes to the reality of the unwanted event, which cannot be prevented or prohibited because it is already a component of the social and environmental milieu under analysis. The operative metaphor of security is inoculation: "The essential function of security is to respond to a reality in such a way that this response cancels out the reality to which it responds—nullifies it, or limits, checks, or regulates it. I think this regulation *within* the element of reality is fundamental in apparatuses of security" (Foucault 2007, 69, emphasis added).

From the perspective of governance, the unwanted event of a mass shooting—not to mention the gun (or guns) used to accomplish it—are already part of the field of intervention. And it is precisely at this point that we gain access to the political aspect of active-shooter scenario play. In my reading of Foucault's lectures collected in *Security, Territory, Population*, security's reliance upon reality as both support for governance and object of intervention naturalizes those elements of the milieu that might otherwise appear political and historical. Foucault (2007, 70) understands the interplay of reality with itself as the political technique of liberalism: "Only ever situating oneself in this interplay of reality with itself is, I think, what the physiocrats, the economists, and the eighteenth century political thought understood when it said that we remain in the domain of physics, and that to act in the political domain is still to act in the domain of nature." He goes on to say: "The game of liberalism— not interfering, allowing free movement, letting things follow their course; *laisser faire, passer et aller*—basically and fundamentally means acting so that reality develops, goes its way, and follows its own course according to the laws, principles, and mechanisms of reality itself" (Foucault 2007, 70). Think, for a moment, of the familiar argument against banning assault weapons: "I don't care what you do, bad guys will still get their hands on guns." A sentiment that is often followed by the assertion that "the only way to stop a bad guy with a gun is a good guy with a gun."

THE AESTHETICS AND ETHICS OF RESPONSIBLE GUN OWNERSHIP

Constructed as a neoliberal problem of freedom—to bear arms, buy assault weapons, conceal and carry guns, etc.—gun violence is not about guns because they are already assumed to circulate within the milieu to be governed. The problem is that we need to tweak the scenario; we need a planned milieu. The coming crisis must be set within a particular milieu, "our" community, scripted as it might occur within one of "our" schools—the bones of which we know so well—and cast with "our" teachers, administrators, mental health providers, police, and kids, precisely because the unwanted event and the instruments used to carry it out are already part of the scenario.

Framed as a neoliberal problem of freedom, gun violence is only a problem when "bad guys" do it. Gun violence appears in neoliberal discourse as something that morally objectionable or emotionally unstable people do. Defense of the free circulation of guns rests on a purportedly *moral* distinction—between those who are capable of handling guns responsibly and those who are incapable of doing so—but, in practice, it rests on an *aesthetic* distinction—between "good guys" and "bad guys." In the rhetoric of responsible gun ownership, "responsible" often serves as a euphemism for white, male, adult, and rural or suburban. The rhetoric of responsible gun ownership presumes a shared, white supremacist aesthetic regarding the types of people presumed capable of exercising the rational use of force versus those presumed to use violence in a fundamentally barbaric and/or animalistic manner. A favorite National Rifle

Association slogan—to which "arm teachers," President Trump's controversial policy solution, alludes—is that the only effective response to a bad guy with a gun is a good guy with a gun. The images of good and bad guys thus conjured up are racialized in a manner that extends beyond the color of their hats. To bring this into sharper relief, consider the National Rifle Association's stunning silence in the Philando Castile case, where a permit-holding gun owner, who calmly informed police that he was armed and had a permit, was shot to death in front of his girlfriend and child during a routine stop for a broken tail light. The case has much to tell us about the racialized aesthetics of "responsible" gun ownership in America today: which gun owners' rights children are protecting by routinely practicing victimization by gun violence in their schools, and which gun owners can neither reach for a permit nor fail to reach for it when under the point of a gun held by a terrified and armed white police officer.

A bumper sticker spotted on a truck outside of a veterans' hospital succinctly communicates the ways in which racism and the gun lobby align in this country. Using the black and white contrast and font familiar from Black Lives Matter visuals, the sticker features a silhouetted graphic of an assault rifle with a scope next to the text that reads: "All Rifles Matter." Read as a mocking response to the Black Lives Matter campaign, it is not too much of a stretch to interpret the bumper sticker as an expression of support for private ownership of assault weapons, which doubles as an active threat issued to the black lives indirectly referenced. The message is double voiced and partisan. It speaks to two audiences at once, and it understands those audiences as engaged in an ongoing, armed conflict.

President Trump alluded to the gendered aesthetics of responsible gun ownership in the wake of the Parkland shooting. As noted above, he proposed arming school teachers and other staff members with guns as an appropriate means of preventing further mass shootings on school campuses. When teachers objected to his proposal on the grounds that they did not want to be armed and that such a policy misses the spirit in which they entered into the field of education, the president responded by feminizing education, saying that most teachers would not prove "capable" handlers of guns anyway. But, he went on to say, perhaps janitors could do the job. The president offered no response to the parents of African American schoolchildren who objected to his proposal on the grounds that if school staff were armed, innocent black children would end up getting shot because of the white supremacist lens through which many of them are viewed in terms of racial stereotypes depicting African American males, in particular, as prone to violence and criminality. Concerned parents were no doubt thinking of the rising death toll of African American men and boys shot by armed police due to tragic misperceptions of situations involving interracial encounter.

The rhetoric of responsible gun ownership is not about the age of the gun owner, in terms of whether or not the person has reached maturation and is, therefore, capable of handling guns responsibly. Rather, it is about the aesthetics of racial, ethnic, and religious differences, as demonstrated in the first episode of Sacha Baron Cohen's satirical series, *Who Is America?* (2018), in which he passed himself off as an Israeli security expert in order to gain access to sitting congressmen. Cohen pretended to be promoting a program that calls for arming "gifted" schoolchildren in Israel, aged "from 12 to 4," with guns so that they might protect themselves and their schools. Current and former members of Congress recorded public service announcements in support of his fake guns-for-kids program. Cohen's parodic proposal to arm schoolchildren as a means of protecting them from gun violence is not quite so absurdly far-out in the context of the performance paradigm in school security.

The rhetoric of responsible gun ownership rests not only on a series of aesthetic distinctions between the types of people who are presumed capable of handling firearms responsibly and those who are not. It leverages this series of aesthetic distinctions in such a way that the gun lobby maintains a flexible position of moral superiority. The gun lobby's "moral" superiority is based on a quiet, social Darwinism for the new millennium, which recharges itself through selective acts of victim identification. The zeal with which states and local communities identify with the victims of mass shootings fuels their willingness to inflict simulated terror on local schoolchildren and their teachers. In her article "Witnessing: US Citizenship and the Vicarious Experience of Suffering," Carrie Rentschler (2004) takes up how citizens learn and are expected to bear witness to human suffering through mass media depictions. Writing about the politics of bearing witness to the terrorist attacks on September 11, 2001, she argues that the politics of whose suffering matters and whose does not is built into acts of bearing witness. Her argument resonates with Judith Butler's (2009) consideration of which lives are deemed worthy of grieving and which are not. For Rentschler (2004), witnessing constitutes a form of selective attention to victims in ways that often make invisible citizens' participation in state violence against others. She worries about how acts of witness can lead to victim identification. When citizens pay witness to acts of mass violence "against our own," it also helps define a national community of victims. Rentschler calls our attention to how the powerful pull of victim identification serves nationalism by collapsing someone else's experience into our own. She writes: "Some people may be more able to identify as and with victims rather than as or with participants in the perpetration of violence because that is how multiple social institutions in the USA have trained them to identify. Victim identity allows people to claim their own sense of injury—from wherever that sense may come—in a way that forecloses their own accountability for violence they help perpetuate, often unknowingly but not always" (Rentschler 2004, 301). The rhetoric of responsible gun ownership quietly reinforces an ethics regarding whose suffering at the hands of gun violence counts and whose doesn't, which types of gun violence qualify as tragic and which do not.

Active-shooter drills are entirely consistent with the aesthetics and ethics of responsible gun ownership in the United States. The performance paradigm presumes that schools, like homesteads, are relatively safe and benign spaces, prior to transgressive acts of violence. This presumption is based on an image of public education borrowed from the early twentieth century, at a time when its primary mission was conceived of as nurturance. But only the most privileged of public school districts within the United States hold to this view of education today. Insofar as the contemporary public discourse about school security presumes that schools are safe, welcoming spaces, it misses the history of what's happened to public education over the course the twentieth century and into the twenty-first. What the aesthetics of responsible gun ownership takes for granted becomes apparent when its logics are considered within the historical context of how Americans have defined the purpose of public education and how those definitions have evolved over time to suit the political desires and economic needs of particular constituencies.

In his geography of school violence, James Tyner (2011) observes that the initial mission of schools was soul work or moral uplift. With the industrial era, schools became disciplinary institutions that trained children to become obedient and efficient factory workers. When child labor laws went into effect, education underwent a feminization. Teachers were to be like surrogate mothers for their students. Tyner exposes the sinister aspect of this apparently benign approach to education in the early twentieth century by noting how such reforms were driven by jingoistic fears of increasing immigration and urbanization. Fear of crime and concerns with public health were closely aligned with fears that the nation was becoming less homogeneously white. Schools and prisons alike were part of the modern institutional network for mitigating these threats and protecting the racial composition of the nation. "In short, the public school was viewed as a key instrument to stave off societal degeneration" (Tyner 2011, 78). But this frozen image of schools as nurturing spaces is appealing as a cultural ideal. And its sinister aspect of keeping societal degeneration at bay is alive and well in the privileged school districts with ample tax bases that still enjoy the luxury of thinking of their schools as spaces of nurturance.

The performance paradigm in school security reinforces strategic absences in the aesthetics and ethics of responsible gun ownership. For example, the performance paradigm in school security presumes that public schools within the United States are unified by their need to defend against threats that are constructed as both external and historically new, in reference to spectacular events like the mass shootings that took place at "Columbine," "Sandy Hook," and "Parkland," among others. Like the aesthetics of responsible gun ownership, the performance paradigm in school security fails to acknowledge racial and class disparities in the United States and how these translate into different educational experiences. During the second half of the twentieth century, and with the desegregation of schools, the disciplinary actions of many public schools shifted from an emphasis on training capitalist workers to an emphasis on the containment and management of "unruly youth" and "problem children" (Tyner 2011, 79). During this period, schools saw a criminalization of discipline aligned with a crime control paradigm. Tyner notes that in the late twentieth century, administrators in poor and urban districts began to approach discipline as a problem of controlling unruly populations. Consequently, school discipline cued off of and began to resemble the crime control paradigms taking hold within cities at the time. He cites zero-tolerance disciplinary policies as akin to mandatory drug sentencing laws in effect at the time. As a result, Tyner (2011, 82) observes,

> masked behind the rhetoric of "security," many schools now resemble prisons. A suite of disciplinary and security practices have been introduced, including the use of book-bag searches, locker searches, and even body searches. These practices have been facilitated and augmented through the introduction of metal detectors, drug sniffing dogs, video cameras, and armed police officers. The school itself has become a fortress, protected also by hi-tech security gates, barricades, and surveillance cameras . . . the daily presence of real police officers (also termed "School Resource Officers") in schools indicates that these public institutions now interpret all young people as potential criminals.

Highly securitized schools resemble the "hardened" look of architectures discussed in this volume as part of the security trend in designing fortresses. Comparatively privileged school districts maintain the look and feel of feminized spaces of nurturance, even as they employ security aesthetics in the form of sensory training and "embedded" infrastructural fixes.

Recent security efforts mean that school populations in privileged districts will be treated more like their less affluent counterparts. Parents in such districts have the privilege of being dismayed when security zealots recommend bag searches for all students entering the schools each day. Those parents are not accustomed to "our" children being treated as a criminal population and are shocked at the prospect. These are the same suburban parents that post signs in their cul-de-sacs that read "Please Drive Slowly, We [heart image] Our Children," as if other parents in less "kid-friendly" neighborhoods without such signs do not. By the same token, security fixes currently being proposed and implemented in more affluent districts borrow on tropes of inner-city policing, like combing schools with bomb- and drug-sniffing dogs, as a means of showing how "hard" they can be.

Finally, whether the school district in question is poor or affluent, the performance paradigm in school security assumes, in keeping with the aesthetics and ethics of responsible gun ownership, that the primary threat facing students is a spectacular act of mass violence by a "bad guy" with a gun. Consequently, the performance paradigm in school security ignores the more mundane violence that characterizes the experience of schooling for many more kids than those who are the victims of mass shootings. Writing in the context of the expansion of school security in the wake of the Columbine shooting, Tyner (2011) observes that schools in the United States are intensely violent places, but not because school shootings are happening every day—although they have become more prevalent since the publication of his work. Rather, everyday violence at school has a more banal character, which Tyner understands as analogous to domestic and partner violence. Many students find themselves on the receiving end of taunting and bullying every day. But, Tyner notes, there is a cultural silence surrounding these acts of violence that enables them to continue unchecked. He suggests that systemic racism and homophobia are important contributing factors. Peers, teachers, and administrators might be willing to look the other way if they share the biases of the students, who taunt and bully poor kids, queer and gender queer kids, and kids of color, or any possible combination thereof. As such, Tyner (2011, 71) understands "the violence of the school as a microcosm of society at large—a place whereby structures of racism and sexism, for example, inform and are informed by our own daily actions." Like a military unit that trains in the use of violent force for national defense, even as some of its members harass, intimidate, and assault others in acts that are decidedly sexist, racist, homophobic, or transphobic, the securitized school imagines itself as united against an external threat—the armed intruder—even as it silently condones more mundane acts of peer-to-peer violence within its halls.

In the spring months of 2018, school districts across the United States held community forums in an effort to assuage the fears and concerns of parents and educators still reeling from the news of another mass shooting on a school campus. Just a few weeks before, Nikolas Cruz had fatally shot seventeen students and staff members and wounded seventeen more at Marjory Douglas Stoneman High School in Parkland, Florida. I attended one such forum held in a gymnasium at an elementary school in an affluent district in the Northeast, where the superintendent framed the conversation in terms of what interventions those in attendance wanted to see, given "the reality of the possibility of a mass shooting in our district."

But of course "the reality" of a mass shooting in "our" district is not a given. Before it can be made available as a "reality," capable of supporting and informing actions to be taken within the district, the threat must be imaginatively incorporated by the community. This can be accomplished discursively, as it was that night. Over the course of the almost three hours that we spent together that evening, the group discussed infrastructural fixes, such as target hardening, especially at school entry points; increased video surveillance of the school interior and grounds; more intensive surveillance of the student population, including bag searches and the installation of metal detectors; increasing the presence of armed police on school campuses by adding more school resource officers; and implementing more systematic threat-screening procedures in the form of risk profiling by school counselors, teachers, and peer-to-peer monitoring by students. Or "the reality of the possibility of a mass shooting in our district" can be incorporated aesthetically through live simulations of active-shooter scenarios in which administrators, teachers, students, and local police play their parts as a means of preparing for the worst-case scenario.

In the performance paradigm of school security, scenario thinking cues off of spectacular news coverage of mass shootings. Citizens and public officials abstract information about how the world works from historical events, based on their mass mediated representation. They discursively and performatively import the active-shooter scenario into their schools, communities, and everyday lives as a template for understanding and acting in the world. Whether the reality of mass shootings is incorporated via talk or performance, the security strategy is roughly the same: a community inoculates itself against the unwanted event of a mass shooting by conjuring its eventuality in elaborate detail. The strategy entails no small amount of magical thinking: let's practice for the unwanted event and thereby shoo it away until it erupts elsewhere, in some other community. As a means of futureproofing their schools against harm, communities accept mass shootings as a new genre of experience and engage in a not-in-my-backyard politics (i.e., "Let's practice being Parkland so as not to become the next Parkland").

The group assembled at the forum that night exercised a quiet, collective refusal to talk about guns. When a person at the table where I was seated tried to raise the issue of assault weapons in our small group discussion, her comment was not allowed to circulate beyond the borders of our table. The designated spokesperson for our group spontaneously edited those comments from her record of what we had discussed when she reported out to the larger group. Near the end of the night, some of the parents became punchy and dared to break the self-censorship in effect up to that point. They called the administration out for recently limiting the freedom of high school students to assemble during school hours to convene a memorial service in honor of the victims of the Parkland shooting in coordination with similar efforts at other high schools across the country. The administration defended its actions as in the best interest of the security of the students. The memorial was framed as an event that promised to bring disorder to the school. It would disrupt the schedule and distract the students from their studies. One parent suggested that the lesson for that day might have been to talk about the history of civil disobedience in the United States as a way of integrating the memorial into the curriculum, rather than treating it as a disruption of the learning process. In response, the superintendent evoked the vulnerability of students congregating outside and said that he could not ensure their safety once they exited the building. He enjoyed the overwhelming support of the majority. Some parents literally patted him on the back and others openly mocked the student activists. While a small minority advocated for their children's rights to free speech and political assembly, the majority anxiously talked through different scenarios in which the threat of a mass shooting might enter into "our" schools.

Americans have largely acquiesced to the active-shooter scenario. In so doing we have accepted a particular threat construction and treat it as an inevitable part of our reality. This construction of reality can then be used to argue the necessity of drills that aspire to a high level of realism—even going so far as to fire guns with blanks in some schools—such that the rehearsal for disaster inflicts real terror. By accepting a particular threat construction, we also accept a particular way of posing the problem. Instead of looking to root causes or complex causality in order to explain and address mass shootings (i.e., the status of mental health care within the United States or the lack of adequate gun control), we start with the problem of mass shootings on school campuses as an inevitable risk of modern life and treat it as akin to a natural disaster. We expect the worst and rehearse for it by performing the aesthetics of responsible gun ownership in order to "save lives," thereby somehow making mass shootings less horrific. Talk of prevention at any level other than the local school drops out because running the simulation reinforces the notion that school shootings are unavoidable at the macro level, even as local communities are encouraged to figure out how to prevent them at the micro level.

In keeping with what Plato called the tragic sensibility, we remain sentimental about "life," in the abstract, by repeatedly mistaking political history for tragic theater. As Halliwell (2002, 26) notes, the mimetic form that troubled Plato more than any other was tragedy:

> Plato understands tragedy to be the vehicle of a worldview, a worldview trapped in an incorrigibly human perspective that sees the fact of human suffering and death as an ultimate, irredeemable negation of the value of existence. This tragic "sense of life," with the grief-directed instinct from which it grows, is embodied at its most intense in the indignant, distraught heroes of Homeric and Attic tragedy; and by "surrendering" to pity for them, Plato's arguments suggest, the souls of spectators are themselves drawn into an implicit acceptance of a tragic mentality that can consequently seep into their psychological selves, corroding their capacity to take responsibility for their own lives.

Within the context of contemporary active-shooter scenario play, the tragic sensibility maps onto a neoliberal biopolitics that values life (in the abstract) and the right to defend it with guns, above all else. The dominant expression of conservative biopolitics in the 1980s and 1990s was the pro-life movement, starring the fetus. The dominant expressions of conservative biopolitics today are security minded: jingoistic national security policies, racist policing of white spaces, and armed preparedness training of what used to be considered civic spaces. Instead of the pathos of poster children, security-minded conservatives mobilize the visual rhetoric of mapping to maintain a sense of control over dreaded cultural futures. In the transition from the dominance of the pro-life movement to the dominance of the pro-security movement, the position of children has shifted from those in need of protection from immoral adults to those in need of hardening in preparation for further acts of gun violence against them. Rather than be protected from the harsh realities of the world, children are mandated to practice the experience of being victimized by gun violence on a routine basis.

It is by reference to the mimetic frame of mass shootings as inevitable tragedies, via collective remembrance of historic and spectacularly mediated atrocities, that legislators, administrators, law enforcement, and private security companies routinely subject students and teachers to terrific scenarios of simulated gun violence. By emplacing students and teachers' bodies within a scenario framed as another (potentially avoidable) tragedy, active-shooter scenario play indoctrinates younger generations into a particular cultural politics—one in which schoolchildren are invited to identify with the victims of mass shootings and, thereby, submit to experiential training in which they play the potential victims of future acts of gun violence. As I have demonstrated, the experiential training to which they are subjected is entirely consistent with the aesthetics and ethics of responsible gun ownership.

Under the pretext of playing the role of the "bad guy with a gun," armed police officers prepare children for terrific futures by aiming their weapons at them. No doubt there is a "playful" aspect to active-shooter drills—at least for the organizers and some of the participants. Simulations are likely a space of fantasy, role-play, and improvisation, capable of producing both terror and pleasure for participants. But, given the sadistic character of active-shooter simulations in which the participation of students and staff is state mandated, it seems pertinent to ask whether pleasure and terror are evenly distributed among the bodies of participants in scenario play. One wonders if the adults running these simulations are having fun playing at disaster, while terrorizing kids with their violent fantasies. Active-shooter scenario play has genealogical ties to other cultural performances in which adults play at being under siege, including paintball, war games, target shooting, airsoft, and the kinds of enthusiastic DIY end-times preparedness cultures that have emerged among what have come to be known as "preppers." Indeed, one effect of mandatory active-shooter drills in American schools is to mainstream the politics of terror and pleasure generated by these adult forms of play—a politics of terror and pleasure based in a racialized victim-identification that justifies a more marshal society (and that includes kids).

NOTE

1 Code Red Personal Training website, http://coderedtraining.com. The website was active from 2004 to 2017.

REFERENCES

Baker, Al, and Alex Vadukul. 2012. "Lockdown Drill Surprises Some, Scaring a School in East Harlem." *New York Times*, December 19. https://www.nytimes.com/2012/12 /20/education/lockdown-drill-scares-school-in-east-harlem.html.

Brady, Sara. 2015. "The Soldier Cycle: Harun Farocki's Images of War," in *The Performance Studies Reader*. 3rd ed., edited by Henry Bial, 193–201. New York: Routledge.

Butler, Judith. 2009. *Frames of War: When Is Life Grievable?* New York: Verso.

California Assembly Bill 549, Chapter 422. "An act to add to Section 32282.1 to the Education Code, relating to school safety." Filed with the Secretary of State, September 30, 2013. https://leginfo.legislature.ca.gov/faces/billNavClient.xhtml?bill _id=201320140AB549.

Capital Region BOCES. 2018. "A Brief History of School Safety Drills." Albany, NY: Capital Region BOCES.

CBS News. 2013. "Illinois School Drill to Include Shooting Blanks in Hallway." CBSNews.com, January 29. https://www.cbsnews.com/news/illinois-school-drill-to -include-shooting-blanks-in-hallway.

Davis, Tracy. 2007. *Stages of Emergency: Cold War Nuclear Civil Defense*. Durham, NC: Duke University Press.

Fein, Robert A., Bryan Vossekuil, William S. Pollack, Randy Borum, William Modzeleski, and Marisa Reddy. 2004. *Threat Assessment in Schools: A Guide to Managing Threatening Situations and to Creating Safe School Climates*. Washington, DC: U.S. Secret Service and the U.S. Department of Education. https://www2.ed.gov /admins/lead/safety/threatassessmentguide.pdf.

Foucault, Michel. 2007. *Security, Territory, Population*. Edited by Arnold I. Davison and translated by Graham Burchell. New York: Palgrave Macmillan.

Fox News. 2013. "Cops in New Jersey Conduct School Shooting Drill." *Fox News*, August 20.

Goldstein, Sasha. 2013. "Gun Attack Drills More Realistic, Intense as Schools Brace for a Possible 'Active Shooter' Incident." *New York Daily News*, May 12. https://www .nydailynews.com/news/national/schools-new-drill-article-1.1341645.

Hall, Rachel. 2020. "Architectures of Risk and Resiliency: Embedded Security in the Redesign of Sandy Hook Elementary School." In *Critical Approaches to Architecture*, edited by Swati Chattopadhyay and Jeremy White, 36–45. New York: Routledge.

Halliwell, Stephen. 2002. *The Aesthetics of Mimesis: Ancient Texts and Modern Problems*. Princeton, NJ: Princeton University Press.

Horn, Jordana. 2011. "Code Red Drills Prep Kids for School Shootings. But Is That TMI?" NBC *Today Show*, June 1.

Massey, Jonathan. 2014. "Risk Design." *Grey Room* 54 (Winter 2014): 6–33.

Massumi, Brian. 2005. "The Future Birth of the Affective Fact." Paper presented at the Genealogies of Biopolitics. Sponsored by the Workshop in Radical Empiricism, Université de Montreal and the Sense Lab, Concordia University.

Moser, Laura. 2016. "Two-Thirds of Schools Have 'Active-Shooter' Drills Because America." Slate.com, May 31. https://slate.com/human-interest/2016/05/two-thirds -of-u-s-schools-conduct-active-shooter-drills.html.

Rentschler, Carrie. 2004. "Witnessing: US Citizenship and the Vicarious Experience of Suffering." *Media, Culture, and Society* 26, no. 2: 296–304.

Schechner, Richard. 2013. *Performance Studies: An Introduction*. 3rd ed. New York: Routledge.

Taylor, Diana. 2003. *The Archive and the Repertoire: Performing Cultural Memory in the Americas*. Durham, NC: Duke University Press.

———. 2009. "Afterword: War Play." *PLMA* 124, no. 5: 1886–1895.

Thompson, Carolyn. 2013. "How Realistic Should School Shooting Drills Be?" *KOMO News*, January 31. https://komonews.com/news/nation-world/how-realistic-should -school-shooting-drills-be-11-21-2015.

Tyner, James A. 2011. *Space, Place, and Violence: Violence and the Embodied Geographies of Race, Sex and Gender*. New York: Routledge.

Who Is America? 2018. "101." Directed by Sacha Baron Cohen, Payman Benz, Daniel Gray Longino, Dan Mazer, and Todd Schulman. Written by Sacha Baron Cohen, Anthony Hines, Dan Swimer, Dan Mazer, Lee Kern, Adam Lowitt, Brian Reich, Kurt Metzger, Eric Notarnicola, and Aaron Geary. Showtime, July 15.

199

8

H5N1 and the Aesthetics of Biosecurity

From Danger to Risk

Limor Samimian-Darash

In the winter of 2012, I received a phone call from William Law, a member of the National Science Advisory Board for Biosecurity (NSABB), who had shared information and insights with me during my fieldwork on biosecurity in the United States.[1] During that conversation, he filled me in on recent biosecurity concerns of the NSABB and the National Institutes of Health (NIH), which oversees the board, and on the effort to establish a policy regarding "dual-use research of concern" (DURC), particularly gain-of-function (GoF) studies related to the H5N1 avian influenza virus. He asked me whether I was familiar with risk analysis and whether I knew any sociologists who were experts on the subject. During the most recent NSABB meeting that had taken place in December 2011, he said, both proponents and opponents of publication of controversial H5N1 studies had agreed that systematic risk analysis could give them a better understanding of the nature of DURC and provide biosecurity guidance for authorizing such research in the future.

A few months earlier, in September 2011, a significant biosecurity event had occurred. Ron Fouchier, a virologist at Erasmus University in Rotterdam, revealed that his research team had managed to transform H5N1 into an aerosol virus possibly transmissible among humans. A group of researchers at the University of Wisconsin–Madison, led by virologist Yoshihiro Kawaoka, had simultaneously reported similar results. Concerns regarding the implications of this research were raised after the studies were submitted for publication: Kawaoka's to the journal *Nature* and Fouchier's to *Science*. The journals' editors had sought the NSABB's advice on whether to approve publication. Their worry concerned the issue of biosecurity—specifically, whether publication would enable someone to use the information contained in the studies in harmful ways.

The fact that such potentially harmful studies were being freely conducted, funded by the U.S. government, and questioned only at the publication stage led to an outcry in the scientific world and raised questions regarding scientists' social obligations and the risks that certain lines of scientific research might pose to the public. The perception that the H5N1 research that had been carried out might have set the stage for the next global pandemic or bioterrorist event shocked many scientists, some of whom raised major objections to publication of the studies. Once the H5N1 papers arrived at the NSABB, the question facing reviewers was whether preventing their publication would neutralize that threat and, beyond that, what kind of biosecurity measures should be taken to avoid such threats in the future.

In this chapter, I examine the aesthetics of biosecurity within U.S. life sciences in the light of the H5N1 research controversy. Rather than focusing on the moral/ethical duties of scientists and a philosophical approach to security, I examine how this case of biosecurity aesthetics evinces a perceptual shift in threat identification and management, namely from danger to risk.[2] Drawing from the modalities of security aesthetics presented by D. Asher Ghertner, Hudson McFann, and Daniel Goldstein (this volume), I in turn argue that the domain of biosecurity captures a parallel movement from "designing fortresses" to "screening threats."

Designing fortresses often includes the use of various disciplinary techniques in an attempt to deter threats and impose order. Using physical and infrastructural built forms to provide signals and orienting signs to the senses, these techniques encode the aesthetic norms of "how security looks, sounds, and feels" (Ghertner et al., this volume). In the biosecurity of life sciences, this modality of security aesthetics is reflected in the creation of a permanent list of dangerous pathogens whose scientific study and use is monitored and permitted within secured spaces that are specifically designed according to a given substance's biosafety level (BSL) (for examples, see Table 8.1 and Figure 8.1). Norms of security encoded within the NSABB's regulatory practice concerning biosecurity (disciplinary techniques to secure from dangers), then, directly shape the work of scientists in their labs. That is, security is exercised

Table 8.1   Summary of recommended biosafety levels for infectious agents

BSL	Agents	Practices	Primary barriers and safety equipment	Facilities (secondary barriers)
1	Not known to consistently cause diseases in healthy adults	Standard microbiological practices	· No primary barriers required · PPE [personal protective equipment]: laboratory coats and gloves; eye, face protection, as needed	Laboratory bench and sink required
2	· Agents associated with human disease · Routes of transmission include percutaneous injury, ingestion, mucous membrane exposure	BSL-1 practice plus: · Limited access · Biohazard warning signs · "Sharps" precautions · Biosafety manual defining any needed waste decontamination or medical surveillance policies	Primary barriers: · BSCs [biological safety cabinets] or other physical containment devices used for all manipulations of agents that cause splashes or aerosols of infectious materials · PPE: Laboratory coats, gloves, face and eye protection, as needed	BSL-1 plus: · Autoclave available
3	Indigenous or exotic agents that may cause serious or potentially lethal disease through the inhalation route of exposure	BSL-2 practice plus: · Controlled access · Decontamination of all waste · Decontamination of laboratory clothing before laundering	Primary barriers: · BSCs or other physical containment devices used for all open manipulations of agents · PPE: Protective laboratory clothing, gloves, face, eye and respiratory protection, as needed	BSL-2 plus: · Physical separation from access corridors · Self-closing, double-door access · Exhausted air not recirculated · Entry through airlock or anteroom · Hand washing sink near laboratory exit

Table 8.1 (continued)

| 4 | · Dangerous/exotic agents which post [*sic*] high individual risk of aerosol-transmitted laboratory infections that are frequently fatal, for which there are no vaccines or treatments

 · Agents with a close or identical antigenic relationship to an agent requiring BSL-4 until data are available to redesignate the level

 · Related agents with unknown risk of transmission | BSL-3 practice plus:
 · Clothing change before entering
 · Shower on exit
 · All material decontaminated on exit from facility | Primary barriers:
 · All procedures conducted in Class III BSCs or Class I or Class II BSCs in combination with full-body, air-supplied, positive pressure suit | BSL-3 plus:
 · Separate building or isolated zone
 · Dedicated supply and exhaust vacuum, and decontamination systems
 · Other requirements outlined in the text |

Source: Reproduced from CDC (2009, 59).

through the design and control of physical lab spaces in conjunction with the deployment of codes, markers, and lists to deter the adoption of dangerous practices in unsecured spaces.

The aesthetic modality of screening threats, by contrast, includes mechanisms of surveillance that go beyond the scope of state control and into the domain of self-securitization. Under this modality of biosecurity aesthetics in the life sciences, the threat is conceived not in terms of danger—lists of pathogens, categorization by BSL, and design of laboratory spaces—but rather in terms of risk—various calculations regarding the scientific research that seek to assess its potential threat. Such a risk mechanism became an especially salient solution in the context of the H5N1 controversy. The NSABB's regulatory guidance produced as a result of that controversy, and the subsequent policy adopted in the United States, promoted threat screening after the earlier disciplinary mechanisms associated with designing scientific fortresses had come to be seen as inadequate.

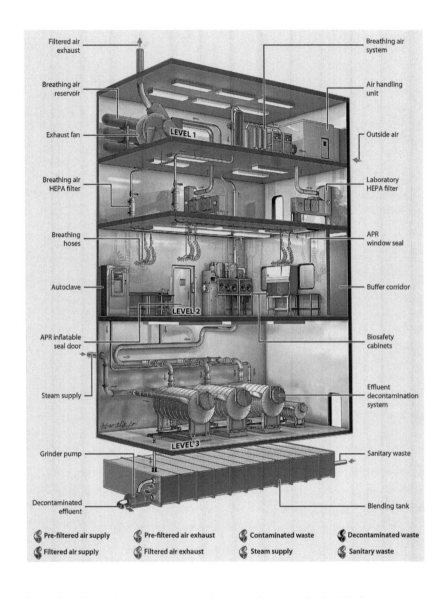

Figure 8.1 Essential features of a BSL-4 laboratory design, as depicted in the "Integrated Research Facility Overview" of the National Institute of Allergy and Infectious Diseases, National Institutes of Health (n.d.).

Following the H5N1 event, the relevant issue concerned not only who could work with dangerous materials and how to prevent the next bioterrorism event (although mechanisms of danger and fortress design are still in place), but also how to design "self-securitizing" mechanisms of surveillance for scientists—that is, how scientists might assess research of concern, develop more honed means of sensing risk, and thereby decide whether that research constitutes a potential threat.

An aesthetic of fortress design within the context of life-sciences danger assessment would have produced questions such as: What is the dangerous substance or list of dangerous substances to be restricted or controlled? How should institutions close off scientific space and protect a laboratory's physical boundaries? Questions shaped by an aesthetic of threat screening, in contrast, ask: What is the likelihood that studies might generate new risks, even those not necessarily related to the use of a particular dangerous substance? Under what conditions should a study "of concern" take place or not take place? What practices might be suitable for making visible and reasonably assessing potential risk? This shift in aesthetic modality thus corresponds to a shift in forms of governing: there is a move from managing the material, physical space of the laboratory to managing the potential risk of the research itself.

BIOSECURITY IN THE UNITED STATES

In the United States, the problem of biosecurity has crystallized over the last few decades around four main fields of threat: emerging infectious diseases, bioterrorism, cutting-edge life sciences, and food safety (Collier and Lakoff 2008; Masco 2014).[3] Especially since the post-9/11 anthrax attacks, there has been increasing concern about bioterrorism and how particular developments in the life sciences might contribute to that threat. Reflecting this concern, "total U.S. government spending on civilian biodefense research between 2001 and 2005 [increased] from $294.8 million to $7.6 billion" (Collier and Lakoff 2008, 10). Most of this funding was directed to life sciences research that sought to improve defense against biothreats (natural and artificial). Worry about biothreats led to a proliferation of laboratories researching dangerous pathogens in order to better counteract them. The number of U.S. laboratories devoted to BSL-4 pathogens (e.g., smallpox, Lassa fever, Ebola) has grown from five before 2001 to fifteen in 2012. Registered BSL-3 laboratories (researching pathogens such as SARS, West Nile virus, tuberculosis, and anthrax) have also multiplied, numbering 1,356 in 2012 (219 have registered with the U.S. Centers for Disease Control and Prevention [CDC] to work on anthrax alone; see Masco 2014).

Ironically, the proliferation of biodefense research has also led to increased concern about possible misuse of both the biological materials involved and the information such research produces. In this regard, Joseph Masco (2014) presents the problem of biosecurity as being central to the emergence of a U.S. counterterror state, asserting that "the biothreat" has become the ultimate all-encompassing potential threat, one that had to be invented to produce the means to counter it, fueling a regime of insecurity. Thus, says Masco (2014, 156), "U.S. biosecurity . . . promises a world without terror via the constant production of terror, creating a potentially endless recursive loop of threat production and response." Carlo Caduff (2014, 116) argues more broadly, through the idea of "insecurity infelicity," that security itself "grows the germs of its own destruction." Hence, rather than a solution, biosecurity has become a self-destructive security mechanism, producing the very threat (risk) it seeks to control.

In the field of life sciences, Caduff (2008) distinguishes between bio*safety* and bio*security*, the former being concerned with the accidental infection of lab workers and with physical materials clearly identified as dangerous, and the latter focused on intentional distribution of dangerous information, an activity whose boundaries are difficult to establish.

Paul Rabinow and Gaymon Bennett (2012, 128) draw on the concept of malice to point to cases in which "good intentions, or what are claimed to be good intentions, in certain situations and under certain conditions, can operate in a mode that is nefarious." Moreover, they argue, "once malice is externalized—there are good and bad uses of technology—once reform and hope for progress falter, no other resources are at hand for understanding or even addressing the issue" (Rabinow and Bennett 2012, 129). While their analysis uses the notion of malice to better understand the conditions under which risk becomes perceptible and governable in the life sciences, malice operates in terms of danger—and, therefore, fortress design. In contrast, I argue that both the situation triggered by the H5N1 event and the policies formulated in its aftermath are embedded within a risk-based security aesthetics characterized by threat screening, where the techniques and terms of rendering risk perceptible differ.

Referring to the H5N1 event, Lakoff (2012, 457) asserts that "rather than a conflict between science authorities and a fearful public, or between open inquiry and the demands of security, the controversy should be seen as a conflict among experts over different conceptualizations of an uncertain situation." Lakoff (2017) further suggests that the case of H5N1 publications illustrates the controversy among the actors of the "pandemic preparedness assemblage." My focus turns from the various perceptions of the different experts involved to how those perceptions become registered as sensible based on the security aesthetic terms in play for governing the threat.

DANGER AND THE AESTHETICS OF BIOSECURITY

In 2004, the National Research Council, which was tasked with investigating the problem of biosecurity in U.S. life sciences research, issued a report titled *Biotechnology Research in an Age of Terrorism*, also known as the Fink Report. On a conceptual level, the report reframed the problem of security in the life sciences from a broadly defined concern to what was specifically called the "dual-use dilemma." The term "dual-use" was borrowed from the language of arms control and disarmament, where it refers to "technologies intended for civilian application that can also be used for military purposes" (Fink et al. 2004, 18)—in order to distinguish a case in which "the same technologies can be used legitimately for human betterment and misused for bioterrorism" (Fink et al. 2004, 1). The report included a list of biological agents that had been identified as dangerous and needed to be controlled in order to minimize the possibility of their misuse and recommended the establishment of a national biosecurity advisory board. In short, exercising security aesthetics through techniques of fortress design, the report sought to cast biosecurity in terms of "good" and "bad" uses and users by creating a space for safe and ethical scientific research, from which dangerous users were to be excluded.

Subsequently, in late 2004, Secretary of Health and Human Services Tommy G. Thompson announced the establishment of the NSABB[4] to "advise all Federal departments and agencies that conduct or support Life Sciences research that could fall into the 'Dual Use' category" (U.S. Department of Health and Human Services 2004). Simon Natcher, an NSABB staff member, emphasized in a conversation with me that the NSABB "wasn't meant to be a biosecurity board, even though it's in the name, but rather its goal was to deal with dual-use research." The committee, in other words, perceived the problem as being caused by *the misuse of scientific material or information by actors outside the scientific community*. In this sense, the NSABB operates through a fortress design modality of security aesthetics, for it casts biosecurity as a problem of boundary maintenance, making insecure materials or actors perceptible based on their location inside or outside the institutionalized science community (including the physical laboratory space). This vantage point, accordingly, forecloses systematic attention to *internal* security risks by rendering threats a boundary problem emergent through the crossing of the inside-outside threshold. Problems emerge, then, when dangers drift beyond the columns in the table to which they are assigned and materials escape or actors breach the securitized laboratory.

As NSABB member Daniel Reynolds described it, the board's concern was malicious use arising from or made possible by the negligent actions of scientists, not intentional malfeasance on their part, a motive usually ascribed to nonscientists:

> I think the general need is to come to a common understanding of how life science might be misused. Most people have constrained their thinking to misuse in a very deliberate, malevolent, premeditated way. There is also a level of misuse that arises from negligence. . . . I think that a major need and goal is to *somehow describe* how these things might come about and where they are most likely to cause problems. . . . So, the consequences are large and therefore there is more of an obligation to *think through the scenarios, to see what the scenario* would look like if something bad happens. (emphasis added)

In conceptualizing threats as external problems triggered when those outside the scientific community take advantage of scientific negligence to intentionally misuse scientific developments, Reynolds sees the NSABB's work of developing means of imagining, making visible, and describing possible threats. Danger scenarios and descriptions emphasizing the NSABB's distinction between the good scientist/normal research and the dangerous nonscientist/abnormal use thus guided its choice of a fortress design for life sciences research based on protecting the boundary between inside and outside, good science and risky nonscience. Since the threat was perceived as lying outside the laboratory space, techniques of biosafety—understood as the practice of producing safe zones and thus preventing material leaking into other nondesignated/secured spaces or people—were regarded as sufficient. The NIH'S biosafety standards thus center heavily on built-form interventions—barrier walls, air pressure doors, and containment zones—with extensive visualizations of laboratory fortification (see Figure 8.2).

Biosafety measurements had already been developed in the late 1970s on the basis of discussions that grew out of the Asilomar Conference on Recombinant DNA, held in February 1975. The meeting followed an experiment by Paul Berg, a biochemist at Stanford, with simian virus 40 (SV40), which could then produce tumors in rodents. The experiment was not completed because Berg's fellow investigators feared that bacteria carrying SV40 DNA might escape and cause cancer in people it infected. This fear gave rise to biosafety principles that were later established in guidance documents issued by the CDC.

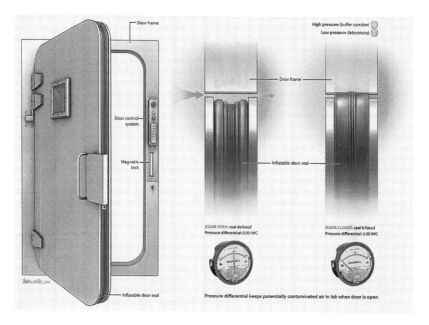

Figure 8.2   Design for stainless steel air pressure door system, as depicted in the "Integrated Research Facility Overview." National Institutes of Health (n.d.).

These principles involved the application of safety guidelines of varying stringency according to the degree of estimated danger. The more dangerous an experiment might be, the more stringent the biosafety measures to be taken—such as using an airlock and placing a laboratory under negative pressure (see Figure 8.2) (Berg 2008). Asilomar was perceived as a success by the scientific community, as NSABB member Stanley Lane told me in an interview: "With the Asilomar, it was purposed exactly the same, that scientists rule and look over the science of their peers and their juniors and their seniors and so forth. Let's not have government run the show. I think it has worked magnificently." As a result, for a long time, NSABB efforts were geared toward educating the scientific community about the biosafety practices and design interventions deemed necessary to avoid external threats.

In March 2006, the NSABB held a meeting in which the term "dual-use research of concern" (DURC) was first presented. This term reflected the idea underlying the work of the board's Dual Use Criteria Working Group (2006, emphasis added), namely, that "*most* if not *all* Life Sciences research *could* be considered Dual Use," and therefore it was important "to identify specific Life

Sciences research that could be of greatest concern for misuse." As NSABB member Christian Venicci explained to me,

> Any piece of information in the life sciences can be misused. . . . From my perspective, it's a little hard because I've been engaged with dual use for a few years now, so it's not a strange concept to me. But, if I did bring it up to my scientific colleagues, I'm not sure what they would think of it. They might respond better to something like "life science research of concern" [that] distinguishes all the rest of research with that very small subset, which really is a very small subset, that has the high probability of being misused.

According to the definition of DURC, then, only certain kinds of life sciences research should be considered "of concern" and therefore subject to special attention. Daniel Reynolds elaborated: "The difference between 'Dual Use' and 'Dual Use Research of Concern' is somewhat semantics. . . . [The NSABB] wanted to acknowledge that everything has potential for misuse, but only a very little of it deserves real attention." At this stage, the DURC definition narrowed the broader problem of biosecurity to a subset of studies that could be characterized as "of concern," and the board agreed that these more dangerous studies needed to be identified in their early stages, before they developed methods or generated data or products that could pose an actual threat in the wrong (nonscientific) hands. However, it was difficult to define DURC and hence which projects deserved increased scrutiny. As Simon Natcher commented, "One of the big issues in dual-use research is, how do you promote [awareness of the problem] when people aren't really clear what it is?"

In October 2010, at the beginning of one NSABB meeting, a board member stated, "We are all scientists, and we are here to protect the 'freedom of science' and to avoid regulation. . . . [We prefer] volunteered oversight." Responding to my surprise at this hands-off approach to biosecurity, Stanley Lane noted of the board, "[It is a committee of] scientists protecting their own discipline."

Such comments are consistent with NSABB reports, which have repeatedly conveyed the message that the scientific community can deal with the dual-use issue, that it can take responsibility for monitoring its own activities through biosafety self-governance practices and facilities, and hence that external regulation is not necessary. At the board's October 2010 meeting, for example, NSABB members voiced ardent support for keeping security mechanisms externally focused, promoted internal voluntary oversight based on a "code of conduct" and a "culture of responsibility," and advocated increasing "awareness" among scientists regarding the problem of potential misuse of their research.

Accordingly, at this point in time, although sectors of the U.S. scientific community had been discussing the problem of biosecurity for more than five years, the way in which that problem was perceived remained rooted in the notion of danger and disciplinary mechanisms designed to secure the life sciences from dangerous others. This framing of biosecurity was made possible by the visual and narrative presentation of biothreats on the terms of fortress design, with pictorial representations of laboratory impermeability the key pedagogic form of securitization offered. Although biosecurity had been presented as a new problem in relation to life sciences research (after 9/11), in practice, then, its security aesthetic framing worked via concerns with danger, and scientists were responsible only for keeping such danger outside their labs; internal threats were imperceptible, mere hypotheticals distracting from the important work of discovery.

With biosecurity's translation into biosafety measurements, it seemed to many that the NSABB had completed its job. The scientific fortress had been strengthened, and known dangers were at bay. At the end of 2011, NSABB member William Law expressed doubt to me about the necessity of its continued existence:

> WL: The question is what are their [the board's] resources? They barely convene; barely manage to participate in meetings. Again, it's the question of importance; I don't think it's urgent [for them]. The impression you get from the energy, the time, and the commitment of the committee members is that it is a very important issue, and they say a thousand times that the stakes are high [but nothing has changed in practice]. . . . [If only] one event happens, the entire scientific world will shut down.

> LSD: Do you think that an event would have to occur for anything to change?

> WL: Yes. And look, there's the issue of the question: "Are we effective, or is there no problem?" [As someone from the NSABB] asked today, "How do you know there is no problem?" And the answer was: "No one is reporting." Now, if no one is reporting dual use, it's either because they don't know what dual use means or there is no problem. . . . If there are no reports, it's because either they don't recognize a problem, or they know how to recognize a problem but there are no problems. I had long conversations with editors [of science journals] that told me, "We have nothing; no one is turning to us."

The focus on known dangers and the security-aesthetic emphasis on inside-outside permeability made dual use a low-activity domain of biosecurity. It was not that risks did not exist, just that they fell outside the terms of sensibility operational within the NSABB.

In September 2011, the NSABB met to discuss its future. A second meeting was scheduled for the end of October, at which time a determination was to be made about whether the committee should continue its work and, if so, what its role should be. That meeting, however, never took place. During October, the NSABB found itself grappling with the H5N1 event. The DURC problem took a concrete form, rendering previous practices of biosafety seemingly insufficient, "redistributing the sensible" (Rancière 2009) by making threats suddenly perceptible inside the fortress of science itself.

CONSTRUCTED THREAT: "AN ENGINEERED DOOMSDAY"

In 2011, researchers Ron Fouchier and Yoshihiro Kawaoka independently created strains of the H5N1 virus that spread via the air among ferrets, considered the best model for predicting how a flu virus might behave in humans. On September 13, 2011, Fouchier presented his study at a meeting in Malta and announced that his lab had "discovered that only 1–3 substitutions are sufficient to cause large changes in antigenic drift . . . [and that] large antigenic differences between and within H5N1 clades could affect vaccine efficiency and even result in vaccine failure" (*Influenza Times* 2011). Fouchier and his team reportedly "introduced mutations, by reverse genetics into laboratory ferrets. They then collected a nasal wash from each infected ferret and inoculated another ferret after a few days. They repeated this process ten times. The result? H5N1 had been transmitted to three out of four ferrets" (*Influenza Times* 2011).

Fouchier's study caused turmoil in the scientific community, especially among virologists and microbiologists. On September 19, *Scientific American* published an article titled "What Will the Next Influenza Pandemic Look Like?" describing an H5N1 pandemic as "topping the worst-case scenario list for most flu experts" and raising the question of whether "the dreaded H5N1" would become transmissible in humans (Harmon 2011). The answer to the article's title question lay in the study by Fouchier and his team, who "mutated the hell out of H5N1" and found that with "as few as five single mutations it gained the ability to latch onto cells in the nasal and tracheal passageways" (Harmon 2011). On September 26, the *New Scientist* reported on Fouchier's work: "H5N1 bird flu can kill humans, but has not gone pandemic because it cannot spread easily among us. That might change: five mutations in just two genes have allowed the virus to spread between mammals in the lab. What's more, the virus is just as lethal despite the mutations" (MacKenzie 2011).

In October 2011, the NSABB was called to review the two studies in relation to DURC. As Daniel Reynolds explained, "The work provides information about [properties of infectious agents]. . . . It's the information that allows someone else to create these things with these properties. Two of the most serious properties to give an infectious agent are *high virulence* and . . . *aerosol transmission between people*, and this was the case with the new H5N1 strain" (emphasis added).

According to *Science* editor Bruce Albert, when Fouchier's paper arrived at the journal, "it was obvious" that it needed special review. The journal "quickly recruited outside specialists, including biosecurity experts who serve on the NSABB. The NSABB itself was first alerted to the studies by NIAID [National Institute of Allergy and Infectious Diseases] in late [summer 2011] and received copies of the papers in mid-October" (Enserink and Malakoff 2012, 20–21).

The research was presented by many scientists as an *internal* security threat (constructed risk): a new lethal virus had been introduced into the world, and it was scientists who were responsible for creating it. Many spoke of it as "a man-made flu virus that could change world history if it were ever set free" (Enserink 2011). Risk created by scientists themselves had become a security problem, precipitating a shift in threat perception away from a narrow focus on external danger beyond the control of researchers and toward the risk inherent in research itself. "Good scientists" had intentionally created a dangerous product (albeit for preparedness purposes) that could put society at risk.

Paul Keim, NSABB chair at the time, said he could not "think of another pathogenic organism that is as scary as this one. . . . [A]nthrax is [not] scary at all compared to this" (Enserink 2011). Laurie Garrett, a Pulitzer Prize–winning science journalist, wrote a piece based on the event titled "The Bioterrorist Next Door" (Garrett 2011). A perception that science had created the next global pandemic or the next bioterror event began to spread. As the *New York Times* (2012) warned, "Defenders of the research in Rotterdam . . . say the findings could prove helpful in monitoring virus samples from infected birds and animals. . . . But it is highly uncertain, even improbable, that the virus would mutate in nature along the pathways prodded in a laboratory environment, so [any such] benefit . . . seems marginal."

As the perception of security risks was refocused onto the core of scientific practice, the critical question became not whether Fouchier and Kawaoka had adequately isolated dangers, but rather whether they had acted responsibly in conducting their studies in the first place. Inglesby, Cicero, and Henderson (2012, 151) criticized the H5N1 research and asked: "Should we purposely engineer avian flu strains to become highly transmissible in humans? In our view, no." They cited three reasons for their position: first, the deadly strain could "escape accidentally from the laboratory"; second, the idea that the engineered strain could help scientists identify similar characteristics in currently circulating strains of H5N1 "is a speculative hope but not worth the potential risk"; and, third, the assertion that the creation of the strain would motivate scientists to search for H5N1 vaccines was also speculative (Inglesby et al. 2012, 152). While the first concern built on the existing biosafety framework, the latter two emphasizing potential risk evidence a shift in risk perception. Enhanced threat screening would soon be required to account for the limitations of fortress design revealed by the H5N1 studies—a shift in security aesthetics that would change spatial measurements into calculations and numbers assessing risk, and render the potential threat imaginable and perceptible.

RISK AND THE AESTHETICS OF BIOSECURITY

In December 2011, NIH officials Anthony Fauci, Gary Nabel, and Francis Collins (2011) expressed their position regarding the publication of the H5N1 studies in a commentary in the *Washington Post*: "Understanding the biology of influenza virus transmission has implications for outbreak prediction, prevention and treatment. . . . The question is whether benefits of such research outweigh risks. . . . New data provide valuable insights that can inform influenza preparedness." This statement reflects a new approach to the H5N1 security dilemma: before a decision could be taken on whether to publish the research, a risk-benefit analysis should take place. In the opinion of these officials, the research constituted "a flu virus risk worth taking," as part of efforts to improve preparedness for flu pandemics.

In parallel with this statement, in December 2011 the NSABB published its own recommendations following its review of the articles: "While the public health benefits of such research can be important, certain information obtained through such studies has the potential to be misused for harmful purposes. . . . Due to the importance of the findings to the public health and research communities, the *NSABB recommends that the general conclusions highlighting the novel outcome be published, but that the manuscripts not include the methodological and other details* that could enable replication of the experiments by those who would seek to do harm" (NIH 2011, emphasis added). While the NSABB recommended that the articles not be published in full, it also emphasized the studies' contributions to public health research, recommending that full details be provided to a closed network of scientists "authorized" to use the information to continue to conduct "responsible" research on the topic.

Unlike the scientific consensus evident in previous biosecurity conversations, the altered conditions of threat perception generated by the H5N1 event produced conflicting assessments and possible responses. Biosecurity became a contested domain, with different communities of scientists disagreeing over the relevant assessment and visualization of risk. On December 30, 2011, for example, the World Health Organization (WHO) released a statement in which it expressed concern that limiting dissemination of information from Fouchier's and Kawaoka's work would undermine the international Pandemic Influenza Preparedness framework, a position it reasserted in early 2012 (WHO 2012). In contrast, Michael Osterholm, a public health expert and member of the NSABB, and physician and biosecurity expert Donald Henderson argued that the risks associated with publication of the two H5N1 papers outweighed the proposed benefits and challenged the rationales offered in defense of the work: "The current circulating strains of influenza A/H5N1, with their human case fatality rate of 30 to 80%, place this pathogen in the category of causing one of the most virulent known human infectious diseases. . . . *We can't unring a bell*; should a highly transmissible and virulent H5N1 influenza virus that is of human making cause a catastrophic pandemic, whether as the result of intentional or unintentional release, the world will hold life sciences accountable for what it did or did not do to minimize that risk" (Osterholm and Henderson 2012, 802, emphasis added).

What both Osterholm and Henderson's and the WHO's critiques of the NSABB decision share, despite their opposing policy implications, is a sense of risk as pervasive and ever-present. The "ringing the bell" metaphor that Osterholm and Henderson invoke indicates this shift in the terms of sensibility, with biothreats no longer imaginable as containable, inside-outside phenomena or discrete material presences or dangers.

In other words, as the controversy surrounding the H5N1 case shows, the security aesthetics of screening threats was driven into the life sciences not so much by the emergence of a new threat but by a new perception—that of an all-encompassing sense of risk. The perception of the H5N1 event as something that could alter "world history," the notion that there was nothing "as scary as this," and talk of the "bioterrorist next door" and a possible "scientific doomsday" all contradicted the belief that the scientific sphere was a secured fortress, separated, and thus controlled. Instead, biothreats suddenly appeared to be circulating within the normal, secured space of science, no longer boundable by known lists of pathogens or containable via biosafety designs and measurements for laboratories. Moreover, what emerges is not only the perception of a potential all-encompassing threat, beyond a particular locality or space, but also the need to make such a threat visible and sensible in order to mitigate it. Risk assessment is then embraced as the appropriate biosecurity mechanism for such a situation.

Following this debate, the NSABB met to reevaluate its previous decision. Soon afterward, the board's formerly open-to-the-public meetings became closed, top-secret sessions. Attendees were subjected to FBI clearance, no documents could be taken out of the meeting rooms, and NSABB members were asked not to discuss matters considered at the meetings with outsiders. It was at this point that experts were called in to help create a tool to assess the level of risk associated with publication of the controversial H5N1 studies. It took NSABB members approximately four months (November 2011–March 2012) to reassess the manuscripts. At different points in this process, they reached opposing conclusions: that the research did and did not present a significant risk to the public.

In February 2012, the American Society of Microbiology hosted a meeting on "Biodefense and Emerging Diseases" wherein an ad hoc session took up the work on H5N1. At this session, Fouchier defended his research and provided a fuller explanation of the issue of pathogenicity. At the same meeting, NIAID director Anthony Fauci announced that he had asked the two lead researchers to revise their papers and the NSABB to review the revised manuscripts. The same month, a gathering of NSABB members and more than a dozen observers, including NIH director Francis Collins and WHO member Keiji Fukuda, took place at the NIH campus. At this gathering, the participants read both the original and the revised reports. Subsequently, the board voted to allow full publication of the revised studies (NSABB 2012a); threats of dissemination had been effectively screened from the public eye.

Following the publication controversy, several changes were made to U.S. policy on life sciences regulation. In March 2012, a new U.S. "Policy for Oversight of Life Sciences Dual Use Research of Concern" was published (NSABB 2012b). The new policy grants the government the authority to terminate funding for research deemed too risky. Other tools provided by the new policy relate to determining the biosafety conditions under which research is conducted and a periodic assessment of research for its potential to be DURC (NIH 2014). Periodic review now allows the government to be constantly updated on the state of the research portfolio it funds, training powers of the biosecurity gaze onto the scientific enterprise rather than focusing on the possible spillage of risky research outside.

To enable a decision on which measures should be applied, the policy articulates a four-step process that indicates what is to be considered an internal risk (though without providing measurements that would enable such a risk to be made visible or perceptible). The first step is to determine whether the research under review involves a pathogen from a list of fifteen infectious agents and toxins that are deemed most lethal. The second step is to determine whether the research performs an experiment that falls under any of the seven categories of experiments listed in the policy. If the study meets these two criteria, a third step is pursued, specifically determining whether the study meets the DURC definition set out in the policy, which is as follows: "DURC is life sciences research that, based on current understanding, can be reasonably anticipated to provide knowledge, information, products, or technologies that could be directly misapplied to pose a significant threat with broad potential consequences to public health and safety, agricultural crops and other plants, animals, the environment, materiel, or national security" (NSABB 2012b, 1–2).

With a few revisions, this definition was based on an earlier definition that the NSABB had articulated in a 2007 report that defined dual-use research as "research that, based on current understanding, can be reasonably anticipated to provide knowledge, products, or technologies that could be directly misapplied by others to pose a threat to public health and safety, agricultural crops and other plants, animals, the environment, or materiel" (NSABB 2007, 17). Though the two definitions are clearly similar, there are two significant differences. The first is that the phrase "by others" was eliminated from the new DURC definition. This phrase was originally intended to express the idea that the threat was no longer or not solely external (and thus that designing fortresses was not enough). The second difference is the addition of the phrase "a significant threat with broad potential consequences" to the new definition. This points to the all-encompassing sense of risk; however, it leaves unclear how threat is to be defined and evaluated—that is, how one might know what "a significant threat" is or which case is considered to have "broad potential consequences to public health."

The fourth step of the policy calls for an assessment of the risks and benefits of studies that are determined to be DURC, in order to address this lack. This risk-benefit assessment is intended to enable a decision on whether any of the tools the policy provides ought to be used: Should the study design be modified? Should it be conducted under different conditions? Should its publication be subject to any limitations? Should its funding be terminated?

However, although scientists agreed upon the importance of risk assessments under this security process, in practice different experts used different tools, thus providing different visualizations and sensibilities of the threat and related questions of mitigation. This would also prove to be a central theme within subsequent scientific meetings and policy debates.

For example, in 2014, the NSABB conducted two meetings with the aim of soliciting public comments on the methods for assessing such studies. The National Academies of Sciences, Engineering, and Medicine (NRC 2015) also hosted a symposium to discuss the potential benefits of and risks posed by GoF research and to identify key principles for its assessment.

At the NASEM meeting, Marc Lipsitch and Alison P. Galvani used a risk assessment model and argued that "alternative scientific approaches [to GoF] are not only less risky, but also more likely to generate results that can be readily translated into public health benefits" (NRC 2015, 27). Going through a series of calculations, they argued that "a release of an H5N1 or other pandemic influenza strain enhanced through GoF research to increase its transmissibility among mammals could result in a 0.01 percent to 0.1 percent chance of 2 million to 1.4 billion fatalities, or an expected death toll of 2,000 to 1.4 million per BSL-3 laboratory-year based on the Select Agent data LAI [laboratory-acquired infection] rate. Using the NIAID data, each full-time person-year of GoF research in a BSL-3 lab could produce a death toll of 10,000 to 10 million" (NRC 2015, 57).

Fouchier responded to these calculations saying: "I prefer no numbers rather than ridiculous numbers that make no sense" (NRC 2015, 58). At the same event, another scientist, Gregory Koblentz, argued that the lack of data about the threat leaves room for speculation and uncertainty, and identified three distinct schools of thought about the nature of the threat: Optimists, Pessimists, and Pragmatists (NRC 2015, 60–61)—thus acknowledging not only that risk assessment models are open to speculation (because of the lack of data) but also that *who* does the assessment affects the result.

Different terms of sensibility thus played out in discussions about, for instance, risk criteria, ethical values, control mechanisms, the implications of risk-benefit-based regulation and funding for research, and even how the expression "of concern" should be defined, and by whom. While all of the above-mentioned policy documents and the commentary presented at the various meetings considered research-related concerns in terms of a risk-registered biosecurity aesthetic of screening threats, they struggled with its concrete measurements and could not come up with a (single) format or structural design for how such risk could be assessed, calculated, and thus managed in practice. An illuminating example for this struggle is presented in a comment by Harvey Fineberg, the facilitator of the NASEM meeting: "Has the NSABB, in its deliberations, gone so far at this point, of identifying the actual, not simply directionalities of transmissibility, virulence, etc., but the actual way to think about when a threshold of concern is passed, either in terms of, for example, a set of reference organisms, or in some other numeric or quantitative way ... how will you judge?" (NASEM 2014, 19–20).

The "passing the threshold" metaphor points out the problem of translating the general sense of risk into something concrete, visible, and manageable—a problem that a risk-registered biosecurity aesthetic of screening threats solves by diffusing that very sensibility across different institutions, disciplines, and actors involved in the research, as exemplified by NSABB member Ken Berns's response to the above comment: "How you predict what the consequences are is a guessing game. I mean you can say, 'Well, this seems potentially dangerous.' The trouble is how you calculate that risk in a quantitative sense is challenging. ... I don't know that, I mean we can only, sort of, do it in a generic sense without being all that specific. I think the question, which we grappled with more is the level at which that decision is going to be made" (NASEM 2014, 20).

That is, rather than "guessing" when the threshold is crossed, or only relying on a "generic sense" of risk, the policy focuses on *who* should set the threshold at different points of the research process. Similarly, the U.S. government (White House 2014, 5) introduced a DURC policy that determined the roles and responsibilities of funding agencies, research institutions, and life scientists in developing and implementing risk mitigation measures. Thus, though assessments and calculations marked a new security aesthetic, the question of how to reach the correct assessment, using which model, remained unsettled.

DISCUSSION

Analysis of the H5N1 case shows how a new problem related to biosecurity (within the prism of DURC) provoked a security-aesthetic shift from "designing fortresses" to "screening threats," and thus from the control of dangers to the management of risks. In the fortress design mode, a distinction was drawn between "good scientists" and "external biosecurity threats," and the former could be separated from the latter through the creation of secured spaces and attunement of the oversight apparatus to identifying encroachments into or leaks out of the pure space of science. This approach was dominant in U.S. life sciences research until the H5N1 event. In the wake of that event, however, screening threats became dominant. As the boundaries between "good scientists" and "external biosecurity threats" (imposed by disciplinary mechanisms encoded with the aesthetics of designing fortresses) collapsed, and scientific research itself came to be seen as a source of potential pervasive threat, parts of the scientific community and the NSABB turned to the self-securitizing tool of risk assessment, in the attempt to identify and anticipate these biothreats.

This involved a shift from long-standing disciplinary mechanisms that separated scientific conduct into particular "spaces" through the use of a pre-existing list of known pathogens confined to BSL-3 and BSL-4 laboratories (a scientific fortress) to risk-benefit calculations and assessments that screen all funded life science research for emergent threat potential. Thus, the probabilistic gaze of the security apparatus shifted the spatially focused aesthetic that defined danger in terms of sphere of use and location of activity into an actuarial aesthetic oriented toward sensing risk potential. However, in their efforts to translate threat screening into concrete designations and criteria of assessment, scientists have not yet reached an agreement. Unlike the scientific consensus evident in previous biosecurity conversations (biosafety in designing fortresses), the altered conditions of threat perception produced conflicting assessments, with different communities of scientists disagreeing over the relevant visualization and evaluation of risk.

As the problem of biosecurity becomes one of potential uncertainty (DURC), recent security aesthetics based on threat screening are thus proving insufficient. But rather than grappling with this as a paradoxical problem of registering threats as risks—where new knowledge and technological developments lead to more uncertainty and ambiguity of threat—the scientific community and U.S. government policy have mostly engaged in discussions that have promoted the diffusion of this sensibility by focusing on who specifically should be screening threats, according to which criteria, and at which stage of the research process. Threat screening, despite the absence of a consensus on how it is to be done, is being pushed forward and duplicated within more specific contexts and stages of the research process, adding more screening layers without clearly defining what a potential threat is. In this sense, biosecurity remains a profoundly aesthetic question, determined by heterogeneous communities of sense relying on different visual, techno-scientific, and biological cues for perceiving risk.

LIMOR SAMMIAN-DARASH

NOTES

1   All names are pseudonyms. Unless accompanied by specific citations, direct quotes are taken from interviews I conducted with scientists, officials, and other relevant parties during fieldwork carried out in the United States between 2010 and 2012. That research focused on the problem of biosecurity in the life sciences, particularly as reflected in the work of the NSABB.

2   Many scholars have distinguished between risk and danger, and this distinction
has become the point of departure for almost every discussion of risk. Ulrich Beck
(1992) and Anthony Giddens (2000) argue that danger is recognized in traditional
societies, whereas risk is created by reflexive modernization. Beck's risk society
approach mainly deals with the production and transformation of "real" risks and
with society's attempts to control the future, which themselves render that future
more "risky." In contrast, Niklas Luhmann (1993) treats risk not as an object in a
first-order observation (which he terms "danger") but as a concept in a second-order
observation.

3   Brian Rappert and Chandré Gould (2009) review seven "national contexts" and
show that although the international discourse on biosecurity has been dominated by the United States, other countries experience biosecurity differently
(also see Samimian-Darash 2016). Filippa Lentzos and Nikolas Rose (2009) argue
that the idea of biosecurity depends on the local political/security rationality. My
colleagues and I have shown that biosecurity emerges as a problem of different
boundary objects in Israel and the United States (Samimian-Darash, Henner-
Shapira, and Daviko 2016).

4   The NSABB is composed of twenty-five voting members who are mostly life sciences experts—microbiologists and virologists—and twenty or so ex-officials from
various government departments, who are nonvoting members. In its attempt to
manage the dual-use challenge, the board can thus be viewed as representing the
broad U.S. scientific community.

REFERENCES

Beck, Ulrich. 1992. *Risk Society: Toward a New Modernity.* New York: SAGE.

Berg, Paul. 2008. "Meetings That Changed the World: Asilomar 1975—DNA Modification Secured." *Nature* 455, no. 7211: 290–291.

Caduff, Carlo. 2008. "Anticipations of Biosecurity." In *Biosecurity Interventions: Global
Health and Security in Question*, edited by Andrew Lakoff and Stephen J. Collier,
257–277. New York: Columbia University Press.

——. 2014. "On the Verge of Death: Visions of Biological Vulnerability." *Annual Review
of Anthropology* 43: 105–121.

Centers for Disease Control and Prevention (CDC). 2009. *Biosafety in Microbiological
and Biomedical Laboratories.* 5th ed. Accessed June 6, 2018. https://www.cdc.gov/labs
/pdf/CDC-BiosafetyMicrobiologicalBiomedicalLaboratories-2009-P.PDF.

Collier, Stephen J., and Andrew Lakoff. 2008. "The Problem of Securing Health." In
Biosecurity Interventions: Global Health and Security in Question, edited by Andrew
Lakoff and Stephen J. Collier, 1–32. New York: Columbia University Press.

Dual Use Criteria Working Group. 2006. "Oversight of Dual-Use Life Sciences
Research: Strategies for Minimizing the Potential Misuse of Research Information."

Accessed February 16, 2013. http://oba.od.nih.gov/biosecurity/biosecurity
_documents.html.

Enserink, Martin. 2011. "Scientists Brace for Media Storm around Controversial Flu
Studies." *ScienceInsider*, November 23.

Enserink, Martin, and David Malakoff. 2012. "Will Flu Papers Lead to New Research
Oversight?" *Science* 335, no. 6064: 20–22.

Fauci, Anthony S., Gary J. Nabel, and Francis S. Collins. 2011. "A Flu Virus Risk Worth
Taking." *Washington Post*, December 30.

Fink, Gerald R., et al. 2004. *Biotechnology Research in an Age of Terrorism*. Washington,
DC: National Academies Press. Accessed November 3, 2012. https://www.nap.edu
/catalog/10827/biotechnology-research-in-an-age-of-terrorism.

Garrett, Laurie. 2011. "The Bioterrorist Next Door." *Foreign Policy*, December 15.

Giddens, Anthony. 2000. *Runaway World: How Globalization Is Reshaping Our Lives.* New
York: Routledge.

Harmon, Katherine. 2011. "What Will the Next Pandemic Look Like?" *Scientific American*, September 19.

Influenza Times. 2011. "Scientists Provide Strong Evidence for Pandemic Threat."
Influenza Times: Conference Newspaper, Fourth ESWI Influenza Conference, Malta,
September 11–14. Accessed February 26, 2013.

Inglesby, Thomas V., Anita Cicero, and D. A. Henderson. 2012. "The Risk of Engineering a Highly Transmissible H5N1 Virus." *Biosecurity and Bioterrorism: Biodefense
Strategy, Practice, and Science* 10, no. 1: 151–152.

Lakoff, Andrew. 2012. "The Risks of Preparedness: Mutant Bird Flu." *Public Culture* 24,
no. 3: 457–464.

———. 2017. *Unprepared: Global Health in a Time of Emergency*. Berkeley: University of
California Press.

Lentzos, Filippa, and Nikolas Rose. 2009. "Governing Insecurity: Contingency Planning, Protection, Resilience." *Economy and Society* 38, no. 2: 230–254.

Luhmann, Niklas. 1993. *Risk: A Sociological Theory.* New York: Aldine de Gruyter.

MacKenzie, Debora. 2011. "Five Easy Mutations to Make Bird Flu a Lethal Pandemic."
New Scientist, September 21.

Masco, Joseph. 2014. *The Theater of Operations: National Security Affect from the Cold War
to the War on Terror.* Durham, NC: Duke University Press.

National Academies of Sciences, Engineering, and Medicine (NASEM). 2014. *Risks
and Benefits of Gain-of-Function Research: A Symposium.* Accessed May 30, 2015.
http://dels.nas.edu/Upcoming-Event/Risks-Benefits-Gain/AUTO-9-61-70-Q
?bname=bls.

National Institutes of Health (NIH). 2011. "Press Statement on the NSABB Review of
H5N1 Research." *NIH NEWS*, December 20. Accessed February 20, 2013. http://www
.nih.gov/news/health/dec2011/od-20.htm.

———. 2014. *Tools for the Identification, Assessment, Management, and Responsible Communication of Dual Use Research of Concern: A Companion Guide.* September. Accessed

June 7, 2018. https://www.phe.gov/s3/dualuse/Documents/durc-companion-guide
.pdf.

———. n.d. "Integrated Research Facility Overview." National Institute of Allergy
and Infectious Diseases. Accessed May 10, 2019. https://www.niaid.nih.gov/about
/integrated-research-facility-overview.

National Research Council (NRC). 2015. *Potential Risks and Benefits of Gain-of-Function
Research: Summary of a Workshop*. Washington, DC: National Academies Press.
https://www.nap.edu/catalog/21666/potential-risks-and-benefits-of-gain-of
-function-research-summary.

National Science Advisory Board for Biosecurity (NSABB). 2007. "Proposed Framework for the Oversight of Dual Use Life Sciences Research: Strategies for Minimizing the Potential Misuse of Research Information." Accessed June 17, 2018.
https://osp.od.nih.gov/wp-content/uploads/Proposed-Oversight-Framework-for
-Dual-Use-Research.pdf.

———. 2012a. "March 29–30, 2012 Meeting of the National Science Advisory Board for
Biosecurity to Review Revised Manuscripts on Transmissibility of A/H5N1 Influenza
Virus." Accessed February 16, 2013. https://www.nih.gov/sites/default/files/about-nih
/nih-director/statements/collins/03302012_NSABB_Recommendations.pdf.

———. 2012b. *United States Government Policy for Oversight of Life Sciences Dual Use Research
of Concern*. Accessed June 17, 2018. https://www.phe.gov/s3/dualuse/Documents/us
-policy-durc-032812.pdf.

New York Times. 2012. "An Engineered Doomsday." January 7.

Osterholm, Michael T., and Donald A. Henderson. 2012. "Life Sciences at a Crossroads: Respiratory Transmissible H5N1." *Science* 335, no. 6070: 801–802.

Rabinow, Paul, and Gaymon Bennett. 2012. *Designing Human Practices: An Experiment
with Synthetic Biology*. Chicago: University of Chicago Press.

Rancière, Jacques. 2009. "Contemporary Art and the Politics of Aesthetics." In
Communities of Sense: Rethinking Aesthetics and Politics, edited by Beth Hinderliter,
William Kaizen, Vered Maimon, Jaleh Mansoor, and Seth McCormick, 31–50.
Durham, NC: Duke University Press.

Rappert, Brian, and Chandré Gould. 2009. *Biosecurity: Origins, Transformations and
Practices*. Basingstoke, UK: Palgrave Macmillan.

Samimian-Darash, Limor. 2016. "Biosecurity in the U.S.: 'The Scientific' and 'The
American' in Critical Perspective." In *America Observed: On an International Anthro-
pology of the United States*, edited by Virginia Dominguez and Jasmin Habib, 79–102.
New York: Berghahn Books.

Samimian-Darash, Limor, Hadas Henner-Shapira, and Tal Daviko. 2016. "Biosecurity
as a Boundary Object: Science, Society, and the State." *Security Dialogue* 47, no. 4:
329–347.

U.S. Department of Health and Human Services. 2004. "HHS Will Lead Government-
Wide Effort to Enhance Biosecurity in 'Dual Use' Research." Press release, March 4.
Accessed February 16, 2013. https://fas.org/sgp/news/2004/03/hhs030404.html.

White House. 2014. *United States Government Policy for Institutional Oversight of Life Sciences Dual Use Research of Concern.* Accessed May 31, 2015. http://www.phe.gov/s3 /dualuse/Documents/durc-policy.pdf.

World Health Organization (WHO). 2012. *Report on Technical Consultation on H5N1 Research Issues.* Accessed February 10, 2013. http://www.who.int/influenza/ human_ animal_interface/mtg_report_h5n1.pdf.

9

Securing "Standby" and Urban Space Making in Jakarta

Intensities in Search of Forms

AbdouMaliq Simone

When residents of Jakarta look out upon their situations and physical settings, what looks secure? What kinds of "looks" enable them to act with a sense of assuredness, while, at the same time, enabling them not to be stuck in particular positions or outcomes? What is security in uncertain environments, particularly when what passes as certainty is not only deceptive but also constraining, limiting what residents can do with the very uncertain conditions that they face and help constitute? What kinds of looks can navigate the supposedly countervailing needs for predictability and contingency? In this chapter I take up these questions in the context of a rapidly changing built environment for working- and lower-middle-class residents of Jakarta—its so-called majority.

Security entails practices that seek to specify optimizing relational circuits among disparate inclinations, behaviors, and contingencies, and that attempt to manage temporalities of events and horizons. Security is necessarily expansive in that it does not act as if contingency is something measurable or subject to contract in the long term. Rather, it entails efforts to instrumentalize the dissensus and uncertainties that ensue in the interaction of specificities registered as life itself (Dillon 2015).

Security instrumentalizes through a process of extending the ways in which things are implicated in each other, in expanding circuits of relations that economy—especially in the financial topologies of securitization, derivation, and arbitrage—brings about. Discrepant places, things, and experiences are articulated and circulate through each other, not just as matters of speculation, but as a complex architecture of accumulating and dissipating energies and attentions (Anderson 2012). Security, then, is architecture with a particular look. So that when one looks upon a situation or setting, it returns a sense of coherence in spite of the disjunctions it offers to suture or subtract.

In Jakarta—whose governance has long emphasized highly circumscribed horizons of aspiration and tolerance for the inefficacy of urban services and the health and educational systems—securing the future becomes an intensely aesthetic exercise of reading between the lines of what policies prescribe, what media reports, and what everyday conversations connote. It entails a practice of being prepared for multiple, disparate dispositions; of finding a way to be "implicated" in various scenarios and projects without making unequivocal personal commitments. Here the uncertainty is productive, instigative of a tactical repertoire of shifting maneuvers. On the other hand, anxieties about the increasing impossibility of verifying anything—of identifying a "real" substratum underneath the profusion of news, tweets, and rumors—has propelled an obsession with the trappings of Islamic propriety and the sculpting of appearances and public action in a highly stereotypical fashion, as if this can then become the guarantor of "real truth."

Here there is an overlap, an implicit contestation among different kinds of looks and modes of visibility. These looks are ways of designing a surface of things that convey no other depth but the assuredness of order in place, even while they seem to connote a depth of conviction and history. Because they are simply surfaces, they open themselves up to ways of viewing that are informed by various concerns, agendas, and styles. As such, people are able to "write themselves" into a setting or find something of themselves within it. So while an aesthetic dissensus among discrete surfaces may prevail over what kinds of orderings are allowed to endure, different kinds of looks and styles can remain side by side and thus potentiate a possible reconciliation to come. Here, the appearance of a built environment or social scenario seems to "stand by" a multiplicity of readings and viewpoints, ready and available to proceed in very different kinds of direction.

STANDBY: WE HAVE A VISUAL

The majority of Jakarta's residents are seemingly on standby. It is the standby of a vastly enlarged transportation sector of drivers ferrying people and goods through a clogged city; it is the incessant attention people pay to their cellphones awaiting updates, announcements, promotions, and more fortuitous social encounters than the ones they are presently engaged in. Standby is the pervasive sense of provisionality that characterizes the very act of residency; the shift from one temporary accommodation to another, as well as the uncertainty as to what exactly a person possesses when they acquire "property."

Given the substantial shift of that residency from dense horizontality to highly formatted verticality, most apartment owners wait for "real certification," new laws that might more precisely define their rights and responsibilities, and more importantly how to seek recourse when the material and managerial conditions of apartment blocks inevitably go wrong or quickly deteriorate. While well-managed residential complexes certainly do exist, they charge highly inflated prices for this capacity, far exceeding what the vast majority of Jakarta residents could ever afford.

Standby characterizes a work career of short-term contracts, long waits for salary increases, of getting out of debt. Standby is a common practice of rent-seeking, acquiring property that is funded through renting to others, while the owner's salary is reserved for paying cheaper rents in short-term accommodation. Standby is the calculated reluctance to make definitive commitments; it is a concession to the speed of urban transformation and the investment that elite urban growth machines make in staking claims to any eventuality, to being part of any eventuality, whether it is profitable or reasonable, or not. Here, residents are largely bystanders to processes to which they are sometimes indifferent or over which they feel they have no control. As residents increasingly recognize that nothing is built to last, they try to squeeze as much money as they can from whatever they have, just as they realize that they, themselves, are being squeezed in the process. This is a constant recalibration of vulnerability, part of an ability to attune oneself to necessarily unstable surroundings that are unlikely to stabilize.

Standby is not only a temporal condition. It is also a particular spatial position. For even if Jakarta now seems driven by the voracious appetites of big developers, the politicians who depend on their money and turn the built environment into a vehicle to "process" the financial leakages from the conversion of land into industrial plantations, the actual management of the results necessitates the enactment of parallel apparatuses of authority, regulation, and provisioning. Developers may seem to exert dictatorial control over their holdings; they may hold residents in a state of capture in terms of arbitrarily imposed costs, rules, and policing, but the circumstances through which people come to be where they are at any given time entail so many heterogeneities that multiple forms of brokerage are required for anything to get done.

Renting spaces in secondary and tertiary real estate markets, organizing the parking of vehicles, delivering any conceivable service anywhere, registering basic citizenship data, getting the sick to a hospital, negotiating the evacuation of sewage when local processors break down and remain unrepaired, accessing labor for a construction site—all are never "straightforward" processes, as the enactment of each function precipitates a wide range of ramifications that have to be addressed outside any available set of standards or rules (Kusno 2013). Yet, in conditions where so many different realities seem to be simultaneously in play, brokerage provides the "look" of translation, of cultivating a sense of things following from each other analogically. It does not subsume differences into some overarching standard, but rather keeps discrepancies in play, in contact with each other. Brokers "screen" particular threats (Ghertner, McFann, and Goldstein, this volume), in terms of trying to filter or block out the impediments that get in the way of different kinds of activities and persons "standing next to each other." At the same time, even though their complicities and collaborations run deep, even though their job is to "smooth the way" for all kinds of projects, they also perform the "features" of these antagonisms, almost like a film screening, demonstrating in their own usually exaggerated style of interacting with each other the fact that these antagonisms exist.

KEEPING THINGS CLOSE

Take the situation of individual units in a large apartment block in Kalibata City, central Jakarta. They all have nominal owners, even though none have outright certification guaranteeing access to the unit in perpetuity. Given the ambiguities of ownership and the rapid deterioration of infrastructure, the normative objective is to squeeze as much money from the units as possible. The owners frequently operate through holding companies—often formed by developers themselves—that acquire thousands of such units across the city. These are made up of individuals, associations, extended families, and informal groupings from all over the country who invest in the acquisition of units in bulk. As most owners do not live in the particular complex in which their unit is purchased, the use of the unit is then brokered by various agents, who handle a varying number of apartments and eventually acquire a diverse portfolio of units to rent out according to all kinds of temporalities—from one-day stays to multiyear tenancies and according to all kinds of different "contracts."

These portfolios are managed in ways homologous to derivatives, where implicit understandings are drawn that enable brokers to acquire various units from each other at some time in the future according to specific conditions that prevail at the time—which can include the rate of deterioration of the unit, its renovations, its floor location, going price, locational advantages in terms of access to amenities, degree of surveillance of illicit activities, availability to be used for various functions, the character of the "social atmosphere" in which the unit is ensconced, and the extent of owner supervision over the conditions of tenancy.

Brokers may attempt to narrow down their holdings to more easily managed standards and similarities around the character, conditions, and temporalities of tenancy. Others may attempt to maximize the heterogeneity of such holdings, and so there are frequent "trades" and "options." Even these implicit understandings—the right of a particular broker to acquire a particular unit at a future time—can be exchanged, optioned among brokers or, as is often the case, converted into "rights of access" to other "managerial opportunities," such as the right to provide services and extract fees from parking lots, markets, traffic intersections, or even access to particular volumes of goods and delivery systems.

What begins as an asset—a unit in an apartment building—becomes something seemingly beyond calculation. What starts out as a particular piece of fixed capital with an assigned yet changing measurable value is converted, through brokerage, into a series of "intensities" that initially have their form in the apartment unit, but then are dispersed and entrained to other rhythms of circulation and combination whose value cannot be calculated.

Multiple apparatuses, logics, and practices of exerting "management" thus all stand by each other in ways that do not necessarily intersect. It is always difficult for actors, looking and speaking from particular positions and perspectives, to garner an overarching story for how things work or don't work, even when they are not entrenched in a particular position, but circulate among different positions as many Jakartans attempt to do day in and day out. There is no definitive contradiction or collaboration; there is no way to tell whether the vast array of makeshift, seemingly improvised regulatory practices are tolerated top-down or whether interventions that percolate from below seep as "facts on the ground" upward through apparent hierarchies of control.

It is almost impossible to tell, for example, how these networks of brokers acquire hundreds of units in a given complex, whether these brokers are working together, and whether the subsequent territories of distinct complexions and trades—whether drug dealing, food delivery, prostitution, the formation of Islamic associations, the consolidation of gay-friendly buildings—are the culmination of planned deliberations on the part of gangs, parties, or associations, or simply the outcome of the incessant pushing and pulling, slippages and openings among groupings whose compositions are only momentarily

SECURING "STANDBY"

stable or appear stable after the fact as the "look" of a fixed neighborhood, building, or floor structure.

Whatever the case, each disposition is experienced as equally plausible; each stands by the others in a simultaneous connection and disconnection; where the grounds of a relationship rest in each disposition seemingly having nothing to do with the others and, concomitantly, each disposition's relative autonomy resting on the fact that all these other dispositions also exist in some relation to it. Rather than amplifying uncertainty or provoking feelings of insecurity among residents, there is instead a general conviction that the "angles are being covered," "the contingencies anticipated," and "uncertainties smoothed over," as several residents of Kalibata City have indicated in conversation with me.

Certainly there is neither equality nor equivalence among forces and forms. Rather the membranes of consolidation are repeatedly punctured in rough intersections that scar the surfaces of discrete identities and compel continuous adjustments through the remaking of boundaries—what or who is included in any enactment, project, or deal. Thus, the elements of any agglomeration that attempts to make something happen are always on standby—awaiting either better offers or more possibilities, or marginalization or eviction from the playing field all together. In part, Jakarta's urban history suggests that conflict has long had an instrumental function as a means of securing new options and sorting through alternative futures, especially conflicts over the disposition of land (Firman 2004; Leaf 1994). The long reluctance on the part of households to specify the terms of inheritance for land normatively precipitated conflicts among the inheritors who, officially, had to all provide their consent for how land would be sold or developed. This would prompt all kinds of undermining and complicities, pulling land in different directions; indeterminacy was often a device for diversifying the content of what took place in a given area.

But in order for such diversification to function, residents and operators within a given district had to be able to witness what was taking place. They had to look at each other and at what each other was doing, tuning their actions to shifting environmental signals. Here, looking is not so much intended to judge or enforce, but rather functions as a "looking out" onto a situation for what it could "hold"; a way of seeing that divergences could indeed sit together within a specific setting. There was rarely anything approaching "community sentiment" or contractual collaborations, but this was not important as long as different "games" could calibrate themselves in relationship to each other, attain a functional indifference to each other, yet remain graspable by a larger public.

But as the financial stakes and consumption aspirations of households have gotten higher, such instrumentality is rapidly disappearing, as the old balances are being swept away. The new spatial products, political networks, and management practices, however, do not so much impose a new coherent order, but instead either explicitly or implicitly (again it is always difficult to tell) fold in varying styles of participation, arbitrary coercion, grassroots populism, religious mobilization, formal governance, clientelism, and accommodation in more opaque ways—where each element stands by to become something else.

In the remainder of this chapter, the objective is to explore some of the conceptual and empirical underpinnings of this notion of standby, particularly the ways in which it operates as a mode for generating a sense or look of security from conditions that offer highly uncertain horizons of what is possible and viable.

DETACHING THE SECURE AND INSECURE

How do urban residents mediate between the compulsion either to turn their bodies and lives into logistical instruments—being at the "right place at the right time," unimpeded by history—or to slow circulation down sufficiently to be able to reflect on their own actions? How do they maintain some ground in order to build a sense of memory and a narrative about where they come from as a means to anticipate possible forward trajectories in order to decide to act, as opposed to succumbing to paralysis or constant anxiety? These are increasingly critical questions facing residents of contemporary Jakarta as they witness the unraveling of familiar modes of residency—an unraveling occasioned, in part, by urban space's normalization to regimens of capital accumulation and the uncertainties they create around what "residency" even means.

In a region of thirty million people, what would residents stake their futures on? How would they decide where and on what to devote their time and their mostly limited resources? Readings of the landscape, in all of its multifaceted physical, social, and political dimensions, would of course be replete with cues and trajectories. Certainly vast alterations of the built environment with their implications for where and how people reside, socialize, and operate economically reinforce an intensive individuation of livelihood, obligation, and accountability. In a city where how the world was to be interpreted was largely contingent upon the everyday pragmatics of residents coordinating markedly heterogeneous backgrounds and ways of doing things within dense, collectively evolved quarters, the ongoing disentanglement of these everyday relations attenuates the accompanying structures of interpretation. Conditions of dissensus increasingly reign.

In order to assess the efficacy of action and decisions, it is difficult to know what is relevant to pay attention to. What constitutes the important variables or considerations? What looks to be secure? It is difficult to exclude things in such assessments. Additionally, even as processes of continuous remaking seem to predominate across the material landscape of Jakarta, the region is replete with "strange contiguities." All kinds of built forms, histories, and economic operations sit uneasily next to each other, and while it can be evident that particular ways of doing things and spaces experience rapid decline, sufficient dissonance exists among that which does emerge to generate confusion and uncertainty as to where things are headed.

The voluminous use of social media proliferates points of exposure to the capsulized versions of other experiences, and specific ethics of orientation emerge based on references to more globalized norms of conduct and consumption. For example, as the world's largest Islamic urban region, Jakarta exudes the full range of markets associated with an Islamic ethos—from fashion and finance to food, lifestyle, and education. Whereas Islam has always been an essential facet of everyday life for the majority of Jakarta's residents, the materialization of everyday practice has largely been contingent upon balancing different sensibilities, regional backgrounds, and procedural diversities that were present in most neighborhoods. But as neighborhoods increasingly become mega-apartment blocks or miles of homogeneous small houses, a more abstracted, uniform version of Islamic propriety comes to the fore—one largely informed by a Middle Eastern–inflected format that long has dominated media outlets and propagation.

Public displays of piety and propriety are actively cultivated as potential assets to facilitate access to opportunities and jobs. It is about having the right look. But at the same time as professions of faith become more homogeneous and instrumental, how do individuals emerge from the crowd to be noticed? For the process of attempting to insure one's future increasingly seems to depend upon the capacity to *act* assured, even in the absence of any actual assurance about what you know or what you are dealing with (Muniesa 2014).

Additionally, both urban sociality and governance circulate through the possibilities of "better deals," of more provisional constellations of actors and affordances where no one can afford to remain where they are. Increasingly the intermeshing of production, servicing, labor, and shelter does not depend upon conventional protocols of ownership, wage levels, and eligibility requirements. The salary, for example, as the primary device marking the exchange of labor is increasingly enmeshed in a thicket of oscillating bonuses, rewards, amenities, and promises of access to opportunities, all of which make the performance of jobs something more diffuse and subject to random interpretations even as the technologies to manage productivity and proficiency are more widely implemented and totalizing.

Despite the persistence of certain anchors of belonging, whether in kinship, territory, or caregiving systems, they are implanted in ground that is being constantly repositioned, resettled, and rearticulated. Residents are compelled to know what they are, to constantly add on to this knowledge, and to be prepared to be many different things simultaneously. But they are also "instructed" to also never forget where they come from, and to articulate all of these possibilities to diverse channels of indebtedness (Berlant 2016). But this compulsion is not easy to address in situations where you have a good idea about *where* you are since everywhere looks pretty much the same and since so much effort is expended in making that look of similarity deceiving. Any place can be so thoroughly networked to different sentiments, evaluations, and operations that there is no way it can seemingly stand on its own, be itself. Rather, particularities simply emphasize the temporariness of any given situation or perspective; they are not anything to "stand on" in order to take a reading of the probable efficacy of particular courses of action.

How, then, is it possible to constitute a position of "standing by," occupying this tension between extensive relationality and the compulsions to be singular in order to experience a "real" sense of movement from "here to there"? How can one constitute or identify a functional interstice that becomes a medium of navigation in conditions where urban dwellers may increasingly feel everywhere and nowhere at the same time?

I want to think through this conundrum by exploring the changing looks of the built environment in Jakarta (see Figure 9.1). On the one hand, as more and more residents move to mega-complexes of vertical towers that seem to materialize an intensive process of individuation and the disentangling of long-honed forms of sociability, the spaces of former residential, commercial, and small industrial districts that had housed the majority of the city's upper poor, working- and lower-middle-class population (the majority) seem to shrink and themselves be subject to more desperate maneuvers to stay afloat.

On the other hand, these residual districts become increasingly contested zones for various forms of speculative activity, some of it generated through the provisional yet nevertheless collectively performed engagements of the nascent residents of the mega-complexes themselves. Here, the older "popular" districts become staging areas for tentative, experimental projects aimed at provisioning the complexes with goods and services cheaper than those offered by the "official" outlets within the complex. What takes place then are

Figure 9.1 The clash of vertical individuation and horizontal sociability found in Cempaka Putih, Jakarta. Photograph by author.

successive layers and styles of *detachment*, sometimes complicit with the widespread disentanglement of localized physical sociability and sometimes giving rise to a burgeoning remaking of collective life along uncertain trajectories and forms.

CHANGING AESTHETICS OF THE EVERYDAY

The intricacies of information economies configure new spatial dimensions of the vertical and the horizontal. In what Benjamin Bratton (2016) calls "the stack," promiscuities of all kinds are superimposed on each other, creating a confluence of interoperable standards-based complex material-information systems. Each place, person, or locale is the superimposition of proliferating signifying systems. What something is or could be, what it can do, and where and what it relates to is something increasingly multiple, all over the place. This takes place in such a way that no place belongs to any particular "sovereign decision."

There can be no easy, even arbitrary, declarations of what belongs or what does not; about who is friend or enemy. Every time a new threat to Islam is discovered, for example, many Jakartans will grow more anxious about the proliferation of threats. The various ways in which entities are located and addressed in networks of information means that there can be many layers of sovereign claims over the same site, person, or event. Bratton (2016) includes the example of ubiquitous computing that will soon be capable of assigning unique addresses to a near-infinite variety of shifting forms of relationships between things. He also cites the ways in which augmented reality directly projects a layer of indexical signs upon a given perceptual field of vision, and literally dislocates it from any single set of coordinates.

When every site becomes not simply the afterglow of averages, samples, and approximation, but can be directly accounted for and mapped, they are the "starting points" for all kinds of emergent relationships and configurations (Negarestani 2013). As it is possible to zero-in on anything and to subject it to demographic, economic, biochemical, and meta-ecological probabilities, what that place is becomes the stacking of a plurality of models and frameworks that produce opacity rather than any kind of knowledge.

Here we see a speeding and a deepening of Michel Foucault's (2009) concerns with how strategies of localization can never keep up with the spilling over of life and places themselves, can never quite contain what takes place. Foucault diagrammed the exposures and folds, stretches and pulls that produce resonance and coordination among constellations of effort and transaction by different actors. Amidst the jumbles of interstices, enclosures, and openings that ensue from the interaction of materials and metabolisms, power is mobilized through constructing architectures of possibilities. These architectures are of specific lines of association and distancing, gathering up things as mutually implicated while separating off other possibilities and matters viewed as disallowed and irrelevant.

The density of the city was not just those of human bodies but of the multiplicity of possible associations among bodies and various materials. While these associations have been subject to various political technologies of governance and control, there has always been something that slips through, leaks out, overflows, or generates long shadows. This is the problem of multiplicities.

Using Foucault's notion of eventalization, John Ploger (2010) talks about how new modes of action can emerge from the very process through which particular ways of connecting encounters, forces, and strategies come to the fore. For in attaining the visibility of what counts as the legitimate connections, official articulations of multiplicity always suggest the possibilities of other kinds of articulations. These are articulations that are not filtered or dictated through sanctioned logics of association, but rather through analogies and other kinds of similarities among the symbolic properties of spaces. As Isabelle

Stengers (2010, 31) indicates, "Agreement may have the character of an event, which may well be an answer to a common matter of concern but without the concern having the power to define its eventual practical consequences."

In the neighborhood where I lived in central Jakarta, for example, seemingly middle-class pavilions fronting a drivable street create the veneer of upward mobility and tranquility. But in the spaces behind these homes often an entire other world has been implanted over time. In the volume of space between parallel streets, in the back lots of property, long histories of subdivision, subtenancy, long- and short-term leasing have created highly dense "interiors" seemingly rendered invisible by the veneer of middle-class frontage. While conditions of density can be overwhelming, as intense crowding takes its toll on available infrastructure, residents of the interior often have more extensive networks into the larger city than the middle-class residents.

Highly intricate circuits of information exchange are forged that enable residents of greater means to circumvent their otherwise claustrophobic reliance upon bureaucratic and patronage networks, typically based largely on place of work. As they are usually trying to complement their official salaries with income derived from various entrepreneurial initiatives that are usually experimental and do not consume large amounts of disposable income, these circuits become valuable "windows" on the larger city, as residents of the "interior" are often folded as labor into them as well.

THE RISK OF FAILURE

In Marilyn Strathern's (2011, 2014) ethnographies the impetus of social life is to both separate and connect. Different social entities can live within their own particular modalities of being, yet they keep each other in view because only those who are separate can tell each other who they are respectively. The view from afar is the only basis from which something can be "told," because orientation is something that emanates in relationship to something else, as it has no significance in its own right.

Separated people need no uniform content of understanding in order to understand each other, but rather each assumes that the other has protocols for working things out, just as they do. Whatever conflicts may ensue may have many different routes for getting there, and these routes do not need an overarching concept, such as ethnicity, as a definitive means of accounting for them. Relations can unfold without overarching reasons for doing so. They can seemingly expand to encompass all kinds of actors and situations. But if relations are to be activated and recognized as operative in the day-to-day lives of given individuals and societies, they must be objectified in some way. There must be some means for them to be recognized. This occurs only if they assume a particular form, a particular aesthetic that enables them to properly appear, to be properly recognized.

As a result, in rapidly changing environments where neighborhoods are destroyed, sites of work lost, and ways of deciding things shift into the domains of impersonal and bureaucratic coding, the sense of being able to know things and to feel a sense of commonality with one's surroundings is disrupted (Candea 2010; Ingold 2011; Navaro-Yashin 2009). This is why it is the case that even when a settlement is relocated to a different site, with people rehoused in more uniform material settings, a sense of strangeness often pervades. This is why even when governments bring certain places and populations into a broader recognition—identifying their needs and priorities—there is often a reluctance to fully embrace such institutional apprehensions; people are not accustomed to or desirous of being known in such fixed ways.

So, knowledge itself, as a process of connecting various parts of a person's or culture's experiences—and, as Strathern has emphasized, cutting off other facets—depends upon the materiality of arrangements, as well as the attainment of a certain look. Objects not only become important mediations between affect and images of self and others, but they help people go back and forth between different versions of themselves, between different scenarios, enactments, and performances on a day-to-day basis. The shrinking, homogenization, or "spectralization" of built environments thus limits the capacities of people to move among heterogeneous perspectives and realities (Anderson 2012; Serres 2008).

The world that inhabitants occupy might evict them at any moment. They, too, may vacate the city as they know it. Much emphasis has been placed on the long-term exodus from the inner city to suburbs, from suburbs to exurban gated communities or back to a substantially remade inner city replete with multiple silos and all-in-one complexes that combine almost every facet of life. Throughout the Global South there appears to be a seamless convergence between desires to live in efficiently managed high-rise complexes away from but still proximate to the urban core and its continuously elaborated lifestyles. The retrofitting of the urban core with high-end, multinational services and amenities also targets residents of poor and working-class areas as objects of eviction and enticement. Much of the violence of forced removals of past years has been replaced with promises of free televisions and washing machines to accompany relocation to cheaply built high-rise accommodation at the periphery of the urban region.

But the vacating of worlds has been a feature of cities for a long time, something reflected in the convoluted patchworks of built environments full of materials emplaced in strange contiguities. Buildings of all kinds and functions in many parts of cities, particularly in those mega-regions of the Global South, are entangled in seemingly improbable embraces, reflecting the bodily movements of a plethora of creatures. I work in inner-city districts of Jakarta still full of an intense mixture of social backgrounds, economies, and built environments. While residents can recall particular sequences of inhabitation, construction, renovation, removal, and destruction in their immediate built environment, they are often hard pressed to account for how their surrounds got to be the way they are today.

The differences in the morphology of districts that began their existence as a result of systematic planning and those that have emerged through various times and logics of self-construction are sometimes indiscernible. Those districts that were laid out with well-ordered grids and demarcations of property could mutate into different hybrid forms. As indicated earlier, the back plots of constructed pavilions could be rented to others who would assemble makeshift structures and, over time, these ancillary settlements could generate a life of their own, proliferating across contiguous back plots, generating further subdivisions or consolidations until all available acreage was filled. Original tenants could intervene in reshaping the arrangements in the back lots, just as those of the back lots might be able to, over time, "make moves" on the frontage. Yet these patterns do not necessarily repeat themselves across contiguous blocks. The "seeding" and spread of such mutations assume no "usual" trajectory. Not dissimilarly, the more random and dispersed insertions of residents in districts that were largely constructed from the ground up with few interventions from municipalities or developers could also tend toward more linear gridded layouts over time, particularly in situations where there existed large-scale collective sentiment to aim for regularization of tenancies.

The point is that the built environment can express the making of relations that operate according to intensely experimental inclinations, as residents attempt to both differentiate themselves from each other and, at the same time, find multiple ways to coexist. The tensions between fitting into a larger collective schema that orients residents to specific forms of optimal functioning—about how to be visible in such a way as to gain access to services and opportunities—and the need to also "stand out" so as to make specific claims and garner particular opportunities are incessant. These tensions are clearly marked in built environments, and particularly in situations in which inhabitation meant not only having access to shelter but also a physical platform from which individuals and households could conduct economic activity and communicate specific messages about who they were and what they were capable of doing to a larger audience.

EXPERIMENTS WITH THE LOOK

Built environments reflect assessments about what can be afforded, which include the trade-offs among various facets of everyday experience: levels of comfort, resource consumption, use of space, public visibility, ease of access, aesthetic preference, flexibility of adjustment, security of tenure, personal safety, and geographic location are all weighed in terms of each other. In the intensely mixed-income, mixed-social-background districts of central Jakarta, residents would navigate across a wide range of decisions—both their own and those of others.

Some residents would commit to substantial initial expenditures, building big in order to hedge against future land divisions and to use the substantial outlay as a way of consolidating particular local advantages, which might include establishing a local power base. Others adopted a more wait-and-see attitude, preferring to install incremental adjustments over time, flexibly moving with the changes of a district's position in relationship to the wider city. The results of many different decisions as to how to deploy available resources and space existed in close proximity to each other, even when they did not necessarily have anything directly to do with each other.

As Wita, a forty-nine-year-old market manager, put it, "We were not looking for mirrors, we wanted to jump beyond what we knew because we were constantly reminded that there was something really possible that we were not aware of, not just silly dreams, but real things that could happen if we could only 'hitch our wagons to them.'" When residents move daily through an intense mixture of living situations marked by the extensive diversity in their field of vision, how, as Ardhi, a thirty-five-year-old artist, muses, "are we going to tell what is proper and what is not, what works or what is useless?"

To make things work, sometimes residents had to take measures that took objects out of their usual context and inserted them as provisional solutions. When the built environment aspires to materialize itself as the model from which it supposedly emanates, things are visualized as in their place. Their integrity is intact; they are where they should be, serving the concept or the realized whole to which they serve as components. A door is inscribed in the house via a specific emplacement and function. It is not to be used as sometimes it indeed is, as a makeshift bridge over a small drainage ditch at the frontage of a property. Bricks used to construct walls are to be laid in their proper quantity, with any

239

SECURING "STANDBY"

excess devoted to decorative or functional supplements inside or adjoining the edifice—and not scattered along the street in piles of varying numbers. Train schedules are not designed to be used to calculate the prices for sex workers who lounge around scores of makeshift bars lining the tracks; the electric pylons that power the trains are similarly not intended to keep the drinks cool and lights just bright enough to make sure the correct calculations are made and the right amount of money is exchanged. But in central Jakarta, things are always spilling over from the uses and models that incorporate them. As such they offer something more than what anyone had in mind.

Here, a general atmosphere is constructed where places are always already inhabited by something more than what anyone had in mind. In urban contexts where the competition for jobs and resources could be fierce, where the uncertainties around security of tenure, employment, and political stability were rampant, it was important for households to aim for the "right pitch." As Mina, a school principal, explained, "The ability to sing in unison as protection against the larger forces that we all knew were there, but didn't know quite what they were, even though we did our best to learn about them and have them see us as only their willing devotees." Rachman, a fifty-five-year-old mechanic, further emphasized that "if we all did the same thing it would be 'one down, everyone down,' and so we understood that we would have to learn to like living in places where there was nothing to really like, but somehow, then, we were safe." Residents, in other words, were always getting something "more than [they] bargained for," says Jo, a sixty-year-old businessman. Living with this "something more" in mind, and seeing it played out in the way in which the built environment was elaborated through all kinds of twists and turns, repairs and adjustments, renovations and demolitions, and seemingly incongruous mixtures of uses of materials, institutionalized a sense of disparate meanderings.

In neighborhoods where decisions had to be made, balanced, revised, and publicized, there was frequently the absence of judgment. By nature, experimentation is an ordeal. It is not frivolous as it not only entails an expenditure of time and resources but has often untold implications for the experimenter. Urban neighborhoods are of course replete with many judgments; this is an inevitable aspect of residents being able to decide what to pay attention to in an environment full of things to pay attention to and what, in a multitude of performances, is important to imitate, complement, or set oneself off from. Judgments in this instance are not about the moral validity of others, but rather a screening device, a way of prioritizing particular parameters of sameness and difference that can be functionally used by residents attempting to orient them within the complexity of urban life.

The judgments can turn into harsh, sometimes debilitating constraints. They can constitute the basis of punitive actions against others whereby stringent conditions are established for the continuity of relationships. They are used to expel, abolish, and destroy. But the willingness of residents to suspend and avoid judgment has been a critical aspect of the capacity of residents to experiment, to piece together the various materials and forces circulating around and through them in different ways. Importantly, it also provides a space for failure. For it was likely that many initiatives and trials would go nowhere. For lives where the sheer pleasure of curiosity often had to be tempered with the demands of efficacy, of making and sustaining viable livelihoods, the productivity of failure could be limited, prompting exasperation and plenty of incentives to simply adhere to the prevailing standards of propriety. But since so many residents failed so often, failure did not necessarily rule out continuous attempts to try even more seemingly outlandish initiatives.

RESECURING THE POPULAR?

But currently, it would seem that a sense of failure is pervasive across the districts formerly housing the urban majority of Jakarta. Even as remaining residents convert whatever they can into cheap rooming houses or commercial spaces, Jakarta churns out more and more mega-complexes, even as it falls behind in providing adequate volumes of affordable housing. As a more transient population of different income levels fills the urban core, much of this nascent population, given its mobility, is not registered and therefore does not count when it comes to budgetary allocations and service provision. As cheap housing in the form of homogeneous lines of small pavilions in the scores of thousands that were rolled out over the past two decades rapidly deteriorate and often remain in the middle of nowhere, there is intense convergence, inward and outward upon a "second ring" of the region, just beyond the former "near suburbs." These near suburbs, too, were replete with popular districts, and now mega-complexes squeeze anywhere from thirty to sixty thousand new residents into existing districts.

As indicated earlier, residents of these large complexes have deployed a wide range of financing mechanisms to acquire a unit or, in many cases, a series of units. In addition to emergent mortgage systems, this financing draws upon intricate debt networks, savings, barters, and swaps, money pooled collectively by different associations and enterprises, proceeds of long-term rental contracts, and laundered money. It is often not clear exactly what is acquired in these transactions, as property remains something fluid. Often titles are not issued until all of the units in a complex are sold—and these sometimes number between fifteen and twenty thousand. Few outright titles have yet to be issued in Jakarta, so this remains a ceaselessly incomplete promise. Residents are sometimes led to believe that they are also purchasing the infrastructural equipment of the flat, its interior pipes, wires, and conduits, only to discover that they have to pay not only for the water and electricity they consume but also a type of rent for these basic infrastructures. Developers of complexes rarely own the land outright and instead secure development rights subject to oscillating terms with landowners who frequently sell the now developed land to someone else with the capacity to renegotiate terms.

As units are typically bought and sold several times prior to completion (in fact, this is largely their purpose), they are also usually subject to intricate subleasing arrangements and brokerage systems that all apply their own particular contractual arrangements. As indicated earlier, the acquisition of a supposedly secure asset that maximizes a sense of individual security in an increasingly uncertain process of urban transformation ends up being infused with peculiar insecurities, in part derivable from its fungibility, its capacity to take on different functions and even forms based on different kinds of tenancy, which can potentially increase the income accruing from such an asset but open possibilities for loss as well. What represents a medium of detachment from labor-intensive extended household and community ties can easily become a feeling of being caught in rapidly depreciating value. This is why the object of acquisition is now often less a unit than a block of units in various complexes.

For many residents of these complexes with whom I have spoken, there is little sense of home, and often little desire for consolidating a home in a specific location now. For them security is located in the possibilities of circulation. As there is little to distinguish one complex from the other, residents cite location as that which was purchased, the particular complexion of the node seen as facilitating access to work, transport, relative anonymity, or as a hedge on where they thought the city was heading. There was little within the complex itself capable of mirroring any sense of progression, of development over the long term; it was seen more as a place to "park" oneself for now.

At the same time, the composition of these complexes is so "all over the place" in terms of the plurality of money brought to the table and subsequent arrangements of habitation that many buildings become intensely cosmopolitan spaces in terms of who is living within them and under what circumstances.

While seemingly aspirant young middle-class residents would seem to predominate, how they actually inhabit the complex is subject to intense variation in terms of temporalities of stay, the social composition of units, and the networks of preexisting connections. In the everyday working out of conviviality, the emergence of residential associations, and the conversion of specific spaces into various social services, residents discover a range of mutual interests and opportunistic possibilities.

Since there are limited spaces of operation to cultivate new activities within the complex itself, the older districts contiguous to the complexes are becoming increasingly used as sites for the development of new small enterprises whose products and services are directed toward consumption by residents of the complex, who are harnessed to a predictable range of standardized stores. These neighborhoods also experience a swell of temporary residents drawn by cheap boarding houses that require no contracts or length of stay. Small eating places that come and go line surrounding streets. Workshops that have lain dormant for years are once again used, but often with a rapid turnover of projects and tenants.

New life is being breathed into popular districts seemingly on their way out, but the terms of their security come not from the logics of the past, where residents of heterogeneous origins, backgrounds, and connections to the city incrementally built a long-term collective life with each other. As long as these areas exist, they will probably do so on standby.

Now, security rests in the status of the popular as a site of provisionality, that no long-term life need be built; that the diversity of the built environment, land statuses, investment protocols, and local actors less inclined to deal with each other—all indications of a district's vulnerability—can instead, momentarily be marshaled into something else, as a kind of a supplement, where a new multiplicity of actors infuse the space with a wide range of agendas and projects that make any broad, uniform transformation of the area into one particular direction or trajectory difficult, for now. As such, a sense of security is anchored in a certain insecurity, whose dispositions may have calculable probabilities in the long run, but provide apertures of all kinds in the short run.

REFERENCES

Anderson, Ben. 2012. "Affect and Biopower: Towards a Politics of Life." *Transactions of the Institute of British Geographers* 37: 28–43.

Berlant, Lauren. 2016. "The Commons: Infrastructure for Troubling Times." *Environment and Planning D: Society and Space* 34: 393–413.

Bratton, Benjamin. 2016. *The Stack: On Software and Sovereignty.* Cambridge, MA: MIT Press.

Candea, Mattei. 2010. "Anonymous Introductions: Identity and Belonging in Corsica." *Journal of the Royal Anthropological Institute* 16: 119–137.

Dillon, Michael. 2015. *Biopolitics of Security: A Political Analytic of Finitude.* London: Routledge.

Firman, Tommy. 2004. "Major Issues in Indonesia's Urban Land Development." *Land Use Policy* 21: 347–355.

Foucault, Michel. 2009. *Security, Territory, Population.* New York: Palgrave Macmillan.

Ingold, Tim. 2011. *Being Alive: Essays on Movement, Knowledge and Description.* London: Routledge.

Kusno, Abidin. 2013. "Housing the Margin: Perumahan Rakyat and the Future of Urban Form of Jakarta." *Indonesia* 94: 23–56.

Leaf, Michael. 1994. "Legal Authority in an Extralegal Setting: The Case of Land Rights in Jakarta, Indonesia." *Journal of Planning Education and Research* 14: 12–18.

Muniesa, Fabian. 2014. *The Provoked Economy: Economic Reality and the Performative Turn.* London: Routledge.

Navaro-Yashin, Yael. 2009. "Affective Spaces, Melancholic Objects: Ruination and the Production of Anthropological Knowledge." *Journal of the Royal Anthropological Institute* 15: 1–18.

Negarestani, Reza. 2013. "The Topos of the Earth." Talk at the Center for Humanities, City University Graduate Center, February 21.

Ploger, John. 2010. "Present-Experiences: The Eventalization of Urban Space." *Environment and Planning D: Society and Space* 28: 848–866.

Serres, Michel. 2008. *The Five Senses: A Philosophy of Mingled Bodies.* London: Continuum.

Stengers, Isabelle. 2010. "Including Non-Humans in Political Theory: Opening a Pandora's Box?" In *Political Matter: Technoscience, Democracy and Public Life*, edited by Bruce Braun and Sarah Whatmore, 3–34. Minneapolis: University of Minnesota Press.

Strathern, Marilyn. 2011. "Binary License." *Common Knowledge* 17: 87–103.

———. 2014. "Anthropological Reasoning: Some Threads of Thought." *HAU: Journal of Ethnographic Theory* 4: 23–37.

Securing the Street

Urban Renewal and the Fight against "Informality" in Mexico City

Alejandra Leal Martínez

Tac, tac, tac: the sound of hammers pounding on metal structures. Pzzzzzzzz: the sound of jigsaws cutting through aluminum bars. It is past eight in the evening in May 2016. The tightly packed, informal[1] street market that for thirty years has stood in the middle of the open-air Chapultepec transportation hub in central Mexico City—now targeted for a major renovation—is slowly being dismantled. Hundreds of street vendors, women and men, young and old, are busy at work. Some are putting their merchandise away in big plastic boxes— from electronics and cellphone accessories to pirated CDs and DVDs; from cheap toys and candy to clothes, shoes, and makeup. Others are disconnecting the wires dangling from the utility poles, for years their source of electricity. Others still are disassembling the metal structures that make up their stands, pulling hard to dig them up from the cement bases that decades ago were built to hold them in place. Many look confused. Numerous piles of rubble start to mount all over the place—plastic bags, crumpled paper, cardboard boxes, pieces of cement, broken metal, trash. The mood is grim. According to the authorities, vendors have until midnight to clear the site and leave.

As we walk around the slowly disappearing street market, Ricardo, a mid-level bureaucrat at the Urban Planning and Housing Ministry, who is overseeing the "removal," as he calls it, is visibly happy that vendors are finally being cleared. He refers to them as a "hindrance" and a "mafia" that for too long

Figure 10.1   The market in the Chapultepec hub days before the "removal."
Photograph by author.

"seized" a public space for private gain. Three police vans are parked across the street, but the officers are nowhere to be seen. Ricardo explains that dozens of policemen are waiting a few blocks away, ready to act in case of disturbances, but the process continues without incident until the early morning hours, when all vendors are finally gone (see Figure 10.1).

A public-private partnership between the local government and an international real estate development firm, the renovation seeks to drastically reorganize and transform the Chapultepec transportation hub into a "secure," "orderly," and "sustainable" space. With its worn-out pavement and numerous potholes, its seemingly endless and chaotic proliferation of ramshackle buses and, above all, its multitudes of informal street vendors, it is often depicted in the local press, in social media, and in everyday talk as a pigsty, a dump, and a dangerous place.[2] Indeed, as is the case with other informal street workers in central Mexico City, street vendors in the Chapultepec hub are seen as a dangerous presence that brings disorder and criminality to the areas that it touches.

A similar discourse underpins the recent installation of parking meters in streets and neighborhoods adjacent to the Chapultepec hub. Also a public-private initiative, this other project, named EcoParq, aims, according to a promotional leaflet, "to improve urban mobility and to recuperate public space by bringing order to street parking" in highly congested central city neighborhoods. Whereas in the hub the term "informal" is applied to street vendors who sell their merchandise to commuters—for the most part middle- and lower-middle-class workers that daily travel to the central city—in the case of street parking it refers to parking attendants, locally known as *franeleros*. These are usually young to middle-aged men who block parking spaces with buckets or boxes, only to remove them for drivers who pay a tip in exchange for the space, to which they direct them using a red rag, or *franela*, hence their name.[3] Like street vendors, informal parking attendants appear in both public discourse and everyday talk as "parasites" that profit from "sequestering" a common space, the street, and who similarly bring chaos and criminality with them.

The eradication of informality has thus been a central premise—and promise—of a variety of urban renewal initiatives that over the past decades have visibly transformed several middle- and upper-middle-class neighborhoods in central Mexico City (Becker and Muller 2013). Positing the informal as a threat to be reined in, urban renewal projects promise not only to produce a secured urban landscape, but also to make the city resemble the cosmopolitan capitals of the world. Put differently, by mobilizing a language of competitiveness, efficiency, and worldliness, these projects have conjured desired images of a future of order and safety—whose promoters associate with global metropolises such as New York and London—which contrasts with a here-and-now of chaos and informality (Ghertner 2015; Roy and Ong 2011). Both the hub's renovation project and the parking meters program thus embody a particular aesthetic of security: a city composed of domesticated and beautified spaces and emptied of threatening bodies and social relations.

247

Based on ethnographic research with promoters and supporters of these two urban renewal projects as well as with street vendors in the Chapultepec hub, in this chapter I explore a double sense of (in)security that runs at the heart of these initiatives and the security aesthetics that they embody. I argue that the construal of informal street workers as the source of middle-class fear in the city is predicated on the displacement of another form of (in)security. This refers not only to the precariousness and insecurities that characterize day-to-day work in the city's streets, but, more crucially, to the forms of political negotiation and belonging that for decades have provided street workers with a particular—albeit partial—form of (work and social) security. In other words, security understood as middle-class perceptions of safety hinges upon a disavowal of both the structural inequities that are at the very center of informal street work and the political mechanisms though which the poor have been incorporated into the urban order. In this context, street informality—and the social relations in which it is embedded—has been temporalized as belonging to the past and has come to appear as an obstacle to a desired cosmopolitan future, indeed, as having no place in that future.

In order to interrogate this double sense of (in)security, the chapter puts in conversation literature on fear and safety in contemporary cities, on the one hand, and literature on neoliberal citizenship and the urban poor, on the other. In doing this, it emphasizes that the global obsession with security understood as the foreclosing of future threats is rooted in larger neoliberal reconfigurations, including the receding horizon of social security (Muehlebach 2012). Let us recall that the second half of the twentieth century witnessed the consolidation and collapse of different forms of the social state. In that context, security meant not only protecting citizens against different dangers but also guaranteeing their well-being. As Nikolas Rose (1999, 247) puts it, "A domain of collective security was envisaged to be maintained by the state on behalf of all citizens, through universal measures ranging from social insurance to the enforcement of criminal law by a unified and socially funded police force."

The national civic collective was thus not only constituted in relation to internal and external threats but also through a particular social contract that put the collectivization of risk, social solidarity, and redistribution—that is, the security of *all* citizens—at the center of the state's legitimacy. Certainly, the ideals of the social state were never fully realized and, to the extent that they were, took rather distinct forms in different regions. Nonetheless, they constituted a common horizon, as well as a commitment and an aspiration, if not an institutional reality, in many parts of the world, including Latin America (Muehlebach and Shoshan 2012, 319).

The transformation of these arrangements under the sign of neoliberalism since the last decades of the twentieth century, and of the sensitivities to which they gave rise, has been discussed at large (Babb 2004; Brenner and Theodore 2002). While collective security presupposed a robust state to guarantee the well-being of *all* citizens, under neoliberal modes of governance each citizen is meant to be responsible for his own and that of his community. In contrast to the supposedly passive and dependent citizens of the social state, neoliberal individuals are expected to actively guarantee their own well-being and security by carefully managing risk, including the risk of crime (Rose 1999, 247). Consequently, each individual, as Daniel Goldstein (2010, 492) has argued, is "encouraged to assume a habitually anxious, cautious engagement with anyone or anything deemed unfamiliar and potentially threatening."

Urban studies scholars have tackled the effects of this individuation of security in the urban landscape, as well as the proliferation of revanchist modes of governance, urban planning schemes, and policing strategies that have accompanied this process (Smith 1998). Some have approached security as a status symbol defined by access to private protective services in fortified enclaves of work, residence, and consumption (Caldeira 2000; M. Davis 1992). Others have examined the consequences for the urban poor of the circulation of neoliberal security discourses and strategies the world across (Rao 2010; Swanson 2007). Others still have focused on the assumed link between perceptual threats and actual danger, which marks the presence of certain bodies in public space as constitutively violent (Feldman 2001). These studies have given less attention to how the disappearance of security as a collective, common horizon articulates with urban securitization processes. And yet, the prevailing emphasis on security as (personal) safety is predicated on the disavowal of security as a collective undertaking and indeed on the reconfiguration of the civic collective itself. As a distinction is drawn between the autonomous and the dependent, the active and the abject, the latter appear as residual, dispensable bodies, cast outside the boundaries of "our" collectivity, indeed, outside the boundaries of citizenship (Yeh 2017).

It is in this context that the urban laws and regulations that accompany urban renewal construe the urban poor's presence in public space not only as dangerous (even criminal) but also, crucially, in terms of physical obstruction and aesthetic disruption. As Nicholas Blomley (2007) has argued in the case of Canadian cities, by emphasizing space, use, and behavior, these laws and regulations create an equivalence between the urban poor and any object that encumbers freedom of movement and ruins the city's aesthetic image, erasing rights-based arguments that support the poor's survival strategies. This is the case in Mexico City, where street activities have been expelled from the universe of socially recognized work. As I will argue, those who engage in such activities are no longer seen as workers deserving (social) security, but rather as abject, threatening, dirtying bodies that must be removed in the interest of a particular aesthetic of security. The central point to be made, then, is that while sensorial dimensions of sight, noise, and smell have historically been central to the perception of the urban poor—and their spaces—as dangerous, something more is at work in contemporary security discourses and strategies. As the horizon of universal prosperity and inclusion—of security for all—has been foreclosed, and as the urban poor have been vanished from the civic collective and from the rights and obligations of citizenship, security mechanisms now maintain the continuous exclusion of those who are already outside.

Following the themes of this volume, I attend to the aesthetic dimensions of this operation in Mexico City or, as D. Asher Ghertner, Hudson McFann, and Daniel Goldstein (this volume) put it, to the "sensory coding of security logics into the design of physical, geographical, and infrastructural milieux." Specifically, I suggest that the redistribution of social entitlements under conditions of neoliberalization must be seen as resting on a concomitant "redistribution of the sensible," or a rearrangement of the self-evident facts of sense perception concerning what belongs or does not belong and what is in-place or out-of-place in the secure and orderly city (Rancière 2004, 12). It is only in a context where certain bodies and voices become unintelligible—and rendered comparable to disruptive and threatening objects rather than as members of the civic collective or, per Jacques Rancière (2009), as citizens "who have a part in the community"—that a renovated, sanitized public plaza or a parking meter can stand as the very embodiment of security.[4]

The remainder of the chapter will develop this argument in four parts. The first two parts discuss the political and social mechanisms through which the urban poor were partially incorporated into the benefits of the social state in Mexico City, as well as the closing of this horizon over the past decades. The next part analyzes how urban renewal projects come to embody a particular promise and aesthetic of security, which is predicated on the disavowal of the structural inequities that shape the contemporary city. It discusses the crucial role of experts—particularly urban mobility experts—in such processes. The final part tackles the effects of these transformations on the already precarious working conditions of the urban poor and the novel insecurities to which these transformations have given rise.

PRECARIOUS SECURITIES

Street work has historically been a central occupation of Mexico City's urban poor, as well as a constitutive element of a street-level urban order (Barbosa 2008). However, there has been a proliferation of informal street activities since the 1982 debt crisis, and the gradual shift from import substitution industrialization and state-sponsored development to an open market economy that came in its wake (Duhau and Giglia 2008). A massive loss of (formal) jobs during the 1980s left a large segment of the population with few other options besides taking to the streets to work.[5] For the city's middle classes, this rise of street informality became inextricably linked to the rise in criminality (Duhau and Giglia 2008, 76). Indeed, with crime rates also rising after the crisis, (in)security emerged as a central concern in Mexico City's public sphere, with calls for tougher approaches to crime and policing becoming increasingly popular.[6]

At the same time, the propagation of (neo)liberal discourses of democracy and citizenship entailed a corresponding loss of legitimacy of long-standing forms of negotiation between the state and the urban poor, forms that have historically enabled the presence of vendors and other workers in the streets and plazas of Mexico City (Leal Martínez 2016b).

These forms of negotiation began to take shape after the Mexican Revolution (1910–1920) and the ensuing ascent and consolidation of a postrevolutionary regime that embraced "revolutionary nationalism" as its guiding ideology. The regime divided the triumphant "revolutionary *pueblo*" into three "corporate sectors" (peasants, workers, and the "popular sector") and promised access to social rights and protections (relating to work, land redistribution, housing, education, and health) through membership in these corporations, and in exchange for loyalty to the regime. This, as Tenorio Trillo (2009) has argued, gave rise to a particular, corporatist form of the welfare state, and to what Lomnitz (2001, 74) has called a "massified" form of social citizenship.

It was in this context, and especially after the 1940s, that the regime slowly recognized street workers in Mexico City as legitimate members of the revolutionary pueblo who could claim a right to work in the streets, even if always ambivalently (Meneses 2011, 45). Therefore, while elite modernization discourses decried (and feared) street workers as disorderly masses, the state also began to recognize their organizations as valid collectives performing legitimate activities that should be negotiated with and regulated (Meneses 2011, 47). Thus, for instance, city authorities granted work permits and licenses to street workers and imposed the use of uniformly designed vending booths in assigned spaces (and proscribed their presence in others). The rules and procedures for these benefits, however, were always highly discretionary and subjected to periodic backlashes that included the criminalization of street work in different periods. Ambiguities and backlashes notwithstanding, belonging to an officially recognized organization provided authorized access to street work and other social protections to the urban poor well into the 1980s.

To be sure, these organizations had a strict hierarchical configuration: leaders controlled who could become a member, in what streets they could work, and the daily amount they would have to pay. At the same time, many provided social protections to their members, such as accessible loans and housing credits, or daycare centers and schools for their children (Crossa 2009, 52).[7] Consequently, these organizations were not merely a vehicle for exchanging resources (or favors) for protections (or support), as the conventional argument about clientelism would have it (Auyero 2014, 115). They involved affect-laden, quotidian social relations of exchange and reciprocity through which the urban poor gained a precarious—and always contingent—access to forms of work and social security otherwise not available to them.

To sum up, Mexico City's street workers benefited from the expansion and consolidation of the postrevolutionary corporatist system, which enabled the urban poor to voice and channel their demands and which, in turn, allowed the state to exert control over the ever-growing urban population (Meneses 2011, 76). Put differently, in a context where social relations of hierarchical codependency have historically taken the place of rights, the state's corporate structures provided the urban poor with a precarious form of security. Moreover, these corporate structures incorporated them into the promise of full inclusion and equality, even if that promise was constantly deferred to the future in the name of modernization.

As mentioned above, informal street work has dramatically increased over the last decades of neoliberalization. According to a 2014 report by the International Labour Organization, 60 percent of work in Mexico takes place in the informal sector.[8] At the same time, street work associations have lost their legitimacy as the state has abandoned its revolutionary rhetoric and as the promises of universal prosperity and (future) inclusion have gradually been foreclosed on (Escalante Gonzalbo 2006). Indeed, much like in other parts of the world, Mexican neoliberalization has entailed the resurgence of liberal discourses of democracy, legality, and citizenship that are vocally critical of postrevolutionary state ideologies for, among other issues, having created dependent subjects. Produced and propagated through a variety of discursive registers—from academic thought to political discourse, from the mass media to everyday talk—these discourses have gained traction in Mexico since the mid-1980s and have gradually become commonsensical (Leal Martínez 2016a). In this context, an idealized figure of the responsible citizen has been delineated as the opposite of the passive subjects of the postrevolutionary regime, which are epitomized by street workers. A temporal reversal has thus taken place: far from being vehicles for inclusion, street workers' organizations, and the corporate practices of which they partake, are represented in public discourse and everyday talk as residues from the postrevolutionary regime and its obsolete corporate structures. They therefore appear as obstacles to modernization and, in the case at hand, to creating a secure and cosmopolitan city, which effectively disavows their claim to a legitimate place in the urban collectivity and, thus, to any form of security.

In this context, the urban poor's presence in public space, especially in the central city, has become legible only as a menace and an obstacle. Urban renewal discourses and projects, and the shifts in the management of street informality that have accompanied them since the early 2000s, have been central to these reconfigurations. As I will discuss below, the evacuation of informal street workers from the urban, civic collective is produced and reproduced by a variety of actors (urban planners, bureaucrats, experts, residents, and so forth) and through a variety of registers, from everyday talk to urban legislation.

WHEN WORKERS BECOME HINDRANCES

One Sunday morning in early 2013, as part of my fieldwork on the introduction of parking meters, I was having Sunday brunch with a group of residents of the hip Roma-Condesa neighborhood, which is adjacent to the Chapultepec hub.[9] Those present at the brunch were part of a group of young professionals in the creative industries (advertising executives, architects, designers, and so forth) who over the past decades have settled in gentrifying neighborhoods in central Mexico City. As I have argued elsewhere (Leal Martínez 2016b), these residents partake of internationally circulating images of the urban as a particular "lifestyle" and accordingly yearn for a cosmopolitan experience of the city devoid of informality (Zukin 1998). They are thus enthusiastic supporters of urban renewal initiatives that aim to move the city in that direction, especially those like the renovation of the Chapultepec hub or EcoParq, which promise to "rescue" public space from informal workers.

The conversation during brunch that morning quickly moved to informal parking attendants, a hot topic at the time. Parking meters had just been installed in the surrounding streets, where many of those present lived, and everyone was hopeful that when the devices began operating a few days later, franeleros would finally be gone. Among those hopeful was Ignacio, an architect in his late thirties, who was an active member of his neighborhood residents' association and who had extensively lobbied state authorities for the installation of parking meters. After reiterating common tropes about parking attendants as aggressive figures who illegally "sequestered" the neighborhood's streets and colluded with car thieves, he said that most infuriating of all for him was that they made "so much money" for "not doing anything all day." Others intervened:

"How much do you think they make?"
"Four, maybe five thousand [pesos] a month" [roughly $380 at the time].
"So much money!"
"Unbelievable!"
"Instead of getting a job!"[10]

These residents participated in widely circulating discourses about street vendors, and especially informal parking attendants, as dangerous elements on the streets; as members of mafia-like, corrupt organizations; and as lazy persons who refuse to work. These discourses posit a link—and a continuum—between informality, illegality, and criminality through their dissemination in a variety of registers: from newspaper reports, which regularly refer to street activities as disorderly, threatening, or openly criminal to opinion pieces that decry their proliferation, calling it a very lucrative business; from crime statistics to expert reports; from social media to quotidian conversations in which street workers are called "dirty," "scroungers," "thugs," and "thieves."

As part of these discourses, consider an opinion column written by a journalist and self-appointed chronicler of the city's criminal underworld, published in the nationally circulating newspaper *El Universal* in 2017, titled "In the Roma [Neighborhood] Criminals Work Everyday." The piece begins with excerpts from a chat-group conversation among restaurant owners in the area, which has in recent years experienced an explosion of hip cafés and upscale restaurants, like the one where the brunch conversation took place. After one chat member reports that his business has been robbed, others reply with similar stories of robberies and extortions, some quite violent, painting a picture of an out-of-control criminality terrorizing the neighborhood. The author writes: "In the chat, members say that Mexico City authorities attribute most of the insecurity unleashed in the neighborhood to the 'secondary economic structure that leeches on the restaurants,' especially the informal parking attendants who function 'as vigils and pass information' to criminals" (De Mauleón 2017, author's translation).

The connection between franeleros and criminals appears as an undeniable fact that does not warrant further examination. At the same time, these commonsensical views of informality construe it as the opposite of work. Indeed, the residents present at the brunch in Roma-Condesa, the bureaucrat that oversaw the removal of street vendors from the Chapultepec hub, the restaurant owners, and the journalist himself do not see them as people in extremely precarious conditions who take to the streets to make a living. Just as importantly, they also fail to recognize that street workers are enabled by, and at the same time reproduce, a quotidian street-level order in which all social classes partake.

In the case of franeleros, this ambivalent and tense street-level order directly involves the middle and upper classes. Some drivers, for example, have long-standing bonds with particular franeleros, entrusting them to park their cars when they arrive at work in the morning. Others rely on onetime interactions with anonymous franeleros, whom they can count on to locate a parking spot when none can be found. Especially these latter forms of interaction are fraught with tension, as the provision of a service is often accompanied by a subtle threat of violence: something could potentially happen to the car—say a scratch could appear—if the driver refused to pay. And yet other interactions are not voluntary, as when franeleros impose the payment of a fee to liberate a spot that has previously been blocked. In this social world, franeleros oscillate between docile service providers and threatening urban figures. Hence drivers simultaneously use their services and condemn them for "seizing" the streets for private gain.

Despite their centrality in the reproduction of this street-level order, not only the public discourse examined above, but also recent urban laws and regulations have played a crucial role both in the expulsion of street work from the universe of socially recognized labor and its criminalization. Consider the Civic Culture Act, a law passed by Mexico City's legislative body in 2004, following the recommendations of former New York City mayor Rudolph Giuliani's consultancy to the local government (D. Davis 2007). As with other laws, regulations, and policies across the world that bear the imprint of Giuliani's "quality of life" approach to policing, the Civic Culture Act penalizes "disorderly" and "antisocial" activities in public space. Building on "broken windows" theory and related approaches to what Ghertner et al. (this volume) describe as "designing fortresses," these policies link such disparate undertakings as street vending, informal car watching, windshield cleaning, painting graffiti, or engaging in street prostitution as petty violations of public order and aesthetic norms, which have the potential to cascade into deeper forms of civility. Street workers thus become symbols not of a need-based economy and a particular street order, but of criminal risk (Goldstein 2016).

And yet, even as street workers appear as the main target of the Civic Culture Act, its legal vocabularies do not target "identifiable persons," but rather proscribe and sanction certain conducts in public space, such as obstructing movement or disrupting tranquility and civic harmony, as administrative misdemeanors (Blomley 2007). The law thus privileges an abstract view of space and use rather than concerning itself with specific categories of users (workers, informal vendors, franeleros) and their particular claims (Meneses 2011, 226). Therefore, according to the Civic Culture Act, informals are no longer workers with rights and obligations, which reflects and in turn (re)produces their erasure from the urban collective. They are no longer members of a community of citizens but obstacles hindering true citizens' right to move freely and at ease through their city's streets and sidewalks.

To sum up, different views converge in contemporary discourses about street workers in Mexico City: they are parasites benefiting from the illegal occupation of public space, not workers engaged in constitutionally protected activities; they are criminal elements on the streets; their organizations are the very embodiment of corruption, and not legitimate collectives that channel the demands of the urban poor. Therefore, all informals are treated as at once a dangerous, threatening presence in the city's streets and as mere obstacles to be removed. Such renderings erase from view the structural inequities that engender informal street activities as well as the extreme precariousness that characterizes the day-to-day survival of the urban poor. At the same time, the security discourses that link informality to criminality, and that have dominated public debates over the past decades, have silenced the disintegration of forms of inclusion (precarious, to be sure) on which, throughout the second half of the twentieth century, the urban poor relied. Security has come to be reflected in controlled, domesticated, world-class spaces with no traces of informality, akin to what Ghertner (2015) writing about Delhi calls a "world-class aesthetic." As I will discuss below, "rescuing" and "cleaning" public spaces appears, then, less as a metaphor and more as a literal act of removing physical hindrances. Aesthetic purification becomes a system of spatial cleansing.

EXPERTISE AND THE AESTHETICS OF SECURITY

Urban renewal projects in Mexico City—from the renovation of the historical downtown, major boulevards, and plazas to the rise of commercial and residential mega-developments—have mobilized a language of modernization, competitiveness, cosmopolitanism, and security. At the same time, promoters of urban renewal have increasingly deployed the vocabularies of "urban mobility" or "sustainable mobility" in such projects. These are loosely articulated fields of policy and expertise that encompass experts and activists who, partaking of globally circulating discourses of sustainability, aim to improve "quality of life" in the city by reducing car dependency and use (Dimitriou and Gakengeimer 2011). They advocate the creation of broader-reaching and more efficient public transportation systems, as well as the production of better public spaces for pedestrians and cyclists (Institute for Transportation and Development Policy 2012).

Urban mobility discourses thus tap into the global imaginaries that are at the heart of urban renewal initiatives. At the same time, they mobilize a seemingly neutral language that approaches urban problems—from informality to traffic congestion to disorderly parking to an obsolete public transportation system—as technical issues demanding technical solutions. Therefore, expert urban mobility languages have been crucial in shaping the security aesthetic of urban renewal. Like the legal vocabularies of the Civic Culture Act, these technical languages construe urban streets and public spaces as sites with specific uses and behaviors to be organized and regulated in a rational and efficient manner, not as contested places occupied by particular persons or collectivities. The ways that different technologies enroll or exclude different actors in forms of economy and livelihood are hence often ignored in discourses of urban mobility. As Mariana Valverde (2005) has argued, this conception effectively displaces discussions of certain rights, for instance the right to work, in relation to those spaces. In her own words, "People have rights: uses, things and spaces do not" (cited in Blomley 2007, 1702).

In this context, a number of expert organizations and international urban mobility consultants have been central in designing the Chapultepec hub's renovation and the parking meters program.[11] Working together, experts and bureaucrats have conceived and presented these projects as part of broader citywide efforts to create a more inclusive, secure, and livable city with fewer cars, better public transportation, less pollution, and a higher number of "rescued" public spaces through knowledge-based, internationally tested strategies. Take, for example, the parking meters program, introduced in 2012. Its stated aim is to bring order into the chaos of street parking in highly congested, central city neighborhoods, some of them adjacent to the Chapultepec hub. As I mentioned before, the promise to eradicate parking attendants is central to this project. However, its promoters have addressed their presence in streets and public spaces only indirectly, as one problematic use of space among many others that would disappear through the ordering and rationality-inducing capacities of parking meters. This was the case in a presentation with which city bureaucrats presented the program to a room packed with residents of the Roma-Condesa neighborhood in a public meeting that took place in a private university located in the area. The presentation started with several slides displaying photographs that depict disorder and insecurity: a cloud of smog covering the city, interminable traffic jams, pothole-filled, worn-out streets overflowing with cars, and informal parking attendants creating chaos (see Figure 10.2).

"Parking meters contribute to solving these problems," read a subsequent slide. Information about the program followed with several slides showing renderings of the same streets, as they would appear after the installation of parking meters, with one payment kiosk distributed along each block: brand-new pavements with no potholes, clearly demarcated parking spaces and stylish (and white) pedestrians leisurely strolling on wide and even sidewalks, few cars, and no informal workers in sight (see Figures 10.3 and 10.4).

A similar logic and aesthetic vision underpins the architectural renderings of the renovated Chapultepec hub, designed by a prestigious local architecture firm, which was presented to the public in fall 2014 by the head of the Urban Development and Housing Ministry and the architect himself. A brand new,

Figure 10.2   Slide from EcoParq presentation to residents of the Roma-Condesa neighborhood in Mexico City. The image shows a plastic bucket commonly used by *franeleros* to block parking spaces. Mexico City's Public Space Authority.

Figure 10.3 (Opposite, top)   Slide from EcoParq presentation to residents of the Roma-Condesa neighborhood in Mexico City. The image shows a complicated intersection marked by double parking, some street vendors, and a strong presence of *franeleros*. Mexico City's Public Space Authority.

Figure 10.4 (Opposite, bottom)   Slide from EcoParq presentation to residents of the Roma-Condesa neighborhood in Mexico City, showing a rendering of the same intersection depicted in Figure 10.3. The image depicts an orderly street, with a notable absence of street vendors and *franeleros*, that the installation of parking meters promised to deliver. Mexico City's Public Space Authority.

Actualmente

Av. Vicente Suárez

Con ecoparq

Imagen objetivo

Figure 10.5   Slide from Chapultepec hub presentation. The image on the left is an aerial photograph of the Chapultepec hub before the renovation began. The market is visible on the right side of the image, covered by blue canvases. The image on the right is a rendering of the same hub as it would appear after the renovation was completed. Mexico City's Urban Development and Housing Ministry.

clean, wide-open, tree-lined public plaza appears where the informal street market once stood; people stroll around or sit on minimalist benches; children run, play, and ride scooters. An imposing forty-one-story concrete-and-glass building that hosts a shopping mall, a hotel, and office spaces overlooks the plaza; brand new buses efficiently go in and out of an underground platform. In these renditions all elements appear in their proper place, from the benches to the plants to the buses, and all behaviors conform to the space's intended uses. Informal vendors simply do not exist in this renovated city of the future (see Figure 10.5).

The seemingly neutral, expert languages mobilized by both projects juxtapose different images of futurity with various images of pastness or, rather, with images of a dangerous and chaotic present that will be surmounted by urban renewal. The current chaotic state of urban space merges with apocalyptic visions of environmental disaster. Consequently, pollution, traffic, potholes, and informal street activities are all positioned on an equal plane, coalescing into the city's dystopic present. For urban mobility experts and activists, confronting this

ALEJANDRA LEAL MARTÍNEZ

dystopic present and creating a secure and livable city entails, to a certain extent, restoring a previous state of environmental equilibrium. Thus, for example, during a televised interview shortly after the Chapultepec hub project's announcement the architect who designed it explained his vision: "We are in a moment where traffic is so bad that many people have begun to change their paradigm and prefer maybe not to arrive by car to these central places. . . . So in a way the aim of [the hub's renewal project] is to propitiate a pedestrian city at the street level, and to propitiate a subterranean city where you have very effective connections between the subway and other modes of public transportation. . . . And this propitiates that we can recuperate, on the streets, a pedestrian and bicycle character for the city" (*Vivienda en Verde* 2015).

The objective, then, is to "recuperate" a certain quality of urban life that has been lost, a city for pedestrians and cyclists. This rendition of an idealized past to be recovered—of an urbanity that never really existed in the first place—effectively erases the long-standing and massive presence of informal street workers in Mexico City's urban streets and public spaces. This erasure recurs later in the interview, as the architect continues to explain his vision by describing what he sees as a paradox:

261

> I think there is a paradox in Mexico City, where each time you think about the subway, and the affectation that the subway produces to an area, I think it is thought about in negative terms. And the example that is always mentioned is the Zona Rosa, the Insurgentes subway and how the Zona Rosa collapsed. And curiously the paradox is because in other parts of the world, where there is a subway the land is most expensive, so I think that as we begin understanding that it is not only the subway as an isolated entity, but this development oriented around it, and around all modes of transport, and this is all integrated, and consolidated, that paradox will be eliminated. And this is what we are slowly moving toward (author's translation).

The architect posits a difference between two spaciotemporal registers. *There*—presumably the cosmopolitan cities that inspire urban renewal projects—the subway and public transportation infrastructures in general are properly valorized and trigger real estate development. *Here*, where there is a subway station, and crucially a public plaza built around it, as with the case of the Insurgentes hub that he mentions, the area is said to "collapse," that is, to become disorderly and derelict and thus suffer a decrease in real estate values. However, he continues, we are slowly moving toward *there*, since we are coming to realize that urban quality of life requires changing the car-centered paradigm of urban development.

What remains unstated in the architect's comments is that where there is a subway station, and particularly where there is a public square built around it, there is an informal street market catering to commuters, most of whom are middle- and lower-middle-class workers moving through the city. Unstated, too, remains the fact that it is precisely the presence of informal workers that leads to these areas being represented as insecure and unattractive for real estate investors. It makes such areas "collapse," to use the architect's word, as informality is associated with disorder and criminality, with an unattractive and dangerous city. Ultimately, what remains unstated is that informal street workers are precisely what must be removed in order to arrive *there*, to the renovated and secure city of the future.

It is worth considering further the architect's erasure of street workers in his comments, since they were indeed massively present in the Chapultepec hub and had to be removed to begin the renovation. This street market, as I noted above, was firmly rooted in that particular space. It had existed almost uninterruptedly for decades, during which the leaders of the various corporate organizations with which vendors were affiliated used a variety of strategies in order to negotiate with state authorities and the police. And, in fact, it was precisely through these organizations that the "removal" could actually take place without violence. It was the result of months of closed-door negotiations between the organizations' leaders, local government officials, and private investors in which all parties reached an agreement that would have vendors leave the hub peacefully in exchange for compensation. While the "removal" received widespread acclaim in the press and among experts and most residents of the surrounding areas, the compensation was harshly criticized for rewarding illegal activities.

There is, then, a different paradox at work here. Since in contemporary security discourses and strategies street vendors are no longer seen as workers—since they have been cast out of the urban collective—the architect and urban mobility experts and activists in general cannot really address their presence in the city's streets and public spaces, and cannot imagine ways to incorporate them into the new city. Indeed, as we have seen, far from reckoning with them as flesh-and-blood people entitled to a livelihood and to security, far from approaching street informality as a social issue that must be tackled, these discourses and strategies posit them as obstacles to be removed or simply erase them from view.

And yet, these multitudes cannot just disappear, as other forms of livelihood have not become available to them. Moreover, as in the case of the Chapultepec hub, state officials, investors, experts, and activists often rely on informal workers' much derided corporate structures and organizations to remove them from the city's streets and public spaces. This not only reveals the endurance of these corporate structures but, more crucially, it discloses that all social classes are involved in these forms of negotiation and organization. Therefore, despite the hopes—and fantasies—of planners, activists, and most central city residents of inhabiting an orderly and clean city devoid of informality, a city where a parking meter or a renovated hub appears as the embodiment of security, informal street workers continue to be constitutive elements of the quotidian urban order, even as their working conditions become ever more precarious and dangerous.

QUOTIDIAN (IN)SECURITIES

In spring 2013, parking meters began operating in the Roma-Condesa neighborhood. As promoters and supporters had hoped, a partial contrast soon started to emerge between the areas with parking meters and the areas without, the former displaying greater availability of parking spaces and less double-parking and parking on sidewalks or pedestrian crossings. But while some franeleros moved to other neighborhoods, many remained and diversified their services by negotiating with the new agents in the area. Some now offer to put money into the devices for drivers when their parking time has expired; others have established complicities with the police, so that they can continue blocking spaces for parking, even if more inconspicuously.

While franeleros are far from (fully) gone, urban renewal projects have put them in more vulnerable positions. This is evident in the experience of Mario, a forty-five-year-old man who works on the eastern edges of the Roma-Condesa. As is often the case in narratives about street work, Mario establishes a contrast between the past—before the Civic Culture Act or before the installation of parking meters—and a more precarious present. *Then*, he claims, when he was able to block spaces with buckets or cardboard boxes and allowed to park cars on sidewalks and pedestrian crossings, work was plentiful and profits sufficient. His twelve-hour shifts provided enough for him to buy a small piece of land in the city's periphery and build his own house. In contrast, Mario relates a more difficult *now*. He continues to work twelve hours a day, he says, but now makes a third of what he once did. Mario tells me that he has adapted to the new reality of parking meters by focusing on serving old clients, mostly students at a private university and regular patrons at local restaurants, who prefer to give him their keys so that he parks their cars just a few blocks away from his habitual spot, in areas without the devices. Now, he says, he has to constantly hide or run from the police, who sometimes demand bribes from him, and at other times take him to the Civic Court, where he has to spend twenty-four hours under administrative arrest, the punishment established by the Civic Culture Act for obstructing public space (Hernández 2017).

Meanwhile, the Chapultepec hub's renovation is moving at a slower pace than planners and investors had anticipated, due to various legal recourses to stop the project presented by local legislators and some residents (who are opposed to the public-private partnership, not the removal of vendors), which have not yet been resolved. Where the street market once stood, there is now a wide, rundown, and empty plaza, but some vendors can be seen there on any given day. Indeed, while some street vendors permanently left, others have returned, albeit without the support of their former organizations, by which many feel betrayed. Instead of fixed stands, they now display their merchandise on shopping carts, in plastic bags, or on rugs that they place on the floor. But as they no longer enjoy the protection of their leaders, vendors have to negotiate their presence every day, and on their own, which leaves them more vulnerable to police abuse. This is the case of Malena, a woman in her late forties who sells prepackaged snacks, candy, and loose cigarettes from a blue rack placed on top a grocery cart, just outside one of the entrances to the Chapultepec subway, on the southern edges of the plaza. She tells me that at least once a day, sometimes twice, several police officers (whom she calls *los azules*) approach her to demand *la pension* (a bribe), usually 150 pesos (roughly $8), to let her continue working, which, as she tells the police, she needs to do: "I eat every day—she recalls saying to them—I'm a woman. I'm sick. I have to work. Or, what? Do you only eat every other week?"

The increasing insecurities that street workers like Mario and Malena face on a daily basis remain unnoticed by most investors, planners, experts, activists, and residents of the area, who often express frustration about the stubbornness of informality, about its refusal to disappear. To be sure, many of these people's vision of the ideal city has an inclusive spirit. In their view, renovated public spaces are both more enjoyable for all and more conducive to civic life. And yet they are caught in an unresolvable paradox. As the urban poor continue to face the disintegration of the precarious mechanisms that allowed them certain rights and protections, and as other mechanisms of inclusion have not become available to them, instead of leaving the streets they remain, even if in more difficult conditions. Therefore, the new normative vision of urban public space looks increasingly unachievable. Put differently, it is precisely the exclusion of street workers that brings about the continuous disruption of the security aesthetics and promises of urban renewal.

In this chapter I have argued that street workers in Mexico City are enabled by and at the same time reproduce a particular street-level urban order in which all social classes partake. This, for example, is how an opinion columnist described the work of franeleros a few months before the installation of parking meters: "[They] make the most of space, so that the largest amount of cars can fit in the street; usually, they offer the additional service of washing the car; direct those who are dumbfounded by the confusing labyrinth of the city's traffic signs; organize traffic in rush hour and their presence chases thieves away, precisely because [franeleros] are invested in neighbors trusting in the safety of 'their' street. Put differently, franeleros produce a certain order—limited, precarious, local—but an order that in many areas has prevented the total collapse of traffic and of our car-related neurosis" (Becerra 2013, author's translation).

And yet, as I have shown above, while street workers continue to (re)produce this precarious order, in contemporary discourses, laws, regulations, and policies street work appears as nothing more than as a sign of danger and as an obstacle that must be removed to bring about a secure, modern city. Such negative representations are far from new, as the elites and middle classes have historically condemned street workers as sources of disorder and as barriers to the city's modernization. However, as I have shown, in the postrevolutionary period street workers were recognized as workers with certain rights and obligations, albeit always contingently and precariously. In this context, the urban poor's use of Mexico City's streets and plazas to secure a livelihood could be read as a visible, material sign of the as-yet-unfulfilled promise of inclusion: of (social) security for all citizens.

This is now a receding horizon, however, as the past decades of neoliberalization have entailed a displacement of security from the social to the personal, from welfare to safety. As a distinction has been drawn between active and dependent individuals, with the former expected to provide and guarantee their own security, the latter have been cast outside the boundaries of the civic collective, even outside the boundaries of citizenship. As I have argued, this redistribution of social entitlements rests, to return to Rancière (2004, 12), on a "redistribution of the sensible," which divulges who and what partakes in what is common to all; who and what can be heard and made intelligible as part of a community; and who and what is relegated to mere "noise."

The urban renewal projects in central Mexico City, such as the renovation of the Chapultepec hub and the installation of parking meters that I have discussed in this chapter, are shaped and in turn shape this "redistribution of the sensible." It is in such a context that urban planners, experts, activists, and residents have invested urban infrastructures—from a renovated transportation hub to parking meters—with the power of producing a domesticated, beautified city emptied of threatening bodies and social relations. Street workers in contemporary Mexico City are thus no longer material, visible signs of a future promise of inclusion and security. They appear as merely an out-of-place excess, a part with no part, in the civic collective. However, as I have shown, it is precisely the receding horizon of social security that spells the permanent incompletion of urban renewal projects and their security aesthetics since, without other options, the urban poor will continue to rely on the streets for their livelihood.

ACKNOWLEDGMENTS

I thank my research assistants Laura Alvarado, Carlos Arroyo, Diego Juárez, and Gala Menendez, whose fieldwork materials and observations are included in this chapter. I also thank D. Asher Ghertner, Daniel Goldstein, Hudson McFann, and two anonymous reviewers for their thoughtful comments on a previous version of this chapter.

266

NOTES

1 I use "informal" and "informality"—local terms that circulate both in Mexico City's public sphere and in everyday talk—to refer to the street work practices of the urban poor and to the urban poor themselves.

2 Officially named Modal Transfer Station Chapultepec, this hub, located at the core of the city's booming financial center, connects the subway system and twenty-six bus lines. Its renovation, announced in October 2014, is part of a larger initiative to "modernize" the forty-nine modal transfer stations in the city. As of June 2018 it has not been completed. This is a different initiative than the Chapultepec Corridor (announced in August 2015), which sought to renovate the entire Chapultepec Avenue but was canceled in December 2015 due to widespread public opposition.

3 They are also called *viene vienes* (come on, come on), for the phrase they use to direct drivers as they park.

4 I thank D. Asher Ghertner for these ideas.

5 As the city recovered in subsequent decades through the consolidation of a service economy, fewer (formal) jobs for the lower classes returned, so street work continued to expand (Duhau and Giglia 2008).

ALEJANDRA LEAL MARTÍNEZ

6 For more than a decade now Mexico has made headlines for its "war on drugs," and the escalation of violence that it has provoked, with entire regions ostensibly controlled by drug cartels. Meanwhile, Mexico City has garnered a reputation for being a relatively safe place, not only out of the reach of war on drugs–related violence, but also showing decreasing crime rates. While this reputation has started to crumble in the past years, Mexico City continues to be perceived as relatively safe in comparison to other cities across the country.

7 The oldest, largest, and better-organized street work organizations are those of vendors, by far the largest form of livelihood of the urban poor. Other forms of street work, such as informally parking cars, emerged in large numbers only in the last decades of the twentieth century, as the influx of cars in central areas of the city grew drastically, but followed a similar pattern of organization. There are, however, important differences between street vendors and informal parking attendants, as well as their organizations. First, the former's customer base is, for the most part, the city's urban poor and lower middle classes, while the clientele of the latter comprises the driving middle and upper classes, which entails different forms of quotidian sociability and of inhabiting public space. Second, large numbers of street vendors work together in the same space, which generates strong bonds. Franeleros, on the other hand, work alone, or in small groups and are thus more vulnerable.

8 The remaining 40 percent, that is, those formally employed, receive between one and three minimum wage salaries per month, according to a 2015 study by the Mexican National Institute of Statistics (Reynoso 2015).

9 I borrow the formulation of this section's title from Meneses (2011). The Roma-Condesa neighborhood developed near the city's historical downtown in the late nineteenth and early twentieth centuries, but it was drastically depopulated and impoverished after the earthquake that shook Mexico City in 1985. In the mid-1990s it began a period of urban renewal, becoming the frontline of gentrification processes that over the last two decades have dramatically transformed the central city (Janoschka, Sequera, and Salinas 2013).

10 While 4,000–5,000 pesos a month was above the minimum wage at the time, it was still a low salary for 12–15-hour workdays without any benefits.

11 One notable example is the Institute for Transportation and Development Policy. This is an international development foundation with a local chapter in Mexico City whose staff has worked closely with state bureaucrats and institutions.

REFERENCES

Auyero, Javier. 2014. "Lessons Learned while Studying Clientelistic Politics in the Grey Zone." In *Clientelism, Social Policy and the Quality of Democracy*, edited by Diego Abente and Larry Diamond, 114–129. Baltimore: Johns Hopkins University Press.

Babb, Sarah. 2004. *Managing Mexico: Economists from Nationalism to Neoliberalism.* Princeton, NJ: Princeton University Press.

Barbosa, Mario. 2008. *El trabajo en las calles: Subsistencia y negociación política en la ciudad de México a comienzos del siglo XX.* México: El Colegio de México.

Becerra, Ricardo. 2013. "Franeleros." *La Silla Rota*, January 28. https://lasillarota.com/yosoitu/viral/franeleros/31967.

Becker, Anne, and Markus-Michael Muller. 2013. "The Securitization of Urban Space and the 'Rescue' of Downtown Mexico City: Vision and Practice." *Latin American Perspectives* 40, no. 2: 77–94.

Blomley, Nicholas. 2007. "How to Turn a Beggar into a Bus Stop: Law, Traffic and the 'Function of the Place.'" *Urban Studies* 44, no. 9: 1697–1712.

Brenner, Neil, and Nik Theodore. 2002. "Cities and the Geographies of 'Actually Existing Neoliberalism.'" *Antipode* 34, no. 3: 349–379.

Caldeira, Teresa. 2000. *City of Walls: Crime, Segregation, and Citizenship in São Paulo.* Berkeley: University of California Press.

Crossa, Verónica. 2009. "Resisting the Entrepreneurial City: Street Vendors' Struggle in Mexico City's Historic Center." *International Journal of Urban and Regional Research* 33, no. 1: 43–63.

Davis, Diane. 2007. "El factor Giuliani: Delincuencia, la 'cero tolerancia' en el trabajo policiaco y la transformación de la esfera pública en el centro de la ciudad de Mexico." *Estudios Sociológicos* 75: 649–681.

Davis, Mike. 1992. *City of Quartz: Excavating the Future in Los Angeles.* London: Verso.

De Mauleón, Héctor. 2017. "En la Roma los delincuentes trabajan diario." *El Universal.* June 6. https://www.eluniversal.com.mx/entrada-de-opinion/columna/hector-de-mauleon/nacion/2017/06/6/en-la-roma-los-delincuentes-trabajan.

Dimitriou, Harry, and Ralph Gakengeimer. 2011. *Urban Transport in the Developing World: A Handbook of Policy and Practice.* Northampton, UK: Edward Elgar Publishing.

Duhau, Emilio, and Angela Giglia. 2008. *Las reglas del desorden: Habitar la metrópoli.* México City: Universidad Autónoma Metropolitana; Siglo Veintiuno Editores.

Escalante Gonzalbo, Fernando. 2006. "México, fin de siglo." In *Pensar en México*, edited by Héctor Aguilar Camín and Enrique Florescano, 19–36. México City: Fondo de Cultura Económica.

Feldman, Allen. 2001. "White Public Space and the Political Geography of Public Safety." *Social Text* 19, no. 3: 57–89.

Ghertner, D. Asher. 2015. *Rule by Aesthetics: World-Class City Making in Delhi.* New York: Oxford University Press.

Goldstein, Daniel M. 2010. "Toward a Critical Anthropology of Security." *Current Anthropology* 51, no. 4: 487–517.

———. 2016. *Owners of the Sidewalk: Security and Survival in the Informal City.* Durham, NC: Duke University Press.

Hernández, Eduardo. 2017. "Con la franeleada pude tener mi casita." *El Universal*, February 8. http://www.eluniversal.com.mx/articulo/metropoli/cdmx/2017/02/8/con-la-franeleada-pude-tener-mi-casita.

Institute for Transportation and Development Policy. 2012. *Transforming Urban Mobility in Mexico: Towards Accessible Cities Less Reliant on Cars.* http://mexico.itdp.org/wpcontent/uploads/Transforming-Urban-Mobility-in-Mexico.pdf.

Janoschka, Michael, Jorge Sequera, and Luis Salinas. 2013. "Gentrification in Spain and Latin America—a Critical Dialogue." *International Journal of Urban and Regional Research* 38, no. 4: 1234–1265.

Leal Martínez, Alejandra. 2016a. "Neoliberalismo, Estado y ciudadanía: La crisis del 'pacto revolucionario' en torno al sismo de 1985." *Relaciones. Estudios de Historia y Sociedad* 37, no. 147: 51–84.

———. 2016b. "'You Cannot Be Here': The Urban Poor and the Specter of the Indian in Neoliberal Mexico City." *Journal of Latin American and Caribbean Anthropology* 21, no. 3: 539–559.

Lomnitz, Claudio. 2001. *Deep Mexico, Silent Mexico: An Anthropology of Nationalism.* Minneapolis: University of Minnesota Press.

Meneses, Rodrigo. 2011. *Legalidades públicas: El derecho, el ambulantaje y las calles en el centro de la Ciudad de México (1930-2010).* Mexico City: Instituto de Investigaciones Jurídidcas, UNAM.

Muehlebach, Andrea. 2012. *The Moral Neoliberal: Welfare and Citizenship in Italy.* Chicago: University of Chicago Press.

Muehlebach, Andrea, and Nitzan Shoshan. 2012. "Post-Fordist Affect: Introduction." *Anthropological Quarterly* 85, no. 2: 317–344.

Rancière, Jacques. 2004. *The Politics of Aesthetics.* New York: Continuum.

———. 2009. "Contemporary Art and the Politics of Aesthetics." In *Communities of Sense: Rethinking Aesthetics and Politics,* edited by Beth Hinderliter, William Kaizen, Vered Maimon, Jaleh Mansoor, and Seth McCormick, 31–50. Durham, NC: Duke University Press.

Rao, Ursula. 2010. "Making the Global City: Urban Citizenship at the Margins of Delhi." *Ethnos: Journal of Anthropology* 75, no. 4: 402–424.

Reynoso, Francisco. 2015. "Los franeleros." *La Brujula: El Blog de la Metrópoli, Revista Nexos,* March 31. http://labrujula.nexos.com.mx/?p=290#_ftn2.

Rose, Nikolas. 1999. *Powers of Freedom: Reframing Political Thought.* Cambridge: Cambridge University Press.

Roy, Ananya, and Aihwa Ong, eds. 2011. *Worlding Cities: Asian Experiments and the Art of Being Global.* West Sussex, UK: Wiley-Blackwell.

Smith, Neil. 1998. "Giuliani Time: The Revanchist 1990s." *Social Text* 16, no. 4: 1–20.

Swanson, Kate. 2007. "Revanchist Urbanism Heads South: The Regulation of Indigenous Beggars and Street Vendors in Ecuador." *Antipode* 39, no. 4: 708–728.

Tenorio Trillo, Mauricio. 2009. "Del Mestizaje a un siglo de Andrés Molina Enríquez." In *En busca de Molina Enríquez: Cien años de "Los grandes problemas nacionales,"* edited by Emilio Kourí, 33–64. México City: El Colegio de México.

Valverde, Mariana. 2005. "Taking 'Land Use' Seriously: Toward an Ontology of Municipal Law." *Law Text Culture* 9: 34–59.

Vivienda en Verde. 2015. "Entrevista con el arquitecto Javier Sanchez de JSa arquitectura." EfektoTV, February 9. https://www.youtube.com/watch?list =PLvyu9gRJBJ5wah-_gHO2sv3BzJvuokwyX&time_continue=18&v=SdbsUe -a280.

Yeh, Rihan. 2017. *Passing: Two Publics in a Mexican Border City*. Chicago: University of Chicago Press.

Zukin, Sharon. 1998. "Urban Lifestyles: Diversity and Standardisation in Spaces of Consumption." *Urban Studies* 35, nos. 5–6: 825–839.

The Age of Security

Didier Fassin

We live in an age of security. There is indeed in contemporary societies both a demand for and a supply of security which are perhaps unprecedented. People's legitimate desire to live in a safe environment is constantly fueled by the convergent logics of sensationalization of violence in the media, the politics of fear conducted by populist leaders, and the economy of safeguard produced by industrial complexes. The paradox is, however, that the demand for security is not only unrelated to the reality of insecurity but also often inversely proportional to it. It tends to reach its peak in the safest countries and safest neighborhoods. Where violent crime has decreased in the past decades, the expectation of more law-and-order policies has rarely declined. In fact, international studies show that the demand for security is correlated with the level of inequality rather than the objective reality of violence and crime, which suggests that the supply of security should be regarded as a response to rising inequalities and a substitute for social justice. When people are worried about their employment or their assets, about the future of their children or the becoming of their identity—depending on their social class and ethnoracial category—their concern is cunningly displaced toward a need for security: more police and military, more surveillance cameras and house searches, more airport screening and border control, more walls and gates. Anxieties about socioeconomic and sociocultural issues are thus converted into calls for tough policies. It is this phenomenon that this volume collectively explores: how security has pervaded contemporary societies. And the authors investigate it from an understudied albeit conspicuous perspective: where aesthetics meets politics.

Yet, the aestheticization of security is not self-evident. After all, law enforcement officers patrolling the streets, broken-down doors and devastated apartments, body scans and metal detectors, roadblocks and surveillance cameras, concrete palisades and barbed wired fences do not easily lend themselves to aesthetics. What the authors demonstrate is that aesthetics is nevertheless omnipresent in the security apparatus in multiple and often contradictory ways. It proceeds through several possible *operations*.

The first of these operations is a process of normalization. The staging of safety and rebranding of neighborhoods to promote gentrification, the installation of specific alarms and preparation for attacks perpetrated by gunmen in elementary schools, and the displaying of counterterrorism instruments and cyberwar weapons in museums contribute to trivializing the idea of the ubiquity of insecurity and normalcy of the security response. The public is progressively habituated to a material and social environment that one could not have conceived of only a few decades ago. Such logics can progressively make the exception the rule as when the French government, after two years of a state of emergency following terrorist attacks, decided to end it in October 2017, but not without having first inscribed into the common law most measures of the state of emergency.

The second operation is that of visibilization and invisibilization. Photographs, videos, posters, maps, and statistics are used to expose facts that can be as abstract as danger or risk, either through the representations of their actual or potential consequences or through the representations of the actions and actors that are supposed to prevent or treat such consequences, such as biologists working on foretold epidemics in the Netherlands and firemen intervening after earthquakes in Colombia. But symmetrically, invisibilization also takes place to obscure uncomfortable realities. The danger of dissemination of viruses may be revealed but not the unequal distribution in the probability of being infected and of dying. The risk of natural disaster can be exhibited but not the housing policies that lead the poor to occupy threatened areas. More generally, disparities are understated or obfuscated.

A third process involves a combination of beautification and uglification. Even the horrors of war, the brutality of policing, and the menace of biological agents are transfigured by dramatizing visual effects. The photoshopped pictures displayed on the front page of newspapers give embellished and tragic visions of battlefields. The heavily militarized harnessing of special law enforcement units provides them with a formidable and frightening look. Scientists wearing full protective gear that resembles spacesuits are the face of the dreaded pandemics. And conversely, uglification serves to vilify the enemy within or without. For middle-class inhabitants of Kingston, Jamaica, the residents of Downtown garrison communities are regarded with fear as they are associated with violence, crime, and drugs. For those who want to stigmatize Mexicans crossing the southern border of the United States, these immigrants are not merely undocumented, they also have to be designated as rapists and murderers.

———

These processes through which aestheticization is effectuated are in turn generative of new facts, or rather of reconfigurations of various dimensions of social life. Indeed, the security apparatus is not only repressive. It is also productive. One can recognize at least four kinds of such *productions*.

First, a multitude of realities are created or re-created, from digital technologies to prevention programs, from risk factors to predictive algorithms, from endangered populations to dangerous spaces, from an imaginary of fortress to an illusion of humane wall, from official representations of the poor to legitimate interventions against crime. Some are made de novo, like cybersecurity devices in exhibits and active-shooter drills in schools; others are recycled, such as vehicles and weapons transferred from the front in Iraq and Afghanistan, where the military use them against remote enemies, to the streets of the Midwest, where the police receive them free of charge from the army to control street demonstrations or intervene in house searches.

Second, temporalities are restructured in the name of the urgency of the situation and the immediacy of responses. The past is often erased, as in the gentrification of neighborhoods formerly characterized by high criminality in Brooklyn or Mexico, and even when the language seems to indicate its recognition, such as the prefix "post" in the adjective "postconflict" applied to the situation in Honduras, much is done to ignore what went before. In parallel, the future is coalesced into the present, which is overwhelmed by disquieting projections of risks and threats.

Third, subjectivities are formed as the discourse of insecurity and the politics of security put individuals in particular circumstances that become the new norm. Messages of caution and invitations to report suspect behaviors on public transport, for example, transform individuals into citizens who can be simultaneously under surveillance and exercising surveillance. Law-and-order policies and police discretion combined with ordinary expressions of racist beliefs and racial discrimination lead certain categories of the population, notably the poor, the migrants, and the ethnoracial minorities, to learn in their everyday lives, and even through their bodily experiences, what it means to be second-class citizens. The formation of subjects, including via this embodiment, thus obeys a dual logic of subjection to the authority of the state and its representatives on the ground and of subjectivation, because they may view themselves as victims or rebels, as oppressed or resistant.

Fourth, economies thrive in two opposed yet not incompatible ways. On the one hand, there is the private and public industrial complex which benefits from the funding bonanza intended to build infrastructures, buy equipment, and recruit workforces for the army and the police, the airports and the borders, the prisons and the hospitals. On the other hand, there are the illegal practices, which take advantage of the expansion of the system to develop their parallel networks, the best-known example being that of the smugglers in North Africa who increase their fees exponentially as the obstacles on migration routes multiply. This distinction between official and criminal activities should however be relativized because collusion between the police and the mafias often occurs. But one should also add to the mix the cost of this security apparatus, both in human and financial terms, for contemporary societies. According to statistical estimates, approximately five thousand individuals die each year trying to cross the Mediterranean to get to Europe, and the more repression there is, in particular from Libyan coastguards, the higher the proportion of deaths. Frontex, the European Border and Coast Guard Agency, has a yearly budget of €250 million, which has been mostly devoted to immigration policing since the interruption of its rescue operation named Triton. Thus, the alleged gain in security for some means a definite increase in insecurity for others.

274

———

The obvious question that comes to mind is: What is the use of this fast-growing security apparatus? Or perhaps, more sociologically, what is its *function*? In the first analysis, the answer seems just as evident: to respond to the people's demand for security. Things are, however, more complex. As mentioned earlier, this demand is largely driven by sensationalism in the media, penal populism among politicians, and the economic interests of companies involved in this activity. The sense of insecurity that is driven by concerns about the present and future is in large part displaced from social and cultural issues to law-and-order problems. While pretending to respond to one demand, the authorities create or at least inflate another one. In this way, they elude the social question, which would imply investment in distributive justice, and they tackle the cultural dimension, but only by blaming migrants and minorities for troubling a supposed identity.

Wondering why the prison system, having been almost constantly criticized since its creation for its inefficacy and inhumanity, was still in place and even flourishing, Michel Foucault famously argued that the function of the prison and punishment more generally was not to reduce crime, as it was claimed, but to distribute illegalisms, not according to their negative impact on society, but according to whom one wanted to punish, the poor rather than the wealthy, the precarious rather than the powerful, and therefore the petty crime rather than the economic crime. In the same way, we must consider whom the deployment of the security apparatus serves—and whom it disserves—to understand what its social function is. Fundamentally, it distinguishes those who should be protected and those from whom they should be protected. For instance, in the case of borders, the nationals of Europe and of the United States from the immigrants and refugees from Africa and the Middle East, for the former, and from Latin America, for the latter; or in the case of crime, the upper and middle classes from the working class, in particular those belonging to minorities, and in fact almost independently from the seriousness of the offense committed. In other words, the security apparatus serves to differentiate between a majority entitled to certain social protection from the state and various sorts of undesirables whether outside or inside the country. What is argued here about national politics would probably also be true in large part for international relations.

However, let me anticipate a possible misunderstanding. By interpreting the rise of the security apparatus in this way I do not suggest that the expectation of living in a safe environment is not legitimate and that policing does not partially contribute to it. But neither of these two elements accounts for the expansion of the security apparatus. Nor do they account for the electoral victories of those who have made it a central plank of their campaigns, from Nicolas Sarkozy to Donald Trump, from Viktor Orban to Rodrigo Duterte, from Abdel Fattah el-Sisi to Benjamin Netanyahu, and the efforts often deployed even by their political opponents to demonstrate that, if they were in power, they would also be tough on immigration and on crime, in a continuous shift of the whole political spectrum toward the right.

Yet, significantly, these discourses and these policies are not judged on their results but on their enactment. It is not the number of migrants deported or the number of criminals arrested that matters. It is the way things are staged and acted out by those who articulate such discourses and apply such policies. The point is not about performance but about performativity. This is where security aesthetics are crucial—and futureproof.

ACKNOWLEDGMENTS

The editors are grateful to the Departments of American Studies, Anthropology, and Geography and the Center for Latin American Studies at Rutgers University for supporting the initial symposium, in 2016, during which this book's contributing authors first presented early versions of their papers. That symposium was generously underwritten by a grant from Rutgers Global as part of its biennial theme, "Global Urbanism." The lively conversations that took place in New Brunswick in the darkening shadow of the aestheticized security regime of the forty-fifth president of the United States helped push those papers into the tight, yet multivocal conversation that has become *Futureproof*. Rick Lee from Rutgers Global was particularly instrumental in encouraging us to think aesthetic politics and security technologies together, and we thank him for his inspiration, as well as logistical support, in making that initial symposium possible. Rick Schroeder similarly pushed us at an earlier moment to consider the aesthetic dimensions of security, particularly in the context of cities of the Global South.

We also thank two anonymous reviewers and the editorial board of Duke University Press for constructive feedback that allowed security's lived and felt dimensions to emerge in these pages with more sensorial richness. Gisela Fosado's editorial oversight improved the book at every stage, and we thank her and her talented team, especially Jenny Tan, as well as Drew Sisk for shepherding the book forward.

VICTORIA BERNAL is professor of anthropology at the University of California, Irvine. Her scholarship explores questions about politics, gender, migration and diaspora, war, civil society and activism, and digital media. Her recent books include *Nation as Network: Diaspora, Cyberspace, and Citizenship* (2014) and the anthology coedited with Inderpal Grewal, *Theorizing NGOs: States, Feminisms, and Neoliberalism* (Duke University Press, 2014). She has carried out ethnographic research in Sudan, Tanzania, Eritrea, Silicon Valley, and cyberspace. Her current project focuses on privacy, cybersecurity, and digital surveillance.

JON HORNE CARTER is a sociocultural anthropologist and codirector of the AppState Ethnography Lab in the Department of Anthropology at Appalachian State University. He writes on ethnographic methods, fictocritical anthropology, punk and black metal, criminality and policing, mass incarceration, and undocumented migration out of South and Central America. He is currently finalizing a book manuscript on gang communities and criminal aesthetics in Honduras.

ALEXANDRA DEMSHOCK is a PhD candidate in the Department of Sociology at Rutgers University. Her recent work includes an historical project of urban planning and the production of whiteness in Philadelphia's University City and ethnographic fieldwork for a team-based, longitudinal study on the impact of NGOs in Léogâne, Haiti. Currently she is piloting walking methods to analyze assemblages of security and fear on urban streets.

ZAIRE Z. DINZEY-FLORES is associate professor of sociology and Latino and Caribbean studies at Rutgers University. Her research focuses on how the urban built environment mediates community life, race, class, and social inequality. Her book *Locked In, Locked Out: Gated Communities in a Puerto Rican City* (2013), winner of the 2014 Robert E. Park Award for best book in urban sociology, investigates race and class inequality as negotiated through fortress architecture in public housing and private subdivisions. Among ongoing projects, she is examining race and class distinctions in the production of urban residential spaces in demographically shifting real estate markets. She currently serves as a board member for the New York City Housing Authority.

DIDIER FASSIN is James D. Wolfensohn Professor in the School of Social Science at the Institute for Advanced Study. An anthropologist and sociologist who also trained as a physician in internal medicine and public health, he developed the field of critical moral anthropology. His current work focuses on the theory of punishment, the politics of life, and the public presence of the social sciences. He writes for the French newspapers *Le Monde* and *Libération*, and occasionally for *The Nation* and the *London Review of Books*. His recent books include *Enforcing Order: An Ethnography of Urban Policy* (2013); *At the Heart of the State: The Moral World of Institutions* (2015); and *Prison Worlds: An Ethnography of the Carceral Condition* (2016).

D. ASHER GHERTNER is associate professor in the Department of Geography at Rutgers University. He has published widely on aesthetic governmentality, gentrification, and urban technics. He is the author of *Rule by Aesthetics: World-Class City Making in Delhi* (2015), an extended ethnographic study of mass slum demolition, and coeditor of *Land Fictions: The Commodification of Land in City and Country* (with Robert Lake, 2020). He is currently carrying out two research projects focused respectively on the cultural and aesthetic politics of air pollution in Delhi and vernacular land markets and flexible law-making on India's urban peripheries.

DANIEL M. GOLDSTEIN is professor emeritus in the Department of Anthropology at Rutgers University. He is the author of three monographs: *The Spectacular City: Violence and Performance in Urban Bolivia* (Duke University Press, 2004); *Outlawed: Between Security and Rights in a Bolivian City* (Duke University Press, 2012); and *Owners of the Sidewalk: Security and Survival in the Informal City* (Duke University Press, 2016). He is the coeditor (with Enrique D. Arias) of the collection *Violent Democracies in Latin America* (Duke University Press, 2012). A political and legal anthropologist, he specializes in the anthropology of security. His current research examines undocumented workers' vulnerabilities and responses in a context of securitized migration in the United States.

RACHEL HALL is associate professor of communication and rhetorical studies at Syracuse University and the author of *Wanted: The Outlaw in American Visual Culture* (2009) and *The Transparent Traveler: The Performance and Culture of Airport Security* (Duke University Press, 2015). Her work has appeared in *Performance Research*, *Women's Studies Quarterly*, *Text and Performance Quarterly*, *Communication Review*, *Camera Obscura: Feminism, Culture and Media Studies*, and *Hypatia: Journal of Feminist Philosophy*.

RIVKE JAFFE is professor of urban geography in the Department of Human Geography, Planning and International Development Studies at the University of Amsterdam. Her anthropological research focuses on intersections of the urban and the political, and includes an interest in topics such as organized crime, popular culture, and environmental pollution, drawing on fieldwork in Jamaica, Curaçao, and Suriname. She is currently leading a major research program on public-private security assemblages in Kingston, Jerusalem, Miami, Nairobi, and Recife that is studying transformations in governance and citizenship in relation to hybrid forms of security provision. Her publications include *Concrete Jungles: Urban Pollution and the Politics of Difference in the Caribbean* (2016) and *Introducing Urban Anthropology* (with Anouk de Koning, 2016).

IEVA JUSIONYTE is assistant professor of anthropology and social studies at Harvard University. Her research and teaching interests lie at the intersection of political-legal and medical anthropology, with a focus on the ethnographic study of state power and the materiality of violence. She is the author of two books: *Savage Frontier: Making News and Security on the Argentine Border* (2015) and *Threshold: Emergency Responders on the U.S.-Mexico Border* (2018). Her research has been supported by the National Science Foundation and the Wenner Gren Foundation, among others, and published in a number of scholarly journals, including *American Anthropologist*, *Cultural Anthropology*, and *American Ethnologist*.

CATHERINE LUTZ is the Thomas J. Watson Jr. Family Professor of International Studies and professor of anthropology at Brown University. Her past research focused on the transformations of war as well as on peacekeeping and gender, military basing and antibasing social movements, and photographic representations of the world of nations. She is currently leading the Costs of War project, an interdisciplinary study of the human, social, and financial costs of the wars in Iraq and Afghanistan. She is past president of the American Ethnological Society. Her recent books include *War and Health: The Medical Consequences of the Wars in Iraq and Afghanistan* (edited with Andrea Mazzarino, 2019); *Schooled: Ordinary, Extraordinary Teaching in an Age of Change* (with Anne Fernandez, 2015); and *Breaking Ranks: Iraq Veterans Speak Out Against the War* (with Matthew Gutmann, 2010).

ALEJANDRA LEAL MARTÍNEZ is associate professor at the National Autonomous University of Mexico's Center for Interdisciplinary Research in Sciences and Humanities in Mexico City. She received her PhD from Columbia University's Department of Anthropology in 2011. Her research interests stand at the intersection of urban and political anthropology. She studies the connection between neoliberal forms of governance and the changing geographies of social difference in contemporary cities, with an ethnographic focus on Mexico City. She is currently working on a book manuscript entitled "'For the Enjoyment of All': Class, Citizenship, and Belonging in Mexico City's Urban Renewal."

HUDSON MCFANN is a PhD candidate in the Department of Geography at Rutgers University. His dissertation project uses archival research and oral history interviews to study the history and legacies of Khao I Dang (1979–1993) refugee camp, established in Thailand in the wake of the Cambodian genocide. His work has been supported by the Beinecke Scholarship Program, the Fulbright U.S. Student Program, the National Science Foundation, and the Center for Khmer Studies. He received his MA from New York University.

LIMOR SAMIMIAN-DARASH is senior lecturer in anthropology in the Federmann School of Public Policy and Government at the Hebrew University. Her research focuses on preparedness and biosecurity in Israel and the United States, the governance of risk and uncertainty in theory and practice, and scenario planning. Her publications include *Modes of Uncertainty: Anthropological Cases* (coedited with Paul Rabinow, 2015) and articles in *Current Anthropology*, *Security Dialogue*, and *Cultural Anthropology*. Her current research on global scenarios examines forms, practices, and conceptualizations of scenarios in health, energy, and security from a global perspective.

ABDOUMALIQ SIMONE is an urbanist with particular interest in emerging forms of collective life across cities of the so-called Global South. He has worked across many different academic, administrative, research, policymaking, advocacy, and organizational contexts. He is presently Senior Professorial Fellow at the Urban Institute, University of Sheffield; Associate Researcher, Max Planck Institute for the Study of Religious and Ethnic Diversity; and Visiting Professor of Sociology, Goldsmiths College, University of London. His recent books include *Jakarta: Drawing the City Near* (2014), *New Urban Worlds: Inhabiting Dissonant Times* (with Edgar Pieterse, 2017), and *Improvised Lives: Rhythms of Endurance for an Urban South* (2018).

AUSTIN ZEIDERMAN is associate professor of urban geography at the London School of Economics and is an interdisciplinary scholar who specializes in the cultural and political dimensions of urbanization, development, and the environment in Latin America, with a focus on Colombia. He holds a PhD in Anthropology from Stanford University as well as a Master of Environmental Science from Yale University and a bachelor's degree in Economics from Colgate University. His book *Endangered City: The Politics of Security and Risk in Bogotá* (Duke University Press, 2016) focuses on how security and risk shape the relationship between citizens and the state in the self-built settlements of the urban periphery. He is currently carrying out research that examines efforts to reconfigure Colombia's geoeconomic space in anticipation of a post-conflict future.

INDEX

Page numbers in italics refer to figures.

epidermalization: Browne's concept of, 129; Fanon's concept of, 15–17

Equal Protection Clause, border wall design and construction and, 101

espionage, museum perspectives on, 40–43

Esswein, Pat, 162

Evangelista-Ysasaga, Michael, 87–88

eventalization (Foucault), 235–36

experiential gap (Bernal): digital media and, 35–37; performance paradigm and, 178–84

expertise, security aesthetics and, 256–63

extortion in Honduras: deportees targeted for, 125–29; economic impact of, 121–25

Fabbri, Paolo, 22

Fair Housing Act 1968, 161–63

Fanon, Frantz, 15

Fassin, Didier, 17, 271–76

Fauci, Anthony, 214, 216

Federal Emergency Management Association (FEMA), 179

Feldman, Allen, 13

Felix, Gilda, 97

Fineberg, Harvey, 218–19

fingerprinting, 15–16

firefighters: border wall injuries and trauma and, 90–91, 101–4; political and legal entanglements for, 91–109; as state actors, 98–101; treatment and transport activities of, 104–6, 109n1

Fiske, John, 15

flexible justice, police corruption and, 123–25

Flores, Alex, 103

food scarcity, security and, 18

"forensic" of built environment, 92

Foucault, Michel, 11–12, 17–19, 118, 186–88, 235–36, 275

Fouchier, Ron, 200–201, 212–15, 218–19

Fourteenth Amendment, border wall design and construction and, 101

Fukuda, Keiji, 216

gain-of-function (GoF) studies: biosecurity and, 200; government policies concerning, 217–19

Galton, Francis, 13–14, *14*

Galvani, Alison P., 218

gang violence: community formation in Kingston, Jamaica, and, 134–53; economic impact of, 120–25; in Honduras, 24, 117–20; Jamaican garrison politics and, 141–42; police corruption and, 121–25, 130–31

Garay-Mariscal, Oscar, 106

Garrett, Laurie, 213

garrison politics (Kingston, Jamaica), 141–42

Garzón, Lucho, 76

Geneva Conventions, 50

genocide, 20

gentrification: glass-house bubbles narrative and, 164–65; prefabricated escape hatches and, 166–67; promise of inequality and, 171–72; quietness narratives and, 165–66; real estate staging and, 161–63; safety narratives and, 163–71; scientific objectivity and, 170–71; technology of security and, 167–68; workers as hindrances to, 253–56

Get Smart (television series), 40

Ghertner, D. Asher, 1–27, 256

ghettoization: of Bedford-Stuyvesant, 156–72; Kingston, Jamaica, don garrisons and, 141–42; security aesthetics in Kingston, Jamaica, and, 142–43, 146–47

Giddens, Anthony, 22n2

glass-house bubbles, real estate safety narratives and, 164–65

Global South, urban space transformation in, 237–39

global warming. *See* climate change

and, 171–72; quietness narrative and, 165–66; real estate narratives and, 163–71
Saldanha, Arun, 149
Samimian-Darash, Limor, 26, 200–220
Sanchez, William, 101
Sandy Hook Promise, 178
San Jose Art Museum, 34, 38, 49–50
scenario thinking: active-shooter drills and, 184–88; media coverage of mass shootings and, 194–97; school security and, 178–84
Schechner, Richard, 183–84
Schneier, Bruce, 37–38
school security: active-shooter drills and, 177–97; educational mission and, 191–93; performance paradigm in, 178–84
Science (magazine), 201
Scientific American (magazine), 212
scientific objectivity, gentrification and, 170–71
"screening threats": biosecurity and, 201–203, 205–6, 214–16, 218–20; definition and examples of, 5–6, 11–17, *14*; in Honduras, 116, 125–29; museums and cybersecurity and, 33, 36, 39, 44, 55, 57–59; real estate in Jakarta and, 228; school security and, 177–78, 194; *sensibilización* (sensory training) in Bogotá and, 84
secrecy, extortion in Honduras and role of, 126–29
Secret Service, 179
Security, Territory, and Population (Foucault lectures), 187–88
security aesthetics, vii–xii; active-shooter drills and, 175–97; on Arizona-Sonora border, 87–109; biopolitics and, 1–27; in Bogotá, Colombia, 23, 63–85, *64*; border wall construction, 23–24, 90–109; cybersecurity and, 33–60; "dark interpretations" of security and, 84–85; definition of, 4;

desplazados (Colombian displaced persons) and, 80–83; in "Downtown" Kingston, Jamaica, 142–46; expertise and, 256–63; Foucault's framing of, 11–12; geography of sensation and, 150–53, *152*; gun ownership and, 188–93; H5N1 research and, 201–20; in Honduras, 114–32; Kingston, Jamaica, "Uptown" and "Downtown" aesthetics, 136–37; life management and, 22–27; ownership ambiguity and infrastructure deterioration in Jakarta and, 228–31; political community formation in Kingston, Jamaica, and, 134–53; politics of difference and, 24–25; power and, 49–58; renovation narrative and, 168–71; responsible gun ownership and, 189–93; school security and, 177–97; spatialized difference and segmented security in Kingston, Jamaica, 139–42; status of the popular and, 240–43; technology and, 167–68; unreality of, 271–76; in "Uptown" Kingston, Jamaica, 146–50; urban space making in Jakarta and, 225–43; violence and, 49–58. *See also* "calibrating vulnerabilities"; "designing fortresses"; "screening threats"
security cameras, recording of corruption by, 129–31, *130*
security warning systems, climate change and, 22
seguridad ciudadana (public safety), 119–20
Seiler, Michael and Vicky, 161–62
Sekula, Allan, 13–17
self-caused fear, 19
self-securitizing surveillance mechanisms, 205
sensibilización (sensory training), Bogotá government's use of, 23, 73–85
sensorial engagement: political geography of, 150–53, *152*; politics of aesthetics and, 137–39, 146–50

September 11, 2001, attacks: biosecurity
in wake of, 205–7; power, security, and
violence in context of, 2–3, 19, 33, 39,
49–58, 93, 95, 99, 205, 211
"Sex and Death in the Rational World of
Defense Intellectuals" (Cohn), xi
Shields, David, x–xiii
sidewalk safety, Jacobs's concept of, 8–11
simian virus 40 (SV40), research on,
208–9
Simon, Taryn, 53, 57
Simone, AbdouMaliq, 17, 26–27, 225–43
Simpson, Ruth, 160–61
Skyfall (film), 41
slavick, elin o'Hara, xi–xii
Smith, Neil, 10
Snowden, Edward, 35–37
social contract: neoliberalism and collapse of, 248–50; security and, 2–3
social media, security vs. insecurity in
Jakarta and, 232–34
"sousveillance" (Mann), 129
sovereignty: security and, 1–2; urban
development and, 115, 234–36
space: cyberspace, 41, 44; defensible
space theory, 8–11; politics of aesthetics and, 138–39; security aesthetics and
management of, 6–11. *See also* built
environment; "designing fortresses";
urban space
"Special Economic Development
Regions" (Regiones Especiales de
Desarollo [RED]), 114–15
"Special Economic Development Zones"
(Zonas Especiales de Desarollo
Economico [ZEDE]), 115
staging in real estate, gentrification and,
161–63
state: border wall violence and, 91–109;
criminalization of street workers and,
254–55; danger vs. endangerment and,
65–66; evolution of security and role
of, 12; firefighters as actors for, 98–101;
national security affect and, 39–43;

patriarchal relationship with, 67–77;
police corruption and, 121–25; street
workers in Mexico City and role of,
251–53
Stay Free! (magazine), 156
Steele, Brent, 20
Stengers, Isabelle, 235–36
Steward, Kathleen, 131–32
Strathern, Marilyn, 236–37
street violence, perceptions of, 19–20
street workers in Mexico City: as economic hindrance, 253–56; organization
of, 267n7; perceptions of danger from,
246–50, 266n5; post-removal activities
of, 264–66; precarious security for,
250–53; erasure of, 256–63
surveillance: artworks as illustration
of, 53–58; biosecurity aesthetics and,
203–20; Border Patrol technology for,
95; digital opacity and, 35–37; don-
based security systems in Kingston,
Jamaica, and, 141–44; historical evolution of, 11–12; natural surveillance,
8–11; weaponization of, 10–11. *See also*
"screening threats"
Sutton, Barbara, 19–20

tactical infrastructure: border wall policies and, 91–109; migrant injury and
trauma and, 92–95
target hardening, active-shooter drills
and, 177–78
Taylor, David, 53, 55
Taylor, Diana, 178, 184–88
Tech Museum of Innovation (San Jose,
California), 34, 38–39, 43–49, 45
technology: artworks as illustration of,
53–58; of espionage and intelligence,
40–43; human control over, in Cyber
Detectives exhibit, 43–49; mediated
surveillance and, 13; security aesthetics and, 7–8, 167–68, 256–63
temporality, security aesthetics and,
273–76